Preface

I wish to thank my wife, Thelma, and our children for their tolerance and support in the writing of this book and its subsequent revision. I also thank them for some editorial advice and for most of the artwork contained herein. I also thank my wife for the back cover text.

I also wish to thank Robert Helfenstine for reviewing a late draft of the first edition. Also, Melody Green for editing a late draft of the first edition.

Wildwood, Florida

Russel Moe
May, 2015

Polyscience and Christianity:

Rational Thought's Long History

ISBN-13: 978-1512010848
ISBN-10:1512010847

Library of Congress Control Number: 2015907944
CreateSpace Independent Publishing Platform, North Charleston, SC

Front Cover: Art by Dave Moe.
"All-seeing" knowledge; empirical knowledge; winnowing; new towers from old; atheoristic thinking.

Library of Congress Cataloging-in-Publication Data
Russel Moe, 1943 -
Polyscience and Christianity: Rational Thought's Long History / Russel Moe
    Includes Index

Around 1980, I visited Japan on business and also attended the English services at a local Christian church. I asked the missionary pastor if the creation-evolution controversy meant anything in Japan. He replied that, strange as it may seem, they saw no conversions to Christianity until after explaining *ex nihilo* creation.

This was so because, to the Japanese mind, God is an absentee landlord, with no direct interest in people. With that mindset, Japanese people could make no sense of Christian words such as sin, atonement, redemption, *etc*. But once they understood *ex nihilo* creation, these words loomed large in their minds.

We need to understand the mindsets of unsaved people. The present world-wide intellectual scene may not seem to descend from the ancient Greek history emphasized in this book. It started with mathematical certainty based on arithmetic, and later on geometry. Mathematics transformed these ancients into rationalists, who still abound. *Their monotruth was hard to criticize.*

There are also reasonable people whose empirical science makes pragmatic use of mathematics. But liberated, rational minds go further. They even "discovered" that the universe was infinite; so the supernatural was not needed. For centuries, they rejoiced in this natural "knowledge," which became the umbrella under which non-empirical disciplines could develop.

About a century ago, mathematics suddenly lost its claim to monotruth. "Certainty" now is said to be based on "data," but data is not grandiosely extrapolatable. *So now what holds the umbrella up?*

For present legitimacy, rationalists depend upon group consensus of learned participants (paradigms). They fiercely defend consensus as objective truth – or at least the best that humans can attain to. *Those sheltered under the umbrella run riot in our day.*

Not all of these are "true believers" in rational truths; some are just liberated. They are cynics and opportunists, confident that their linguistic and rational capabilities let them "get away with it." They can pull the wool over the eyes of the old fogies, governments, universities and even funding agencies. *Their "new" is sheltered under the ancient natural umbrella.*

To understand the rational mind, look to both Genesis and ancient Greece. Granted, Genesis is where we find God's revelation. However, if the rational remain loyal to ancient mathematics or saving the appearances, few will turn aside from the associated "unaided" reason and look to the Genesis account of *ex nihilo* creation, the flood, or Christ's Incarnation.

Ancient history is unknown to most people, yet trying to clarify truth by only analyzing today's worldviews has little success. Worldviews can form labyrinths; in which many are comfortably lost. Thus, to me, to understand truth, we first need a prelude on the curious history of rational thought!

Ancient Greek thinkers used "unaided" reason to search for truth ("aided" by mathematics, but not by the supernatural). They deduced an utterly large cosmos, materialism and atheism. To this day, their followers remain proud slaves of reason. Success in mathematics and astronomy makes them adopt the ancient "way" to truth. Their scientific "way" to the utterly large cosmos rules out a God worthy of that name. To them, religion is a diversion of the psyche – not a rational interaction with reality.

To their continual surprise, Christianity remains vigorous. The Christian cosmos, young and complex, stable and reasonable, is a created fact. We are complex entities, with body, soul and spirit. His inspired Word, only-begotten Son, Holy Spirit and history bear witness to God's continuing involvement in His *ex nihilo* creation.

But many people consider science foundationally objective, so they reject or "up-date" Christianity. "Updated" Christianity sounds an unclear note. Sensitive souls realize that life without "outsiders" is inauthentic. As a defense, Christians generally ignore science or resist its misuse primarily in geology, biology or the social understandings.

Alongside empirical science, engineering, technology and tinkering, some scholarly disciplines attempt to make limited sense of their corners of reality. Their "data" does not squeeze out the supernatural, yet such data is of little interest to rationalists. *They seek salvation in various universal natural monotruths!*

Reading scholarly books is hazardous, for not all learned authors agree, so theory, paradigm and viewpoint multiply. The confident mind's eye can filter what one sees and hide such wordy subjectivity. Woe for me, books have diverted my attention to a hidden, yet obvious, path.

The hidden path follows the history of early mathematics and science. The path leads up to the present – and supports empirical science, yet highlights the ancient subjectivity residing in the "way" of rationalism and mathematics.

Science, falsely so-called drives mankind.
Paradigms expand.
Objectivity diminishes.

But witnesses remain:
Creation and salvation for mankind.
History and science witness to God's ongoing care.

Polyscience and Christianity
Rational Thought's Long History

Table of Contents

1 Introduction   iii

2 What Doth Science Mean?   1

3 The Lure of Objective Truth   21

4 Old Mathematics; Old Biases; Old Science   57

5 Confusion, Syncretism and Christian Criticism   97

6 More Visions; Still Old Mathematics   133

7 Pitfalls of Reason   167

8 The Specter of Attenuation   193

9 The Divorce of Mathematics from Reality   243

10 *Extrapolatio Grandis Mythi*   279

11 Epilogue   287

12 Appendices   289

13 Bibliography   331

14 Index   341

"What indeed has Athens to do with Jerusalem?" Tertullian, an early church Father, thus pondered reason and faith. He concluded that Athens' reasoners were more subjective than scientific; they competed with reason *and* faith!

Eighteen centuries later, do we agree with Tertullian? Can faith even question reason? If we answer no, perhaps we are unfamiliar with rational thought's history. Words like reason, rational and science are freely used, yet hint at vagueness.

Rationalists' dismiss religion – and Christianity in particular. They say that "God's existence is not in *rational proof.*" And rationalists are, above all, rational.

They seek world dominance – so that they can "free" the world from mental shackles. They are fed by ancient visions; fed by the fading enlightenment which is mesmerized by the even more ancient Mathematic's Word.

Yet rationalists ignore that arithmetic, geometry and logic are *also* not in *rational proof*, (but have empirical usefulness)! Anciently, they "knew"[1] these were rationally proven, but not now, so the sciences (of the inaccessible) are also not in rational proof. Now, theory or paradigm consensus substitute for that lost rational proof.

Further, while God's existence is not captured by human rational proof, God's works are in rational sight! The cosmos – the created fact – is His handiwork and He has transmitted to mankind Scripture. These are reasonable objects.

This book is a prelude on reasonable and rational thought, beginning with Greek thought. What can be wrong within the foundation of science? Most conservative Christians find nothing significant; they criticize Charles Darwin and his sequel. Rationalists also find nothing significant. Both groups ignore ancient through near-modern history. They have a "book-ends" view; the centuries-long "between-years" hold no crucial interest. (Many recognize only one book-end – today's world.)

Dictionaries no longer define science, but provide explanations that satisfy present seekers – but not those of the past or deconstructed future. "*Systematically arranged truths*" or "*showing the operation of general laws*" are mentioned. These explanations seem neutral, even to theism. As *homo scientificus*, rationalists confidently generate confusion, enlarging "truth" within a framework of theory and paradigm. Thus the Biblical concern over science, falsely so-called, remains valid.

If science, itself, is unexplainable, why argue about "is evolution science?" or "is Creation science? For disciplines from A to Z, what is the definition of science that anchors them in truth, (without reference to any specific discipline)? Sigh! …. I can get my attempt down to only several paragraphs.

Some may respond with "*Several paragraphs! Don't you know that science can*

---

1   Many times I use quotation marks " " to indicate words or phrases that have a common usage but which seem inappropriate when studying rational thought. The context will help determine if this additional usage is intended.

be defined with four easy words? Science is objective truth!" I agree that that is the general definition, but that means a science purged of subjectivity – no paradigms, schools of mathematics, extrapolative infatuation, *etc.* If you agree, your view of science is as restrained as mine! *Welcome, friend!*

Have you ever fallen for a trick question? Something like "Can you see that elephant camouflaged up in that tree?" You look up and respond "I don't see any elephant up in that tree!" And the trickster says "Pretty good camouflage, eh!"

In a similar manner, we may be told that science's domain is the entire universe. It is better to say, "Where applicable, science can be utilized." If I walk in the woods and discover a cave or a mineral deposit, have I discovered scientific truth? No! I have merely discovered a fact that can be added to our knowledge base.

We have forgotten that science is not a domain, but a search methodology for facts. (Science is a verb, not a noun.) Is scientific knowledge more objective than facts found otherwise? No, again! Science is a limited experimental methodology. Nor should we overlook engineers, technicians, craftsmen and tinkerers. All these folk are fact-gatherers. They do leave some room for scientists!

However, DEEP knowledge wants to discover, not caves or the like, but *Universal Connected Knowledge*. Beginning with the ancient Greeks – this is science. To do this, the needed solvent is numbers. Hello – mathematics!

Christians believe "*the fear of the Lord is the beginning of knowledge*," Proverbs 1:7. Rationalists believe something like "*the fear of mathematics is the beginning of knowledge*," Reason 101:1a. These two statements parallel the tension between creation *ex nihilo* and the belief that God is an absentee landlord.

Christians frequently visualize this clash by contrasting:

God's Word versus Man's Word

Yet, a person molded by Plato's philosophy would view it as:

Mathematic's Word versus Man's Word

These ancient Greeks definitely would not call it "Mathematics' Word" or "Mathematician's Word." No, *mathematic* transcends both man and mathematics. It is incarnate in matter. Recognize it and you find truth! Mathematic (law) causes all things. Mathematic is an astonishing possibility!

Mathematic may be a new word. Mathematic is connected to *Universal Connected Knowledge!* In contrast, mathematics is connected to empirical science. If we are unsure of the difference, perhaps the wise old Gandalph might advise us: "Mathematic is similar to the one ring that rules them all." More on this later.

Dictionaries present rational and reasonable as almost indistinguishable adjectives. My experience and reading make me see an additional dimension to the words, not frequently expressed. My dictionary has 4 uses of Reasonable and 9 uses for Rational. Consider also:

Rational … 10. One who accepts no limits to extension, witnessing to the Platonic mathematical root of the word (ratio). One who believes that all real things have mathematical dimensions. No secondary qualities or other nonmathematical possibilities exist. If such a one cannot calculate, then he is dealing, at best, with secondary qualities.

Reasonable ... 5. One who accepts limits to extension, witnessing to the reality of complexity and nonmathematical objects. Only portions of reality can ever be mathematical.

In this important respect, the rational and the reasonable hardly inhabit the same conceptual world! *Rationalism is not pure reason*, but belief in an unprovable mathematical utopia.

To say that you are rational or reasonable is easy. To prove it is difficult! What the ancient Greeks said about reality, we, today, mostly find antiquated or embarrassing. Their rational "proof" for science and its *Universal Connected Knowledge* was mathematic – so it requires patience to comprehend what that meant.

The ancient Greeks imported Egyptian and Mesopotamian mathematics and transformed it into foundational truth. "Unaided" reason's triumphs began when they found mathematical predictability in the heavens. This confirmed their naive rational sense of superiority over others.

The subjective and the supernatural ceased to exist for them. Yet the mathematical "universals" long ago proclaimed by Pythagoras and Plato remain defective – as well as the methodology and logic of Aristotle!

Some accommodating Christians say God created according to number, weight and measure. Such may conclude that "God is the Great Mathematician." But which dialect of number, measure (geometry) or even logic does God prefer – and do we even know His dialect? Dialects in science surprise most people!

Today, we demand a better accounting of "unaided" truth. Who still accepts "pure" reason? Or "pure" intuition? And logic – how many theories of logic are there? Mathematic, mathematics – mathematical models of reality – do they unfold from one master equation without human tweaking of the constants or selecting sub-equations appropriate for each arena of explanation? Can people wend their way through this "explanatory" maze and remain *objective*?

Amazingly, rationalists know, "aided" by mathematic, that we live on an insignificant spec of planetary dust, adrift in a deterministic, impersonal, unimaginably cold and old universe. They freely apply a "radical doubt" to whatever contradicts this axiom. Miraculously, their "radical doubt" does not criticize science.

The ex *nihilo* Creation account, complete with the Garden of Eden and Noah's Flood, is foolish to rationalists. *Ex nihilo* creation, that created fact, is a discontinuity, which is known with the "aid" of revealed truth. It limits mathematic's methodology. Discontinuity is the original problem caused by the created fact! So we require some familiarity with rationalism's history – and convenient rational omissions.

The Greek view of science lasted over two thousand years, but failed around A.D. 1850 due to mathematical failures. This was science based on "first principles" or a physical mathematic. Few disciplines could join this exclusive club. After it failed, science moved to various consensus paradigms, including Darwin's evolution. Most retained the "concrete realities" emerging from past rational failures.

A puzzling subjectivity surrounds rational thought, which emphasizes theories and paradigms, and thus distorts science and truth. Much in this early mathematics and astronomy is silently passed over. This shortened historical perspective obstructs the search for truth. Thus the need to enter that hidden, yet obvious, path and retrace reason's history.

Ancient missteps still affect reason's endeavors. In fact, rational subjectivity is hidden in plain view. The early church Fathers, (from the time of Christ up to the Council of Nicea in A.D. 325), had long conflict with heresies spawned from false reason. After this prelude, the present-day claims for science can be evaluated.

Philosophy, like science, is also puzzling. Initially, it was not considered erudite word-smithing or crystal-ball gazing, but an intellectual encounter with the mathematic or logic building blocks of the universe. After mastering philosophical truths, science could then proceed to its *subsidiary* task. Yet philosophy's cosmic encounters repeatedly failed, so unaided reasoning was again exposed as subjective.

Because many of today's "truths" spring from ancient errors, reviewing the musty dusty history within the between-years is not a search for antiques but for error recognition. This task risks offending both sides of the intended audience. Rationalists dislike frank discussion of science's mystical roots. Indeed, the following chapters show good reasons for no longer defining science! Also, the early church Fathers bewilder many Christians, who (rightly?) wonder if the Fathers' ancient writings support present-day theology and/or practice. Going back (only) one hundred and fifty years is not a deep historical review!

Serious problems afflict both reason and faith, yet rationalists "know" that they are objective. They grant that not all of reality is in the experimental domain, but insist that mathematic (and logic) thereby find their finest application. These inerrantly extend the experimental reach with grandiose theories and exemplify puzzle solving. *Knowledge is Universal.* Surprisingly, mathematic (or logic) cannot inerrantly support this endless grandiose assumption; elements within them require choices. *Puzzle solving* beyond the experimental domain risks becoming well-reasoned *storytelling*.

Men of faith also seek to understand our world, but many move away from the sacred and inspired Scripture and listen to well-reasoned storytellers. Disconnected from history, the world, and the Word – they think their own thoughts are God's theology for today.

Rationalists vehemently say the Bible was "put in its place" a long time ago – that, at best, the Bible is an honored pre-scientific myth. Christianity gained supremacy in the past with a noncurrent, but unified, account of the cosmos, thereby *temporarily* satisfying reason and faith. From the heavens, to the earth, to the individual, to the souls of men and the afterlife – all was in its rational place. This was a supernatural, stable and rational cosmos. Biblical revelation harmonized faith and reason.

Rationalists believe the ancient Greeks, thankfully, ruined this harmony with Mathematic's Word, proved in mathematics and astronomy, revealing that we live on this insignificant spec of planetary dust adrift in an utterly large, old, and material cosmos. Besides, they say, Christianity is only one of many religions – all being subjective. Their *radical doubt* rejects articles of faith.

Their science now has the "unbiased" superiority, "revealing" the "unsuper-natural" beginning – and history – of everything. They proudly confront truth – facts – and are compelled to assent, thereby avoiding the taint of faith – or faith's documents. So fortified, they neither bow to religion nor reevaluate reason's accomplishments. (For over two thousand years the subjectivity in mathematic and logic were not widely recognized. A false sense of objectivity increased their courage.)

I reassure such thinkers that they are our model of objective truth! (*sic.*) In our troubled age of uncertainty, relative truth, and no absolutes, it is comforting to know that rational thought reigns unshaken. It's science and puzzle solving activity stand above quibbling relative truths, theories, paradigms or well-reasoned storytelling!

Woops! Now these same thinkers get apologetic, saying they didn't mean it so absolutely. They may reluctantly concede that science is provisional due to new data. Rather, unwise foundational visions and demotion of empiricism may give the better major reason for provisionality. Unfortunately, *paradigms* and *truth* are *not equivalent*. No wonder deconstructionists, acidic philosophers of science, disgruntled scientists, old-fashioned Christians, or Oriental-minded philosophers criticize the edifice of their science.

So, the Bible *is not* put in its place by reason! Rationalists conveniently fail to apply their radical doubt to Greek mysticism and mathematical visions that have endured in various forms. Ironically, their "assent" to truth is now assent to rational storytelling.

The beginning of science contains storytelling, and a later transition to objective foundations cannot be demonstrated. Much of the inaccessible remains unconquered. Some science requires reclassification as science, falsely so-called; their claims to focus on puzzle solving, not storytelling, are not reasonable. Assumptions and mathematical choices means that such as *astronomy contain marvelous rafts of data adrift on oceans of mathematics.* Like the old toy, the *kaleidoscope*, making "sense" of rafts of data with mathematics may overwhelm our ability to distinguish truth from systematics. In contrast, (true) science is constrained.

The present edifice of science has had much time and money lavished on its understanding of facts. Do not conclude that its grandiose extensions are approximately correct, but wonder what the Biblical understanding would be with a similar expenditure of time and money.

Verbally dexterous rationalists use wordy subjectivity to fight the faith and reason built on Biblical Revelation. It is a clash between faith in subjective rational wordiness versus Christianity's revealed faith.

This controversy contains the current creation and evolution debate, but the controversy is broader. Look again at Genesis 1:1: "*In the beginning God created the* **heaven** *and the earth....*" Volumes are written on "beginning," "created," and "earth" (applied to systematizations such as geology and biology) and "days." Yet little is said on "heaven," even allowing for the fact that on day one of the creation week, heaven was an empty place. Systematizations of astronomy are dangerous interpretive signposts, being afloat on an ocean of mathematics.

Granted, the rationalists goal was to know reality and banish the subjective or mere "saving the appearances." In the process, rationalism nurtured materialism, which sought objective status. Supernatural discontinuities grated on their extrapolative infatuation.

In contrast, Christian reasoning accepts the Revelation ("aided" truth) that God created the universe *ex nihilo* (out of nothing), as Genesis 1:1 reveals. The earth and the universe had a recent beginning ... and will have an end. God's purpose rules history – teleology. Dimensionally, the universe is finite. The created fact is rather small for rational tastes.

Beyond the universe is God's abode, the third heaven. God, in the universe's design and in sundry times and places, manifests His care for His *ex nihilo* creation. Supernatural visits by God and His angels (and the Devil and his troupe of fallen angels) are also part of reality. The Christian worldview: "*The earth is the Lord's, and the fullness thereof*" (Psalm 24:1).

Christian thought and Greek "objectivity" both spread across the Mediterranean arena in the between-years. They clashed over worldviews – comprehensive understandings of reality. The Biblical epistles warned against "philosophy," "knowledge" and "*science, falsely so-called.*" We today little appreciate the clash.

Some thinkers reconciled Greek "science of that day" with both nature and God, naively assuming all "science" revealed details of God's marvelous handiwork, highlighting creation's underlying beauty and order. The mathematical relationships evident in nature muted concerns about the mysticism and materialism embedded in Greek mathematics. A truce ensued, allowing God's handiwork and supernatural encounters to remain foundational.

In that era, believers did not live as aliens or automatons in a cosmos unvisited by the supernatural. Worshipping God was being in God's presence. The modern fashion of living by "pure faith" was alien.

Nor could Greek science hide its many internal squabbles or shameful pleasures. Christianity defeated – or subdued – this science, falsely so-called.

This ancient world fell apart some centuries after Christ.

A thousand-plus years later, Europeans rediscovered many Greek ideas in the Renaissance and the Enlightenment eras. Some philosophers, astronomers and mathematicians then emphasized the long-dormant Greek mysticism and mathematical visions. They chaffed at Christian restrictions to Greek ideals. Freeing themselves from Christian restrictions and basking in a newfound mental autonomy, they ironically chained themselves to the extrapolative infatuation inherent in mathematic. Scholarly disciplines gained increasing respectability as long-sought truth, but not all this respect was well-deserved! Some were orderly veneers over word fogs.

Soon, the new astronomical understanding of Copernicus nurtured their existing "expansive" thoughts. The Bible could no longer be true, at least in its astronomical statements. Later, Newton's mathematical systematization of gravity was interpreted to exclude any relationship between God and His *ex nihilo* creation.

This unhinging of the mind from the Bible encouraged recent folk such as Charles Darwin and Sigmund Freud. They saw man as an irrational animal in a materialistic cosmos. How ironic – *irrational animals make "rational" scientists!*

When inconsistencies appeared later, such were for Einstein and the quantum mechanics folks to paper over. Such new systematizations, now the "sciences of our day," conflict with the supernatural – and each other.

Supposedly, this is the liberating influence of science. Mathematics is the medium of scientific laws, but mathematic masks some illusions. (Simple) natural laws are the siren calls of rational utopias. Also, (complex) natural laws that grapple with our complex world can fall prey to creative freedom. Dangers lurk for "pure" rational thought. Empirical criticism was not rational, thus unwelcome.

Through those same centuries, Christianity grew and conquered many false lifestyles and rational worldviews. Daily living provided practical questions to answer. Christians relied on the Bible, and the tradition once delivered to the saints, and prayed for the Holy Spirit's guidance.

An example from the late Middle Ages reiterates how even death held no terror for Christians. An aged monk was asked why he did not fear death. He replied that the universe is God's. At death, he would merely open another door in God's house, enter, and continue living. Death was of little consequence to his life in God's world – which is bigger than the cosmos.

The passage of centuries, however, can allow compromise or error to distort Christianity. This leads to calls for reformation, such as that identified with Martin Luther, but change presents new dangers! Times of Reformation, radical Reformation, Counter-Reformation, or Renaissance may unwittingly allow the entry of differently flavored errors. *(Out with old compromises, in with new compromises!)* The mind's oversight of reason exhibits fallibility by misjudging the "sciences of the day" and unwisely accepting some as truth.

Old and new misjudgments mix storytelling and truth, subtly revising Christianity in efforts to correct, cleanse, defend or defeat it! At best, Biblical miracles were allowed to remain, but later miracles were definitely out. This naturalizing trend disrupted Western culture's spiritual balance and put Biblical revelation and Christianity on the defensive. Some gave up their spirit and soul. Others embraced a previous antagonist, philosophy, then specifically existentialism, identified with Søren Kierkegaard. Accepting the storytelling about an infinite cosmos, such thinkers retreated beyond the grasp of reason by believing religion to be a "leap of faith."

Once again, rational thought and faith clashed over the source and content of truth. Biblical revelation is upsetting, even within Christianity! Even though I Timothy 3:15b says that the church ... is the pillar and ground of truth, some fear(ed) to apply it against the "neutral" juggernaut of science. Christianity was (and is) thus ill-prepared to resist rationalism.

Surprisingly, in our day, the long-expected showdown between Christianity and rationalism is distracted by the intrusion of other ideas – Oriental or New Age. A duel of words has grown into at least a triad of conflict, and neither sect or myth nor paradigm wants to be excluded.

This enlarged conflict exists because rational subjectivity grew more obvious before its showdown with Christianity. Philosophy, mathematic and mathematics were tainted with pluralism and subjectivity! Theories, paradigms and many "laws" have degenerative half-lives. Like the kaleidoscope, "unaided" reason can be storytelling or puzzle solving. Rationalists stumbled; they failed to out-argue other rationalists! They still do not believe in faith – but their wordiness hides a subjective faith. Conflicting rational word systems were losing their exclusive grips on rafts of facts. The orderly veneers were unravelling. Their competitive edge slipped!

A cloud of uneasiness settles over mankind. Contradictory mathematical, philosophical, scientific or political "objective truths" seek our loyalty. Far from correcting these, grandiose science clings to this ancient vagueness – some of its reasons are subjective. In this flawed landscape, rational thought falters. Language's ability to communicate strains under these contradictions – and some people are happy about that! Most ominously, truth – even scientific truth – retreats into private preferences, which yet demand preferential respect! Contradictions increasingly paralyze many people's minds. They mark our age.

Some rationalists have lost the secular faith. They see "assent to truth" as window dressing. They retreat to cynicism or modern sophistry, confident that their linguistic and rational capabilities let them "get away with it." They can pull the wool over the eyes of the old fogies, governments, universities and even funding agencies.

This conflict between rational thought and faith highlights the need for a *prelude* on rational thought before the Gospel is "hearable" by rationalists. In missionary settings, like the Japan incident, Christians recognize the importance of understanding a local culture's cosmic perspective and word meanings. Scientific rationalism is a (cosmic) cultural barrier – but between people speaking the same language!

Without a prelude on reason and science, including its between-years expressions, rationalists easily confront Christians with naive statements like, "It is unfair to invoke God into the experiments." Really. I reply, "God is not mentioned in explanations of superconductivity, electron transport through ultra-thin computer circuitry, or the strength determination of composite graphite structures – other than as being the universe's designer." (The list goes on.) Additionally, such things as the irreducible complexity of cell structure point to a designer – such intricacies cannot be mathematically or logically modeled, negating the desire to show progress through blind chance. There are also the geological markers of catastrophe. Invoking God into experiments is not where the clash occurs.

Rather, *rationalists invoke grandiose extrapolation to go well beyond the experimental realm* – as when "explaining" the heavens. When challenged, the audacity of questioning science astonishes them. They typically cover their extrapolative infatuation by accusing their questioners of invoking God into science.

Their extrapolations are "objective" because their *mathematic "aid" is value-free.* They say the tools of science are; *Arithmetic:* 1 + 1 = 2; *Geometry:* point, line, triangle, cube and conic section; and *Logic.* A scientific explanation, generously smothered in arithmetic, geometry, and logic, should not be questioned by any "rational" person.

Rationalists may make statements like, "We follow reason, alone, as far as it can go. Then, if barriers are encountered, we will 'incorporate' religion." Humbly though, a foundationless reason, with creative subjectivity and unbridled extrapolation, can not recognize the difference between puzzle solving and storytelling. Rather, recognition of reason's limitations causes disillusionment with the myth of "unaided" reason.

Many say science (and its vast domain) are too well understood to criticize it, but do not be distracted from a review of rationalism's claims and defeats. The quest for truth is a welcome contrast to the swamp of paradigmatic subjectivity. Wordy subjectivity undergirds rational thought.

Yet, undaunted rationalists heroically plod on, continuing to devise laws and systems. But their minds are distracted by people! People are so unmathematical. Individuals don't mirror their laws, but they hope the "statistic-able" masses do! The truth remains: Life's perplexities are intractable to "unaided" reason.

The trendy religious help them by rationally updating religion. They do not listen to actual religions, but create "Religion." Bleached of specifics, this super-religion bypasses creeds and founders; names are retained but with new meanings.

A vague unity results, it is the best that can be constructed with unaided rationalism! Nonetheless, the Bible remains the source of truth which transcends science. (True) science is reasonable by restricting itself to experimental environs.

The early church Fathers are instructive amidst this relative and reasoned subjectivity; the dangers they faced are returning! The Fathers engaged in reasonable debate and apologetics – in addition to witness and compassion – and converted their world. The Christian mind in action defeated Greek science due to an open secret: Greek science was guided by science, falsely so-called. This "overburden" was more important than mere science. The "residue" of mere (empirical) science remains compatible with Christianity.

So, today, *learning, intellect, reason, science, mathematics, engineering, philosophy* and *knowledge* remain respected by Christianity. STEM – science, technology, engineering and mathematics remain amenable to Christianity. Most thinkers have an over-rosy evaluation of science – and a resultant over-gloomy view of Christianity. Christian apologists should not accept this evaluation; compromise is driven by subjective concepts embedded in science, falsely so-called. I call these concepts "*well-reasoned.*"

Well-reasoned folk, intentionally or not, promote science, falsely so-called. They present science as a seamless fabric of knowledge, with no flaws, cracks or gaps. Their undefined science – containing "vast distances and long ages" – prohibits the supernatural.

Many people wonder what religion is left to deal with. The answer requires a prelude on the between-years. Too often, well-reasoned folk replace faith with subjectivity!

Another question often asked is "What use is this history in facing life's challenges today." Apart from the evident continuity of the Christian faith, consider the following example:

A family member once asked me about early church beliefs so he could respond to a cult member he was witnessing to. He mentioned the name of Arius (third century A.D.), who had been favorably mentioned by the cult member, even though Christianity long ago rejected him as a heretic.

Reflecting on the Greek philosophy then predominant, I described the cosmos that such thinkers used to fashion their science and "updated" Christianity. Arius, to harmonize with the Greek science of the day, postulated: a Christ separate from Jesus, (so the Savior was untainted by birth or execution); disdain for the Old Testament and Jehovah God; no hell; perform careful editing of the Scriptures, an unapproachable master god; and other such views. The family member said these items are beliefs of this present-day sect!

The science of that day is still operative! Can one present the Gospel to this sect by Bible-study, or must we preface the study with a prelude on that long-forgotten science of that day? Not to downplay Bible-study, yet we must use scholarship to assist in understanding the mind of the unsaved.

Rationalists do not understand Christian writers who try to repair the "sundering" of reason and faith – to live and write in His presence and not by "pure faith." The aura of His presence partially accounts for the attraction of recent writers like George MacDonald, G. K. Chesterton, C. S. Lewis, J. R. R. Tolkien, and Francis Schaeffer.

My prelude is creationist – yet somewhat unfamiliar. The history of mathematics and astronomy is emphasized, instead of their progeny: materialism and evolution. It begins with thinkers in ancient Greece – some of their lasting mental structures are strange.

This study does not talk about reason versus faith, but rationalism versus faith. *Reason, understanding, and faith co-exist.* Also, the sundering of faith from rational thought was not a clear break for all people through the centuries. It was more like a tearing, a fragmenting. Inter-mediate belief or assent positions abound.

This subject matter, spanning centuries and having prolific writers, is an enormous challenge. I pray that professionals in these complex subjects will tolerate my words. Words can have shades of meaning, so I sometimes use nonstandard expressions to convey ideas.

Some may object to the Bible translation I use. They think the King James Version (KJV) of the Bible has poor scholarship and antiquated language. As I review the Biblical quotations used herein, few are that hard to read. Concern over scholarship and language are overdone.

Some may not like the KJV practice of using the words, *mankind, he,* or *him,* to refer to people in general. The KJV translators found such wording inescapable. They used the ancient Biblical Received Text (*Textus Receptus*), a work still worthy of respect.

Modern phraseologies are sometimes awkward, sometimes evolutionary-minded (like humankind). I trust you see that *mankind* communicates best. Scripture quotations will be from the KJV, unless otherwise noted.[2]

---

2   The KJV text is actually from 1813, in a family Bible printed by M Carey, Philadelphia!

We do not want to lose sight of the inadequacy of discussing God and our relationship with Him by using logic or formula. Few are so naive as to think they can describe themselves or family members with logic or formula! How do you describe a heart of compassion or a sensitive spirit with logic or formula? Words – or equations – just never say so many things correctly. Stories or personal experience convey that which eludes logic or formula. Even more so, this applies to human discussion about God.

By keeping the opening chapters general, I seek recognition of – even agreement on – *concepts* before exploring whether they conflict with "scientific" knowledge. We then can better understand the verbal gymnastics so many use to avoid the obvious – as they use extrapolative infatuation to anchor "reason" and thwart true reason and faith.

Why did the *Introduction* sound so skeptical of reason and science? This chapter provides the technical historical basis for skepticism.

The Search for Knowledge. People seek to know the world by their unaided efforts. Indeed, people can find certain truth! The discovery of a cave or a mineral deposit yields *direct facts...* yet such accessible but fragmented knowledge is a letdown for many. It deflates their noble human ego! Surely people can do more than make lists of facts; *scientific knowledge is universal!* We therefore seek U*niversal Connected Knowledge* about the accessible and inaccessible. Inaccessible implies things such as history, things too small (atoms), and things too large or far away (heavenly objects).

As science began in Greece, Greek pagans provided answers for at least history and astronomy. Actually, they gave many answers. Their oral and written records are viewed as a jumble of facts and storytelling.

Soon, other Greeks sought Universal Connected Knowledge as philosophers, but they emphasized unconnected facts. These pre-Socratic philosophers (before 400 B.C.) were the "earth, air, fire and water" folks. Their many answers showed some orderliness, but were not widely accepted.

Thus a new search methodology was needed:

The Atomic Search. Democritus (*ca.*460-*ca.*370 B.C.) was an early philosopher with a difference. He theorized that *reality is composed of atoms*. These were inaccessible, indivisible, infinitely small, infinite in number, in an infinite cosmos and moving due to chance. Randomly cohering atoms "create" our emerging reality, according to his view of atheism and materialism. His theoretical need for universal disorder contradicted the empirical reality of order.

Democritus was a noted mathematician but did not offer a methodology to advance knowledge. Therefore, atomism received little support among thinkers, as the subject was inaccessible. Later, Plato and Aristotle showed other ways to access the inaccessible. Also, Democritus's atheism repelled pagans and philosophers. In Greece, atomists led almost a quarantined existence. Epicurus (342? - 270 B.C.) and Lucretius (*ca.* 96 - *ca.* 55 B.C.), a Roman, continued the school. St. Paul, in his visit to Athens around A.D. 55 recorded in Acts 17:1-34, encountered the Epicureans, who were atomists. But St. Paul's listeners included the Stoics, who were anti-atomists! The followers of Plato and Aristotle are not mentioned; they were then in decline. Athens' thinkers were a quarrelsome crowd. By A.D. 300, atomism had died out, yet it lived on for years in Rome. Atomism survived in writing – in the criticism it received in the works of Plato, Aristotle and various Roman sources, particularly Cicero.

The Mathematical Search. Beginning a new phase, Plato (*ca.* 427-347 B.C.) a disciple of Socrates (*ca.* 468-399 B.C.), reached back to Pythagoras (*ca.* 582-500 B.C.), a pre-Socratic philosopher, and both sought order and universal connectedness by a curious process. *They postulated and then studied a hidden "substance"* – which was *mathematic*: arithmetic for Pythagoras and (primarily) geometry for Plato. An ethereal repository in a heaven contained the master "pure" substance – and trained thinkers could access it! Pure, but inaccessible, mathematic was then said to be incarnated as sensible reality. This *top-down* view of reality means that mathematical "properties" cause physical properties. **Mathematical LAW causes ALL things; this is Mathematic's Word! Law is self-evident truth!**

To explain everything, this theory had more superstructure than just mathematic. It even included a fated god.

This was the theory – and they took over the word, *theory*. In common Greek usage, "theory" meant sightseeing or reading a road map.[1] Theory became an overarching vision – a "clear intuition" – in the "mind's eye." Theory frequently was sightseeing on the road to becoming "all-seeing."

This theory was developed under the continuing shadow of polytheism. In contrast, *mathematic was monotruth.* 1 + 1 = 2 and the angles of a triangle always add up to 180 degrees – and gods could not change these. Sensible facts were united by their common mathematical ancestry! Man's "unaided" efforts were aided by mathematic – and their first "success" was in mathematics itself and then in astronomy. Direct facts were eclipsed by this search for connected inaccessible facts. The abstractions: number, point, line, curve and circle were the only true facts. These grounded *rationalism* but it is better called *mathematic-ism*.

Science was the understanding of (and communion with) these universal but ethereal abstractions. Indeed, as monotruth, mathematic grew and many examples of incarnated mathematics were said to be found in reality. Incarnated mathematic might be "saving the appearances" (storytelling) instead of describing objective reality. Predictably, there were casualties. Pythagoras was defeated by irrational numbers. Plato's view was ultimately defeated by the logical coherence of Aristotle, multiple geometries and the belated recognition of inherent subjectivity in mathematics.

The Accessible Search. Plato's most famous pupil, Aristotle (384-322 B.C.), agreed with many sensible items in Plato's thought, but disagreed with the top-down Mathematic. (He spent about twenty years in Plato's Academy.) He found no rational proof for a mathematical heaven, nor its incarnation into reality! That theory required belief, not analysis, to arrive at truth. Instead, he said that *all knowledge comes in through our senses*. He reportedly said that mathematics comes through "playing with marbles or drawing in the sand." Complex mathematics arises from thinking about this

---

1. Theory: To understand a map is puzzle solving; to create a map may be storytelling; to understand the difference may challenge the wisdom of King Solomon!

rudimentary data. Numbers are for counting; geometry is for figures and measuring; but *Science is to know things through demonstrated conclusions.*

Aristotle was a master mathematician who studied accessible reality, but without a reverence for mathematics. He thus could see nature directly, and it was a challenge in its own right! Direct facts were to be discovered and then connected via the methodology and logical categories he developed, thus showing the common ancestry and structure of reality. His theory was a *bottom-up* search for knowledge. He was not adverse to direct facts, observation or working with lists. It was *proto-empiricism.* But he faced a similar danger: He could be logically "saving the appearances" instead of describing objective reality.

His logic removed some muddles existing in the minds of thinkers. Logical syllogisms begin with IF, then another IF, and ends with a THEREFORE conclusion, but not necessarily a fact or truth. His logic developed some First Principles required for clear thought. Even the later monumental *Elements* (of Geometry) by Euclid respected his logic.

Conflict and Compromise. The atomist, top-down, or bottom-up systems had questionable long-term success, despite being "clear intuitions" in their minds' eyes. Plato criticized Democritus without ever mentioning his name, and Aristotle criticized both many times. (Some philosophers point out that Democritus' indivisible atoms, Pythagoras's indivisible numbers and Plato's indivisible triangles have a strange similarity![2]) And the systems of the Stoics and the Cynics soon entered the struggle. (At various times, these were more popular than the "big three.") After the deaths of these masters came an unsettled time. Contending top-down or bottom-up systems were transformed or merged into neo-this or neo-that.

---

2.   Empirical science and engineering would say that they share the strange property of non-deformability, *i.e.,* infinite hardness. In contrast, real things are deformable. They form mass-elastic systems, with a specific "natural frequency" that is also their "resonant frequency." If an outside force rhythmically impinges on a mass-elastic system at its resonant frequency (and the system has insufficient dampening), that system will be driven to destructive amplitudes of motion.

In a later chapter we will mention the famous "Galloping Gertie" suspension bridge. It was destroyed by a light, but rhythmic, wind months after its completion.

Planets also form mass-elastic systems. Sir Isaac Newton's "uncommon unintelligibility," otherwise known as gravity, is the spring. Engineers ask, what is the system's natural frequency? With matter having infinite hardness, this was a question and a concept the Greeks never thought about.

We now suspend this discussion until later chapters. Some uncertainty is good for our over-rationalized souls!

Also, neither Pythagoras, nor Plato nor Aristotle was a pure atheist. However, a strict materialism later arose which stressed logical rigor, the unaided power of reason, an infinite universe, geometry, and atheism. (And there was the separate path to atheism of atomism.) Thinkers now had many ways to reason, but where was truth? None of these relied solely on public knowledge. But did one, at the least, point in the correct direction?

Interestingly, three other prominent individuals may not have been members of philosophical schools. They were Archimedes of Syracuse (*ca.* 287-212 B.C.), Ptolemy of Egypt (*fl.* A.D. 127-151) and Euclid (*fl.* 300 B.C.).

Archimedes is remembered as an engineer and developer of military weapons. He also discovered the principle of buoyancy, the Archimedean screw pump, principles of levers and he wrote important mathematical treatises.

Ptolemy is remembered for his *Almagest* which showed how to calculate planetary positions, assuming geocentricity. (Its accuracy was unsurpassed until well after Copernicus.) Also important was his *Geography*, which was on mapmaking. He also wrote the *Tetrabiblios*, the standard handbook on astrology! Back then, astrology was a serious endeavor, indeed, a branch of philosophy.

Euclid wrote his celebrated *Elements* of Geometry and Number, and it remained the standard textbook for about 2,000 years. Euclid did not originate all of this material, but he collected and organized the existing scattered material. Euclid required less than two pages to list 23 definitions, 5 axioms (postulates) and 5 common notions. Then followed 400 pages of elaboration (in thirteen books), each of which includes additional definitions and lemmas.

Only the gifted few can tackle the *Elements* without help. The two most noted commentators are Proclus (A.D. 410-485) and Sir Thomas Heath (A.D. 1861-1940). Proclus and Heath each required more than 100 pages to explain Euclid's beginning two pages. To understand the *Elements*, Proclus and Heath quote some of Euclid's sources and, ironically, a major source is Aristotle, who discussed mathematical particulars and history, and his logic set the standard of rigor that Euclid followed. As the two commentators said, the *"**Divine Plato**"* and the *"**Inspired Aristotle**"* were both required.

The Scientific Method (of the Greeks). The *Elements* became celebrated because, with those two pages of beginning notions, the entire edifice of geometry and number was constructed. At the least, it is an abstract intellectual exercise.

The foundational definitions, axioms and common notions are undefined terms. They are accepted without proof. They are obviously true – clear intuitions. As Aristotle had said, each science must be based on undefined terms in order to avoid an infinite regress. The *Elements* also accepted Aristotle's dictum that reality was not infinite, as that notion went beyond sense experience – and got entangled in contradictions.

Geometry and number are abstract subjects, but Euclid does not mention Plato's ethereal repository in a heaven. Proclus has no doubts that Euclid was a committed Platonist, but Proclus was a prominent neoplatonist (and an anti-Christian). Heath agrees that Euclid was a Platonist (in education) but that he followed Aristotle's logical outlook. As abstractions, how do the beginning notions apply to the real world? (*The question is not even asked in the Elements.)* Nonetheless, the abstract *Elements* was easier to understand than the complex sense world.

Greek science was based on foundational principles – that were undefined but obviously true. It was called the *axiomatic method,* providing self-evident truth independent of man. It guided the search for Universal Connected Knowledge.

Clearly enunciated steps led to ... knowledge. Each step must save the appearances of reality. Wrong notions were not to be used, even if they led to correct results, but there were some lapses. The *Elements* inspired a "passionate search for truth and beauty"!

(Greek mathematics was restricted to arithmetic and geometry. Their conceptual outlook prevented the development of trigonometry, algebra and some other branches.)

There were several Achilles' heels: Where does pure geometry reside? What does it mean to apply an abstract number or geometry to the causal real world? Is the real world as constant as mathematics? Or is the present time an exception to the normal? To a Pythagorean or a Platonist, these presented no difficulty as the real world was incarnated mathematics. To an Aristotelean, these statements required caution, as matter may have features not captured by mathematics. The non-philosophically-minded Greeks supposedly weren't interested in these questions.

Yet, a greater obscurity existed. People are inclined to say to doubters of science. *"Don't you believe that 1 + 1 = 2?"*

But that is the ancient version of the question. Does it mean the same to say today; *"Don't you believe that .... →?"*

$$e^{jx} = \cos x + j \sin x$$

$$e^{j\pi} + 1 = 0$$

$$E(x) = \mathbb{A} \langle x \in \mathcal{U} \wedge x \in \hat{a})$$

$$\sigma_x \, \sigma_p \geq \frac{\hbar}{2}$$

$$\hat{e}_i = \sum_j R_i^j \, e_j$$

$$\langle \Psi_1 | \Psi_2 \rangle \equiv \int_{-\infty}^{\infty} \Psi_j^*(x) \, \Psi(x) \, d(x)$$

While some may say that these later equations are built upon 1 + 1 = 2, *can they say several other things?* Are they built solely upon 1 + 1 = 2; does sensible reality display these; and do all scholars with the same PhD degrees agree upon the proper usage of them? I doubt all three possibilities.

So, Greek science contained a tension. While they disputed among themselves for many centuries, *Universal Natural Law was the key mark of Greek science.* Arithmetic and geometry were abstract truth, but were they also objective truth?

In good mathematical fashion, their timeline of history became infinite! Mathematics easily affirms the reality of the eternal stability of nondeformable matter.

Yet what measurable truths did philosophy provide? Its truths were invisible!

Atoms, mathematics and logic could not be seen. Further, the actual timeline they could document were a few centuries in the past, but nothing about the future.

So, we should look again at:

The fear of the Lord is the beginning of knowledge.

No wonder Greek "rational wisdom" did not conquer reasonable Biblical peoples.

The Christian Search. The Christian era soon began and conflict arose over worldviews: the orderly overarching universal knowledge of the accessible and the inaccessible.

Nonetheless, Greek thinkers insisted that there was "guilt by association" with anything connected to the name of god. (In lands immersed in polytheism, atheism seemed like progress!)

The Biblical record, though, was orderly and connected, but full of events. *Events (history, discontinuity)* contradicted the eternal mathematical and logical order Greek thinkers favored – exemplified by a mathematical line. *Mathematical order (mathematical determinism) has no "events," it is ahistorical, it is axiomatic, it is abstract, it is rational!*

But sense observation can invalidate the application of abstraction to reality. So, science informed by Christianity was to struggle to utilize mathematics and observation, while respecting events and avoiding unwarranted extrapolations or elaborate superstructures. Indeed, Christianity provides universal knowledge, but indicates that rational thought cannot provide unlimited extension. God and his *ex nihilo* creation were an ancient example of Occam's Razor – challenging thinkers! Mystery and the unknown remain – as a principle – another Achilles' heel. And if abstraction and sense experience argue for superiority, is our noble human ego an impartial referee?

Not surprisingly, Plato was vague about many details of his extensive superstructure and Aristotle instead focused on sense observations. Plato does mention the "myth" of the lost city of Atlantis. He mentions universal floods at intervals, which no longer occur because the constituent "triangles" of matter are now hardened. And there was the memory of the violent earthquake and tsunami that destroyed the Minoan civilization on the island of Crete many centuries earlier. Aristotle mentions some reported astronomical events but dismisses them. So, did the ahistorical mathematical line prove "eventless" truths about the (real) universe?

    Historical evidence includes what earlier observers have reported. One does not investigate the Peloponnesian Wars without reading the Greek reports on these wars. "Myth" can be a word used to discredit earlier observers. We honor macro-historical statements about events in the Bible by investigation: *ex nihilo* creation, Noah's flood and Joshua's long day. Worldwide records also report them. Are these history or inter-continental synchronized mythology? Nor should mundane events like earthquakes, volcanoes or tsunamis be overlooked. Indeed, events mean that sight-seeing or "knowledge" regarding the inaccessible may be "unclear" intuitions.

    There is little evidence Greek philosophers tried to reconcile events to mathe-matics or logic! Rational omissions were common. Mathematic prevailed!

    Ex Nihilo creation stands as a witness to God's power and creativity – which are not foreseeable by unaided humans. When the Bible talks about "science, falsely so-called" or the "winds of human wisdom," a major target was Greek mathematic-ism, which extended knowledge beyond history into an ahistorical "reality."

    There was to be no peace in the word wars! Aristotle, as mentioned earlier, said that science is to know through demonstrated conclusions. In his logic, he also said, when you encounter a contradiction, to make a distinction. Because he and Plato disagreed on much, a distinction was in order.

    The key contradiction regarded the word, *demonstrated*. Are conclusions about reality demonstrated through mathematics; or observation (saving the appearances), by experiment (then practically unknown), or sometimes is it that reason cannot make a judgment? This, in summary, was the argument. It still is.

    This discussion stands near the "beginning bookend" of history. Yet rationalists do not like to stand there and ponder what they were "before science." Further, they immediately claim an advantage by possessing reason, science and mathematic. But these words are loaded with ambiguity and lack exclusivity.

    At the beginning bookend, there were pagans and monotheists. Their various outlooks influenced the ambiguity referred to. To avoid having to critique reason, science and mathematic, beginning Greek thinkers (and their later disciples) relied on strange concepts – as the next chapters elaborate.

    Around A.D. 50, shoulder rubbing began between Greek knowledge and Christian revelation. Foundational ambiguity and non-exclusivity confuse the situation. Intense contact would soon occur.

    This contact heightened the fervor of the emerging gnosticism, which tried to synthesize science(s) and religion(s). It was a heady brew, but was subdued by around A.D. 350. A major subject in the writings of the early church Fathers was refuting various forms of gnosticism. Irenaeus (A.D.? - 202) pointed out that system (and mathematics) comes from the Creator (not vice-versa), thus partially coinciding with the bottom-up attitude.

    Christian thinkers did find useful bits in the contending philosophical systems. St. Augustine (A.D. 354-430) used some of the moral and political tones of Plato. St. Thomas Aquinas (A.D. 1225? - 1274) used the logical rigor of Aristotle. With the destruction of the Western Roman Empire in A.D. 476, Greek writings gradually became lost to Europe, but were preserved in Constantinople, the seat of Byzantium, the Eastern Roman Empire. Christianity, both in Rome and Constantinople, survived and flourished. Their witness subdued paganism and rational sight-seeing.

In summary, atomism died out, Plato's moral tone was valued but his top-down mathematics from an inaccessible ethereal heaven was eclipsed by Aristotle's bottom-up analysis of the accessible. Yet neoplatonism later breathed new life into Platonism. Also, Aristotle's logical rigor made some crucial physical mistakes which centuries later allowed Plato's reemergence. Euclidean mathematics, which was easily applied to astronomy, concurrently offered "promise" of also conquering the accessible. But its ancestry was unknown and, further, its relationship to reality was assumed as known.

With this as an introduction, can we decide whether God is the Great Mathematician or is God the Great Craftsman? Either answer has echoes relating to the argument between Plato and Aristotle! Or to the grandiose versus the accessible!

A New Dawn. About a thousand years later, Europe began to recover from the destruction of the Western Roman Empire, the devastation of barbarian invasions, deadly plagues, warring kingdoms and mass migrations. This was the Medieval Period (Middle Ages), derogatively called the Dark Ages by humanists. Improvements to living standards occurred due to native ingenuity, and some scholarly advances also occurred. Prosperity brought trade and travel, which, in turn, brought then unknown Greek manuscripts, which were hypnotic.

Thus began the Renaissance (of Greek science). Indeed, much knowledge was recovered, but also mathematical or philosophical mysticism or "clear intuitions." Pre-1800 writers such as Voltaire, Spinoza, Bruno, Descartes, Leibnitz, Diderot, Hobbes, Hume, Thomas Paine, Laplace, Rousseau, and Edward Herbert were not concerned with evolution, atoms or mundane things. (They were atheists or philosophical theists, but definitely not event-believing Biblical theists.) *They were "expansive" Platonists, rebelling against the "confining" Aristotle.* Their human ego favored a rigid mathematical determinism, materialism, an infinite universe, and unaided reason, coupled to Euclidean geometry. *In sum – rationalism – mathematic-ism!* These ideas vividly influenced science in the 1800s, yet present-day thinkers mostly ignore them.

First Principles in Science. At this transition from the Middle Ages to the Renaissance era, fact-finding continued, but there was concern over how to guide the quest for knowledge. The axiomatic method was, itself, entangled with saving the appearances. To say that one's theory is comprehensive, causal and true is easy. To prove it is not so easy! Indeed, excesses of partisans for Plato and Aristotle caused wariness. They also quarreled over who should take credit for empirical, craft, engineering and technological advances. In reaction, Leonardo da Vinci, (A.D. 1452-1519), the famous Renaissance painter and engineer, said:

"Mental things which have not gone in through the senses are vain and bring forth no truth except detrimental." *What is detrimental are the universal statements which close our mind to reality....* This [Leonardo's] use of mathematics is essentially different from that of *the Greeks, which had led them to organize a world of abstract entities fit only for contemplation,* and to geometricize the heavens into a system of eternal and uniform circles.[3] (Emphasis added.)

Thinkers in the Christian world utilized **First Principles of Science** to make sense of knowledge, which I have grouped as follows:

A. The universe is real. Its origin is *ex nihilo*; the created fact.
B. The universe is reasonable (orderly), witnessing to the "mind of the Maker."
C. The human mind can understand much about the accessible universe because the mind is a major feature of being "created in the image of God."
D. After the *ex nihilo* creation event, material actions proceed due to cause and effect relationships – with few exceptions. Events occur, laws may not acknowledge them, but nothing happens because of definitions.
E. There is unity in the cosmos. One God and His common laws govern the universe.
F. Sense observation uncovers additional direct facts. Open eyes and creative minds, in all walks of life, were successfully improving living standards and knowledge. Experimental rigor was gradually recognized as needed to help distinguish between storytelling, saving the appearances and cause and effect relationships. Knowledge was expressed mathematically to limit ambiguity.
G. Mathematics reflects the rational design of reality.

These First Principles reflected Christian belief as well as various Greek principles of logic and mathematics. Creation *ex nihilo* implies that a rational mind can explore an event-filled, yet orderly, unified, rational, finite universe. Cause and effect rejected the belief in astrological "spirits" or of "essences" directing physical processes. First Principles frame science; principles reflect belief, with evidence.

Mathematics, in G, came with a caution. The growing experimental domain is limited, so extrapolation of mathematical summaries requires assumptions about interactions between the components of reality. Grandiose extrapolation is even more dependent upon assumptions, specifically infinite hardness, infinite precision, and no events. Sense experience and wisdom – informed by Biblical revelation and science history – must be added to the process! Is reality uncreated, infinite, material, event-less and resulting from a top-down mathematic "incarnation?" Or does bottom-up mathematics shadow the interaction of especially created/existing units of matter? Is mathematics summarized as Universal Natural Law or useful equations? As long as the meaning was optional, different folks could agree to G!

A few thinkers began to espouse atomism. Their influence is hard to judge. Atomism received harsh criticism for its link to atheism. Also, its chance motions were anathema to mathematical determinism. Pierre Gassendi, a French priest, attempted to reconcile atomism to Christianity around 1630. Mercene and Descartes later attempted the same.

Resulting Scientific Progress. The following centuries saw great advances in knowledge (and theorizing) regarding reality. Witness the engineering, industrial, craft

---

3.   *The Age of Adventure,* edited by Giorgio de Santillana, pages 69 - 70. Emphasis added. The first sentence is by da Vinci. The rest is by that editor.

and scientific revolutions of the 1600s to 1900.

First Principles underwent stress during this time. For example, Sir Isaac Newton's Universal Law of Gravitation left gravity as a result without a cause and understood without experiments. Newton (1642-1727) was pragmatic. His equations at least saved the appearances, but he offered no theory as to how or why gravity worked. (On other subjects, Newton readily theorized.) He recognized that causal gravity eluded his grasp.

As an expert mathematician, he recognized the two-fold character of mathematics: a servant to empiricists; but a Janus master[4] to seekers of Universal Connected Knowledge. His celebrated fluxions (calculus) upset mathematical purists by replacing astronomical objects with mathematical points. The resulting gravity, *his uncommon unintelligibility*, caused Newton to be accused of occultism! While points were a convenient calculating device, everyone could see that astronomical objects *were not* mathematical points.

His failure to explain the cause of gravity did not inhibit his contemporaries or later generations. (**Paradoxically**, Sir Isaac Newton is one of the few thinkers who did not believe in Newtonian gravity!) To understand gravity, other thinkers tended to theorize, with mathematics as a top-down "incarnating" causal phenomenon, and thereby easily "explaining" why $F = M \cdot A$ and $F = G \cdot M_1 \cdot M_2 / r^2$! These, in turn, fostered thoughts reespousing determinism and atheism.

Blaise Pascal (1623-1662) had warned that "the heart has more reasons than reason is aware of." It is also true that mathematics and logic have more answers than reality is capable of.

But, all-in-all, great advances were made: common folk continued to discover direct facts; mechanical, chemical and craft tinkerers and engineers made instruments, processes and machinery; experimenters made discoveries. These individuals made the great advances in empirical science, engineering and technology. The printed word now spread information rapidly, which stimulated additional minds. Observers, such as in astronomy, also made discoveries; while thinkers, mathematicians and philosophers made models regarding the heavens.

Intermediate First Principles in Science. Approaching A.D. 1900, rationalists unfairly took credit for all achievements of the previous centuries. They considered engineering and technology to be "applied" science, yet there was little science relevant to practical things! The Intermediate First Principles revised the original First Principles. As a result of their growing mathematical confidence, item H was added. Finding direct facts happened less because so much had already been found:

A. The universe is real.
B. The universe is rational (orderly), not chaotic.
C. The human mind can understand the universe because of its mathematical structure.
D. Activity proceeds due to cause and effect relationships.

---

4. From the title to Arthur Koestler's *Janus: A Summing Up*. Janus, a Roman god, had two faces.

E. There is unity in the cosmos. One set of natural laws governs the infinite universe.
F. Scientific experiments and observations uncover facts. Experimental rigor distinguishes between storytelling, saving the appearances and cause and effect relationships. Observations in astronomy approach the objective standards of experimental sciences. Scientific results are expressed mathematically to limit ambiguity.
G. Mathematics reflects the ahistorical rational order in nature; *mathematical law is a science!*
H. Rational thought can safely extrapolate into the inaccessible.

These austere Intermediate First Principles had reduced Christian guidance. The question of origins was either ignored or thought to be answered within geology and biology. Rationalists rejected supernatural or historical limits to ahistorical physical processes – thus opting for infinity. Subsequently, many Christians began to talk less about God's action in historical events and more about "principles." As before, principles reflected belief, with evidence.

These changes also reflected the demotion of Aristotle and the re-elevation of Plato. So mathematics again hardened into that incarnated top-down "commander!" Reality was becoming infinite, material, eventless and uncreated. Dissent began to cause exclusion from the ranks of science, as scientists must "believe" in the infinite universe – assisted by "clear intuitions" in their mind's eye.

The impact of "clear intuitions" was most notable in the theory of evolution as *mathematicians and astronomers now "explained" the over-arching nature of reality.* They published theories that the universe was much larger and older than *ex nihilo* creation could accommodate. *This obligated geology and biology to fall-in-line and develop a "connected account"* that began with an utterly large and old universe.

Yet *mathematics changed from 1600 to 1900.* It entered as *mono-mathematics;* relatively simple concepts that could be physically modeled and easily accommodated to Euclid's *Elements.* It exited as *poly-mathematics* – with all the democratic pitfalls that implied! Was this progress on the road illuminated by Mathematic?

In the decades prior to 1900, observation and experiment uncovered phenomena that were hard to understand. Heat, chemical reactions, electricity, fields, violin strings, *etc.* were such. Accordingly, mathematics grew in complexity and rose in importance as an aid in "understanding."

Atomism was now reviving, and it or its critics drew little distinction between atomism (a philosophy of chance and materialism) and atoms (the structure of elements). Chemistry and the budding study of elements gave atomism some prestige, suggesting another rationale for a resurgent atheism.

God and *ex nihilo* creation were replaced by a postulated mathematical certainty. Sight-seeing explanations exhibiting universal connectedness were expressed mathematically, so rationalists (mathematic-ists) knew these were "incarnated" geometrical truth, not mere foundationless saving the appearances. Further, experimental proofs about the accessible implied that whatever was mathematically said about inaccessible reality also had to be true. It became a grand edifice! *Theory led to mathematics, which led to truth!* This was **Classical Science**. It looked much like Intermediate First Principles of Science, but with more confidence and less faith!

Two items hinted at impending problems. First, mathematics and logic encountered hard times. Subjectivity was rife in their advanced dominions. They looked like creatures of imagination, not monotruth commanders.

Second, all previous research had been on a "macro" scale. No one could enter into the atom. Such research would certainly support the then existing "science."

Shifting to Paradigms from Intermediate First Principles. Well, the optimism was unwise and a great disaster soon followed in the early decades of the twentieth century. Classical Science collapsed within decades of its celebrated maturation!

First, although abstract mathematics had great modeling capability, there was now uncertainty about its internal consistency and, hence, its *truth-guaranteeing power*. Attempts to rigorize geometry instead discovered non-Euclidean geometries. Attempts to rigorize arithmetic finally succumbed to the 1931 paper of Kurt Gödel on his *Incompleteness Theorem for Formally Undecidable Propositions*. The cloud of discredit remains, applicable to all four foundational schools of arithmetic: logicist, formalist, intuitionist and set-theoretic.[5] The sister discipline, logic, likewise splintered into many schools of logic. Rationalists reluctantly recognized that God and *ex nihilo* creation were not replaced by axioms, causality or mathematic, as originally thought, but by unprovable consistent connected saving the appearances of inaccessible realities. *Science became a provisional consensus, not a certainty!*

Second, the Intermediate First Principles had been strained by James Clerk Maxwell's recent mathematical treatment of electrodynamics. The Intermediate First Principles were then violated by the relativized non-Euclidean extension of this electrodynamics and by "explanations" of the inner workings of the newly found atom. The atom is almost impossible to see; its component parts or fields are impossible to see. Researchers carefully observed the atom, but what they saw made "sense" only after being massaged by top-down poly-mathematics. They could not see causes. Models of the atom were offered, but they had known defects. Finally, in 1913, Niels Bohr swept them all aside with his theory of the solar-modeled atom as a point-particle quantum phenomenon, using poly-mathematics to "open" the atomic black-box. All noticed that causality was sacrificed to definitions, but few admitted that the definitions were expressed with ununderstandable poly-mathematics.

(The rise of poly-mathematics muzzled the leaders of Classical Science. They were uneasy about poly-mathematics, but had loudly proclaimed their allegiance to mathematics. They were superseded by those fluent in the new poly-mathematics.)

Perplexing experimental results led to increasing use of poly-mathematics in the growing theory of quantum mechanics. That was the price paid for unfortunate allegiance to the "clear intuition" that the unseen electron "point" exists within a solar model of the atom. Since then, mathematics twists and turns to save the appearances of the atomic and electromagnetic black-boxes. In revenge, atomic science became a complicated, congested labyrinth!

---

5.   See *Mathematics: The Loss of Certainty*, by Morris Kline and *What is Mathematics, Really?* by Reuben Hersh.

The mathematical triumph of relativity and quantum mechanics; the transition from (certain) mono-mathematics to (interpretable) poly-mathematics; the unexpected continued reasonable defense of *ex nihilo* creation; the rise of sociologies of knowledge and science; post-modernism; and finally an enigmatic deconstruction caused rational thought to falter. *Had event-based truth been traded off for ahistorical continuity?* Classical Science now needed so much revision that thinkers knew that a revised universal mathematical or logical basis for science was unlikely. *Thus science splintered into various specialized paradigms* – consensus agreements of learned participants. (Outsiders, of course, were not learned.)

Indeed, such disciplines were so immersed in poly-mathematics that outsiders were not capable of understanding them. But they were not alone, as most insiders could not comprehend them either, but could use them by following the rules.[6] Rules replace causality. Was this the "new reality" of scientific truth or evidence of falling back to saving the appearances?

The rise of paradigms allowed additional "disciplines" to acquire the mantle of science – such as economics, psychologies, social sciences and political sciences, for they were also guided by consensus agreement of their learned participants. Yet, the complexity of reality revealed weakness in consensus. Learned participants rely on many theories, much mathematics, much consensus, but little certain truth! So, paradigm shifts occur and have scholarly subjectivity. Some learned participants opt-out to post-modernism or deconstruction or New Age beliefs or Christianity or .... ? And consensus groups many times splinter into sub-groups. All-in-all, Modern Science (Inaccessible Science Paradigms) is a heady brew! In this milieu, direct facts remained curiosity pieces, with minimal influence against the startling new picture of reality.

Inaccessible Science Paradigms. "General" consensus of learned participants reflects this catastrophic overhaul of science:

A.   Reality is an illusion. The inaccessible micro- and macro-worlds are "known" with top-down poly-mathematics. The bottom-up mathematics of the intermediate real-world is lower-level experimental science – or mere engineering or technology.

B.   Micro-reality is nonpredictable, not causal. Experimental results are therefore put into data arrays – to be algorithmically retrieved as needed. Micro-reality is imprecise and indeterminate – within experimental limits. Supposedly, at the real-world level, Classical Science reappears!

C.   Actions proceed due to whatever is in those data arrays, as cause and effect predictability is replaced by rules, definitions and indeterminacy. This loss of causality is the "death of (classical) science." Science becomes a game – with

---

6.   "I can safely say that nobody understands quantum mechanics," by Richard Feynman, as quoted in the *Passion of the Western Mind*, by Richard Tarnas, page 489, note 2. Or Murray Gell-Mann, "One supposes that (quantum mechanics) is exactly correct. Nobody understands it, but we all know how to use it.... And so we have learned to live with the fact that nobody can understand it." As quoted in *How is Quantum Field Theory Possible?* by Sunny Y. Auyang, page 229.

(To understand means to anticipate future events as causality works its course in nature.)

strict rules, paying homage to the non-causal quantum mechanics.

D. In spite of chaos, there is unity in the cosmos, but there is no TOE (Theory of Everything).

E. Experiment and observation uncover some facts. To find "all" the facts, it is necessary to extrapolate with "inferences to the best explanation."

F. Mathematics proves that nature is infinite or unbounded. *Mathematics is the Foundational Science!* We know nothing about the micro- or macro-worlds, only their Natural Laws. (This reflects the dark-side of submission to the Janus mastery of mathematics.)

G. Rational thought, based on the above, can safely extrapolate into the past or whatever had been considered inaccessible. Consensus teaches that science no longer "sees through a glass, darkly." The "unaided" noble human ego was proud of its *consistent connected mathematical models that display the "unaided" proof of the rational unity of the materialistic universe.*

Eight centuries ago, science had been helped for some time, then hobbled, by *Aristotelian logical Scholasticism.* Today, science is helped, then hobbled, by a *Platonic mathematical Scholasticism.* While experimental science, engineering and technology thrive, Inaccessible Science Paradigms struggle to present themselves as responsible for this success.

Few see what is hidden in plain view: that which thrives and paradigms that struggle both use mathematics – but not with the same attitude! Empirical science is comfortable with a bottom-up attitude toward reality, for explanatory failure is a frequent companion of accessible science. On the other hand, inaccessible science is euphoric about its top-down "explanatory" successes. But the success/failure comparison is too jarring. It hints that science's provisional nature is due to saving the appearances, or unwise extrapolative confidence or reflects mystical aspects of rationalism.

Trails Leading to False Science. Mankind is now as modern as can be, yet inaccessibility and black-boxes remain. Scientific truth has a history of "half-lives." Failure analysis indicates that a major cause is "clear intuitions" about opening black-boxes using current "research," but with a life-line back to unprovable articles of Greek rationalism. Top-down mathematics "creates" a reality that may be other or larger than reality actually is.

First, to use a paradigm consensus to uphold the infinite (or unbounded) universe and to exclude the supernatural begins with an IF and ends in a THEREFORE consensus. To investigate what "is", without grandiose theories, would be like utilizing creation *ex nihilo*, or experimental science (and its bottom-up mathematics), not Inaccessible Science Paradigms (and its top-down mathematics). Fossils do not come with age tags attached; so also, subatomic parts do not come with equations attached.

Second, mathematics still suffers from hard times. This goads some thinkers into mathematical tinkering not sanctioned by the consensus Paradigm. *Ad hoc* tinkering with the already *ad hoc* equations under-girding relativity, quantum mechanics, or the big bang upsets defenders of the consensus Paradigm. But such tinkering retains the twisting, turning, poly-mathematical dance! Even more incomprehensible to them is to question the nature of gravity and electromagnetism, or the structure of the atom.

Defenders of inaccessible orthodoxy see such questioning as a threat, not a lifeline.

Third, to investigate the inaccessible past requires belief in uniformitarian processes – the adherence to the ancient ahistorical mathematical line. Yet historical earthly processes include attenuation, resonances, and catastrophic events, such as earthquakes, volcanoes, hurricanes and tsunamis. (Recent such events are minor compared to what has happened over the last several thousand years – and even smaller than events associated with Noah's Flood.) Therefore, *uniformitarianism is underdetermined*, an ahistorical "clear intuition," but not a reasonable thought!

Fourth, it is fashionable to say that science includes such as astronomy, which substitutes multiple observations, manipulated by consensus equations, for experiments. However, an orbiting satellite observes, it does not perform experiments. (The distinction is real, but brilliant engineering and technology still pay generous dividends!)

Fifth, research into micro nature now includes sub-molecular features of life. Is there really biological "Irreducible Complexity?" Direct facts do not support consensus Paradigms!

Sixth, consensus paradigms claim experimental support to which they may not be entitled. Many cite, but do not read, foundational research papers. In relativity, this includes Sir A. S. Eddington's paper on his 1919 eclipse expedition, published in *Nature*. In 1922, the astronomer, Charles Lane Poor, critiqued this report with his *Gravitation versus Relativity*. More recently, *Sky and Telescope* reported that the 1919 eclipse expedition's "results were of only 20% accuracy and plagued with systematic errors. Later eclipse expeditions show only minor improvements in accuracy!"[7] Ironically, Relativity Theory is so firmly believed that the *Nature* article receives benign neglect.

Seventh, consider such groups as the Natural Philosophy Alliance and the John Chappell Natural Philosophy Society. Their consensus of learned participants is that General Relativity, Special Relativity, (Copenhagen) Quantum Mechanics and the Big Bang are all wrong! They have at least 1800 degree'd members who "agree on little more than that something is drastically wrong in contemporary physics and cosmology."

In like manner, consider such groups as the Creation Research Society. They have over 600 members with graduate degrees, along with many others. They accept the foundational axiom of creation.

Sifting the wheat from the chaff is hard work. These groups illustrate the important point that a "proof of a theory" may be claimed as proof for another theory, (presented, of course, by an equally degree'd expositor). Equal academic degrees don't lead to equal scientific thoughts about the inaccessible!

The above list blasphemes the Inaccessible Science Paradigms! The supporting consensus of learned participants is dependent upon refereed journals (and editing), tenure tension, clear intuitions, grant applications, easily swayed by dominant personalities and replete with "confirmation bias" bolstering inaccessible truths. Rational orthodoxy is not free-thought!

While Christianity says that *"love covereth a multitude of sins,"* mathematic-ists say *"the noble human ego covereth a multitude of gaps."* Science needs a life-line back to reality!

---

7 *Sky and Telescope*, October, 1983, page 198.

The Minority Report. Part I, The Human Response – The Rest of the Story.

During the long between-years, not everyone rejoiced in the "passionate search for truth and beauty" that Euclid's *Elements* had inspired…or at least they did not like where it was going. They did not like what a un-event-filled ahistorical mathematical line said about themselves. *It consigned all mankind to meaninglessness and uncreativeness,* so it became a virtue to be alienated from science.

Romanticism sprang up in the mid-1700s. It opposed rationalism and emphasized arts, music and literature. They tried to find personal meaning by bravely facing untamed nature, usually as creative loners.

Existentialism began about a hundred years later and was first stated by the Danish philosopher, Sören Kierkegaard. In the twentieth century, men such as Jean Paul Sartre were the leaders. They emphasized emotions, decision-making and a "leap of faith in the dark," in spite of the absurdity of an un-event-filled life on an ahistorical mathematical line.

Phenomenology began with Edmund Husserl. It is a study of conscious experience, consciousness and the meaning of phenomena.

Modernism is against tradition, even enlightenment thinking, as well as against a creator. It rejects the verbosity of philosophers and extrapolative "scientists." They marveled at how quickly philosophers went non-current. Reality has unexplainable complexity. Philosophical schools should stop arguing over the supremacy of their unconvincing creeds.

Post-Modernism gets more uncomfortable. Even science has wisps of subjectivity. "Scientific" thought has enough freedom to be bent by social needs. Knowledge of reality is relative.

Sociology of Scientific Knowledge. This probes in taboo regions. Are "free thinkers" willing to defend their knowledge – without biases?

Deconstruction began with Jacques Derrida. Words form traditions. *De-Sedimentation* is the process of separating the layers of meaning. Truth no longer has meaning, beyond the consensus of participants! So the important truth is that which the recipient thinks it means!

In a parallel manner, other thinkers praised the science resulting from Euclid's *Elements*.

The earlier mentioned pre-1800 atheists and philosophical theists expressed contradictory roadmaps as to how to find "unaided" truth.

British Empiricism and later, John Locke, emphasized sense experience coupled with skepticism.

Pragmatism meant much the same thing, but sprung up in America.

Positivism began with August Comte and emphasized the "scientific method." It was against anything metaphysical.

Immanuel Kant, and many others such as Hegel, struggled to "objectify" what all moderns knew to be true. Indeed, "*The technical jargon of one school shortly becomes the gibberish of the next.*"[8] While these thinkers disagreed on what was science – they generally only agreed that Christianity was wrong! This agreement was an unsecure foundation for rational thought.

For those who considered themselves scientific, the Minority Report was un-understandable, irrational and embarrassing. Yet none of these knew how to rationally modify the inhuman principles of science or its "proven" accomplishments in the previously inaccessible.

The lack of personal meaning is troublesome. The historical disarray of thinkers continues! No wonder Christianity continually surprises rationalists. Its events (and other discontinuities) witness to an alternate reasonable worldview.

The Minority Report. Part II, Empirical Science – The Rest of the Science Story.

Consider the mathematical triumph of Relativity and Quantum Mechanics; what did they triumph over? It was the Intermediate First Principles of Science – about the same as the short-lived Classical Science.

All factions praise the axiomatic method of Euclid's *Elements*, but some wonder how to apply that abstraction to reality.

> [T]he elementary particles of modern physics are even more abstract than the atoms of the Greeks .... [I]t is not a material particle in space and time, but only, in some sense, a symbol whose introduction gave the laws of nature a particularly simple form.[9]

Was this a science of storytelling or puzzle solving? These investigators perhaps over-relied on a flexible mathematics. Amusingly, Albert Einstein said the following about the beginning of quantum theory:

> Einstein appeared to have a similar opinion (of Heisenberg's 1925 paper) .... "The most interesting development produced lately is the Heisenberg-Born-Jordan theory of quantum states. The calculation is pure witchcraft, with infinite determin-ants (read matrices) in place of Cartesian coordinates. *It is most ingenious and, owing to its great complexity, safely protected against any attempt to prove it wrong.*"[10] (Emphasis added.)

Beware of the labyrinth nature of poly-mathematics! Also, few thinkers want to admit they do not understand esoteric mathematics, so they bow to the consensus of learned participants.

> Quantum electrodynamics gives the most precise predictions of any physical theory. Yet physicists have known from its birth that it is self-contradictory. They make *ad hoc* rules for handling the inconsistencies. Divergent series of divergent terms are manipulated and massaged.[11]

Classical Science did not "roll over and die" just because consensus paradigmers told them to. Classical Science adhered to the cause and effect criteria. Ernst Mach

---

8.   *The Age of Ideology,* edited by Henry D. Aiken, page vii.
9.   *The Atom in the History of Human Thought,* by Bernard Pullman, page 309. A quote from Werner Heisenberg.
10. *The Atom in the History of Human Thought,* by Bernard Pullman, page 390.
11. *What is Mathematics, Really?* by Reuben Hersh, page 31.

(1838-1916) enumerated a number of criteria centered around a rejection of unseen entities and undue trust that mathematical constructions exhaustively reproduce the real. Classicists accused the paradigmers of accepting saving the appearances instead of requiring the more rigorous cause and effect criteria. No one has disproved what may be called the *irrefutability theorem*, that an incorrect theory, given access to much poly-mathematics, cannot be proven wrong!

Paradigmers said "get over it! This is the nature of reality! The micro- and macro-worlds no longer use cause and effect criteria. You need to learn modern poly-mathematics, its data arrays and rules as you are unable to otherwise explain sub-atomic phenomena. (*Oh. They slyly ask,* "Explain the atom without us, if you can!")

Classicists replied with, "Get over your mathematical infatuation! Platonism is dead. Retreat from its ethereal mathematical heaven and replant your feet in the intermediate real-world."

And on ... and on ... the non-communicative conversation goes. Both forget that the rising living standards largely came about without credit to either of them! For that, thank native ingenuity of laypeople, craftsmen, engineers and technologists.

The accessible portion of Classical Science did not die, but survives and thrives as **Empirical Science**!

    A. What can be manipulated and measured is our domain. Other studies we cannot comment upon; perhaps some have scholarly results. Theory has limited realistic extension, such as the Periodic Table of the elements. Science is one of the ways to acquire knowledge.

    B. Experimental science is orderly. Well – mostly! Natural or manmade objects can exhibit resonances or other instabilities.

    C. The human mind can understand processes. But understanding utilizes a toolbox. A toolbox witnesses to pragmatism – not to rational determinism.

    D. Activity proceeds due to cause and effect relationships. We see but do not see into these relationships. Mystery and beauty abound.

    E. There is unity among phenomena, but distinctions and unique characteristics remain. We cannot follow this unity into the inaccessible. Science is performed "now" – not as a "stand-in" for elsewhere or other times. Be wary of extrapolative infatuation!

    F. Facts are owned by no model or procedure. "Anything goes" in the search for facts! Keen eyes and agile minds are a blessing. Observation is less-discerning than experimental interrogation.

    G Mathematics is a tool, but its plurality highlights an ingenuous garden of choice, not a tree of determinism. Mathematics provides useful formulas.

    H. Reasonable thought, to avoid disasters, should not gamble with pliable mathematical dice! Nor have allegiance to rational paradigms.

Empirical Science has developed amazing tools, but hesitates before exploring such as the subatomic. That paradigm labyrinth witnesses to the need for a believable, robust model of the atom. Also, Inaccessible Science Paradigms seek to enfold and smother Empirical Science.

Over the entrance to Plato's Academy reportedly was a sign, "*Let no one destitute of geometry enter my doors.*" Likewise, over the gate to paradigm science is a sign, "*Let no one destitute of the solar model of the atom enter my doors.*" Indeed, there is an abstract ethereal similarity between the two.

The Minority Report. Part III, The Atom – The Rest of the Science Story.

Fulfilling this desire for a robust model of the atom is the major interest of a Christian group, Common Sense Science[12]. Utilizing Empirical Science, they reject the solar model of the atom, thereby rejecting the sly temptation offered by the paradigmers. Their Toroidal Ring model of the electron holds great promise of exercising Occam's Razor. The atom: a small item – yet enormous impact!

The resulting model of the atom does away with the un-understandable poly-mathematics of relativity and quantum mechanics! The paradigm labyrinth is becoming a museum curio.

A Christian Comment.

Christians frequently warn against the "Primary Axiom: Evolution and Natural Selection." Yet awareness of the tumultuous times within the between-years broadens the concern. This prelude *re-recognizes the MORE Primary Axiom: "Mathematics and astronomy show that the universe has 'vast distances and long ages.' The subsequent job of geology and biology is to fill in the details."*

Not surprisingly, this re-recognition makes some Paradigm Protectors sense that their orthodoxy faces a scholarly challenge. They may lash out at scholarly dissent and charge that learned Christians illustrate "belief without evidence." But the paradigmers' ahistorical consensus is belief with insufficient inaccessible evidence – an extrapolative group-think. Equating paradigms with science is not wise.

Reality provides no guarantee that *consensus* explanations of an inaccessible, complex, congested reality are more than saving (some of) the appearances. Top-down mathematics and logic may fail within the event-filled reality. To claim that "scientific" extrapolations are not limited by the supernatural presupposes uniformitarian extrapolation to the uttermost. Such theorizing frames the answer ahistorically before the investigation starts; such a far-reaching "clear intuition" is subjective and self-serving.

Paradigmers generally say that they are God-less, but they are not vacuum-filled. No, the God-less are self-filled or idea-filled. Those most likely to disagree with this book would say that, as God-less thinkers, they are science-filled thinkers. Some of these, due to an interest in the genealogy of rationalism, would say that they, as mature God-less thinkers, are Paradigm-filled thinkers. This conclusion is a two-edged sword. Upon reflection, it becomes a dark, embarrassing cloud over their "rational" substitute for the Garden of Eden.

---

12   This chapter first appeared in the May 2011 Journal of Common Sense Science, Foundations of Science News (FOSN). (www.commonsensescience.org) Used by permission. Revisions have been made.

It seems best to leave the paradigm labyrinth and go back to the beginning, the search for knowledge. It is not known if our Creator God can also be understood as "The Great Mathematician" or "The Great Artisan or Craftsman!"

Doubt is becoming rampant among the younger generation. They have read the *philosophers of philosophy* and other leading lights but sense an ingrained haze. Some have advanced to the foreboding *philosophers of science* who delve into inaccessible science and surprisingly struggle with the ingrained haze. (What a pity the desedimenting Deconstructionists do not critique modern science.)

Present rational confusion calls for a reconsideration of historical events versus the reigning paradigmatic consensus that guards the ahistorical mathematical line. The irrefutability theorem renders inefficient the Christian attempt to clean house in labyrinths by merely tweaking consensus paradigms. While separating direct facts, engineering and technology from consensus overburden is helpful, the greater need is to step outside the labyrinth. Christianity, which takes Bible history seriously, offers cleansing from tarnished "clear intuitions" which forbid events due to the "reality" of the ahistorical mathematical line.

Part of the confusion about what science means is due to a (deliberate?) obscurity about mathematics. Mathematics studies relationships between things – it does not study things! It can save (some of) the appearances of things, but cannot address causality – why things do what they do or are what they are.

Empirical science finds a non-rigid, complicated, accessible reality. Thus it resorts to *ad hoc* modifications to mathematical summaries. Studying the present cannot provide Universal Connected Knowledge.

On the other hand, extrapolative science of the inaccessible cannot openly tolerate the *ad hoc*. The *ad hoc* mocks the extrapolative assumptions of Paradigm-filled thinkers and their loyalty to Mathematic's Word.

Thus there are two main views of science. Both utilize mathematics but with opposing mindsets. Nay – opposing dialects! One provides (limited) knowledge; the other provides universal probabilities or stories.

So what are we to make of history, astronomy, psychology, economics, social science, political science, and other disciplines?

What doth science mean? Science is a reasonable, finite, experimental and measuring endeavor to find truth, by distilling out regularities and expressing them with mathematics. Empirical Science gladly works with others who investigate reality: theologians, craftsmen, engineers, technologists and tinkerers. Unfortunately, they are surrounded by a rational, consensus, wordy, mathematical haze that struggles with how completely reality is understood, how far the data is valid, and how to defend their universal "knowledge" of the inaccessible. (The created fact must be myth!)

Philosophers of science diplomatically agree. They seem to say, "I have written a large book on science, but, in a few words, I cannot say what science is."

Thus, we have good reasons to enter that hidden, yet obvious, path that wends backward in time.

To be ignorant and simple now – not to be able to meet the enemies on their own ground – would be to throw down our weapons, and betray our uneducated brethren who have, under God, no defense but us against the attacks of the heathen. Good philosophy must exist, if for no other reason, because bad philosophy needs to be answered.
     C. S. Lewis

There are tragedies caused by war, famine, and pestilence. But there are also intellectual tragedies caused by limitations of the human mind.... [C]alamities ... have befallen man's most effective and unparalleled accomplishment, his most persistent and profound effort to utilize human reason – mathematics.
     Morris Kline

The secret things belong unto the Lord our God: but those things which are revealed belong unto us and to all our children for ever....
     Deuteronomy 29:29a

Have you noticed that few books about science actually say what science is? Well, don't blame them; it probably can't be done.

How does Christianity interact with the human desire to acquire Universal Connected Knowledge? Jesus Christ ministers to the spiritual needs and trials of mankind. He also lifts our eyes to heaven wherein all truth is anchored. There, reason and philosophy meet truth – and find it difficult to synchronize with their rational ahistorical mathematical line!

Ignoring the (unseen) world of ideas is dangerous. Old ideas still influence us; some bad ideas survive the test of time. Ideas shape political, philosophical, religious, and scientific movements. In fact, morality – Christian life – is anchored in the unseen. Mankind constantly endures verbal assaults from the world of ideas. These are word wars; they thicken into clouds of well-crafted, but bad, philosophy.

Word wars torment mankind. The combatants are serious thinkers, but partisans for conflicting "truths," applying ideas in their various attempts to improve the lot of mankind. Do Christians face these "evangelists" squarely? We do mourn the casualties, yet seem uninterested in the principles used to assault everyone.

Word wars are very old. The New Testament epistles contain warnings against such verbal assaults – and not only from Judaizers and pagans. The Bible highlights its caution concerning the pride and prize of rationalism with the concepts of "*science falsely so-called*" (I Timothy 6:20) and "*philosophy and vain deceit*" (Colossians 2:8). These warnings continued after the New Testament era closed. False reasoning is a seedbed for heresy. In harmonizing Christianity and science, often a concord is instead made with a science of the day!

The need for a prelude to the Gospel depends upon the audience. St. Peter, in his Jerusalem exhortation recorded in Acts chapter two, did not need a prelude. His listeners were Jewish people; they understood the Biblical worldview. Other listeners needed a prelude to the Gospel. St. Paul, in Athens, in Acts chapter 17, had to present a prelude of a Biblical worldview before converts were made. (And missionaries have always seen the need for preludes.)

The early church Fathers critiqued many philosophers. Pythagoras, Democritus, Plato and Aristotle are some of those mentioned. The numerous references may surprise modern readers.

Ancient philosophers had many disciples and close-knit schools – and strange systems of well-crafted words. They founded science and once they achieved that exalted position, associated ideas became harder to question. Reasoners, like everyone else, yearn to escape from subjectivity into assent to "true" truth. Yet Tertullian had asked; "*What indeed has Athens to do with Jerusalem?*"

The "indeed" is this: Christianity and rtionalism both claim to explain universal truth. Around A.D. 100, the debate would likely proceed as: *Christians turn to* events and revealed truth (by and about God) in Scripture; *rationalists turn to* the autonomy and rigor of mathematic and its "unaided proof" that the "vast distances and long ages of the cosmos" reveal no Godly involvement in the cosmos.

Christians pointed out that Jesus said: "*I am the way, and the truth, and the life*" (John 14:6a), and His disciple John said, "*All things were made by him*" (John 1:3a). But a jaded and cornered Pontius Pilate asked, "*What is truth?*" (John 18:38).

Ancient Greek reasoners creedally said, "We have a visible truth, a physical mathematic. We know that 1 + 1 = 2 is incarnate in matter. Because of mathematics' infallible characteristics, our earth-based observations of the sky can be extrapolated to reveal the structure of nature."

Biblical revelation or mathematical rationalism? At the beginning of the long-running conflict between "revealed" faith and "unaided" reason, such were the choices – and they still are, regarding the cosmic big picture.

These competing visions undergird methods to find truth. Presented this starkly, it is not obvious that Christians have to "theologize away" a conflict with science. Grandiose reasoners, indeed, may need to rethink their universal yardstick: extrapolative infatuation.

Christian conflict with science, falsely so-called, predates Galileo or Darwin. Science has a very technical language, yet a consensus alleges that science avoids word wars or story-telling – bad philosophy being foreign to objective enterprises. The consensus elevates science to the pedestal of objective truth. That, however, is hasty and inaccurate.

Science began in ancient Greece when thinkers joined mathematics with reason. An early thinker, Pythagoras, coined the word, philosophy.[1] To him, it meant *Phile-Sophia*: "love – truth." Love of truth inquires into foundational matter – the building blocks of the cosmos. Pythagoras knew these building blocks were number, but he did not think he or his contemporaries had uncovered all facets of truth. He pursued truth as a mystic, a reasoner, a philosopher... as a lover of truth.

Everyone may reason about the world and its meaning, but thinking can yield false conclusions. Laypeople and professional thinkers have the same problem.

As said earlier, facts can be discovered without the aid of science, such as the discovery of a cave or a mineral deposit. Yet, reason wants more than fragmented knowledge; it wants connected facts about accessible and inaccessible phenomena. It seeks the discovery of "causes;" interwoven physical, logical or mathematical threads which connect to even more facts. The highest prize is universal connectedness – a rock at your feet – a distant star – or an event of long ago! Indeed, *reason strives to be "all-seeing!" Thinkers seek Universal Connected Knowledge!*

Scientific knowledge is a commons – available to all. But the commons can contain litter, some "knowledge" may be imbedded ideas mistaken for objects or truth. Such is the fate of some logic, mathematic, faith or hope. Also, choices exist regarding which ideas to systematize facts with. Imbedded ideas and choices can undermine truth. Thinkers try to hide this unexpected freedom. Reason's methodlogy is not purely objective; well-reasoned storytelling or bad philosophy exist.

Be forewarned, philosophers are not neutral sages. Their concentrated thinking has a dual goal: to study the foundation of the cosmos and to shape everyone else's thinking to conform to their ideas. Failure abounds! For example, Pythagoras, the lover of truth, bound himself to false systematizing concepts. Yet, philosophy is not inherently anti-Christian – but it cannot serve as the foundation for all reasoning. Rational thoughts do not infallibly lead to universal truth or unity.

The lure of objective truth is formidable. It seeks to anchor itself in the building blocks of reality, yet the lure can be diverted. People often trust the experts or trust the tradition of science or religion rather than think afresh about a subject.

To understand word wars, a historical review is needed. Social upheaval drove Greek thinkers to formulate new understandings of reality. The earth was center stage in their inquiries, but what did it mean? What did these "lovers of truth" find that they called science?

As an opening summary, these Greek thinkers were (or became) rationalists and, after much argument, viewed reality somewhat as follows: The earth is a finite, material object within an infinite cosmos.[2] Mathematic's Word confirms this conclusion. Man is just complicated matter. The supernatural does not exist or

---

1   Some students of Pythagoras were called *mathematekoi;* "Those who studied all." (B1, page xvii.)

2   COSMOS: original meaning: well-ordered, and applies to the totality of reality, the universe. The cosmos can be complete and well-ordered without being infinite, but the finite option was abandoned as Greek thought matured. An infinite cosmos leaves no room for God; two infinities were not possible.

invade (or intervene in) the cosmos. *The cosmos is unperforated.*[3]

Greek thinkers lived among Greek pagans,[4] who believed the earth was a living organism. Even the stars had life – imbued from the gods! *The cosmos is alive!* This was viewed with unease because the gods could be capricious or uninterested. Their cosmos was finite.

Greek thought conflicted with Christianity, so consider how Christianity and Judaism view reality. Infinity[5] belongs to God's nature, so the finite material earth exists within a finite material cosmos. Man is matter plus a mind and an ensouled spirit. All in the cosmos results from the recent *ex nihilo* creation, and God reportedly still intervenes in cosmic affairs. *The cosmos is perforated!*[6] Additional examples of this supernatural perforation are: revelation in the inspired Scripture; the Incarnation of the Son; and the ever-present Comforter.

We confront three understandings: Greek thinkers, paganism, and Christianity? While tempted to disqualify paganism, we note a reviving interest in neo-paganism. We also see a newcomer to Western regions: *pantheism*; Oriental and New Age religion – *the Cosmos is God.* Both paganism and pantheism survive and thrive, even among thinkers. Their survival warns against overvaluing Greek thinkers. Also, there is an increasing unbelief in any truth, religious or scientific – a movement known as postmodernism or deconstruction – but perhaps better called *modern sophistry. Thus, mankind continues to face a choice among three – four – maybe five – understandings!*[7]

The preceding summarizes the initial battlefield of the word wars. The earth became peripheral; disputes soon centered on the big picture – the cosmos. *Is the cosmos unperforated, infinite (or unbounded), and materialistic?*

Did ancient Greek thinkers arrive at truth via reason? No, but, with serendipity, they championed principles helpful to clear thinking, albeit principles supportive of more than their "way" to explain reality. The scientific and technological wonders up through the twenty-first century make sense within the Christian cosmos.

Greek understandings are commonly called science, or at least proto-science. Without recognizing science, falsely so-called, that label is premature and would tacitly herald the defeat of Christianity.

Word wars still bewilder, weary and divide Christians.

Conservatives say that movement away from historic Christianity decimated Christian ranks and stymied the outreach to mankind. Christianity grew through the

---

3   UNPERFORATED: No outside forces or causes affect the cosmos. (So used by the theologian, Dr. Rudolph Bultmann.) The cosmos is materialistic. Atheist rationalists say the cosmos contains everything, so there is nothing to perforate it. Alternatively, religious rationalists insist the supernatural exists but does not directly interact with the cosmos.
4   PAGAN: Followers of primitive religions – including worship of many gods: polytheism.
5   INFINITY: a mathematical term, not a Biblical term. It is convenient but can be misleading. Biblically, God is all powerful, all knowing and ever present.
6   PERFORATED: The (inanimate) cosmos, and the life existing therein, can be affected by outside (*i.e.*, supernatural) causes.
7   Many "unbiased folk" claim this picture of philosophy does not include them. Somehow, they have risen to objective truth!

centuries until the mid-1800s, when the false science of Darwin appeared. The mid-1800s were the high-water mark for Christianity.

Liberals agree Christianity was successful before the mid-1800s, but due to a touch of serendipity or spiritual elitism. Then, they say, the rising tide of scientific truth forced Christianity to begin purifying itself ... and truly begin to love humankind.

Where do I fit into this? Conservative, but with the qualification that all was not well in the world of ideas before the mid-1800s. Ancient misunderstandings (bad philosophy) – fascinated by mathematic and astronomy in the between-years – only began to bear *visibly threatening fruit* around the mid-1800s.

This major division within Christianity is a reaction to the vagueness in *science*. Everyone – in all ages – tends to uncritically accept science, and may unwisely dwell on the latest findings of "cutting-edge" science. This frequently short-circuits thinking; the purported "facticity" of cutting-edge news stops the (backdoor) analysis of any deeper paradigmatic foundations. Rather, to recognize errors in fact or systematization, begin at the beginning bookend.

Acknowledged truth fosters unity, so well-crafted ideas in bad philosophy seek to be identified as objective truth. Such maneuvering for advantage by well-reasoned storytellers seeks to control communication systems and thus promote their truth. But strategy runs into a problem; people already have worldviews[8] and experiences that affect their evaluation of things or words. Music and sports may be trite examples of universal communicators, but note that the Beatles and Bach evoke different responses among people. Even more so do whole systems of well-crafted words clash and cause confusion.[9]

When our Lord presented the Gospel, His listeners also had worldviews. (While most were Jews, some were influenced by Hellenism or other cultures.) The Truth He spoke addressed both their hearts and minds. His Truth may be hard to comprehend against the backdrop of today's worldviews, as some also found it in that earlier day.

Communication barriers were on the mind of the philosopher, Alfred North Whitehead, in his 1927-1928 Gifford Lectures:

> When you are criticizing the *philosophy of an epoch*, do not chiefly direct your attention to those intellectual positions which its exponents feel it necessary explicitly to defend. There will be some fundamental assumptions which adherents of *all the variant systems* within the epoch unconsciously presuppose. Such assumptions appear so obvious that people do not know what they are assuming because *no other way of putting things has ever occurred to them.* With these assumptions a certain limited number of types of philosophic systems are possible, and this group of systems constitutes *the philosophy of the epoch.* (B2, page 184. Emphasis added.)

To me, the philosophy of modern epochs flutters around mathematics and

---

8   Worldviews: understandings with a cosmic perspective.
9   "Education" is given the additional task, by many, of overcoming discordant worldviews. But education – beyond the 3 Rs – requires foundational ideas. So the maneuvering for storytelling privilege struggles to control education.

rational certainties. Three concepts seem to allow rationalism to go beyond reasonable investigation. *First,* mathematical abstractions are (or accurately model) all of reality. *Second,* reality, as a mathematical mirror, is uniformitarian and "stops" at infinity! *Third,* basic matter is non-deformable, like marbles.

Thinkers, like men of goodwill,[10] continually dispute about Christianity, its mission, and God's involvement in His cosmos. Communication barriers abound! Frustration over opponents' lack of objectivity is rising. No peace in the word wars is in sight! They fight with words mistakenly considered value-free and mutually agreed upon! *Science, mathematics, reason,* and *God* are such words, but *the meanings are optional.*

Unspoken assumptions determine how key words are understood and built upon as they stretch toward universal connectedness. These assumptions often are vague, yet thinkers find them a solid basis. They become "colonies of thinkers" arguing within their own bubble of subjectivity. Dialog rarely leads to communication.

Erudite spokesmen see no deficiencies in their appeals for support! This suggests despair, philosophic tiredness, historical naiveté or overconfidence in one's own rationality – a blindness in the mind's eye. Communication barriers are hidden in plain view! Elusive words undergird the many well-crafted systems used by the well-reasoned to "explain" reality *and* keep God at arm's length[11].

Study of God's exceedingly complex creation increases our skepticism of well-reasoned storytelling claiming to reveal grandiose knowledge of the cosmos. Particularly in the realm of the grandiose, words – or equations – never say it just right. Nonetheless, naive Christians adjust their theology, unaware of vagueness in the "objective" pictures of reality thus drawn. They comply with the most effectively presented thought system, the "science of the day" or "philosophy of the epoch."

Subjective science(s) and the "Christian" trend to reconcile faith to anything "reasonable" are untrustworthy, yet popular and lack wisdom. Objective truth becomes lost amid this agreeable uncertainty. In examining communication barriers, reason will be considered first.

Subjective science! Science, falsely so-called! Are such contradictory and blasphemous notions real? Many quickly affirm that religion is subjective, but is some science subjective? Am I jesting, or have you also encountered this subjectivity? In case you have not, consider two small incidents from my experience.

On a business trip, I met a fellow who had just received his master's degree in economics. As our dinner conversation turned philosophical, he said that many pronouncements of economics seemed false, and he could not understand why his professors called it a science. Neither could he fathom how anyone in his right mind could call *any* "social-science" a science! Further discussion revealed deep disillusionment. Life no longer made sense, and his desire to help people was

---

10   Men of goodwill: Men and women in the general public who have not thought deeply about philosophy and worldviews, but who are open to truth.
11   This desire to exclude God from the cosmos shows that many thinkers have been mesmerized by sticks, stones, strata, or mathematics. St. Paul said we also face unseen enemies in principalities and powers ... (Ephesians 6:12).

paralyzed by the competing claims of contradictory sciences. Yet, these same sciences proved to him that spiritual things are useless abstractions. Stripped of faith by his prelude, he withdrew into self-preservation in a meaningless world.

On another trip, in the People's Republic of China, my host boasted that Chinese science is superior to Western science. I finally asked what he meant since I (naively) thought of science as a unified commons, not competing parties. He replied that Western science had concluded that China had few land-based petroleum reservoirs because it lacked proper sedimentary formations. Nonetheless, considerable oil was found. This, to him, proved Chinese "science" was superior.

Further, you may have read articles showing the well-reasoned on college campuses range from strident materialists to oriental mystics to neo-pagans to modern sophists. You may also have your own personal incidents that make you wonder what science really is.

Anecdotes like these are a necessary corrective. *"Science" is an overused word.* If "subjective science" is offensive, revert to the Biblical phrase; "science, falsely so-called."

Some consider such incidents trivial. What then is science?

Being forewarned that we cannot provide a concrete answer, we must, nonetheless, return to ancient Greece. Science[12] is derived from the Greek word, *epistëmë* (*scientia* in Latin), which means "to know" or "knowledge."

Thinkers in ancient Greece saw the living cosmos of paganism as an error. Paganism was gross, unpredictable, open to too many interpretations, and the pagan factions could not convince others. To these new thinkers, the emerging "structure" and "truth" in mathematics sharply contrasted with the interpretive elasticity of paganism.

It probably was a delightful shock to these thinkers to stand in the presence of truth after their previous experiences. Certainly, 1 + 1 = 2 and the sum of the angles of a triangle equals two right angles![13] These truths were independent of any god! Knowledge quickly sought refuge in mathematics.

Anything opposing mathematics was thereby "exposed" as mythology (religion). With revelation nonexistent, mathematics was the key to truth. Thinking with mathematics became their peculiar type of reasoning – *scientia*. This circular thinking led to a comfortable conclusion: "Reason versus faith" summed up the intellectual alternatives; only *scientia* answered the lure of objective truth. After several false starts, *scientia* was based on "understandings" of Mathematic's Word – rational concepts few openly accept today.

Greek thinkers feared a science lacking cosmic proportions[14]. Such could not be the COURT OF LAST APPEAL, the anchor for truth. To be "all-seeing," *Scientia* had to own the "big picture," thereby excluding polytheism! Accordingly, science applies to a stone at their feet, the distant stars and events of long ago. *Ahistorical*

---

12   The word "science" did not come into common use until about A.D. 1840. Prior to that, the phrase used was "*Natural Philosophy.*"
13   Per Lev Shestov in *In Job's Balances*, reluctantly quoting Spinoza.
14   Cosmic thinking – thinking in the big picture – was (is) not restricted to "cosmology."

mathematic was the universal connector between these. As such, science's (assumed) objectivity stood in stark contrast to the earthboundness, subjectivity, and interpretive pluralism of polytheism.

This dawning awareness of "unaided" science offered a *tantalizing prize* – the acquisition of *truth* and, thus, the *good* and the *beautiful. Only then could authentic love exist!* The lure of objective truth had (and still has) a worthy claim upon one's intellect. However, one does not have to be religious to have an "evangelical" fervor (fever?)!

Epistemology[15] is an old word which wisely examines the objective status of our knowledge. Too often our science words are not knowledge, but are better identified as rationalism, belief, conjecture, theory, understanding, paradigm, storytelling or myth.

The simple (and mathematical) epistemology of the unperforated cosmos advocated by Greek rationalists is alluring but subjective. A good definition of science eludes us. Collapsing all facets of thinking into "science versus religion" intermingles with the vagueness that the well-reasoned live with, fight against, yet also propagate! This is not a reasonable or wise methodology!

Some readers may accuse me of science bashing. They may say I overlook the obvious: *Science is objective truth!* Thus I speak as if I have not learned the textbook definition, a wording such as the following:

All nature is orderly. Order originates from (or with) mathematics. This is the "unaided" starting point of science. There is nothing supernatural that can be invoked, and science is the servant of self-evident objective truth.

Science investigates (and tries to connect) all phenomena in the cosmos. The first tentative explanation is called a *hypothesis,* which is subjected to manipulative tests, called *experiments.* Deductive reasoning[16] then finds cause and effect relationships – and predicts new data or wider application of the underlying mathematical relations. After repeated experiments and deductions by many researchers, successful hypotheses rise to the status of *theories.*

This rigorous methodology advances until the prize is attained – *monotruth: the single repeatable answer ...* written with mathematics to exclude bias. This satisfies the lure of objective truth. Indeed, a *Universal Natural Law* has been discovered. Natural Laws, being mathematical, reveal *uniformitarian necessity* – why laws *must* control things. (The objects of astronomy also obey laws, even though inaccessible to experiment. Observation in astronomy is thus scientific.) Laws are

---

15   Epistemology: The study of the soundness of ideas. It attempts to unmask subjective elements mistaken for knowledge. Based upon the known, it tries, sometimes unsuccessfully, to distinguish between puzzle solving and storytelling.

16   Deductive Reasoning: The process of starting with principles held to be true and then predicting conclusions or action that should result from their use. It begins with an IF and adds another IF to arrive at a THEREFORE conclusion.

universal; they reach all times; past, present, and future, and all places in the cosmos. History is unneeded. Equations can be extrapolated to tell everything about nondeformable matter. If interpretive doubt occurs, *theory trumps (local) experiment!* Science shows that reality is like an ahistorical mathematical line. It makes the inaccessible accessible. Laws are *ahistorical and all-seeing.*

The tool of science is mathematic, meaning arithmetic: 1 + 1 = 2; geometry: point, line, triangle, cube and conic section; and logic. With these tools, science has no axe to grind or hidden motivations. Due to their accuracy, we know mathematics is the "really" real. When science produces arithmetic, geometry, or logic, *all arguments must cease.* Unbiased people merely assent to truth. The accumulating facts may at times be disconcerting – but truth is truth. This is the scientific engine that generates such great confidence and enthusiasm.[17]

With this tool and methodology, science infallibly distinguishes between subjective and objective. By many small fact-gathering steps, researchers reveal "all-seeing" true truth. They know how to verify data, equations and the logic required for discernment. Science finds Universal Connected Knowledge – a commons for all mankind. Experimental science provides an umbrella under which other sciences can flourish.[18]

This is the *public version* of science. The *private version* is: "*Science dissolves matter into mathematic and Universal Natural Laws are the result.* Any part of matter that does not resurface into mathematics is thus identified as lower-class secondary phenomena."

The public version sounds like a clear definition of science, so why quarrel with it? But then ... qualifying words may be added that negate or modify the preceding affirmation. Why are qualifications needed if the single, repeatable Universal Natural Law has already been found?

New advice also seeks our attention. New thinkers soothingly tell us, with objectivity dripping from every syllable, "Do your own thing;" "Create your own reality;" "You can pop in and out of various manifolds of reality;" "You need to understand the *Yin* and *Yang* principles of physics;" and so forth.

More reasons for concern appear later, such as multiple solutions to equations, competing schools of mathematics and physical processes that aren't ahistorical. Most thinkers now shy away from a clear definition of science – hoping that specialized consensus agreements are sufficient. Lastly, a specter haunts some thinkers; does a systematic understanding exist that correlates with *ex nihilo* creation, for *the created fact is an event, not an ahistorical theory?*

Also, *a sense of history catches up with me.* A hundred and fifty years ago, and stretching back for over 2,000 years, the textbook definition of "natural philosophy" was, instead, something like the following:

Philosophy revealed the true essence of reality – all nature is number or geometry, whose clarity and rigor were a continual delight. "Unaided" Mathematic's Word's necessity stands over gods. Science (Natural Philosophy) searched for (Euclidean) geometry in stuff with pure thought – or was assisted,

---

17   As we ponder such facts as dialects in mathematics and that these laws are formulated on the surface of the earth, we are puzzled as to how they became *verified* as "universals."
18   To my knowledge, this is my wording. Admittedly, I have read many relevant books, but I cannot remember specific influences.

when necessary, by simple experiment, measurement or observation. Hypothesis thus rose to theory and then to Universal Natural Law. As Plato said, science is the knowledge of Universals. All-seeing ahistorical universal mathematical mono-truth was the product of Natural Philosophy.

The tool of Natural Philosophy was (Euclidean) geometry. Geometry and its axioms had no axe to grind, hidden motivation or inherent subjectivity. This was science by definition and deduction yet, it didn't outlive the demise of Euclidean geometry.

Also, we look to the future, at least as modern sophists see it:

Nature is orderly, but its essence is an inaccessible puzzle. "Unaided" experiment and/or measurement can only go so far – after which comes hypothesis and theory. Then thinkers extrapolate, "aided" by their consensus paradigms. Grandiose science is a learned consensus systematization and investigation of "lower level" results. We rarely get close to Universal Connected Knowledge. Frames of reference or points of view limit or enslave us. *We are plagued by mathematics, logic and paradigms.* As we reach for Universal Truth, we can rarely distinguish between puzzle solving and storytelling, because cloudy experiments and saving the appearances are protected from refutation by such as fortuitous *ad hoc* auxiliary hypothesis. Science proves theoretical necessity – but what "unaided" necessity? Use de-sedimentation to find meaning in all word systems – and believe no word system.

The thinker's "all-seeing" goal fosters self-deception because, admittedly, the tools of science resemble those used in the past: arithmetic, geometry, and logic. But these simplistic facets are now restricted to pre-college instruction. Today, our mathematics is fragmented, has more concepts, is more labyrinthine, and lacks foundational objectivity. Subjective preferences, alternate methodologies, and creative viewpoints provide wide maneuvering room for dominant personalities. Choice is an inevitable companion when we leave the comforting confines of the "unaided" laboratory. Thinkers may have axes to grind and hidden grandiose motivations. We sophists "understand" the resulting labyrinth.

Poetic justice – multiculturalism has swallowed up extrapolative infatuation. Note that all three definitions assume that science is "all-seeing," which goes well beyond "unaided" empirical science.

...or is there a fourth definition – that of shorn science? Science that recognizes its limited domain and mercurial tools, as described later in this chapter. This is empirical science, almost like classical science, yet a science comfortable with the accessible facets of the created fact.

In spite of these historical cautions, the modern confidence is expressed by Corliss Lamont, famous twentieth-century skeptic and humanist, when he wrote:

The development, over the past four centuries, of a *universally reliable method* for attaining knowledge is a far more important achievement on the part of science than its discovery of any single truth. For once men acquire a thoroughly dependable *method* of truth-seeking, a method that can be applied to every sphere of human life and by anyone who *faithfully conforms to certain directives,* then they have as a permanent possession an *instrument of infinite power* that will serve them as long as mankind endures. *Scientific method is such an instrument.* (B3, page 22. Second emphasis in original.)

Without a sense of history, this endorsement of the "unaided power of reason" (philosophy of the epoch) answers the lure of objective truth. The referenced method uses arithmetic, geometry and logic and is highlighted by astronomy.

Mathematics cannot bear this burden; listen to the acidic philosopher of science, Paul Feyerabend:

> *Ad hoc* approximations abound in modern mathematical physics.... *Ad hoc* approximations conceal, and even entirely eliminate, qualitative difficulties. They create a false impression of the excellence of our science.... In most cases modern science is more opaque, and much more deceptive, than its 16th- and 17th-century ancestors have ever been. (B4, pages 63-64.)

So rationalists have no infallible extrapolative method *and* I am limiting science, *but* that is realism, *not* science-bashing. Philosophers of science lay aside textbook definitions of science and grapple with universal truth as an elusive concept. They end up talking about "conjectures and refutations,"[19] "revolutions of science,"[20] or "paradigm shifts."[21] I prefer "*intellectual adventure*" or "well-reasoned storytelling," tributes to the adventure (and rational subjectivity) in most Universal Assumptions. Philosophers of science end up with bewilderment, not affirmation! They frequently sigh and confess: "Well! I have written a large book on science, but in a matter of a few words, *I cannot say what science is, except that it has not detected anything supernatural.*"

No wonder men of goodwill are wary of "science?" *What is the Bible warning against when it speaks of science, falsely so-called?*

"Unaided" reason cannot provide Universal Connected Knowledge! The alternative, "revealed" truth, has many claimants. What is mankind to do? Be cynical? No! Begin with the BB – not the "BB!" (The beginning bookend – not the "big bang!") The BB is before reason, science and mathematics were operative. Nonetheless, "reason" claimed an advantage!

At the beginning bookend, we face "Athens and Jerusalem." Or is it "*Unaided reason*" and "*revealed reason*." The time

---

19   Conjectures and Refutations: A phrase introduced by Sir Karl Popper, pointing out that "scientific" perceptions change with time. New data or new visions undermine previously accepted interpretations.

20   Revolutions of science: A phrase introduced by Dr. Thomas Kuhn. It focuses attention on the sudden and radical shifts in perception occasioned by such as the discovery of radiation.

21   Paradigm: Concept popularized by Dr. Thomas Kuhn. Universal connectedness is achieved with systematized data under a consensus worldview of learned participants. Other worldviews exist, but it is confusing to dwell on multiple systematizations.

would be around 1,000 B.C. – some refer to the subsequent years as the Axial Age – the beginning or flowering of Greek thought, Hebrew revelation, Buddhism and Confucianism.

At the beginning bookend, at least Hebrew and Greek thought used reason. The Greeks did so loudly and proudly – but with little empirical content. Reason, as a dictionary term or an internet search result is (or allows) a veritable forest of possibilities. Reason is not a refuge for objectivity.

The views can be contrasted as:

Athens: proto-"unaided" reason, immersed under polytheism.

Jerusalem: monotheism and revealed truth ("aided" reason), surrounded by polytheism.

So, at the beginning, Athens and Jerusalem both used reason. At Jerusalem, accepting revealed truth, they reasoned about an *ex nihilo* beginning event, present stability, providence and evident miracles. At Athens, hoping they had an "unaided" guide, they used Mathematic's Word to reason about an event-less past, present stability and an eventless future.

Too often, disappointed extrapolators find that the going gets easier if they say "science says" instead of "my paradigm says." It is wise to restrict usage of the word, science. When the context allows it, say science. At other times, say "investigators or thinkers or theoreticians say …."

What does the future hold for rational thought? This we return to in a later chapter.

Following is a discussion of concepts used in this book:

Knowledge: That which is true, factual – some call it justified true belief. Knowledge can be public or private. Public knowledge is accessible to everyone and undistorted by worldview or theory or bias. It is a "commons" for all mankind. Such knowledge can be static – a fact. Or it may link facts – which requires a causal mechanism.

Private knowledge can include such inner experiences as hunger, pain, love or observations through the senses; such as by being the sole witness to an accident or crime. Private knowledge has the challenge of verification. Many times, private knowledge is not suspected of being ephemeral, subjective, or unimportant – even if unverifiable.

Reason: Mental capability for consistent thought – to connect things together in the "true" way. Intensely applied, it ponders the flux of appearances and postulates some first principles.[22] Reason is identified with our brain.

Reason may also be described as a ground or cause for belief, making sense of things, relating cause and effect, applying logic or arguments to the best expla-

---

22   First Principles: All of reality is not public knowledge, so foundational assumptions are required, such as: an external reality exists and is ordered; the law of the excluded middle is a valid proposition; the cosmos can be mathematically described; cause precedes effect; *etc.* Thinking accepts first principles; it cannot prove them. Yet, few would advocate dispensing with them. Thus, philosophy, reason and blind chance cannot prove Universal Truth. Universal assumptions, such as uniformitarianism, must be "vetted" against the events of history.

nation. But these are not grounded statements. There is no "yardstick" in use.[23]

Reason is not unique to ancient Greek rationalism. However, in ancient Greece, philosophy connected reason to a *primary-object: mathematics*. Possessing Mathematic's Word seemingly "promoted" the philosopher to the highest level of objectivity, allowing him to make true "unaided" statements about the inaccessible.

Mathematics is a complex abstraction, which many think affirms the unperforated ahistorical cosmos of conventional textbooks, thereby justifying the passionately held paradigms. This bundle of related concepts may be storytelling, private knowledge, or assent to complicated puzzle solving.

Intellect: Relating to the mind and its primacy over the brain. The Greeks frequently referred to the mind's eye. Only later would the mind be denied.

Systematic understanding: In our well-ordered cosmos, regularity is the common way things occur. Patterns of regularity can be discerned. We get hungry daily; thus, we can systematically conclude that meals are to be a daily affair. (Or, like Sherlock Holmes, we may thread together various clues to solve a mystery.)

On a mundane level, this is called consistent thinking – or common sense. Systematic thinking can be complex, employing rules of logic and symbolic expression. It can find hidden linkages between "rafts of data." Prudent extrapolation of results or linkages can be made. Wisdom is required to discern when saving the appearances or grandiose extrapolation – and subjectivity – predominate.

We may say, for example, "All men are mortal. Socrates is a man. Therefore, Socrates is mortal." The phrase "All men are mortal," is such an elevated systematic understanding, but what about Enoch, Elijah, and Jesus? Even the cliché, "The only certainties are death and taxes," has qualifications. It assumes that you die before the end of the world and are not in the underground economy.

IT'S AS IMPORTANT TO KNOW WHEN TO STOP AS IT IS HOW TO { START.

Beware: When someone says Christianity is unreasonable, are they accusing Christianity of being *unscientific?* Or merely accusing Christians of rejecting the critic's own *rational system of universal connectedness?* (Reason would rather have "free inquiry" without a cosmic commitment.)

Extrapolation: The non-experimental process of extending the application of accessible knowledge, which depends upon an assumed or tested regularity – and preciseness of phenomena. Accessible knowledge can be built upon to predict what is yet unknown or unrelated. The process is like mathematics, *i.e.*, 1 + 1 + 1 + ...

(Due to imprecision inherent in phenomena, extrapolation has limits – *unless one assumes perfect phenomena. The "perfect" phenomenon is a nondeformable precise mathematical object. Then, it is forcibly imposed upon increasing portions of reality* – like the ancient Greeks did.)

---

23 A recent book is *Plato at the Googleplex* by Rebecca Goldstein. She is the honorary chairperson of FFRF (Freedom From Religion Foundation). But she does no better than just provided.

Caution is required. Insignificant factors can grow enormously with high values of multiplication. Take, for example, calculations of the wide range of money paid out on home mortgages under various rates of interest or years to maturity. You, thus, can appreciate the variability thinkers face as they extrapolate to trillions. For example, the Voyager I and II spacecraft are "only" 0.002 light years from earth. What does that inerrantly confirm about objects at so-called millions or billions of light-years away? (It is safer to connect and understand accessible facts than remote "facts.") Wisdom is required when encountering *grandiose extrapolation*.

Mathematically connecting theories is a process of addition, but the probability that the results express truth has multiplicative vulnerability, expressed as follows:

$1 \times 1 \times 1 \times$ (infinite times) = **1**, but
$1.001 \times 1.001 \times 1.001 \times$ (infinite times) = **infinity**, and
$0.999 \times 0.999 \times 0.999 \times$ (infinite times) = **zero**!

You have to get it exactly right, which only rational mathematicians can do! To use a theory to explore inaccessible reality is *extrapolative storytelling*.

Fact: Technically, there should be no need for words on facts. Facts are real, actual experience or observation. Unfortunately, some are tempted to "upgrade" ideas to "facts." Some ideas have an abstract "solidity," like evolution. Others say that mathematical summaries are the only facts. Thinkers say they carefully distinguish between facts and ideas, but their actions are not so convincing.

An interesting exception to mathematical distillation is provided by the mathematician, Reuben Hersh. "I phone my doctor for an appointment. He's booked way ahead, but his receptionist finds me an opening…. The opening in his schedule can't be weighed, or measured, or analyzed chemically. It's not a physical object…. Is it a mental object?... No. The opening in the schedule really exists…. It has the right to be called an object. (B14, page 72.)

Consider the following:

Direct Fact: This is the above-mentioned fact. It can be called a datum (or data, in the plural). Direct facts are found in nature, yet ambiguity can occur. Consider a witness

to an accident. If the weather wasn't clear, the scene was some distance off, or the lighting was poor – is the direct fact fully reliable? Yet find a cave and that fact is easily verifiable.

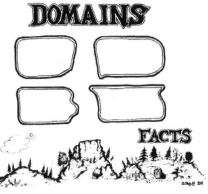

As we will see, direct facts were disdained by mainline Greek philosophers. Their mind's eyes were instead looking for Universal Connected Knowledge.

An organized search for facts divides nature into various areas of investigation called *domains*. Domains are not actual objects but areas where the search uses specialized tools. Domains such as physics, chemistry, *etc.*, have many sub-specialties and sub-domains. How many domains are there? Well, in how many different areas in such as physics or chemistry is it possible to get a PhD degree? Different direct facts are found in these domains but they may investigate the same object, such as a rock.

Mathematical Fact: Mathematical relations are generally defined – and hold true abstractly. The phrase, "according to my mathematics ...," is a means to upgrade a theory into a fact.

Theory and Theoretical Fact: Direct facts are the easiest to understand, even though not satisfying to the "all-seeing" mind's eye. To see further, the mind's eye assumes mathematical precision and stability and constructs a tentative road map of the unknown. Is a theory closer to storytelling or puzzle solving?

In empirical science, theory is controllable. But in inaccessible science, theory can have a life and "reality" of its own. This is where continued – nay, careless – use of the word, theory, provides certainty, where certainty cannot exist!

Investigation proceeds on the assumption that the theory provides a correct description of inaccessible reality. If confirming instances are found, this lends credibility to the theory (roadmap). But how many confirming instances are required so that truth and saving (all of) the appearances are equivalent? What about alternative roadmaps? Mathematical predictability is not the same as causality.

Paradigm and Paradigmatic Fact: Paradigms are a latecomer to intellectual endeavors. They arose when the totality of theories in science lost universal connectedness. Thinkers then retreated into specialized consensus agreements of learned participants. Paradigms attempt to bridge the gap between experimental domains (or theoretical domains) and the totality of reality. They begin as supra-visionary roadmaps in the mind's eye. They try to place all facts into a hierarchy of facts! This "stitching together" is another use of mathematics. Yet rationalism has a poor track record in being all-seeing.

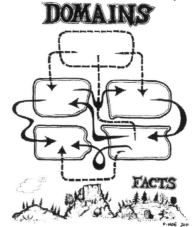

Theoretical or paradigmatic facts are vulnerable to dissolution. Such facts frequently require *Promissory IFs*: "We'll prove it later." Unredeemable Promissory IFs exist.

The resulting connections become tenuous *paradigmatic facts* – and builds a collection of *Layered Paradigmatic Facts*. If X direct fact is true, then Y organizing fact is true, then Z paradigmatic fact is true, and domain becomes connected to domain. Or the opposite may be said: Z is true. Then Y has to be such and such. Then X has to be so. If X isn't, then fix your instrument! (Theory trumps [local] experiment.) *Higher domain "facts" rule!*

Connecting domains together is hazardous, yet a worthy occupation. Indeed, science is not all laboratory work. Many researchers can spend their entire career pondering the interconnectedness of facts in various domains.

As has been said, some domains have an inherent vagueness – they ponder the inaccessible. These are such as the subatomic, astronomy, the human person-ality, or history. Consider an atom-smasher. The result is cloud-chamber tracks. It takes copious theory to get subatomic particles from these tracks. Is this interpre-tation of the direct facts objective? Also, what if the interconnecting mathematics says more than the domains contain? What if a dominant investigator imposes his own "clear intuitions?" He can outrun his headlights; "confirmation bias."

Also, time, itself, cannot be examined, even though it measures intervals. No instrument can measure the "alpha and omega" of time. Time is outside of science.

Likewise, fossils present challenges – they witness to *Life, Place* and *Time*. They witness to events; events do not witness to the ahistorical mathematical line!

So, a fossil in the ground is a direct fact. It is in a domain of *place*, but with a domain of *time*. To say the fossil is millions of years old is, at best, inferred, based on a theory. (*IF* reality proceeds on an ahistorical mathematical line and *IF* fossils are buried deep underground, *THEREFORE*, fossils are extremely old!)

We frequently hear talk about the Theory of Evolution. After 150 years, why is it not called the Fact of Evolution? Why? Be-cause the standard of causality is a very high standard. Layers of explanations may only save the appearances.

Fossils do not come with age tags attached. Some will say that the geologic strata can date the fossil. (This draws in geologic theory.) Some say that nuclear decay dating methods can date the fossil or rocks. (This draws in nuclear decay theory.) Some will say that ... (This draws in ....) Some will say that uniformitarian theory makes sense of all these theories. (This draws in uniformitarian theory.)

But others who agree on the data (the fossil and strata) will say that Noah's catastrophic worldwide flood explains the fossil's location and age. (This draws in discontinuity, hydrology and flood sorting theory.) Some will say that dating method calibrations make dating methods unreliable. (This draws in the analysis of dating method assumptions.) Some will say that catastrophic phenomena explain sediment layering. (This draws in initial condition assumptions on planetary shaking, hydrology, mountain uplifting, etc.) (*IF* reality proceeds on the basis of equilibrium and *IF* disequilibrium occurs, *THEREFORE,* fossils can witness to short lives!)

Theory is not competent to choose between explanations that transcend the known! Was it time (T) or water volume (V) that formed the earth's landscape? The above can also be expressed mathematically:

1,000,000,000 T x V = PDGF   (Uniformitarian)
or is it:
T x 1,000,000,000 V = PDGF   (Catastrophic)

T = Time in years
V = Volume of water
PDGF = Present Day Geological Features
(Expressed this way, the second formulation is incomplete because high water volumes and pressures "activate" additional phenomena, such as cavitation erosion!)

T x 1,000,000,000 (V + extra's) = PDGF   (Catastrophic)

Was it vast amounts of time or vast amounts of water that formed geological features and biological fossils? We can wonder where all the water could come from. But, (as Don Batten of Creation Ministries International points out in a pamphlet, *Noah's Flood – What about all the water?*), if the earth's surface is flat, there would be about 1.7 miles of water on its surface. Historical events such as shifts in the earth's mantle or the breaking of the "fountains of the deep" (Psalm 104:8) limit extrapolative certainties!

Researchers can agree on direct facts, but disagree on inter-domain facts, their layering or extrapolation. Refereeing these disagreements is not easy. *But science studies "what is"* without presuppositions about the inaccessible. These disagreements also show how it is possible for such as a Christian to hold a PhD in a domain of science and, yet, have "scientific" disagreement with another equally "PhD'ed" researcher about *inter-domain relations.*

We will see further examples in later chapters. Did Edwin Hubble discover the fact of an age indicator in the red-shift in the color of stars? Or did Halton C Arp instead discover parentage relations in the same red-shift data? There are many interpretive quarrels in inaccessible science!

Arguments among investigators are concentrated in the inaccessible or inter-domain regions. Sometimes explaining these domains unfortunately results in *Layered Potpourri*! Potpourri includes saving (some of) the appearances, because the "stitching" mathematics may not reflect causality; and mathematics has "wiggle-room" that experiments do not have. The history of science is littered with these appearances – the science of yester-year.

The inter-domain hierarchy can be a *complicated conceptual labyrinth*, to recast a statement of Bertrand Russell. The mathematician, David Berlinski, calls it an "*immense inferential trail.*" It breeds modern sophistry. The multiple inferences yield low overall probability. In summary, to be factual beyond direct facts is a rare accomplishment! Complicating the issue is the frequent suspicion that not all the facts are presented, but only those supporting a preferred explanation.

You may have felt the ground beneath you getting slippery! The person experimenting in a domain is a scientist. In the inter-domain regions he may be a scientist, a researcher, a technologist, a thinker, or a philosopher. It is no longer so easy to say what someone is doing.

Science: A domain of objective truth – truth not captive to bias or theory. Beware though; this arena of repeatable controlled experiments is not as large as many desire. *(Laboratory) science deals with the accessible, not Paradigms, Universal Natural Law or Universal Connected Knowledge.* It uncovers stable, repeatable relationships in the laboratory, which can be prudently extrapolated, but extrapolative infatuation may creep in.

Laboratory science – experimental science – may also be called empirical science. "Extrapolative" science, if it is science, gathers at the higher altitudes so that it can be "all-seeing." Extrapolative science is inaccessible science – paradigm science – ahistorical science – intellectual adventure – science, falsely so-called. *Paradigms, Universal Connected Knowledge and Universal Natural Law are grandiose extrapolations; they are not a commons of public knowledge.*

Associated with experimental science are other people who work with real things: engineers, technologists, craftsmen and tinkerers. Alert eyes and agile minds – even among hikers – are needed. Professional accreditation is optional!

In case you have forgotten, *discovering facts is not rationalists primary interest,* but rather Universal Connected Knowledge. Direct facts and events are down-played! (Such are for engineers, technicians, tinkerers, or hikers.) Instead, their "science" focuses upon the inter-domain regions. It organizes – and discovers – new facts "seen only" with the aid of inter-domain theory. Otherwise, buyers beware!

People who visualize mathematics as being as rigid and uncomplicated as 1 + 1 = 2 easily conclude that Universal Natural Laws *can be* discovered. Contrari-wise, visualizing mathematics as possessing subjective features makes it easy to conclude that Universal Natural Laws *cannot be* constructed; only useful formulas are expected. One's degree of assent to Mathematic's Word determines the amount of "knowledge" in Natural Laws, *i.e.*, whether puzzle solving or storytelling is predominant. As said earlier, ancient Greek thinkers searched for "unaided" truth, but "aided" by mathematics and its infinitely precise and rigid matter. They deftly operated by faith; they did not doubt the value-free status of mathematics!

Science is paid many justified compliments due to its value-free methodology, but a price is paid. Science is praised because it fulfills the lure of objective truth; *therefore,* where choices or ambiguity occur, science is sidelined. For example, the transition from a technical language to well-crafted words is such a gray area.

Where experiments are absent, is there science? Facts exist outside of science, but astronomy, social understandings or historical investigations are observational, not experimental. They catalog data, can be scholarly and useful, but lack causality. They may be saving (some of) the appearances or storytelling!

Understanding, not knowledge, results from extrapolative science. As said earlier, knowledge even exists outside of empirical science. It is presumptuous to think otherwise. Yet, workers in other disciplines should not label their work as scientific – but as knowledge. In this context, "scientific" is an unnecessary adjective.

Additionally, the adjective, "scientific," is easily forged. Keep science (natural philosophy) in its empirical context. This is realism. Let's not fool ourselves.

We frequently hear that "science is self-correcting." Yes and No! Because of the presence of theories, paradigms and types of facts, fortuitous *ad hoc* mathematical tweaks may become hard to recognize, much less to refute. History also shows that corrections rarely come from the developers or promoters of specific theories. Outsiders or successors do the job.

This is where one would expect the philosophers of science to step in and desediment the "sciences." But they don't! Facts can be hostage to paradigms! And paradigms can have powerful human sponsors.

Mathematics: Mathematics is science's handmaiden and is important to communication and analysis in science, yet choices exist in certain aspects thereof. The orderliness of creation allows the units of matter and their relationships to be discernable. Mathematics results from observing objects; it is not a physical reality – either here or in some other "world" – but is a shorthand notation to summarize highlighted features of experimental results or observations. An unrelated set of equations is required to describe the associated experimental apparatus. Mathematics and logic are tools – not science – nor the real.

Many years ago, mathematics and logic were much simpler, making them easier to assent to as truth. Thinkers now argue because extrapolative infatuation becomes vulnerable if mathematical objectivity is questioned.

In Greek times, mathematics was considered private knowledge of the philosophers. Science turned it into public knowledge! Once mathematics lost its earthy nature, strife began within rationalist ranks.

Law: Laws do not cause anything. Physical processes do not "digest" equations to learn how to act! Instead, laws shadow unseen causal physical processes.

(But, many causal physical processes remain cloudy!) No one has ever measured forces between 1 and 2 – or any other numbers! See Appendix B, *Algebra for Tinkerers*, for additional information.

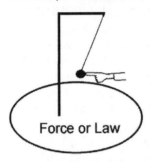

Force or Law

Laws are human formulations that try to model the interplay of forces to become statements of physical predictability, as demonstrated by repeated experiments. The mathematical data so obtained can hint at features of stuff otherwise not discernable. Models and laws are at least true within experimental confines. Extrapolating the law can cause uneasiness. [24]

Some still say that laws or mathematics control or create the cosmos. Some say mathematics is in the "mind of God," that matter "springs out" from (causal) or top-down mathematics. It seems better to say that mathematics shadows reality, as illustrated by children learning mathematics by playing with marbles. Such bottom-up activity can derive basic arithmetic – and geometry. *In this alternative view*, matter comes first – and mathematics arises from viewing deformable matter and its interactions. Friction exists between top-down and bottom-up mathematics, reflecting continuing disagreement between Pythagoras and Plato on one side and Aristotle on the other. (Rationalism versus reasonableness.)

Beyond its accessible utility, the nature of mathematics causes arguments. It seems dubious to say that God created with mathematics. If physics came first, then it seems better to say that God created in His craftsman shop!

Properly labeled, law describes a cause and effect relationship. Sometimes the law label is hastily applied and really describes a coincidental relation. Some-times, the most that can be said is that it can "save the appearances"[25] of phenom-ena. Revolutions of science may be waiting in the wings and affect the whole hierarchy of laws. Reason, science and law cannot determine if the cosmos is perforated or unperforated – nor its dimensions.

Mathematics and Causality: The relationship between these two is puzzling, as the following drawing illustrates. Consider the example provided by planetary motions and how mathematics models them. Ptolemy used epicycles and circles to make his system work; likewise for Copernicus. Kepler dispensed with circles and Newton built on Kepler's work, but motions were still reduced to geometry.

---

24   Experiments assume interrogative manipulation. Even though experiments require obser-vation, observing, by itself, is passive and less objective – be they observations from one or many perspectives. Astronomy tries to substitute observations of multiple phenomena for experimental manipulation. The grandiose application of this assertion is tenuous.

25   Save the Appearances: A Greek epistemological concept mentioned in an earlier footnote. It recognizes that all causes are not public knowledge. In such cases, thinkers must be content to describe (or save) the appearances. An example is Ptolemy of Alexandria's ancient use of epicycles to model planetary motions. Ptolemy was satisfied that such devices saved the appear-ances. That they were literally true could not be ascertained, therefore physical truth need not be required of them. They were useful "calculating fictions." (Alternatively, Aristotelians said the crystalline spheres and epicycles in their planetary model were "physically real.")

With a modern view, some facets of reality can be said to be in black-boxes, thus inacces-sible. One can probe the black-box with x-ray like tools and thereby discern some features – but not all.

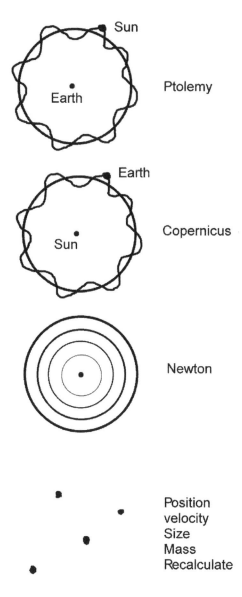

Ptolemy

Copernicus

Newton

Position
velocity
Size
Mass
Recalculate

In the first two, little physical data was used. Geometry of circles was the primary factor. They could have been modeling planets or apples! Once the proper values for the various circles were determined, the calculation could continue without looking at the planetary bodies. Neither were causal systems, it was saving the appearances. Data was used to fine tune the mathematics.

With Sir Isaac Newton it is more complicated. His fluxions (calculus) dealt with motion along curves. (He used curves, not circles.) His equations did not "need" the actual bodies either. His equation, $F = G{\cdot}M_1{\cdot}M_2/r^2$, could not be directly applied to imprecise curves.

In recent years, many calculators have moved to an arithmetical framework. They start with initial conditions for position, velocity, size, mass, *etc*. Then they calculate the forces between the various planets and then let the planets "move" a small amount, say one seconds worth of time and then recalculate all the values. This is endlessly repeated and the orbits are detailed. Yet, we again don't actually "see" how the physical objects "grab" each other. Mathematical "equivalents" to the physical forces are used. It is more accurate than the circular procedure, but still is an example of saving the appearances, but with greater accuracy and a hint of causality.

So just because equations are generously used does not equate to a knowledge of causality!

Intellectual Adventure: An extended systematic understanding with open tribute paid to the power of grandiose extrapolation (sightseeing or theoretical "thinking"). Thinkers should – but are reluctant to – step back and explore alternate systematizations. Rafts of data may be adrift on (competing) oceans of mathematics[26]. If all the "facts" line up, monotruth has been found and supposedly

26   Proving the objectivity of mathematics has always been a "goal." Even the eminent British mathematician, the late Bertrand Russell, recognized this was a present failure – the visions of Pythagoras and Plato are still unrealized.

cancels any need to search for rational alternate monotruths. Unfortunately, a *consistent explanation does not rule out alternate consistent explanations.*

Some thinkers say grandiose extrapolation is objective because we can *define* the stability of the properties under consideration. However, man can only define his creations – mental abstractions which embody mathematics and logic. A hard transition follows. The nature and extent of any relationship between the abstraction and reality are matters of inspection, not definition. We know what a "one" is and what a "rock" is. But how does "one" relate to a "rock" – especially a rock an utterly long distance away?

Well, mankind "traverses" such utterly long distances with grandiose extrapolation – which assumes a homogeneous universe: a manifestation of the ahistorical mathematical line. (Every place is just like where we are. *How convenient!*) Followers of Mathematic's Word are adamant on the homogeneous universe – even before exploring it. They "know" (extrapolative) science is not possible without this assumption – *but that is special pleading to "objectify" their "unaided" assumptions, which are not public knowledge.* Predictably, they are silent on the subjective element in mathematics.

Rather, whatever the universe is – whatever mathematics is – reality works. The commitment to truth recognizes grandiose extrapolation as subjective. In truth, a non-homogeneous universe cannot be traversed by mathematics, only local precision is attainable.[27] Anything more inflates into storytelling. Likewise, a malleable mathematics cannot retain precision when grandiosely extrapolated. In either case, universal conclusions are invalid. In summary, intellectual adventure is easy to *understand* but difficult to *know*.

Noncurrent Adventures: Scientific truth has a history of half-lives. Examples are: Platonic and Aristotelean physics, Ptolemy's and Copernicus' epicyclic theories of planetary motion, Kepler's three laws of planetary motion, Newton's corpuscular theory of light, the phlogiston theory in chemistry, steady state cosmology and Pythagorean numerology. Today, some paradigmatic thinkers promote various flavors of "big bangs." Some search for the TOE: Theory of Everything.[28]

Man's ability to explain outruns his ability to prove. That is a common feature of non-current adventures. Where facts or observations fall short, clear intuitions or confirmation bias of dominant personalities can provide a missing assurance. Also, critics may have a herd instinct or respect for their elders that mutes their criticism. "Current scholarly consensus" may not reflect a democratic vote of peers!

Materialism: An intellectual adventure, dear to atheism! All in the cosmos is determined, hence unperforated. It is an extrapolation broad enough to include atomists, relativists, quantum phenomena folks and string theorists. It can be called "methodological naturalism."

For over 2,000 years, rationalists promoted an infinite material cosmos. They

---

27   A nonhomogeneous universe is not necessarily chaotic, but its distant regularities may reflect force levels that differ greatly from earthbound assumptions. It reflects matter in regular motion in the created cosmos.

28   TOE: Theory of Everything – like a flower beginning to bloom, the blossoming arises from a single equation! This acronym is not a joke. Many thinkers spend their life looking for this "Holy Grail." Einstein tried and failed.

visualized mathematic as rigid and uncomplicated, so they "knew" what (or where) the other end of 1 + 2 + 3 + ... was. Present-day rationalists accomplish the same unperforated cosmos by promoting a finite, unbounded, but expanding, cosmos.

In accepting only mathematical models as real, they yet must observe a physical reality corresponding to the mathematics with measuring instruments. The senses are required to read these instruments, yet they believe the resulting unseen mathematical models are real – making reality a secondary phenomena. Can the nonmathematical reality of the world be recovered? Or is it even worth the attempt? Do not be deceived by the senses, they say. But also do not be deceived by the rationalism and mathematic-ism that captivates the mind's eye.

There is an unstated requirement for materialism. *Its universal mathematical models must unfold from a master equation without human intervention.* The mathematics must flower forth on its own. We don't want a "Wizard of Oz" in the background (a transplanted empirical Dr *Ad hoc*), inserting various equations or adjusting "constants," at critical junctures. Furthermore, an algorithm is like a computer program (an intellectual effort), so it cannot substitute for the flowering "master blind equation."

A brilliant theoretician is another problem. Such can leap from preliminary mathematical equations about a phenomenon under measure to a broad systematization. His co-workers are justifiably amazed; his result is not computable from the available data. His mind's eye is not restricted to the reasoning ability of his brain. Rationalism has a state of inner contradiction between mind and brain.

Turning their attention from the cosmos to man, rationalists reject human attributes not reducible to mathematics, since their deterministic philosophy allows no exceptions to mathematical distillation. Mind and spirit are banished as secondary phenomena.

Lastly, this cosmic meaning of materialism predates the current popular usage that generally means "a pursuit of possessions."

Quantity and Quality: Determinism requires that everything real can be measured – which means everything must be a quantity.

Qualities are not measurable. The only way qualities are acceptable to a determinist is to somehow change them into a quantity. What can't be changed is thereby judged to be a "secondary phenomena." Rene Descartes acted on this. He famously said that "matter and extension" are all that exists! (Though, he did postulate "soul atoms," but few believed him on this.)

An example of a transformed quality is heat. With a thermometer, temperature can be measured – that is a measurable item. But the quantity of heat is not. Taste, odor, love, beauty, a sensitive heart and compassion are unmeasurable qualities. *Can a determinist love his spouse and children?*

Thus far in this book, the word quality, has occurred several times. More usage will occur. Quality is not a secondary phenomena. (Remember the opening in the Doctor's appointment schedule.) Unmeasurable, yes; quality is another indicator of the limited range of science – and the omissions extrapolators require.

Philosophy: A slippery word about reasoning. Greek philosophy dealt with the essential building blocks of reality, *i.e.,* atoms, arithmetic, geometry, or logic and their appearances in reality. For centuries, a scientist, a mathematician, and a

philosopher were the same – a lover of truth. A "physical" mathematic tied philosophy to science.

Today, philosophy concentrates on "mathematical" physics (*i.e.*, inaccessible
physics) – but arithmetic and geometry are now esoteric constructs, no longer like
1 + 1 = 2. Philosophy becomes saving the appearances, with erudite crystal-ball
gazing, storytelling, or proselytizing – vainly avoiding the embarrassment of being
religious, utopian, or subjective. It frequently is a secular "god of the gaps," tuck-
pointing gaps in Universal Connected Knowledge.

Myth: A story from the past about an earlier historical event, but which is
inaccurate – at least it doesn't agree with "today's" science. Myth rarely intrudes on
the domain of empirical science. As said earlier, the Biblical report is orderly and
connected, but full of events. Events contradict the mathematical and logical order
Greek thinkers favored – exemplified by an ahistorical mathematical line. As said
before, *mathematical order has no events, it is ahistorical.*

Myth frequently is a word used to discredit earlier observers. We honor macro-
historical statements about events in the Bible by investigation: *ex nihilo* creation,
Noah's flood and Joshua's long day. Worldwide records affirm these events. Are
these history or intercontinental synchronized mythology? (Synchronized mythology requires some interesting ocean trips long ago! Defining these required trips as
mythological is a theory less believable than believing the historical events!) Indeed,
events set a limit to knowledge – the inaccessible may not be so large.

God: Atheists do not accept the concept of God – much less the person. The
deist and the philosopher's god is a god of the unperforated cosmos. He may provide the original chaotic material and impart motion to it. But – the theist's God is
the God of the event-filled perforated cosmos of *ex nihilo* creation.

Revelation: Communication from the transcendent God – it is Godly news.[29]
Revelation deals with knowledge sent into the cosmos and written down. These
supra-rational (*trans*-empirical) Scriptures are required for total comprehension of
reality. Granted, Scripture must be evaluated by humans but in a manner appropriate to its transcendent status, as mankind's public knowledge lacks cosmic
dimensions. Reason cannot fully evaluate what is beyond its capabilities.

Biblical revelation causes an unequal contest, similar to the challenge of how
the clay evaluates the potter (Isaiah 64:8). The Potter (God) must provide the
information. This perforation (information) into the cosmos came to individuals who
wrote it down in the God-breathed (inspired) words of the Bible – sacred Scripture.
God continues to perforate the cosmos. At least part of this activity[30] is intended for
individual exhortation or comfort, but Christians are to test even this private comfort
against sacred Scripture.

Critics may say Biblical revelation is subjective. It is better to say that public
verification of historic communications may not be neat and tidy.[31] Revelation can
sorely test popular reasons and extrapolations. When dealing with the uniqueness

---

29   Godly news. Taken from *Quam Dilecta,* by Peter van Inwagen, in *God and the Philosophers,* edited by Thomas W. Morris.
30   God has other business to be about that He has not revealed to mankind.
31   Transcendent reports are studied by Biblical interpretation, archaeology, geologic excava-
tions, and historic investigation.

of historical events, you can't be ahistorical! Declaring history to be irrational or mythical is only consistent with a prior "faith" in rationalism and Mathematic's Word!

The original documents of Biblical Revelation are gone. The many extant ancient fragments, translations and quotations respected Jesus' admonition that "not one jot or tittle"[32] shall pass away. Yet, some relics do show variations due to scribal error or deliberate distortion. Even anciently, the church pruned away many of these accretions.

Wisdom: Last but highest, wisdom is that "sixth sense" quality regarding the discernment of knowledge, understanding and appearance. It is related to the mind and intellect. It provides a "feel" for epistemology, common sense, and when a thinker's wish fathers the fact. Yet, human wisdom has a poor track record when being grandiose, like the clear intuitions that bedevil philosophies of the epoch.

So ends the general discussion of concepts used in this book.

In summary, I am not science bashing. Universal science, falsely so-called, is a potpourri of science, ideas and layered theoretical facts. This mixture leads to posturing and self-righteousness.

We have had many examples of frustration and communication barriers. Ironically, lovers of truth fail to recognize potpourri. Before we come to cures, we need further illustrations of the extensiveness of this irony. Only then may people be convinced that a trek through the musty dusty history of the between-years is worthwhile.

"Science" is an ill-defined and overused word:

> In German speaking countries, every serious (but not necessarily meaningful, coherent, and verifiable) discourse is entitled to be labeled scientific ... In other languages of the European continent ... every discipline making verifiable state-ments – or at least striving to make them – whether requiring empirical confirma-tion (like those of biology) or not (like those of mathematics), is usually called a science. Finally, in English we find the paradox that mathematics and logic, though both admittedly scientific in the highest degree, are not usually included in science; indeed, in that language the word "science" ordinarily covers the study of nature, spiritual activity, and society.... (B5, page 223.)

Rationalists love universal connectedness, but reality remains embarrassingly elusive. The existing potpourri, complete with national flavors – cannot exclude such systems as the Oriental Tao of science.[33] Even the voluminous *Encyclopedia Britannica* avoids defining science, yet accepts these universal statements. Most science writers are oblivious to this loss of objectivity. "Creation 'science'" leads to a proper appreciation of reason, conjecture, and faith.

What did reasoners overlook? Why is science so elusive?

In its Greek origins, besides the good things mathematics provided, mathe-

---

32   "Jot and tittle" refer to Hebrew language grammatical markings. The closest English similarity would be to "dot your i's and cross the t's." See Matthew 5:18.
33   Pity the high school (or even college) student who now has to *decide* how to write THE objective definition of science.

matical misconceptions existed. These went beyond direct facts to guarantee their grandiose extrapolations. The next chapter views these misconceptions, which were fossilized into the "science of measure." They still shield intellectual adventure from scrutiny.

Many centuries later, exploration, experiment and observation unleashed data explosions – not-so-subtle hints of Creation's extraordinary complexity. The science of measure could not systematize all the resulting facts, so cherished grandiose extrapolations failed. Later thinkers reluctantly faced falsification, paradigm shifts, and revolutions of science. Modern science, (falsely so-called), commingling understanding and knowledge, and ornamented with unverifiable universal statements, at least is a *great intellectual adventure*.

This troubling description of what once was truth again indicates that the text-book definition of science – and the cliché "reason versus faith" – is inadequate. Too often, truth eludes our grasp. Reason and faith are examined in the following chapters.

Also, instead of awkwardly compressing thought into "reason versus faith" or "science versus religion," people should talk about "reason, *conjecture*, and faith" or "science, *understanding*, and religion."

Conjecture or understanding indicates a middle ground of pragmatism, proto-religion, or proto-science. This middle ground cannot be well defined, yet is a pool of necessary – and rational – words. The middle ground may make some thinkers uncomfortable, but the lure of objective truth should restore comfort.

Science's "subjectivity" results when cosmic thinkers eliminate the middle ground and equate paradigms with knowledge.[34] They express their potpourri with science words, so subjectivity may escape notice. Sadly, most people accept the resulting "simple" opposition between objective and subjective, but cannot unravel whether understandings – or paradigms[35] – are objective or subjective.

This struggle between understanding and knowledge renders the word "science" unclear. Poetic justice applies reductionism to science,[36] since that word covers the work of tinkerers, experimenters, engineers, technologists, observers, mathematicians, thinkers and explainers. Indeed, by popular use, a scientist can be almost anything (as long as he is systematic) – including historian, literary critic, astrologer or metaphysician. Appeals to "secular" truth (to shut out the Christian worldview) are based on intellectual adventure, not on direct facts.

Pluralistic interpretive possibilities, where admitted, challenge the objectivity of

---

34   This anticipates subjects to be covered – and already hinted at in the uneasiness of philoso-phers at the textbook definition of science.
35   The contemporary objective-lined buzzword.
36   Reductionism: Reducing a system or process to its constituent parts – real or imagined. A useful procedure but it can be an inverse extrapolation to the extreme, such as by reducing life to atoms. Unfortunately, reductionism allows baffled thinkers to hide from uncomfortable facts by proclaiming that they will carry the analysis to "deeper levels." Problems are postponed, then conveniently forgotten, through this process of moving to deeper levels of analysis. The result is usually nihilism: they have seen to the deepest level! They have seen nothing ... all is mirage. They place uncritical trust in the tools of reason. Such thinkers see nothing because their tools, themselves, contain freedom and subjectivity. (I once read something similar to this.)
   Some thinkers refer to reductionism as knowing more and more about less and less until you know everything about nothing. From that narrow base, you can understand whatever!

rationalists. They insist that any "working with" facts must be science, so they cringe at the suggestion that they should not wear the mantle of science. They hope further research will harmonize all systematic understandings.[37]

Commingling paradigm and knowledge corrupts science. Hygienically, such science is only provisional. Once every generation or so, revolutions of science, paradigm shifts, or *gestalt* shifts provide partial correctives.

Undaunted by these criticisms, rationalists remain smug; *they retain a long-held secret truth!* Reason is rational, unbiased and autonomous – only if it is atheistic.

But cosmic perspectives are not "free" inquiries – they are "aided" in some manner. Therefore, *free and autonomous reason is uncommitted: it is rationally agnostic[38] and atheoristic[39] – not atheistic.[40]* An atheist may not be religious – yet has subjective faith. Atheorism is blasphemy to those who sight down the ahistorical mathematical line and "see" only a simple opposition between reason and faith, with no broad spectrum to blur their extrapolations!

Two concerns now intermix. **One**: Does God exist or is it atheism? **Two**: Can our reason, resident here on earth, objectively reach all of history and distances and thereby rationally explain reality? Can 1 + 1 = 2 and associates really accomplish this?

The rationalist assumes that concern **One** affirms atheism. He further hopes that concern **Two** need not even be brought up, and that people should just accept science and not insult reason!

The rationalist is frightened if both concerns are addressed. A negative answer to concern **Two** nullifies answering concern **One** in favor of atheism! Do not give the rationalist the linguistic advantage of treating the two concerns in isolation. Without a prior belief in "vast distances and long ages," no atheist is comfortable. *Is any atheist an atheoristic rationalist? That is a discontinuity!*

Reluctance to return reason to its servant status carries on the Greek (mis)understanding of mathematics. They saw it as mathematical matter, not as a systematic understanding.

As a servant, reason[41] cannot rigorously critique the middle ground or first principles (secular or supernatural) or mathematics for none are purely public knowledge. Despair and/or cynicism follow as the mind senses exceptions to or inconsistencies in unwarranted universals. This also applies to thinkers' current

---

37   Resultant contradictions cannot be explained away as being due to imprecise data. There may be misguided and/or falsely grounded paradigms.

38   Agnostic: One who cannot decide if God exists. He is a rationalist – but is repelled by its meaninglessness and uncreativeness. He is a lapsed atheist. (I once read something like this.) Agnosticism is unstable because *unbelief* in God *should be coupled* with *unbelief* in any grandiose explanation.

39   Atheorism: Disbelief in grandiose extrapolation; an awareness of learned ignorance. Imre Lakatos, in *The Methodology of Scientific Research Programmes*, uses the word, atheorism, once.

40   Atheism: The faith of rationalists. The belief that no god exists – or if he/she/it does, that he/she/it has no contact with or interest in the unperforated cosmos.

41   We now know that "the savage mind" and "crazy" people are reasonable and logical. They just utilize savage or crazy assumptions.

preeminent universal: *All is relative.* The well-reasoned praise this gem of bad philosophy as the pinnacle of truth and tolerance, so a paradox continues into the twenty-first century: *Rationalists are absolutely certain* they exclusively certify and guard truth. Accordingly, they are pleasant to those who express gratitude for their historic destiny. But woe to those who question their methodology or resulting corpus of "objective" truth! Thus, in spite of a veneer of tolerance, relativistic thinking is violently antagonistic to Christianity, which adheres to Biblical revelation, which denies physical truth to the mind's grandiose extrapolations.

Perhaps you now better appreciate the paradox that science is not synonymous with truth. Extrapolative "science" hinders atheoristic interest in facts. Rationalists "know" that a Universal Natural Law is as objective as experimental proof – helped with fortuitous *ad hoc* auxiliary hypothesis. In contrast, experimental science sticks close to laboratory facts. *No wonder rationalists believe* **theory trumps (local) experiment** – *extrapolative "science" trumps (local) empirical science!*

Universal statements proliferate; rationalists see no need to blush. For them, *science is systematic knowledge.* Yet "systematic" is an elusive word. As Karl Popper said, "Consistency is not the criterion of truth, but all truth will be consistent." Yet, up until the beginning of the twentieth century, systematization allowed it to be "scientific" knowledge that Mars had canals and vegetation, and that Mars, the moon, the sun, and other planets were inhabited.[42]

Nonetheless, disillusionment with "science" occurs, yet "scientific" hostility to Christianity continues unabated. You may now sense that two opposing ideas fight each other – but both are called science. Extrapolative science needs a new name – perhaps the old name of science, falsely so-called, is best.

Frequently, the general public's only alarming contact with "science's" vagueness is through the (derivative) social ~~sciences~~ understandings, where well-reasoned folk, desiring to be burden-lifters[43], squabble about how to spend our money and control our lives – for what *they* consider to be *our* highest good.

People praise science and technology. Science, falsely so-called, wants to share this aura of success in spite of warnings that science has limits. Rationalists do not intend to give up and accept the vestments of philosophers or storytellers or mystics or theologians. Chastened, they now artfully describe, though not define, science as a process of experiment plus mathematics:

> The history of *modern* physics has taught us that the analysis of the problem of causality has been decisively assisted and furthered by two basic methods which were foreign to Greek antiquity – systematic experimentation and the mathematization of science. The refinement of experimental techniques on the one hand revealed the *complexity of apparently simple phenomena* and on the other hand made it possible to decompose them into a number of *isolated occurrences.* It could further be shown that some of these occurrences were connected with others, and that a *clear and unambiguous description* could be given of the connections between them. The language most suited for this description is mathe-

---

42   For example, see *Planets and Perception,* by William Sheehan.
43   Burden-lifter: One who does good with a golden rule based on imagined mathematical objectivity. People are reduced to objects. Dispensers of compassion become bureaucrats.

matics, and the success of mathematical physics became indeed an overwhelming proof of the possibility of *describing* increasingly large complexes of the
physical world. Mathematical algorithms, such as differential equations, tensor
analysis, matrix algebra, and statistical methods, have been successfully used or
adapted to describe the evergrowing sum total of our knowledge, to assist in the
detection of new facts and to serve as instruments of prediction. (B6, page 49.
Emphasis added.)

Contrary to this statement, Greek "science" was incarnate mathematics,
although only with Pythagorean number or Euclidean geometry. The above writer
assumes organic and inorganic stuff are conceptually the same, and that "increasingly large complexes," in fact, includes the cosmos. He certainly accepts grandiose extrapolation, highlighting mathematics as the extrapolative tool of science. He
"objectively" oversteps science's empirical domain.

Is mathematics really untainted by subjective and ambiguous understandings?
Is mathematics a discovery of things or relationships, rather than a vision / invention of the mind? Some may think these questions view mathematical dexterity as
only a style of presentation, as in art. As one extrapolates beyond science with
universal connectedness, mathematics as invention becomes truer!

A thought occurs: alternative systematizations may exist that save the phenomena, *i.e.*, retain facts, but without postulating universal statements. Systematic
understandings with the least extrapolation are the more objective.

Many thinkers overlook alternate systematizations. As they manipulate
paradigmatic "facts," *they master the art of subjective choice without also being
religious!* This cosmic delusion tarnishes science. Some left religious communities
to escape vagueness – but *"colonies of thinkers" – the current scholarly consensus
– can be subjective paradigm communities.* Some, in turn, leave "colonies of
thinkers" and become modern sophists or even return to Christianity.

Concurrently, naive Christians perilously compromise their faith by saying
science forces them to retreat from manifest Christianity into airy "spiritual niches."
A noted minister recently warned the Church, "We almost reached the point where
no one had the right to speak except scientists." (B7, page 36.) Unfortunately, that
point may yet come.

You may have experienced, as I have, some bright young people who reject
Christianity because "science" renders it obsolete. The only thing still bothering
them is that science itself is so flaky. No wonder many turn to the fourth or fifth
understandings ... and read crystals, recite guru formulas or accept rational
incoherence. It rarely occurs to them to travel down the hidden, yet obvious, path
and examine the original rational alternative of God's *ex nihilo* created fact.

A paradox continues: Christian faith manifests itself in observable actions
such as personal sanctification and loving one's neighbor as oneself, but "moderns" regard *all observable action* as science's exclusive domain. Therefore
moderns (*in the Church as elsewhere*) try to make Christianity surrender its
leadership role in intra- and inter-personal life to secular burden-lifters. Supposedly,
this allows Christians to concentrate on spiritual abstractions! Yet, paradoxically,
science will not separate itself from science, falsely so-called, thereby retaining an

accumulation of contradictory rational theoretical edifices.

Well-reasoned folk study ... and resist ... *and propagate* ... intrapersonal and societal (interpersonal) tragedy! The smoke of conflict occurs in the arena of secondary "sciences," yet the spark-generators are in the deeper sciences, falsely so-called. Science's good name is imperiled. Too often science functions as an oracle giving answers that are paradigmatic, but not truthful – a truly hideous strength! (This, as C. S. Lewis warned, is a multifaceted danger.)

Cosmic thinkers are reluctant to acknowledge their ignorance, learned though it be, for fear the good they promote is not good. If adventuring is subjective ...

After all this, can science be defined? Some may say, "Science is empirical and experimental," so are theories unscientific? Some may say, "Science deals with observable quantities," so are forces, fields, masses, *etc.*, unscientific? Some may say, "Science is well-ordered knowledge, and predictions can be based on it," so are systematic philosophy, theology, and astrology science? Some may say, "Science is mathematical," so why bother with experiments – *and on it goes!* Like previous attempts, these mutually exclusive phrases are inadequate, each trying to acknowledge known problems, yet retain "science's cosmic dimensions."

Confusion results from overusing the word, science. Many think separating science from intellectual adventure is too daunting a task. Admittedly, a gray area exists, yet at this early point in our study no great obstacles exist. Later, a retreat may be required, but beware of an interest in only cutting-edge "science," which can become a security blanket – obscuring the epistemological question of whether consistency rules out alternative systematizations.

Paul Kurtz, the humanist, shows this obscurity when he says:

> [The] scientific approach unreservedly is to accept as ultimate in all matters of fact and real existence the appeal to the evidence alone; a court subordinate to no higher authority, to be overridden by no prejudice however comfortable. (B8, page 109.)

Kurtz does not consider that science's mathematical tools contain subjective freedom or that "all-seeing" rational "evidence" may not be facts but may be layered potpourri. "*Appealing to the evidence alone" frequently appeals to paradigmatic facts to say what accessible facts cannot say.* This lack of a critical eye should be replaced by an atheoristic look for any ensnaring extrapolative infatuation. Therefore, those with ready answers to our concerns should wait awhile. Studying the foundation of science is a prelude and a curative; it deflates rational storytelling.

Cosmic-minded thinkers have outrun science's exalted goal and, moreover, what "men of goodwill" consider science to be. Men of good will do not say, "Scientists are people who have esoteric quarrels with each other." Indeed, most people still think science is objective truth; truth not captive to bias, theory or word system. This recalls the ancient Greek understanding, flawed though it was. Can some of science's credibility be regained? Science is not intellectual adventure, nor is science whatever scientists say it is.

In response, and after many pages written to show that science is an over-used word, consider the following:

Science is objective.

Science respects atheorism.

Science dislikes intellectual adventure.

Science, therefore, produces an unexpectedly small body of knowledge derived from those facets of the material world amenable to experimentation.

Physics exemplifies this; its inorganic experimental domain excludes unmathematical arenas such as qualities, animate nature, human personality, and teleology. Yet even physics must ponder the unverifiable or the otherwise subjective: within its mathematical tools; in its first principles; in formulating laws or theories that transcend their experimental domains; in encountering phenomena that are not ahistorical; and when pursuing the macro- or microscopic. Knowledge and useful understandings may also be found via observation – to save the appearances – but science does not wander far from unencumbered experiments.[44] The works of tinkerers, craftsmen, engineers and technologists are generally independent endeavors and are heartily welcome! Extraordinary complexity requires a lack of dogmatism. (No wonder the fiery philosopher, Paul Feyerabend, was "against method.") Thus, science uses atheorism to respect the lure of objective truth.

Extrapolation – at least grandiose extrapolation – is subjective. This learned atheorism acknowledges that God's creation is orderly and complex. Order (and attendant repeatability) allows the systematic analysis of the observable. Order offers the tempting vision that perceived patterns can be reduced to (unbiased) mathematics (*i.e.*, 1 + 1 = 2 and associates), then combined with theories and paradigms and extrapolated without loss of coherence or conformance with complex reality. Complexity, however, assures that ultimate error results from using grandiose extrapolation! We then see through a glass, darkly!

The above description of science, while worded differently from typical descriptions of science, has no conflict with the lure of objective truth. But it exposes the subterfuge of joining accessible complexity and experimentation with grandiose extrapolation and Universal Natural Law. Science is finite and earthy because of complexity, the predominant earthboundness of experimentation, and that this is where mankind lives.

Strictly speaking, the phrase, *"Universal Natural Law,"* is a cliché. Atheorism shows it to be, at best, bold extrapolations from "geo-apparent natural regularities." Expressed cautiously, traveled distances and recorded history generally describe science's playing field – the finite material earth, thus friendly to the created fact.

Attempts to rectify defects in Universal Natural Law run afoul of paradigmatic facts or the creative choices available in modern mathematics and logic. Philosophers of science and modern sophists recognize this problem but fear to retreat from extrapolative infatuation and rationalism. The limited and perforated cosmos of Biblical revelation haunts them; it is not falsified by science. Atheorism reveals rationalism to be storytelling based on simplistic mathematical concepts.

Mathematics describes features of God's *ex nihilo* creation; yet creation is not mathematical. Did top-down mathematics spring out of the "mind of the maker" and

---

44   The methodology is discussed at the end of chapter 9.

subsequently matter come from (causal) mathematics? Or was matter "forged" in the Creators workshop and bottom-up mathematics comes from examining the resulting relations between the created objects?

The latter seems more probable. The simplistic concepts in the (soon to be studied) science of measure are inadequate, and correctives smuggle in creative freedom. Complexity shows that the regularities experimentally manipulated (or observed) may be subject to irregularities, error bandwidths, or sharp cutoffs, with time, distance, or unusual combinations. Words such as *entropy, attenuation* and *catastrophe* hint at this. (The perforated cosmos is stable, but its distant regularities may not be as expected from our earthbound "vantage point.") [45]

Universal Natural Law rules science, falsely so-called, and believes that mathematics and astronomy prove that the cosmos has "vast distances and long ages." The subsequent job of geology and biology is to fill in the details. When Christians unwisely agree, their disagreement with rationalism slims down to an origins dispute regarding geology or biology. The description of science stated herein retains these disputes – but is not limited to them.

All nature is orderly – thanks to its Designer and Creator. Order allows modeling, especially so for solid inorganic matter, under constant ambient conditions. Other inorganic matter, possessing more elasticity, and liquids, gases or plasma, are more difficult to model. Likewise for organic life or the otherwise inaccessible! Understanding people is further complicated because people think and act. Marks of supernatural involvement may sit in test tubes but more likely in some large events, system designs and human hearts.

The scientific method extends human knowledge about the lawful creation. It is the unbiased manipulative investigation of accessible phenomena; thus experiments can only probe so far. The first tentative explanation is called a *hypothesis,* which is subjected to manipulative *experiments.* Deductive reasoning then finds cause and effect relationships – and predicts new data or wider application of the resulting mathematical relations. After repeated experiments and deductions by many researchers, successful hypotheses rise to the status of *theories.*

This rigorous methodology advances until the prize is attained – *monotruth: the single repeatable answer –* written with mathematics. To exclude bias, the choices within mathematics must be respected. Experimentally repeatable results are distilled into formulas which model (local) *necessity,* but cannot say what is the *extent* of the necessity, *why* nature has a specific arrangement nor *how* the specific arrangement came to be. Mathematics shadows the interaction of forces; reality is more than formulas or algorithms. Respecting atheorism helps to satisfy the lure of objective truth.

It is difficult to consider a natural law to be universal (possessing infinite precision, infinite hardness and unattenuated). Clearly, science seeks truth about the experimentally accessible; mathematically modeled and systematically arranged to show generalized relationships. However, extrapolation of the results and creating inter-domain facts requires wisdom due to the subjectivity inherent in certain aspects of mathematics, mathematics' partial portrayal of reality, the non-equivalence of reality (and events) and mathematics, and wise timidity due to Creation's complexity.

---

45   Organic aspects of reality add further levels of intellectual challenge. Organic reality almost changes their subject to information programming.

Mathematics, the tool of science, can be an unruly servant. It is used for curve fitting and puzzle solving, but it can also be storytelling. Beyond experimental confines, arguments will never cease. Experimental facts may at times be disconcerting, but truth is truth, limited though it may be. This is the engine that drives technological, engineering and scientific advances. Atheoristic scientists, engineers, technologists, craftsmen, and tinkerers are servants of objective truth. This is the limited knowledge commons! Observation (such as in astronomy) and extrapolation may save some appearances.

Atheorism shuns extrapolative infatuation and dominant personalities, respects mathematical limitations and realizes that the supernatural is a hard potter for the clay to investigate. "All-seeing" thinkers may have axes to grind, hidden motivations, and accept the "unaided" philosophy of the epoch. Resulting systematizations bolster the pride of ivory-tower builders – it is not a commons. Such science, falsely so-called, is an unfortunate ongoing hypnosis. Patient atheorism and humility is the reasonable option!

This definition reflects empirical science, for man's "all-seeing" desire outruns public knowledge. God's revelation transcends the cosmos and is the court of last appeal. It also addresses spiritual reality but resists subjectivity or "spiritual adventure." As the Designer and Creator of this specific finite cosmos – and that within us which responds to the lure of objective truth – God questions the objectivity of some secular "knowledge."[46]

This definition of science may sound like a radical empiricism, but scientific knowledge covers less ground than expected. It is not enough to live by. Faith and the middle ground of conjecture and understanding are needed in order to get on with our lives.

To limit sciences' domain sounds hostile to the "science" of astronomy, which extrapolates to the uttermost. Yet the lure of objective truth must not be censored by any fancied slight to astronomy. The late physicist, Henri Poincaré, once wondered what science would be like if the earth were perpetually covered by clouds. If that sounds claustrophobic, what would science be like if the solar system were surrounded by some sort of sea. Even more so, what if the ancient Greeks realized that they only saved (some of) the appearances instead of saw Universal Natural Laws? Be wary of extrapolative infatuation!

Intellectual adventures, such as those within astronomy, may be systematic and fruitful, but integrity is best preserved by avoiding the *misconception* that such an admixture with subjectivity remains science. Like a still, small voice, science reminds us that direct facts do not rule out *ex nihilo* creation; *i.e.*, "God's little short

---

46   Philosophers of science struggle with this. The concepts expressed in footnotes 19, 20, and 21 express uneasiness with grandiose extrapolation. Yet, their lifework uses the selfsame grandiose extrapolation to avoid science being finite. Further, some say that direct facts do not exist; that all facts are tainted with "all-seeing" theory. Such are mesmerized by the tangled webs involved in considering "inaccessible" issues such as: "which big bang is proper?" They never stoop to consider the facts in such mundane situations as; "It is going to be -20 degrees Fahrenheit tonight ... it is going to freeze;" or "Watch out! Do not drive that truck over that old bridge, it will collapse;" or, "Did you really discover a cave? Show me!" The mesmerized prefer science, falsely so-called, over mere science or knowledge.

story."[47]

Rationalism is plagued with failed extrapolations generated in their flight from this "little short story." Our present age, containing so many shattered worldviews, should force people to be "open, relevant and unbiased." A deflated description of science should be acceptable; but it is not. The proud and lofty goal of a cosmic science is obscured, but not shattered. Atheorism finds real problems to solve, but atheism must begin with "vast distances and long ages" for the cosmos.

Typical definitions of science tiptoe around this subjectivity. They seek to retain as truth all sightseeing presented as science. Yet reason cannot harmonize all claimants to the name of science! (Why is no autopsy performed on the ensuing SILENCE?)

Hearkening back to my dinner table conversation – Why is economics called the "dismal science"? Is it not rather, "many dismal understandings?" Likewise, why is astronomy called a science? Astronomy is systematic understandings of rafts of data adrift on oceans of mathematics!

Such statements cause anger and resentment. They commit sacrilege against the cosmic outlook of SCIENCE, falsely so-called; hinting that its cherished interpretation of "truth, goodness, and beauty" cannot endure; cannot fulfill the lure of objective truth; or replace Christianity[48] as the means to unite men of goodwill. Universal truths come via Biblical revelation, but the well-reasoned say they are discovered by "(unaided materialistic) reason and (its extrapolative) 'science.'"

Science cannot disprove God – nor prove God. Science cannot address the universal, the distant, the historical or the otherwise experimentally unmanipulable – or even arithmetic, geometry and logic. Science can address the experimentally accessible, and thinkers can grapple with the observable or inconsistent. To prefer atheism – to disdain atheorism – brings up matters of the heart and soul. Understanding why a thinker chooses his worldview involves more than an earnest desire to "love truth" or "love mankind." It also involves rational or reasonable outlooks.

Inquiring about preludes can cause uneasiness, anger and resentment. More than scholarly pride is at stake; our individual souls are in danger. Also at stake are the reasons for living and consequent motivations of mankind for good and lasting endeavors. The soul's "desire for good" does not deny original sin, for not all evil delights in immoral deeds. Even lovers of truth are sinful and can advocate untruthful understandings.

Followers of the unperforated understanding seek an advantage in the word wars by wrapping their adventures in the mantle of science, that magic word above criticism. Science, falsely so-called, upon assuming the authority of science, thereby renders its critics irrational. Once your storytelling is as objective as $1 + 1 = 2$ and associates, you can be educational, therapeutic, or even benevolently authori-

---

47   The truthfulness of this affirmation may be acknowledged by writers candidly discussing the "search for truth." Some acknowledge that Biblical *ex nihilo* creation is not ruled out by the *facts*, only that the *current scholarly consensus* points in other directions. "God's little short story" is the way someone I once heard on the radio express his disdain for Biblical *ex nihilo* creation. That person viewed reality as an endless, mindless, soap opera.
48   Christianity is more feared than religion in general. Only the Judeo-Christian perspective contains offensive absolutes and documentable perforations of the cosmos.

tarian toward disbelievers.

Sadly, many Christians accept extrapolative infatuation as science. Bewildered, weary, and divided Christians uncritically accept the prevalent commingling of understanding and knowledge and retreat into airy spiritual niches, which *they* tell us is the only refuge in an unperforated cosmos from science. Oneness with the Spirit and spiritual vitality are subsequently replaced with therapeutic up-to-date-ness. They find it demeaning that their therapeutic up-to-date-ness needs to walk alongside soul ministry. They have surrendered their domain of expertise – the human soul and its works. As a result, they devalue – then replace – soul ministry with therapy for physio-chemical animals, while avoiding Biblical archaeology, apologetics, or soul ministry. Such is a fruit of bad philosophy and the lack of a prelude to rational thought.

Well-meaning Christians often naively respond to the challenge of the well-reasoned by saying: "The solution is to purify our faith – or doctrine." (Personally, I think that has been done very well already, but perhaps too ivory-towerishly.)

Science needs purification from intellectual adventure. *Christianity conflicts with grandiose extrapolation, not with objective truth.* Christianity conflicts with some theoretical facts, mathematical facts or paradigmatic facts, not with direct or experimental facts! Systematic errors of ancient origin run through all-seeing science, falsely so-called, which men of good will are asked to respect.

Christians oblivious to these errors blame science for causing Christianity's present tribulations – as particularly evidenced in the treatment of origins or interpersonal relations. Resist the temptation to say, "Let us reform social science," or "Let us reform geology." In reality, such tribulations flow from the avoidance and/or denial of the ancient errors embedded in grandiose science. Not surprisingly, many Christians shy away from science and discuss faith without examining any connection to science. Christians must discard the simple opposition between faith and reason and then reappraise their apologetics.[49]

Pragmatically, if we do not challenge bad philosophy ... but only want to show Jesus' love – we will not be "all things to all people" as St. Paul admonished. If Christians do not resist bad philosophy, the appeal of new versions of bad philosophy – Oriental and New Age "science" or modern sophistry – increases!

Christians many times must present a prelude to the gospel. It bears repetition: people speaking the same language may not understand each other. (Reconsider St. Paul in Athens.) This communication barrier includes communicating with people nurtured by scientific rationalism! They may recognize our words, but their unperforated worldview negates any useful meanings for our words.

Significantly, it was reported some years ago that forty percent of the American public cannot be reached by the Gospel because of a "mindset of

---

49   Christian parents regularly bemoan what happens to most of their children when in college. Far too many enter as Christians and exit as cynics, agnostics or atheists. What specifically happens in college to cause this result? Case studies should be numerous, but the response is muted. This illustrates the skittishness of so many Christians to well-reasoned dangers.

scientific rationalism"[50] – which reflects a loss of the Biblical knowledge of their forefathers. In other countries, and among society's "movers and shakers," the percentage probably is higher. The "philosophy of the epoch" is a major communication barrier, for much one-on-one evangelism confronts scientific rationalism. Granted, we may break through to such people by solely concentrating on the Gospel, but the example of the missionary efforts of St. Paul and later folks shows that preludes render vital assistance.

Thus, we begin to examine a dreary and yet surprisingly ill-explored subject: *what is science – and science, falsely so-called?* Most histories of science (reverently) trace how the past leads up to today's marvelous "scientific" truths. Rather, practice atheorism: Discern which ancient or modern "scientific" truths unwisely transcend direct facts. Do not let such "truths" rest unchallenged, for they will rise to thwart you when later addressing seemingly unrelated modern concerns. To repeat, *start at the beginning bookend.* Does mathematics prove that we live in an unperforated, infinite material cosmos. Properly introduced to atheorism, readers are more resistant to being tossed too and fro by the winds of human wisdom.

Accordingly, the next several chapters about the musty dusty history of science are an antidote to most descriptions or definitions of science, which make vague references to "ancient principles" we *must* accept. If such vagueness is not recognized, *a misguided love of truth* urges people to mold their lives to "principles" and follow them to their ultimate, and surprisingly bitter, consequences.[51]

God speaks to the three, four, or five understandings of paganism, rationalism, Christianity, pantheism and sophistry. He knows the cosmos is not an unperforated, infinite, material cosmos ... or a living or divine ... cosmos. Jesus Christ can thus correct bad philosophy. His love is grounded in His care and concern for the Father and His creation. Jesus' love speaks first to the mind and then creates, sometimes unlocks, the loving heart.

Unsaved thinkers must be encouraged to ponder well-crafted word systems that exclude God and His perforated cosmos. Likewise, disillusioned people need to see how their distaste for historic Christianity, the irrelevance of modernized Christianity (its fascination with spiritual niches), and the vagueness and flakiness in the storytelling within science, falsely so-called, are interrelated.

Despite the prevalent intellectual atmosphere of relative and systematic words, he who has the banner of objective truth best speaks to men of goodwill.

We have reviewed many topics in this chapter. They form a complex backdrop to history. As we move forward, we begin to see their relevance amongst events that occurred at the beginning book-end and in the between-years. Thus we can better appreciate the confusion in the "other" book-end: the modern world.

Now we are ready to begin the prelude, our journey on that obvious, yet hidden, path wending back through history.

---

50   Mentioned in *Reasons to Believe* of the Dr. Hugh Ross organization.
51   This last phrase comes from Ayn Rand.

I say this, Socrates, because, as I think you yourself are aware, we Pythagoreans have a theory of the soul… (Simmias in *Phaedo*.)
Plato

Greece, a cradle of the arts and mistakes.
Voltaire

As the history of mathematics teaches us, rationalism and mysticism are very close to each other.
Dijksterhuis

Scientific rationalism did serve man well as long as it was moving towards its false ideals from a great distance. But this could not last. Eventually the truthbearing power of its absurd ideals are bound to be spent and its stark absurdity to assert itself.
Michael Polanyi

Proclus' reference to the "geometrical number" of [Plato's] Republic 545e ff is a good index of the way passages of Plato which are now treated as mumbo jumbo or heavy-handed humor were taken to be deep "symbolic enigmas" by the Neoplatonists.
Glenn Morrow (on Proclus)

Whenever the mind perceives a mathematical idea, it makes contact with Plato's world of mathematical concepts …. Mathematical ideas have an existence of their own, and inhabit an ideal Platonic world, which is accessible via the intellect only …. [E]ach [mathematician] is directly in contact with the same externally existing Platonic world!
Roger Penrose

Being quotedly forewarned, we proceed. Roger Penrose's quote is to tempt those who find musty dusty history irrelevant. In *The Emperor's New Mind,* he finds Plato's ideas necessary, not irrelevant. Some thinkers require Plato's private knowledge of mathematics to comprehend the cosmos.

Writers building up to modern science present a history devoid of the ancient thinkers' mystical outlook. They discuss the Greek individuals who made physical discoveries, but the mathematics of Pythagoras and Plato are only hygienically mentioned, even though they are the backbone of science. Such writers find Greek mathematics embarrassing or outdated. Other writers are not so timid. This forewarns us that there are many experts on Greek thought. It is best to read a sampling from many disciplines: philosophy, mathematics, history, politics, mysticism, *etc.* (And some disciplines are divided by internal quarrels.)

Many writers are quick to label as mythological (mumbo jumbo) anything that contradicts their *present* scholarly consensus. But that avoids asking if the ancient authors or their students considered specific doctrines to be fact or mythological.

We thus begin our journey on the hidden, yet obvious, path that wends backward in time to when mathematics and astronomy were young.

Once upon a time, a long time ago, (*c.a.* 600 to 300 B.C.), well-reasoned
Greeks reasoned themselves into a dilemma and it gradually became everyone's
dilemma. The unperforated cosmos began to rule their minds, forcing acceptance of
Godlessness, materialism, and meaninglessness. They assumed these extrapolations – from a few principles – were unbiased.

This "truth" never set well with man's spirit, so the dilemma in mankind's spirits,
souls and minds continues. Most thinkers imply conflict between "reason and faith"
has been resolved – at the expense of faith. They believe reason is already purified.
Nonetheless, science must be examined carefully due to an admixture of vagueness.

The mists of history hide when or why earlier peoples abandoned the monotheism of the "sons of Noah" in favor of polytheism. When St. Paul later visited
Athens and preached on Mars Hill, he commented upon their many gods. They
even left room for an unknown god, (Acts 17:16-34). Intellectual security was absent.

As said in the previous chapter, pagan Greeks thinkers observed and made
lists. Therein they recorded unusual weather, historical snippets and traveler's reports, but with "fanciful" reports intermingled. Sifting of reports for credibility seemed
absent. They gathered direct facts, a necessary prelude to understanding reality,
but failed to find a common thread connecting the phenomena in their lists.

They probably would have agreed with Christians that only God can answer
man's ultimate questions about himself and the cosmos: Who am I? Where am I?
Why am I here? What happens hereafter? What is the cosmos? However, consort-
ing with many gods made it hard to hear one god make sense of their lists or hearts.

The gods of Greek paganism were not interested in man's welfare. The myths
record adultery and betrayal be-
tween these deities and
mankind. Tragedy is a
Greek concept; it
represents man's
betrayal by one of
the gods, some-
times only for
the god's
amusement.[1]
Greek
philosophers
said the
number of
pagan gods,
their rank,
and concepts

1   Aristotle would later say that tragedy was not due to the gods, but due to man's pride and
violence.

of the cosmos were hostage to whichever poet was speaking.[2] The irrationality of polytheism stymied efforts to find order, meaning or Universal Connected Knowledge. An interpretive babble existed, making the thinkers' self-entrancement palatable to themselves.

Unlike Biblical revelation, pagan "knowledge" of the gods caused spiritual discomfort and insecurity. As G. K. Chesterton commented:

> There comes a time in the routine of an ordered civilization when the man is tired [of] playing at mythology and pretending that a tree is a maiden or that the moon made love to a man. The effect of this staleness is the same everywhere; it is seen in all drug-taking and dramdrinking and every form of the tendency to increase the dose. Men seek stranger sins or more startling obscenities as stimulants to their jaded sense.... They try to stab their nerves to life... (B9, pages 164, 166.)

The polytheistic interpretive babble was socially acceptable. Not surprisingly, early Greek thinkers reacted to this demoralizing babble, boredom and pretending. One new group of thinkers called the Sophists[3] criticized this babble because they saw no truth in these fables – or in early attempts at mathematics or science. They found no truth anywhere except, perhaps, in pragmatism. One of their members, Protagoras, famously said, "Man is the measure of all things."

Another emerging group of well-reasoned folk stood out by their disgust for polyanswers, but they also rejected the wordy unbelief of the Sophists. Socrates is recorded by Plato to have said: "I asked for one [answer] and I got many." Unlike Sophists, these "scientists of their day" found certainty in reason and mathematics.

Thus began an uncoordinated search for an alternative understanding of reality using a new idea permitted by the emerging mathematics and determinism: no theism – atheism. As "proto-atheists," the transition was gradual and carefully advocated, they being a tiny minority in a polytheistic culture. Socrates (c.a. 470-399 B.C.) had to drink poison because anything less than Pagan polytheism was deemed to be atheism.[4]

Doubt of polytheism, however, still leaves a choice between atheism and monotheism. Not knowing the Lord, they did not recognize this. Additionally, their simplistic epistemology, commingling understanding and knowledge, allowed an easy entrancement by their own new "scientific" ideas.

With no knowledge of Scripture, these thinkers tried to understand matter and man *without* pagan gods – or God. They sought Universal Connectedness, the

---

2   Plato wanted to banish poets from his ideal city for this and other reasons.
3   Sophists were itinerant Greek teachers who taught for a fee. (Presumably, they became disenchanted with truth and turned to cynicism and self-interest.) For several decades prior to Plato's appearance, their teachings were very disconcerting in Greek society. Their subject was primarily oration, rhetoric – how to win arguments and sway juries. Plato despised and critiqued them for not accepting any truth, thus for not being "lovers of truth."
4   Socrates is portrayed by Plato as an impartial searcher for truth, but it may not be that simple. Socrates' arrest, conviction and death occurred shortly after Athens' defeat in the Peloponnesian Wars, and Socrates had expressed sympathy with the culture of the victorious Spartans. The charge of atheism may have included his lack of commitment to broader Athenian "values."

Also, Athens was then ruled by a "tyrant" and Socrates refused to help him unfairly arrest someone, according to Plato, suggesting that Socrates was judicially killed in revenge.

common thread connecting the many phenomena of reality. They wanted to advance beyond collating lists, mere saving the appearances or wordy unbelief. They
began as philosophers, initially explaining the building blocks of matter in such
terms as: "everything comes from water," "everything is earth, air, fire, or water," *etc.*

These are
known as the
pre-Socratic
philosophers,
prior to 450 B.C.
They were such
as Thales of
Miletus, who said
all things are made
of water – yet he
predicted an eclipse
of the sun. Anaxi-
mander criticized
Thales – Anaximan-
der preferred a
boundless source of everything. Anaximenes said all things are made of air.
Heraclitus said all things come from a strife – an opposition – between opposing
tendencies – all things being in flux. But he preferred fire as the basis. He also
admonished others to grasp the underlying principles of things – a hint of what
science strives for. Parmenides said, "What is, is." Empedocles said all things come
from "earth, air, fire and water."

Another group, the atomists, began with Anaxagoras, who said matter had
infinite divisibility. Leucippus said matter is made of innumerable constituent
particles. Democritus said reality consists of atoms in motion – through an infinite
void. This motion caused random contact, from which matter gradually built-up.
Later, Epicurus introduced a random swerve into the motion of the atoms.

These ideas were not flippant – but had little "staying power." After mastering
such theories, the question was: "What next?" And there was little that could be
offered. (Plato was to say that these folk could explain many things, but not where
earth, air, fire, and water, themselves, came from.) These early thinkers were not
above criticism; witness the critical and financial success of the Sophists.

Susceptibility to criticism meant these explanations could not replace gods.
Some realized the need for a rigorous and objective truth, *i.e.*, self-evident;
impervious to criticism; acceptable to men of good will; and yielding one precise
answer. They walked a precarious tightrope – to avoid both "religion" and the
"subjective." *There must be no more polytruths – of any kind.*

Surprisingly, several founders of Greek "science" were not atheists, most
notably Pythagoras and Plato, and perhaps Aristotle, nor were they pagan. Instead,
they revered philosopher's gods, the thirty Æons, (Eons), whom we meet in the next
chapter. The Æons, (plus assorted others), while incestuous, were unrelated to
pagan gods, such as Pluto or Zeus.

Next on stage were Greek thinkers famous for their interest in mathematics, but they did not invent mathematics. Instead, they acquired it from Egyptians, Assyrians, Chaldeans (Babylonians), and Persians, who already had extensive mathematical dexterity. In these nations, mathematics was for scribes, surveyors, astronomers and accountants. The Greeks brilliantly advanced mathematical capabilities; but in their flight from polytheism, they transformed mathematics into the sacred oracle of science, falsely so-called. (*And mathematics transformed thinkers in confident rationalists.*) Mathematics was hypnotic, providing *monotruth,* seemingly based on public knowledge. *Monotruth became the mark of science* and penetrated the many appearances disguising the phenomena of reality. It became their key to truth and made science impervious to criticism.

In contrast to the pre-Socratic philosophers, Pythagoras, Plato and Aristotle had answers to "What next?" The answer: "Study arithmetic … or geometry … or logic … or observe." While many of their concepts had defects, they kept lively minds going and much was discovered.

The word, "science," was not used then, instead scientists were *natural philosophers.* In contrast, philosophers got the most attention; they strove to be "all-seeing." Universal Connected Knowledge was their goal. Natural philosophy held little interest to philosophers. The exception being Pythagoras and Aristotle, who are well-known to have dabbled in experiments and observation.

Pythagoras, (*ca.* 582 - *ca.* 500 B.C.), was a pre-Socratic. He had the first notable success in explaining the building blocks of matter and thus unifying thought – and *the unifying "substance" was number,* and nature was a numerical reality. He remains important in that, while "all philosophy is a footnote to Plato," according to Alfred North Whitehead, some add that *Plato is a footnote to Pythagoras.*

To Pythagoras, mathematics meant number and arithmetic; even geometry was subordinate. Number provided Universal Connectedness; physically incarnate and thus superior to direct facts. His intellectual adventure had a twofold creed: *Matter is number and number is self-evident truth.* These possess necessity. *Number is rational thought!* Man is free only if he assents to this top-down truth!

Pythagoras' view of mathematics does not match ours. On one hand, he was seemingly concerned with the details of reality: finding number in things. On the other hand, he had his "eye on the sky," for out there, somewhere, was where the real "really" was. He could see it very

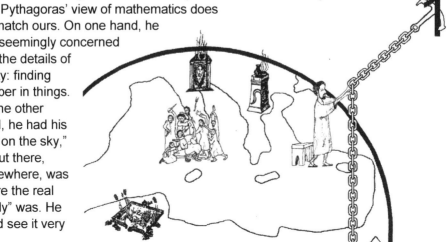

clearly with his mind's eye. This outlook is commonly called *idealism*, but *mathematic-ism* is more accurate, as his abstract ideal was a numerical object – in a remote location. [*Arithmetic and geometry helped liberate the soul from the domination of the senses.*]

Scholars cannot agree how Pythagoras came to these convictions. He reportedly spent 12 to 30-odd years studying "mysteries" and "science" in Phoenicia, Egypt, and Babylon. (Some say he met the Persian, Zoroaster, and his Maji.) The Orphic[5] cult was also influential.

In the introduction, we mentioned that some of Pythagoras' followers were called *mathematekoi* – those who studied all. *Mathematekoi* has also been translated as "inner light." This hints at the mind's eye and the transcendent mathematical world that was so prominent in Pythagorean thought. Other students of Pythagoras were called *akousmatikoi* – the word refers to magic and ritual.

Pythagoras was secretive. He wrote nothing, relying upon oral teaching for his initiates. His word was not for the common man. He admonished his followers[6] not to disseminate his truths to outsiders.

Pythagoras was pious, devoted to the (philosopher's) gods, and a vegetarian, except for beans. (Supposedly this prohibition was enacted because the resulting gaseous indigestion prevented dreamy contact with the gods.[7] He prohibited his followers from even going through a bean field to escape from enemies!) *He believed in reincarnation* – occurring at 216 year intervals, *i.e.*, 6^3, *e.g.*, 6 x 6 x 6 = 216. He freely referred to his past lives and attributed some of his truths to them!

Pythagoras believed in a finite cosmos, centered on the earth. The next chapter elaborates on the philosopher's gods entwined (at least, later) in his cosmos. The planets and stars were home to various gods – or were gods themselves. Man sojourned with them between reincarnations.[8] The peculiar properties of numbers he espoused were invested into the various planets and stars. Arithmetical "knowledge" was a crucial navigation aid on the death journeys "back" to the "higher" stars.

He was a proto-atheist, even though he did not believe in rationalism, in the strict sense. Physical number gave him a firm foundation for dispensing with pagan Greek religion, but he offered sacrifices to any and all, as needed. *To Pythagoras, physical number was the medium and content of divine revelation and the cosmos!*

As a proto-atheist, Pythagoras prayed as follows to the number 4 (and its triangular culmination in 10, called *tetraktys)*:

Bless us, divine number, thou who generatest gods and men! Oh holy, holy tetraktys, thou that containest the root and the source of the eternally flowing

---

5   Orphic cult: A Greek religion that, among other things, emphasized reincarnation and that the soul is imprisoned in the body. Escaping this imprisonment and safely returning to the cosmic home required mystical knowledge. Pythagoras substituted (added?) "mathematical knowledge." The Orphic cult was immersed in magic – understood as the supposed ability to master nature, the weather, or even converse with the dead. There is evidence Pythagoras was a magician, who tried to put magic upon a numerical basis.

6   Pythagoras – after his travels – lived in something like a monastery or commune. His followers faced prescribed rituals and years of training.

7   See *Ancient Philosophy Mystery and Magic*, by Peter Kingsley.

8   Reincarnation makes no sense without an appropriate astronomy providing heavenly "homes" (and hosts) between "trips."

creation! For the divine number begins with the profound pure unity [ONE] until it comes to the holy four; then it begets the mother of all, the all-bounding, the firstborn, the never-swerving, the never-tiring holy ten, the keyholder of all. (B10, page 73.)

Pythagoras was a number theologian! This seems strange to believe, but various sources attest to his numerology: equating number, things, and the divine.

This early Pythagorean doctrine is puzzling because to us numbers are abstract ideas, and things are physical objects or substance. But *we have made an abstraction of number which the early Pythagoreans did not make. To them, numbers were points or particles.* (B11, page 12. Emphasis added.)

Tetraktys

Pythagoras' philosophy was not built upon the abstraction we call mathematics, but upon a "physics" of the numerical particles (units) of matter. In this he had a systematic foundation – except no one could see these units of matter as numbers. His challenge was to show his initiates how to use their mind's eye to "objectively" see these numbers in matter and the "godly" origin of number.

Each of these physical numbers (units of matter) could not be broken or modified in their individual wholeness. (They were 1, not 1.001 or 0.999.) They were like indivisible marbles whose unchanging wholeness meant one number was as good as any other – an early cosmological principle. With number having such precise and simple wholeness and "physicality," (the universal yardstick), grandiose extrapolation merely "assented" to rational mathematical truth, like 1 + 1 = 2; certainly, it was not an act of faith.

Physical number was so strong a concept that a "proper" philosopher did not count as we do: one, two, three, ... No! No! He said: One apple, two apples, three apples. Numbers were not abstractions, they were not detachable from things.

Further, it seems that the numbers 1 through 10 were "special." Each had their own unique existence – 2 was not 1 + 1, but 2, and 5 was not 4 + 1 or 2 + 3, but 5. Numbers above 10 were subject to addition, subtraction, *etc.* This "special" nature of 1 through 10 carried over into Plato's outlook.

Pythagoras was very observant and resourceful. He developed the octave scale in music and discovered the numerical relationship between sound tone and string length, or sound tone and air chamber size. Such discoveries showed him that numerical properties existed in nature. Other examples were the music[9] of planets and the rise and fall of fevers. Even justice was mathematical:

The Pythagorean definition of justice, which is: "The power of repayment of what is equal and appropriate, being encompassed by the mean of a square odd number." (B12, page 70.)

Pythagoreans endowed each of the 10 numbers in the tetraktys with special properties. (The aforementioned earth, air, fire, and water were related to the

---

9   Much later, the astronomer and mathematician, Johannes Kepler (A.D. 1571-1630) tried to write the score for this heavenly music!

numbers one, two, three, and four.) They also dedicated various geometric angles to assorted gods.

In viewing number as physical, Pythagoras' intellectual adventure was firmly anchored in the philosopher's gods and their numbers. Number, as the basic unit of matter, was the key to rational thought. It fulfilled the lure of objective truth. In his mind's eye, number was "assent" to truth, not belief in a philosophy of the epoch.

In the last chapter, we mentioned that Greek thinkers had some strange ideas. Here we meet one, yet so far outside our realm of experience that it is hard to see.

Pythagoras said number started with "1" and arithmetic started with "2." His arithmetic excluded "1" because of its status as the source of unity and because it takes more than one to count. His followers, and later those of Plato, considered the problem of "the *one* and the *many*" to be the central problem of thought.

A hierarchy of numbers existed; physical number was not alone. Broad hints were given regarding an ascent to divine number, even though details of the early Pythagoreans are sparse. Iamblichus (*ca.* A.D. 250-325), a reviver of Pythagorean-ism, said the following:

> But if you knew of the variety of number, you would have asked me about intel-ligible, essential, and ideal number .... Physical numbers ... [are] manifest in the rotations and the revolutions of the heavens .... Indeed, the measures of number determine health .... In physical number the unlimited[10] is the cause as regards plurality, the limited[11] the first cause as regards the one .... Neither in nature nor in physical number is there void .... And as there is a physical, so there is an ethical arithmetic .... Soul's powers are related to number forms ... mean and perfect[12] numbers fit natural virtue, superabundant[13] and deficient[14] [numbers] [fit] excesses and deficiencies in relation to virtue .... And courage as manliness relates to odd[15] numbers, but as constancy it relates to square[16] [number]. What is female such as cowardice is to be fitted to even[17] [number], inconstancy to oblong[18] [number]. Fitting temperance, cause of symmetry, is 9 which is multiplied from the triad[19] ....

10   Unlimited: A divisible number, hence weak. Numbers such as 4, 6, 8, 9 ... were divisible.
11   Limited: An indivisible number, such as 1, 2, 3, 5, 7 ... They were "manly," unchanging. Indivisibility implied order and stability.
12   Perfect Number: Numbers which are the sum of their divisors (factors). For example, 6 and 28. 6 = 1 + 2 + 3 and 28 = 1 + 2 + 4 + 7 + 14.
13   Superabundant Number: Numbers of which the sum of their divisors (factors) are greater than themselves. For example, 12 < 1 + 2 + 3 + 4 + 6.
14   Deficient Number: Numbers of which the sum of their divisors (factors) are less than themselves. For example, 10 > 1 + 2 + 5.
15   Odd number: 1, 3, 5, 7, *etc*. Many odd numbers are indivisible. Indivisibility symbolized strength. One (monod) being the supreme strength!
16   Square number: The beauty the Pythagoreans saw in square numbers is illustrated on the next page. A diagonal drawn through successive levels always intersected whole numbers, so 1, 4, 9, *etc.,* were held in high esteem.
17   Even number: 2, 4, 6, 8, *etc*. Even numbers are divisible, thus not stable and were identified with cowardice. (2 was an exception as it could only be divided by itself.)
18   Oblong number: A variant of the square number, but whose results were held in distaste. The diagonal, in this case, did not always pass through whole numbers. It might even be irrational. So 6, 12, 20, *etc.* were held in low esteem. (2, again, being an exception.) (See drawing on the next page.)
19   Triad: Three, the breadth of a geometric number. (Length, width, and height produce area.)

Thus of divine number there is a uniform divine principle, prior as cause to the causes in all numbers .... The first then, the one properly speaking, God as *we* would say, is henad[20] and triad ... and the intelligible and the brightest monad[21] ascends to the highest cause ... (B13, pages 219-228. Emphasis in original. Footnotes added)

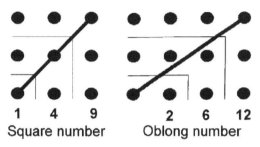

1   4   9   2   6   12
Square number   Oblong number

Numerous books describe the characteristics of Pythagorean number. Whether they make sense is for the reader to conclude. How did this top-down outlook bias their science, falsely so-called?

The crucial consequence of the Pythagorean creed was that mathematical number ruled matter. *Physics is incarnate number. With matter simply mathematical number, then mathematical impossibilities limit physical possibilities.* This top-down Mathematic's Word imposed itself upon nature and created Universal Natural Laws as

an immediate "fruit" of his creed. Number promised the ability to be "all-seeing."
We now understand rational thought better:

Reason 101: 1:
The fear of mathematics is the beginning of knowledge.
Our "all-seeing" mind's eye thus soars as on the wings of eagles.

We now can understand Greek thinkers if they said: "Rational thought has a visible truth – a physical mathematics. We know that 1 + 1 = 2! Because of arithmetic's infallible characteristics, our earthbound observations of matter can be extrapolated to reveal the structure of all nature." (This was not so much Universal Connectedness as "universal is-number-ness.")

(This would again be a good place for the "critical" rationalist to display his radical doubt of this mathematical "truth." But they are silent. The beliefs and consequences of Pythagorean thought are not superior to: "*In the beginning God created the heaven and the earth.*")

"The Pythagoreans are not talked about in philosophy courses.... Plato himself [found] in Pythagoreanism the chief source of his inspiration.... Bertrand Russell [1945] said, 'Pythagoras was intellectually one of the most important men that ever lived .... The influence of mathematics on philosophy, partly owing to him, has, ever since his times, been both profound *and unfortunate.*'" (B14, page 95.

---

20   Henad: Ten, the sum of the tetraktys.
21   Monad: Another word for One. Especially significant because it meant wholeness, indivisibility. It was the source of all being.

Emphasis added.)

Pythagorean physical number had many ramifications. For starters, it extended to the absence of number ... zero! We note the reference to 1 + 1 = 2. What does Pythagoras say about 1 − 1 = 0? To him, this was an absurd question – emptiness or void did not exist[22]! Pythagoras' "scientific" understanding lasted up to the not-too-distant past. Even space was not empty; it contained the fifth element, aether, with properties appropriate for the number 5^{23}. The dictum, "Nature abhors a vacuum," reflected this *banishment of zero,* because number started with 1 and arithmetic started with 2.

As shown in the long quotation from Iamblichus; zero, the void, was banished! In short, the mind's eye of Greek thinkers would not permit, and so their physical eyes could not see, any physical example of zero once they "knew" it was mathe-matically impossible[24]. Accordingly, the Greek number system did not include zero, and algebraic equations were "written" in the form, $x^2 + ax = b.^{25}$ (About A.D. 1630, Harriot introduced the modern form, $x^2 + ax - b = 0$.)

Since zero was taboo, what about negative numbers like, 1 - 2 = -1? Another absurd question! *Negative numbers – negative matter – did not exist!* While this may seem like an ancient, naive belief, fragments of this belief are evident through the nineteenth century A. D.

[Negative numbers] became known in Europe through Arab texts, but most mathematicians of the 16th and 17th centuries did not accept them as numbers or, if they did, would not accept them as roots of equations .... Vieta [1540-1603] dis-carded negative numbers entirely. Descartes [1596-1650] accepted them to an extent. He called negative roots of equations false on the ground that they claim to represent numbers less than nothing .... Pascal [1623-1662] regarded the subtrac-tion of 4 from 0 as pure nonsense. He said in his *Pensees,* "I have known those who could not understand that to take four from zero there remains zero" [*e.g.,* 0 - 4 = 0!] .... Lazare Carnot [1753-1823], a well-known French geometer ... asserted flatly that the notion of something less than nothing was absurd. (B11, pages 114-115, 154.)

As further evidence of this long-lasting belief, August DeMorgan, an eminent mathematician, wrote in *1831:*

Above all, [the student] must reject the definition still sometimes given of the

---

22   In A.D. 1657, the German, Otto von Guericke, demonstrated the existence of a vacuum. He made two half-moon-shaped spheres, whose mating surfaces were sealed and a vacuum pump created a vacuum within. Two teams of horses could not pull the two halves apart.
23   For some, aether was the element of the stars and planets. This "unearthly" element gave a "physical" reason for their freedom from change, decay, or falling to the (central) earth.
24   Today, the phrase, "the mind's eye," is little used. We would more likely say *theory* or *law.* Entrancement by the mind's eye or theory or law can hide in plain view the subjective.
25   The Greek language then did not have symbols for numbers. Instead, certain letters in the Greek alphabet were "marked" and thus utilized for computations. That is why, in Revela-tion 13:18, the Greek name of the man is his number 666. Greek mathematical texts looked like prose, not equations.
       The Roman number system was different, but very cumbersome. You may have seen the Roman numerals: I, II, III, IV, V .... Beyond elementary computations, they are unwieldy and did not extend back to zero.

quantity -a, that it is less than nothing. It is astonishing that the human intellect should ever have tolerated such an absurdity as the idea of a quantity less than nothing. (B15, page 72.)

Notice that DeMorgan refers to the "quantity -a," not to the "number -a." Mathematics was not an abstraction to be manipulated as one pleases, as is present usage. As a "physical" emphasis, the philosopher John Stuart Mill (1806-1873) said:

All numbers must be numbers of something. There are no such things as numbers in the abstract. (B16, page 34.)

How would John Stuart Mill have explained why one quart of water added to one quart of alcohol makes only about 1.8 quarts of vodka! Kline further points out that not only do some things not add up when brought together – they explode! And chess moves cannot be modeled with mathematics; they require logic. Physics as incarnate mathematics had some difficulties!

Joseph Ray, in 1866, published his *Primary Elements of Algebra.* In it, he does use zero and one, but not negative numbers:

If a monomial is *negative*, the extraction of the square root is impossible, since the square of any quantity, either positive or negative, is necessarily positive. Thus, $\sqrt{-9}$, $\sqrt{-4a^2}$, $\sqrt{-b}$, are algebraic symbols, which indicate impossible operations. Such expressions are termed *imaginary quantities*. When they result from an equation or a problem, they indicate some absurdity or impossibility. (B17, pages 172-173. Emphasis in original.)

The tradition of avoiding zero is evident in a mathematics exercise book, *Oral Arithmetic,* published in 1910 by Wentworth and Smith.[26] It is 215 pages of exercises in addition, subtraction, multiplication, division and some advanced applications. However, nowhere in the book does zero, one or negative numbers appear, in the numerous equations or answers. A page from the book is shown on the next page:

---

26   David Eugene Smith, known for his many contributions to mathematics.

SUBTRACTION 113

8. Subtraction of Integers

Subtract the following :

1. 39	4. 42	7. 55	10. 65	13. 205
16	25	28	28	90
2. 36	5. 44	8. 57	11. 125	14. 204
16	28	39	18	94
3. 32	6. 54	9. 63	12. 125	15. 207
16	37	26	28	98

16. If a room 32 ft. long has a rug 18 ft. long on the floor, how much of the length is not covered ?

17. If a man having $225 in the bank deposits $65 to-day and draws out $75 to-morrow, how much will be left ?

9. Subtraction of Decimals

Subtract the following :

1. 2.7	4. 5.4	7. .47	10. .70	13. 30.2
.9	3.5	.28	.29	2.6
2. 3.2	5. 7.5	8. .52	11. 2.04	14. .463
1.6	4.9	.37	.65	.058
3. 4.3	6. .32	9. .66	12. .208	15. .090
2.8	.09	.48	.072	.018

16. If I have $3.06 and spend 88¢, how much is left ?

17. If the distance between two stations is 23.14 mi., and a train has gone 6.2 mi. from one station towards the other, what is the remaining distance ?

Oral Arithmetic

1910 (B18)

Wentworth and Smith

Compared to what we have reviewed about addition and subtraction, the ancients regarded multiplication and division to be truly "higher" mathematics.

The perplexity regarding the operations continued until recent times:

> Multiplication was at first rightly viewed as *repeated addition* of concrete units .... There is a dialogue between master and scholar in the sixteenth-century arithmetic of Robert Recorde, [1510-1558] in which the pupil struggles with the difficulty that in some cases multiplication should make a thing less. [*E.g.,* while 3 x 3 = 9, so also 3 + 3 + 3 = 9; yet while 1/3 x 1/3 = 1/9, nonetheless 1/3 + 1/3 + 1/3 = 1.] The master finally explains [multiplication with fractions]. To which the scholar replies with great courtesy, "Sir, I do thank you much for this reason; and I trust that I perceive the thing." But his politeness is more conspicuous than his understanding ... (B19, pages 168-169. Emphasis in original.)

The absence of zero and negative numbers, even the number 1, also applied to multiplication tables. Consider the following:

"1910 style"	"Modern" Multiplication
	0 x 4 = 0
	1 x 4 = 4
2 x 4 = 8	2 x 4 = 8
3 x 4 = 12	3 x 4 = 12
4 x 4 = 16	4 x 4 = 16

This material brings up the question of fractions. So, what about 1 + ½ = 1½? Again, another absurd question! *Matter is number, there is no fractional (fractured) matter.* The profound pure unit or monad (one) was the foundation of "science," so discussion of fractions long met with "cultic" disapproval:

> Official Greek mathematics before Archimedes [287-212 B.C.] does not have any fractions at all. *This was not because they were not known, but rather because one did not wish to know them.*[27] For, according to Plato, the unit was indivisible and, in Plato's own words, "the experts in this study" were absolutely opposed to dividing the unit .... Instead of operating with fractions, they operated with ratios of integers .... [*Republic* 525e.] The reason why fractions were eliminated from the theory is the *theoretical indivisibility of unity.* (B20, pages 49, 115. Second emphasis in original.)

Many fractions had another bad feature; consider the fraction, $\frac{1}{3} = 0.333...$

The "..." indicates an endless number. (Centuries later, equations were found to describe this as an indefinitely extended decimal expansion.) To the Pythagoreans, that was irrelevant because matter is (indivisible) number and "..." is not a part of number or matter.

---

27   Fractions were freely used by their Babylonian fore-bearers – and even by Greek mathematicians not associated with philosophical schools and probably used by merchants.

If you don't do the division, what remains is a ratio. But how does the ratio $\frac{1}{3}$ differ from the fraction $\frac{1}{3}$? There were marketplace uses for fractions, but it seems "mathematician's" honor kept fractions out of pure arithmetic! Plato emphasized this:

Must not it be said that the arithmetic of the crowd is one thing, and that of lovers of wisdom another? (B21, page 22. *Philebus* 56d.)

Should someone attempt to partition such a unit, so Plato himself says (*Republic* 525 E), *all the expert mathematicians* "would laugh at him and would not allow it, but whenever you were turning it into small change, they would multiply it, taking care lest the one should ever appear not as one, but as many parts." (B21, page 39. Emphasis added.)

Aristotle summarized the Pythagorean mathematical belief as follows:

The Pythagoreans first applied themselves to mathematics, a science which they improved; and, penetrated with it, *they fancied that the principles of mathematics were the principles of all things.* (B22, pages 10-11. Emphasis added.)

Aristotle further reported in his *Metaphysics*:

For example, as the number 10 seems for them the most perfect thing and appears furthermore to embrace the whole realm of numbers, as a result there must also be 10 bodies circling in the sky as stars [planets]. But as there are only 9 visible ones, they invented a special tenth body, an invisible counterearth.[28] (B23, page 15.)

What was the thrust of Pythagorean rational thought? First, mathematics was not primarily concerned with the units of matter, but with mathematics' control of the cosmos and ability to purify the soul for the "higher" wisdom appropriate for "lovers of truth!" The logic of reincarnation required mathematical skill as a valuable navigational aid during the hazardous birth and death journeys through the planetary orbits. (Purification freed "lovers of truth" from the imprisonment or influence of the body and its passions, which hindered one's concentration on their reincarnation needs.) Pythagoreans considered themselves philosophers, divine-like souls, not cut off from theological truth. They were called "descended souls" or "Daimonions."[29] These "truth-bearers" had no need for democracy.

---

28   Peter Kingsley, in *Ancient Philosophy Mystery and Magic,* says the Pythagoreans had a "central fire" within an underworld in the earth (to be the 10th unit). Plato and Aristotle supposedly substituted for this the "invisible counter-earth."
    The "invisible counter-earth" is attributed to Philolaus, a second generation Pythagorean. He is mentioned in a later chapter.
29   Proclus, (A.D. 410-485), the neoplatonic authoritative commentator on Euclid's *Elements*, discussed *daimonions* in his *Commentary on the Timaeus* (of Plato):

[Proclus] discusses at various points the different degrees in the descent of the soul in the world. At the top Proclus places the souls of the gods that do not descend into the world .... These divine souls are "accompanied" without interruption by lower souls who never descend. Below these come souls who do descend .... [This] represents a formalization of the divine company of the gods and their followers, fallen and unfallen, of [Plato's] *Phaedrus* .... [Heracles] is one of a class of 'heroic souls'... Such heroic souls descend so as to benefit mankind.... (B13, page 150.)

Demons were not mumbo jumbo, but integral to the Pythagorean (and later Platonic) ideas on the cosmos. Demons were both the gods of the various planets – and the planets

The second thrust of Pythagorean number was that physical number could construct the cosmos. I have read a book entitled, *A Beginner's Guide to Constructing the Universe*, (B1). That is not mere poetry to a Pythagorean.

In spite of these utopian visions, the enduring Pythagorean Theorem of geometry is attributed to the Pythagoreans, but it wrecked their intellectual adventure. The Pythagorean theorem: $AC^2 = AB^2 + BC^2$. Its origin can be traced to ancient Babylon.

Therein they encountered *irrational[30] numbers* while trying to calculate certain square roots of triangular relationships. *(Fractions had been bad, irrationals were worse.)* The first irrational encountered was $\sqrt{2}$ = 1.414213 ... The (...) answer yields fractured matter – not calculable or reducible to a simple ratio.

Another major irrational is π *(pi)*. Instead of saying that π was approximately 3.14159 ..., they said that π was bounded by the ratio of the integers 223/71 and 22/7. While these ratios "looked" like fractions, they were never converted to decimal form [3.140845 and 3.142856] or reduced to 3 10/71 and 3 1/7.

Technically, irrational numbers are not numbers. Lacking physical existence, they were abhorred – they broke the (assumed) continuum of (whole) numbers. Like fractions, irrationals could not be real and exist between adjacent whole numbers. Irrationals would outnumber fractions – and scandalize mathematical law. It would be over 2,000 years before "creative" solutions to this dilemma were developed. Such pseudo-numbers (along with zero, fractions or negative numbers) were not of the same caliber as the profound, pure, indivisible unity. They were *unlawful!*[31]

---

themselves. Between reincarnations, souls navigated past unfriendly demons ... and dwelled with friendly demons between "trips."

The Greek word in the New Testament translated as devil or demon is generally the same Greek word, *daimonion*. Most usage of the word relates to our common understanding of demon. A passage such as 1 Timothy 4:1 may relate to the dangers of Greek thought: *"Now the Spirit speaketh expressly, that in the latter times some shall depart from the faith, giving heed to seducing spirits and doctrines of devils."*

Likewise in I John 4:1 we read: *"Beloved, believe not every spirit, but try the spirits whether they are of God; because many false prophets are gone out into the world."* Contact between Christianity and Greek philosophy was already happening. It is difficult to associate thought systems (doctrines) with demons. But descended masters, false prophets, starry-eyed philosophers ... these are another matter!

False Prophets may not mean individuals who left the Christian faith, but rather individuals who were captivated by Greek philosophy – or its later revisions!

30   Irrational number: A number that cannot be expressed as the ratio of two whole numbers. Its exact determination is impossible; it can only be approximated. There are websites where you can download the *first* million digits of "numbers" like $\sqrt{2}$ or π!

31   In the *Manual of Harmonics*, by Nicomachus the Pythagorean (A.D. 100), the translator and commentator, Flora Levin, says the Pythagoreans discovered the irrational due to a musical problem instead. The midpoint of a musical octave is an irrational number. (A logarithmic number, which was unknown then.) Nicomachus, as Levin points out, wrote obscurely as he evaded defining this midpoint. He finally confessed that note, interval, and system were musical terms, not mathematical terms, thereby confessing that all was not number.

Plato later [denounced] as a national crime the fact that young people were left ignorant of the distinction between rational and irrational quantities. (B24, page 94. A free translation and summary of *Laws* 820B – E)

Why did the Greeks not simply adopt Babylonian algebra as it was, why did they put it in geometric form? ... [I]t is the discovery of the irrational, which, as Pappus tells us, actually originated in the Pythagorean school .... Nowadays we say that the length of the diagonal is the "irrational number $\sqrt{2}$," and we feel superior to the poor Greeks who "did not know irrationals." *But the Greeks knew irrational ratios very well* .... That they did not consider $\sqrt{2}$ as a number was not a result of ignorance, but of strict adherence to the definition of number. *Arithmos* means quantity, therefore whole number .... In the domain of numbers, the equation $X^2 = 2$ can not be solved, not even in that of ratios of numbers. But it is solvable in the domain of segments [geometry]. (B20, page 125. Emphasis added.)

Matter, that solid weighty material of which stuff is made, could not derive from such numerical indefiniteness. Even worse, the elements of the Tetraktys became "un-divine" in such a fragmented number world. Reportedly, the Pythagoreans swore a special oath of secrecy never to reveal the existence of irrational numbers, but one of their members divulged the secret.

The paradoxes of motion propounded by Zeno of Elea, (*fl ca* 475 B.C.), also criticized Pythagorean physical number. Zeno's "paradox of infinity" showed Pythagorean number concepts to be full of irrationals. It rendered motion absurd – as a physical mathematical object! [32]

HALFWAY THERE!

WARNING: Runners can run a race in minutes while mathematicians take years proving it can't be done! (Mathematics is inadequate for some things.) Like a century or so ago, mathematicians covered blackboards with impressive formulas proving that rockets can't work in space or trains cannot go over 60 miles per hour! Granted, in the late 1800s several mathematicians refined the definition of numbers and related concepts. So today, Zeno's paradoxes of motion aren't so threatening.

Pythagoras did not let his senses deceive him; his mind's eye deceived him. We can sympathize with the commonsense criticism such thinkers received from their neighbors – first from their pagan and Sophist countrymen, then from some philosophers, then their barbarian neighbors, then their Jewish and later Christian neighbors.

Pythagoreans were not impervious to criticism. Their "knowledge" that number

---

32   Paradoxes of motion: Technically, motion is not paradoxical but some mathematical attempts to model motion lead to paradoxical mathematics. Zeno's examples of a runner traversing a track or the flight of an arrow were mathematically insoluble by a "physical" arithmetic.

Aristotle solved Zeno's paradox by postulating the difference between an actual infinite and a "merely" potential infinite.

*was the foundational building block of reality was downgraded to a science, falsely
so-called.* What survives is belief that reality can be mathematically analyzed – but
their "belief" in "an incarnated arithmetical cosmos" is no longer truth. Can another
branch of mathematics replace it?

Words – or equations – did not say it right. The pragmatism of the Pythagorean's pagan neighbors seemed justified by this debacle[33]. Why search for "hidden"
things with the unreliable mind's eye – abstractions they called "theory" or "mathematical truth?" Pythagoreans were well-reasoned storytellers – arithmetic was
neither matter nor rational thought. Fatefully, their abstract Universal Connected
Knowledge was a physical error! *Free and autonomous reason had failed*[34].

(Pythagoras was separated from Christianity by five centuries. Pythagoras said
"number is matter." Christianity said "System does not spring out of numbers, but
numbers from a system." [Irenaeus] And the "system" was the recent created fact. *If
units of matter came first,* mathematical relations automatically "pop-up" due to
matters placement and not due to a top-down causal "power" in mathematics. Others
said "matter is atoms," but it took "almost all of infinity" to get atoms organized. Yes,
1 + 1 = 2, but to who or what to attribute this to is not a matter of computation!)

The Pythagorean failure caused a scandal and crisis among Greek thinkers.
An intellectual void occurred and other "scientists" of the day searched for a new
anchor for truth. Parmenides is such a "scientist," a later Pythagorean remembered
by having one of Plato's dialogs named after him. Parmenides is known for denying
the reality of change; having said: "What is, is." As an old man, he visited Athens
and talked with the young Socrates, (later to be Plato's teacher), so the Platonic
setting for the dialog is plausible.[35]

Fragments exist of a philosophical poem Parmenides wrote, discussing the
"way of truth" and the "way of seeming." The philosopher's goddess of truth,
Alétheia, one of the 30 Æons, is the speaker in this poem. The poem attempts to
reestablish the validity of the continuum of whole numbers (*i.e.,* banishing fractions
and irrationals). Parmenides is criticizing the fragmentation of the "one," which
resulted from the discovery of irrational numbers. He also denies the existence of
"space" (the void).[36] To support these objectives, Alétheia uses words that hint at
the philosopher's reincarnational heaven. She admonishes on the need to use the
stars for guidance. A phrase captures the poem's outlook on where truth resides:

... far indeed from the beaten track of men. (B25, fragment 25.)

Alétheia goes on to criticize the "way of seeming," the way of opinion – or
sense impressions (relying on sight and touch). Its advocates were said to be prag-

---

33   Pythagoreanism survived for centuries as one of many philosophical schools. Early
Christian writers referred to it as still influential.
34   This again would be a fine place to hear the rationalist's radical doubt. Instead, there is
the usual radical silence. Over this silence, "*In the beginning God created the heavens and the
earth,*" can be heard.
35   Most authors think Plato distorted whatever were Parmenides' ideas.
36   As whole numbers followed each other in a "touching" continuum, so particles of matter
also could not be separated by a void.

matic, empirical and non-mathematical. Alétheia undermines this position by saying the earth is an illusion, so pragmatists are limited in what they can know. They cannot attain the highest all-seeing category of Universal Connected Knowledge. Consequently, a "true" philosopher knew that sense experience – empirical knowledge – had limited value. Only what is intelligible to the mind's eye is important – meaning the all-seeing truth discernible only with mathematics. Thus, they can "soar as on the wings of eagles" and inspect their valued ahistorical mathematical line.

Cosmic truth cannot be derived by studying the earth, but the observational exactitude of the soon-to-appear Aristotelian school contradicted the necessity of this other-worldly emphasis. (And the craft, engineering and technological wonders of the modern world contradict the notion that an earthly focus cannot yield great bodies of truth.) Those who believe in the mind's eye "know" it yields infallible cosmic truth. Such specs of dust frequently get in the mind's eye.

In all this maneuvering, one can sense that insecurity and fear of the fractured (divided) "one" were very strong. The mathematical term, *fraction*, is related to the word, *fracture*. The Latin word, *fractus*, means broken. As Proclus (A.D. 410-485) later points out:

> Every *divisible* thing is an obstacle to our returning upon ourselves, every *formed* thing disturbs our formless knowledge, and every *feeling* is an impediment to passionless activity.... [S]o long as we remain in bondage, with the eye of the mind closed, we shall never attain the perfection to which we are adapted. (B26, pages 37-38. Emphasis added.)

In their attempt to find and anchor Universal Connected Knowledge, they followed Pythagoras' example, looking for uniting abstractions and abandoning the mere observation of nature and compiling lists. The acidic philosopher of science, Feyerabend, commented upon the new methodology of the philosophers:

> The "rise of naturalism" in ancient Greece is a fascinating example of [the] attempt to transcend, devalue, and push aside complex forms of thought and experience .... [Philosophers discovered] that statements composed of *concepts lacking in details* could be used to build new kinds of stories, soon to be called proofs .... The discovery was interpreted as showing that knowledge could be detached from traditions and made "objective."
> The leading representative of this view was Parmenides. [He said that] "*far from the footsteps of humans*"[37] is [what is] "appropriate and necessary."
> ... [Thinkers,] like Parmenides, were not overly interested in crude empirical matters and objectivized their lack of interest by saying that *such things were not real.*[38] (B27, pages 65, 66, 70. Emphasis added. Footnotes added.)

Alétheia's disparaging attitude towards the earth was linked with a hoped-for certainty provided by their mind's eye belief in a cosmic mathematics that provided Universal Connected Knowledge, which mathematicians could directly access with their mind's eye. Things of the mind's eye weren't public knowledge, so philoso-

---

37   At some point, this was restated as "not being deceived by the senses," which has more staying power. In either case, top-down abstraction was given prominence over bottom-up observation. I suspect most people are cautious about these statements. Too often, we have been led astray by unverifiable claims. This wording varies slightly from that quoted earlier.
38   Again, we hear Alétheia speaking.

phers were vulnerable to the proto-empirical commonsenseness of pagan Greek thinkers and the acidic doubt of the Sophists. The fervor for – and against – abstractions such as "everything comes from water" or "everything is number" can now be appreciated. Were such cosmic statements merely well-reasoned story-telling or saving the appearances, or were they really the prized universal truth of puzzle solving? (In fact, a word they liked, *theory*, is a Greek word meaning sight-seeing.) Thinkers like Pythagoras and Parmenides thought the transcendent vision provided by arithmetic was all-seeing and would conquer the cosmos and so they devalued the earth. This fixation with the Æon's advice ran contrary to common-sense and generated reaction, even among reasoners.

Feyerabend did not accept the modern party-line that Greek science exem-plifies puzzle solving rather than storytelling. As Feyerabend further reports:

> The Sophists objected that truth that is not part of a tradition[39] is an impossibil-ity .... *[Aristotle] rejects the entire approach.* The task of thought, he seems to say, is to comprehend and perhaps to improve what we do when engaged in our every-day affairs; it is not to wander off into a no-man's land of abstract and empirically inaccessible concepts. (B27, page 71. Emphasis in original.)

A battleground in the word wars was looming regarding searching "far from the footsteps of humans." To get there, one had to avoid "being deceived by the senses" – this "soaring" advice was the lure of arithmetic! The passionless contemplation of Pythagorean number could not compete with sensation and feeling and "down-to-earth" events and concerns for all but the dedicated few philosophers. Plato, like Pythagoras, repeated the call for ~~arithmetic~~ mathematics to provide an abstract solidity and foundation that substituted for worldly sensations, feelings, concerns or experiment! As Plato later said in his *Timaeus*:

> That which is apprehended by intelligence and reason is always in the same state, but that which is conceived by opinion with the help of sensation and without reason is always in a process of becoming and perishing and never really is. (B28, page 1161, [*Timaeus* 27d – 28a].)

(Talk about using word meanings to sway people!) This cosmic predisposition for mathematical "jewels" downgraded experimentation (sensation) in the eyes of Greek thinkers. *But Plato promised a practical payoff:*

> *Should we not settle things by calculation, and so come to an agreement quickly.* (B28, page 175. Emphasis added.)

However, before the Æon's advice could be fulfilled, the scandal of irrational numbers had to be resolved. Plato accomplished this by synthesizing various dis-cordant themes he inherited. Yet, the intellectual milieu in ancient Greece was in turmoil:

> In philosophy [the fifth century B.C.] was the period of the enlightenment ... of rationalism. The ancient religion and ethics were ridiculed by the intellectuals. The sophists taught that all truth and all values are only relative. Materialistic systems, such as that of the atomist Democritus, were at a premium in wide circles .... In contrast to this view stood the [reclusive] religious-mystical metaphysics of the Pythagoreans .... It was not until the fourth century [B.C.], the century of Plato, that

---

39   In this context, tradition meant a cosmos-wide statement.

philosophy and mathematics reached their zenith.[40] (B20, page 106.)

Plato (427? - 347 B.C.) restored calm among thinkers by initially revising Pythagorean number concepts and, later, by championing the new geometric tools of Eudoxus [408-355 BC]. Plato was also a gifted communicator.

Plato was born into a noble family, with inherited wealth to support him. He seems to have initially intended to enter politics, like some of his relatives, but events soured him on the profession. He began his teaching / philosophical career at the age of forty.

Before his public career, he traveled to a Greek colony in Italy where the main Pythagorean thinkers were then located. By then, we can presume Plato was aware of the problem of irrational numbers.

This trip led Plato to an intellectual discovery, which he called his "second wind" or "second-best sailing" idea. All thinkers before him he considered to be "physicists," including Pythagoras. Their fault was that they were seeking to understand the cosmos by studying earthly things, with "sense" explanations. They were in disarray and Plato concluded that knowledge should be pursued with another methodology. This was his "second wind," which he discusses in his early dialogue, the *Phaedo*.

> Surely the soul can best reflect [on absolute truth] when it is free of all distractions *such as* hearing or sight or pain or pleasure of any kind – that is, when it ignores the body and becomes as far as possible independent, *avoiding all physical contacts* and associations as much as it can, *in its search for reality* .... Don't you think that the person who is likely to succeed in this attempt most perfectly is the one who approaches each object, as far as possible, with the *unaided intellect*, without taking account of any sense of sight in his thinking, or dragging any other sense into his reckoning – the man who pursues truth by applying his *pure and unadulterated thought* to the *pure and unadulterated object* .... So long as we keep to the body and our soul is *contaminated* with this imperfection, there is no chance of our ever attaining satisfactorily to our object, which *we assert to be truth*. (B28, *Phaedo* 65c – 66b. Emphasis added.)

Plato, like Pythagoras before him, thought reality was to be understood with pure thought – rational mathematical abstractions – from a "higher" reality. Incidentally, the "mind's eye" was a phrase coined by Plato. He did not mention that his "unaided" thought was already filled with Mathematic's Word and theory!

Also, at that time, the Greek language was not well-articulated. Plato thus spent a lot of time introducing distinctions amongst words. Some of his early dialogs have seemingly wearying discussions of concepts, but this was necessary to help people see distinctions otherwise overlooked. For example, "to be or not to be" was a fortress phrase. Plato showed that there were more choices than yes or no. There was also "to be – but different, but not nonexistent."

Language vagueness may have influenced Plato's teaching style. Plato favored oral instruction, not written instruction. The written word was only a "memory

---

40   The zenith of Greek culture was probably due to the statesman, Pericles, rather than to philosophers.

jogger" to those who had already been instructed. To prevent misunderstanding, Plato never wrote down the "important" things. Well, some may have been written down later in his career.

> ... Plato had firmly denied the appropriateness and utility of writing, *because they [philosophical subjects] require a series of discussions made with persistence and with strict communion between teacher and pupil.*...
>
> Wherefore, Socrates, if in our treatment of a great host of matters regarding the Gods and the generation of the universe we prove unable to give accounts that are always in all respects self-consistent and perfectly exact, be not thou surprised; rather we should be content if we can *furnish accounts that are inferior to none in likelihood,* remembering that both I who speak and you who judge are but human creatures, so that it becomes us to accept *likely accounts* of these matters and forbear to search beyond it.... (*Timaeus* 29c – d.)
>
> I was afraid that by observing objects with my eyes and trying to comprehend them with each of my other senses I might blind my soul altogether. *So I decided that I must have recourse to theories, and use them in trying to discover the truth of things* .... *I started off in this way, and in every case I first lay down the theory that I judge to be the soundest, and then whatever seems to agree with it – with regard to either causes or to anything else – I assume to be true, and whatever does not I assume not to be true.* (*Phaedo* 99d - 100a.) (B29, pages 12, 32, 40. Emphasis in original.)

Secluded teaching and belief in theory were part of Plato's top-down outlook; his "second-wind." (His dislike of "sense" experience was contrary to the soon to be articulated position of Aristotle in favor of bottom-up searching.) Plato elsewhere said:

> To maintain that reason orders it all does justice to the spectacle of the ordered universe, of the sun, the moon, the stars, and the revolutions of the whole heaven, and for myself I should never express nor conceive any contrary view on the matter. (B28, *Philebus* 28d.)

So Plato downgraded contemplation of physical facts. Pure thought was in the mind's eye – indeed, in the *infallible* mind's eye! Pure theoreticians were the only people objectively pursuing truth! Manual labor and physical investigation were to be discouraged for the philosophically minded. Plato emphasized his scorn:

> And plausibly, said [Plato], for other *manikins* ... so these gentlemen joyously bound away from the mechanical arts to philosophy, those that are most cunning in their little craft .... [A]nd this is the ambition and aspiration of that *multitude of pretenders unfit by nature*, whose souls are bowed and mutilated by their *vulgar occupation* even as their bodies are marred by their arts and crafts. (B28, *Republic* 494d – e. Emphasis added.)

To stay in Plato's good graces, don't get your hands dirty. Plato's pure thought required thinking in mathematical terms, but with a subtle difference from that of Pythagoras.

> Aristotle never tires of stressing that Plato, in opposition to the Pythagoreans, made [number] "separable" from objects of sense, so that they appeared "*alongside* perceptible things." (B21, page 70. Emphasis in original.)

In addition to the Pythagorean incarnated numbers, Plato added several layers. These intervening layers "sort-of" acted like transformers between systems!

Aristotle reports on these Platonic concepts:

> [T]here are three kinds of *arithmoi*: [41] (1) [on top] the *arithmos eidetikos* – idea-number, (2) [at the bottom] the *arithmos aisthetos* – sensible number, (3) and "between" these, the *arithmos mathematikos* ... which shares with the first its "purity" and "changelessness" and with the second its manyness and reproducibility. (B21, page 91.)

This changed outlook on number was not enough to overcome irrational numbers. For that, he was to champion the founding of mathematics upon the geometric tools of Eudoxus[42]. By comparing lengths instead of calculating distances, geometry avoided irrationals.

The intervening layers were complex – and Aristotle was to reject them. These additional layers allowed ideal number and (sensible or counting) incarnate number to be viewed as separate.[43] Arithmetic became a derivative of geometry and was no longer used on problems that produced irrationals.

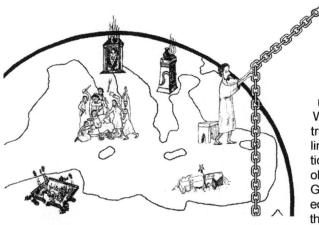

The resolution of the problem [of the irrational] ... was to think of all magnitudes geometrically .... When 1 and $\sqrt{2}$ are treated as lengths, that is, line segments, the distinction between 1 and $\sqrt{2}$ is obliterated .... The classical Greeks solved [quadratic] equations geometrically so that the roots appeared as line segments and again the need to use irrational numbers was avoided .... Only geometry could handle incommensurable ratios. (B11, page 105.)

Arithmetic – number – was downgraded to be a servant of geometry. The scandal of irrational numbers was swept under the carpet. Mathematics now meant geometry, with an undercurrent of arithmetic. As Plato emphasized:

> That [study] is the knowledge of that which always is, and not of a something which at some time comes into being and passes away.

---

41   This book by Jacob Klein, the mathematician, is a technical discussion of how latter Pythagoreans, Plato, and the neoplatonists came to grips with the traumatic discovery of irrational numbers.

42   Eudoxus: A one-time student of Plato who was perhaps the most renowned astronomer and mathematician of his day. Much of the fifth book of Euclid's *Elements* is his work. Eudoxus' "Method of Exhaustion" was the tool that bypassed the irrational.

Somewhere it is said that the relationship between number and geometry is something like: "A point is a number; a line is a sequence of points / numbers; a triangle is an arrangement of lines." So number, line and geometry remained intimately related.

43   Plato was distancing himself from the magical aspects of Pythagorean thought. It is not known if he did this deliberately or because this magical depth had not been taught to him.

That is readily admitted, he said, for *geometry is the knowledge of the eternally existent.*

Then, my good friend, it would tend to draw the soul to truth ... directing upward the faculties that now wrongly are turned earthward. (B28, *Republic*, 527b. Emphasis added.)

[Ironically, many commentators cannot see in Plato's writings the redemptive value of geometry. Such say little on Plato's mathematics. They, instead, focus on his ethics and politics. Mathematicians and historians of science predictably dwell on his mathematical and science preoccupation. He also had his "unwritten doctrines" and they were commented upon by some of his pupils. More indicators of his geometrical focus are discussed later in the chapter.]

Plato realized that he needed a complex explanatory superstructure – best taught orally but hinted at in his "unwritten doctrine."

The Good (One), God (Demiurge), Principles, and Ideas/Forms were needed to avoid an infinite regress. You might call this "Plato's ladder." Whether the ladder succeeded or merely made the thought process too complicated to criticize is an everlasting debate. For example, Plato said:

Moreover, the receptacle participates "in a very complicated way" in the intelligible, because this participation ... takes place "in a way that is ineffable and marvelous," by means of complex numerical and geometrical mediation, as Plato later explains in connection with the constitution of the four elements. This complex participation implies the intermediate realm of mathematical entities and the soul and all that that involves. Finally, it is invisible because of its lack of form ... because what can be seen is in some way determined and formed. Nevertheless, it continually makes itself visible under the appearance of things which it from time to time receives. (B30, page 380. Refers to *Timaeus* 51A1 – B6.)

I don't think this is the only instance where Plato made mystical rationalizations to justify his superstructure. The founder of neoplatonism, Plotinus, later had to offer another such explanation because of "difficulties" in his own superstructure:

The quality now manifested may be probably referred to the conduct of a former life; we may suppose that previous actions have made the Reason-Principle now governing within us inferior in radiance to that which ruled before; the Soul which later will shine out again is for the present at a feebler power. (B31, page 214.)

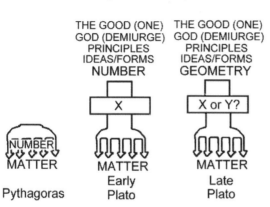

Pythagoras
Early Plato
Late Plato

These drawings are not adequate to fully illuminate what is said about Plato's system:

The level that we call the lowest is made up of sensible objects in motion. The second level is made up of mathematical natures, which are intelligible and immutable, but that insofar as they are individuals still do not belong to the archetypical universals.

On the third level are located the universals, which are not a multiplicity of individuals, but each is of an ideal uniqueness. The final level is composed of the principles that are above being; they are themselves of a purely universal character, and therefore can be grasped only by going through and beyond the remaining ideas. These four levels, distinct according to precise ontological criteria ... are further subdivided.... (B32, page 83.)

The text continues on and on with further clarifications and additions.

(Mathematicians who want to talk about mathematics or philosophers who want to talk about philosophy *can endlessly feast on the interpretive possibilities!* We will say little on these interpretive layers other than that the "demiurge" was a servant to the mathematical One. There is no Christian connection to this super-structure.

Plato was probably not aware of the transcendent God who *ex nihilo* created the cosmos. Plato made a valiant attempt to build a rational substitute superstruc-ture, but failed. Matter comes from the creator, not from a layered superstructure.)

Plato also took a shot at Protagoras:

Now it is God who is, for you and me, of a truth the 'measure of all things,' much more truly than, as they say, 'man.' (B28. *Laws*, 716c.)

Like that of Pythagoras, Plato's intellectual adventure had a two-fold creed: *matter is geometrical, and geometry is self-evident truth.* These possess necessity. Geometry is rational thought and "all-seeing." Man is rationally free only if he assents to this top-down mathematical truth.[44]

Geometry became "physical," (or controlled the process of how number became "physical"), much like number had been earlier. Geometry, in turn, was buttressed by the concurrently formalized deductive proof.[45] Deductive proof and geometry reinforced the practice of "objective" extrapolation on a grandiose scale; this extrapolative infatuation provided the prized Universal Connected Knowledge. Geometric thinking – cosmic thinking – became synonymous with knowledge. Once again, they could reject the pragmatism of their pagan neighbors, sophists and physicists. This new methodology had a clear foundation (the geometry of the mind's eye) and a clear terminus (the cosmos). Yet, philosophy was not for the common man!

These elements set the Platonic adventure apart from the detested polytheism with its subjective oracles, divinations, and sacrifices. Ironically, the methodology was so impervious to criticism that it, in turn, was (and is) respected as a secular

---

44   Matter to the Greeks was like marbles, numbers or triangles. They shared a vision of matter as "hard." But what if Plato had said that matter is like "jello with a halo" (charge and fields)? Such deformability was beyond their mathematical vision. Their matter had infinite hardness and infinite precision.

45   Deductive Proof: The process of applying a general rule to a specific situation to judge its truth or falsity. Geometry illustrates this as its few simple rules (axioms) were (supposedly) used to construct the entire edifice of geometry. (However, recent mathematicians have concluded that its codification in Euclid's axiomatic structure was flawed. These flaws weren't noticed for the previous 2,000 years because all learned people "knew" that Euclid's axioms were such remarkably "clear" intuitions.)

"sacred" oracle. It exemplified *monotruth – the priceless single answer.*

Greek thinkers still said: "Rational thought has a visible truth – an incarnated mathematics. We know that 1 + 1 = 2 *and also* that the sum of the angles in a tri-angle always equal two right angles. Because of geometry's infallible communica-tion to the mind's eye, our earthbound observations of matter can be safely extrapo-lated to reveal the Universal Connectedness ingrained even in inaccessible nature."

Plato's heritage of Pythagorean mysticism is acknowledged by the historian, Giorgio de Santillana:

> Behind Plato there stands the imposing body of doctrine attributed to Pythagor-as, some of its formulations uncouth, but rich with the prodigious content of early mathematics, pregnant with a science and a metaphysics that were to flower in Plato's time. From it come such words as "theorem," "theory," and "philosophy." This in its turn rests on what might be called a proto-Pythagorean phase, spread all over the East but with a focus in Susa [in Persia]. And then there was something else again, the stark numerical computing of Babylon. From it came that strange principle: "Things are numbers." (B33, page 6.)

As Numenius of Apemea (of Syria, second century A.D.) was to say: "Plato Pythagorizes."

Like Pythagoras, Plato was a proto-atheist, but did not believe in materialism either, in the strict sense. As number had for Pythagoras, so geometry gave Plato a firm – physical – foundation from which to dispense with pagan Greek religion. Plato retained the Pythagorean cosmos but with geometrical significance. *For Plato, ge-ometry was the medium – and content – of divine revelation and the cosmos!*

Only three (observable) dimensions exist: the parameters in Euclidean geom-etry list them as length, width, and height. From these, area and volume are geometrically derived. Since no geometric figure can be drawn with four or more dimensions, there could be no equations containing the fourth or higher powers.

> The classical Greeks regarded the product of more than three numbers as meaningless because the product had no geometrical significance. (B10, page 106.)

> All references to a geometry of more than three dimensions before [A.D.] 1827 are in the form of single sentences pointing out that we cannot go beyond a certain point in some process because there is no space of more than three dimensions, or mentioning something that would be true if there were such a space. (B34, page 524.)

For over two thousand years this physical geometry influenced what philoso-phers saw – such as in astronomy. And philosophers, in turn, told other people what to see.

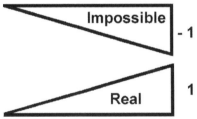

Because zero and negative numbers were nonexistent according to the axioms of Pythagorean / Platonic mathematics, a tri-angle with a side of length "-x" was merely an upside-down triangle. (Also, Greek geometry worked with lengths, not with positions. Positions came with the later coordinate geometry of Descartes.)

Rationalists considered the mind's eye to be vindicated. Geometry reigned – and breathed life back into a subordinated physical number. Both were lawful and objective! *Mathematics gave solidity to storytelling about astronomical appearances.* More on that later.

Looking ahead for a moment, we know twenty-first century mathematics includes algebra (and trigonometry – plus others) in addition to arithmetic and geometry. In Greek times, algebra, while known, was discriminated against, like arithmetic was. *Scandalously, algebra easily produced irrational numbers!* Therefore, geometry was used to solve algebraic problems, such as those for area and volume.

Consider the algebraic equation, $x^2 + 4x = 5$. This was not viewed abstractly, but as a problem to solve for the resulting area of 5 units. As the following figure shows, the geometric methodology required "completing the square."

The 4x is broken up and the square completed. Thus the side is 3 units or x + 2, so x + 2 = 3. The answer is: x = 1.

This procedure reduces quadratic equations to ones of first degree. A similar reduction could be made to cubic equations, but with more difficulty.

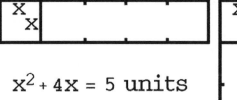

$$x^2 + 4x = 5 \text{ units}$$
$$x = 1 \text{ unit}$$

This figure also illustrates why Greek mathematicians never constructed the equation as: $x^2 + 4x - 5 = 0$. The equation represents an "area," and "0" is not an area.

Ominously, solving the above equation with algebra results in *two* answers:

$$X^2 + 4X - 5 = 0$$
$$(X + 5)(X - 1) = 0$$
$$X = -5$$
$$X = 1$$

However, the Greeks emphasized that zero and negative numbers did not exist – and *multiple* answers also didn't exist in a monotruth environment! Again, *specs of dust get in the mind's eye!* We return to this early indicator of contradiction in chapter six, where the work of Diophantus, a later Greek algebraist, is discussed.

It is, in fact, quite impossible to arrive at the concept of "negative" and "irrational" number by way of Diophantus' [and his teachers] concept of number. Therefore, in order to avoid "negative" and "irrational" solutions, a "restrictive condition" is introduced in each case. (B21, page 138.)

The geometric approach was cumbersome, but was the alternate way to solve algebraic equations, to avoid the embarrassing "restrictive conditions." More importantly, geometry was all the science of measure was comfortable with.

Algebra was not the only embarrassment to Platonic philosophy. Continuous (smooth) motion was impossible within Pythagorean and Platonic mathematics. Such motion implied that moving objects pass through an infinity of intermediate positions, some of which would be irrational. The dual transgressions of infinity and irrational were an information overload for the science of their day. No wonder Zeno's paradoxes of motion terrified rationalists. Acknowledging Zeno, the accepted theory said motion occurs in "little" instantaneous jerks from one stationary position to the next,[46] such as in the flight of an arrow.[47] This corresponded to the discreteness of Pythagorean physical numbers – the mathematical continuum. Mathematics ruled physical possibilities.

(Much later, both Galileo and Newton were severely criticized by their "scientific" colleagues because their mathematical procedures implied continuous motion. Continuous motion is a fact of life today, but the universities and monasteries of late medieval Europe witnessed numerous controversies regarding the still mathematically unconquered nature of motion. It was controversial, like trying to decide how many mathematicians can stand on the head of a pin! Both pins and motion show the science of the day's fallacies.)

Discontinuous events were another embarrassment. *Discontinuity* is motion of short duration, but of rapid change, *e.g.,* historical events are such as earthquakes, volcanoes and tsunamis, or a more drastic example, Noah's flood. Discontinuities highlight *historical* events, *not ahistorical continuity.* This offends mathematical incarnation, which considers number to *smoothly* follow number *forever.* Numerical sequences, such as 1 + 2 + 3 + ... do not "break," (*e.g.,* 1 + 2 + 3 + 26 + 27 + ...). Geometry, it postulates, has the same continuity. The mind's eye could not see discontinuity, so the physical eye grew blind to it also. *Mathematic's Word provides Universal Connected Knowledge!*

This use of the mind's eye is called *uniformitarianism.* It easily deduces the familiar cliché, "The present is the key to the past ... *and* the otherwise inaccessible." The cliché, in a larger sense, is: The changeless present (reduced to its ahistorical mathematical measure) is the key to the past." Again, all-seeing grandiose extrapolation received approval!

In this cliché, how long is the present? Is it only this year? It should be all of history! *Yet history testifies to overwhelming discontinuous events!*

---

46   This is similar to today's Quantum Mechanics, which requires real and "virtual" particles to accomplish "motion." It incorporates the annihilation and recreation of particles between positions to account for the required instantaneous movement between the selfsame positions!
47   Aristotle provided an ingenuous "physical" explanation for motion, but Plato is the one who said it had to be explained in some such way.

Because rationalists knew that reason and objective truth and mathematics and grandiose extrapolation and monotruth and atheism were inseparable, discontinuous events were summarily dismissed as physically impossible. *Mathematically impossible motion does not occur* in Greek science and *ex nihilo* creation was the most discontinuous of all!

Some may think Plato's writings are not connected to the preceding discussion of Greek science. The Pythagorean roots of Plato's thought may be overlooked because much of his writing seemingly emphasizes politics, law and government. A further challenge is the fact that Plato never wrote about his central truths; they were only for oral transmission. In his letter to the tyrant, Dionysius,[48] he said:

> Take precautions, however, lest this teaching ever be disclosed among untrained people, for in my opinion there is in general no doctrine more ridiculous in the eyes of the general public than this, nor on the other hand any more wonderful and inspiring to those naturally gifted .... It is a very great safeguard to learn by heart instead of by writing .... That is the reason why I have never written anything about these things ...[49 & 50] (B28, page 1567. Footnotes added.)

One can almost feel some wounds on Plato from the comments of the general public due to their empirical disdain for the philosopher's "far from the footsteps of humans" mathematical mindset. One is left with the impression that studying Plato's written legacy hides some central features. This silence invites speculation and the schools of Greek thought willingly fill in the blanks.

While many writers downplay mathematics in Plato's thought system, the following data show that mathematics was the highest priority for Plato:

First: Close reading of Plato's writings shows that behind the apparent eccentricity of his style is a Pythagorean outlook. In his *Phaedo*, (86b), recounting the death of Socrates, Simmias says, "We are all Pythagoreans." (B28, page 68.)

Plato's educational curriculum ranked, in the following order, the most important subjects as: Number (arithmetic), geometry, astronomy, and music (harmony). His outlook is obvious in passages such as the following:

> Now for divine begettings there is a period comprehended by a perfect number. ... Whereof a basal four thirds wedded to the pempad[51] yields two harmonies at the third augmentation ... the other dimension of a hundred cubes of the triad. And this entire geometric number is determinative of this thing, of better and inferior births. And when your guardians, missing this, bring together brides and bridegrooms unseasonably, the offspring will not be wellborn or fortunate. (B28, page 775.)

---

48   Dionysius was tyrant (ruler) of Syracuse, a city-state Greek colony on the island of Sicily. Plato, at one time, thought he could mold Dionysius to his truth. As a wealthy aristocrat, Plato went there to teach him. Dionysius loved the "good life" too much and soon put Plato under house arrest, but later allowed him to leave (or he escaped).

49   For example, Iamblichus in *The Exhortation to Philosophy* mentions the same "silence about the mysteries." He attributes it to a ban by Pythagoras. Aristotle, in his *Physics* 209b, also mentions Plato's unwritten teaching. The unwritten doctrines were discussed among his students. See *Plato and the foundations of Metaphysics* (B32), by Hans Joachim Krämer.

50   One is tempted to speculate that Plato was also a shrewd marketer. He conferred high status by giving what others cannot have.

51   Plato used this term, but no authority now knows what it means.

There being as it appears three pleasures .... the tyrant in his flight from law and reason crosses the border beyond the spurious .... The tyrant, I believe, we found at the third remove from the oligarch ... and the oligarch in turn is at the third remove from the royal man .... Three times three, then, by numerical measure is the interval that separates the tyrant from true pleasure .... But by squaring and cubing it is clear what the interval of this separation becomes .... He will find on completion of the multiplication that [the king] lives seven hundred and twentynine times as happily and that the tyrant's life is more painful by the same distance. (B28, page 815.)

The series of equations, $1 \times 3 = 3$, $3 \times 3 = 9$, $9 \times 9 = 81$, $81 \times 9 = 729$, were not considered mumbo jumbo! According to Plato's logic, democracy was also at a "remove" from the king. Plato preferred rule by philosopher-kings; bureaucrats are a modern equivalent.

Second: Plato also evidences Number in his method of argumentation: he uses only either-or constructs in his *Dialogs*.[52] There are no intermediate positions (fractions), only brave-coward; smart-dumb; hot-cold, *etc.* Thus, his analysis becomes even more tenuous when noting the absence of graduated scales, *i.e.*, the absence of fractions.

Third: Late in his life, Plato did speak somewhat openly on his "science" in the *Timaeus*.[53] For example, he describes how the physical world is built out of elementary triangles:

Of produced things, the substratum is Matter, while the reason of each shape is abstract form; of these two the offspring is Earth and Water, Air and Fire.
This is how they were created. Every body is composed of surfaces, *whose elements are triangles,* of which one is right-angled, and the other has all unequal sides .... Now let [this] be called a *scalene* triangle; while the other, the half of the square, is the principle of the constitution of the Earth. For the square produced from this scalene triangle is composed of four halfsquares and from such a square is produced *the cube, the most stationary and steady form* in every way, having six sides and eight angles.[54] *On this account Earth is the heaviest and most difficult elemental body to move, and its substance is inconvertible, because it has no affinity with the other types of triangle.* Only Earth has a peculiar element of the square, while the other triangle is the element of the other three substances, Fire, Air and Water ... (B35, page 291. *Timaeus* 53c – 56b. Emphasis added.)

First, there was the moon in the orbit nearest the earth, and the next the *sun, in the second orbit above the earth;* then came the morning star and the star said to be sacred to Hermes ... (B28, *Timaeus* 38d. Emphasis added.)

---

52   Plato was an accomplished mathematician. See the *Manual of Harmonics* by Nicomachus the Pythagorean, about 100 A.D. (and an accomplished arithmetician), translated by Flora Levin. She points out various examples of his computations regarding musical problems. Another reference is to *Timaeus* 35b - 36b, where Plato summarizes a lengthy calculation on the formation of planetary motion – here understood also as the diatonic musical scale (the harmony of the spheres), including his proof that there is no center to the octave scale in music; his concluding infamous irrational ratio of 256:243 is not compatible with Greek mathematics.
53   Plato does preface this discussion in the *Timaeus* as a "likely myth," but he also had said to "search no further." What he meant by "likely myth" certainly did not keep his followers from considering it as a rational certainty. *We may treat it as mumbo jumbo, they didn't!*
54   In the writings of Iamblichus, we saw favorable symbolism in these numbers.

The earth, which is our nurse, *clinging around the pole* which is extended through the universe, he framed to be the guardian and artificer of night and day, first and eldest of gods that are in the *interior of heaven.* (B28, *Timaeus* 40b. Emphasis added.)

[M]*otion never exists in what is uniform* …. In the revolution of the universe are comprehended all the four elements, and this being circular and having a tendency to come together, compresses everything and will not allow any place to be left void. (B28, *Timaeus* 57e. Emphasis added.)

The 5 Platonic Solids

The **tetrahedron** (greek "tetráedron" = four-sided) is bounded by 4 regular triangles. The faces are bordered by 6 edges of equal length and 4 vertices. 3 triangles meet at each of the vertices. The tetrahedron has the least ratio of volume to surface area. According to Plato it symbolizes dryness or fire.

The **hexahedron** (greek "hexáedron" = six-sided) is bounded by 6 squares. The faces are bordered by 12 edges of equal length and 8 vertices. 3 squares meet at each of the vertices. The tetrahedron rests solidly on its base. According to Plato it stands for the stable earth.

The **octahedron** (greek "oktáedron" = eight-sided) is bounded by 8 equilateral triangles. The faces are bordered by 8 edges of equal length and 6 vertices. 4 triangles meet at each of the vertices. It can rotate freely when grasped at opposite vertices and symbolizes air.

The **dodecahedron** (greek "dodécáedron" = twelve-sided) is bounded by 12 regular pentagons. The faces are bordered by 30 edges of equal length and 20 vertices. 3 pentagons meet at each of the vertices. It represents the universe and, according to Plato, its faces symbolize the 12 signs of the zodiac.

The **icosahedron** (greek "eikosáedron" = twenty-sided) is bounded by 20 equilateral triangles. The faces are bordered by 30 edges of equal length and 12 vertices. 5 triangles meet at each of the vertices. It has the highest ratio of volume to surface area and, according to Plato, symbolizes water.

www.3quarks.com/en/PlatonicSolids/index.html

The neoplatonists elaborated on "natural" and "forced" motions:

In sum, then, no outside body is necessary to the heavens to ensure their permanence – or to produce their circular movement, for *it has never been shown that their natural path would be the straight line; on the contrary the heavens, by their nature, will either be motionless or move by the circle; all other movement indicates outside compulsion….* (B31, page 103. Emphasis added.)

(If you thought Plato was not responsible for these long-lasting ideas, then you have only read sanitized versions of Plato's writings!) Thus Plato – not Aristotle – gave the geometrical ("physical") reason for the central position of the "heavy" earth associated with geocentric astronomy. (Plus this quotation criticizes Democritus' atoms.) Also, the four elements of earth, air, fire and water were earlier than Aristotle. Some added that the stars were composed of the 5th element, aether, which was light and unchanging. And "natural" motion was circular, thus dispensing with gravity. Other motion was "violent," due to outside compulsion.

And … Yes …. All this truth was discovered without benefit of experiment, telescope or electron microscope! As Plato further elaborates:

> At first, however, [the four elements] were all without reason and measure. But when the world began to get in order, fire and water and earth and air did indeed show faint traces of themselves, but were altogether in such a condition as one may expect wherever God is absent. Such, I say, being their nature, God now fashioned them by form and number. (B37, page 1179. *Timaeus* 53a – b.)

As a further example, Plato explains body growth as follows:

> When the frame of the whole creature is young and the triangles of its constituent bodies are still as it were fresh from the workshop, their joints are firmly locked together …. Accordingly, since any triangles composing the meat and drink … are older and weaker than its own, with its new-made triangles, it gets the better of them and cuts them up, and so causes the animal to wax large. (B37, page 97. *Timaeus* 82b – d.)

Fourth: All these fit Plato's creedal statement. When well-reasoned Greeks said, "Everything is mathematical," they really meant it! With extreme mathematical seriousness, the sign[55] over the entrance to Plato's Academy summarized rational thought:

Ah Son! What a handsome set of new made triangles you are!

> *Let no one destitute of geometry enter my doors.*

Why did Plato attach such tremendous importance to the cultivation of Mathematics? Why did he require all his pupils to obtain a thorough knowledge of mathematics before being initiated into his philosophy?… [I]t was because in mathematics one can learn that it is possible to reason about things which are neither seen nor heard, but exist in thought only. (B20, page 148.)

I think that is a partial explanation. The fuller answer includes the all-seeing promise of Mathematic's Word – which is the heart of Greek philosophy!

Fifth: Plato carried on the ideas of Pythagoras. He had a form of godliness. The atheism of the atomists, the moral relativism of Sophists and the sexual perversions of Athenian trendsetters scared him. His teaching had a moral basis. In commenting upon the *Epinomis*,[56] a posthumously published work of Plato, a recent author examines his indebtedness to Pythagorean views:

> The lofty conception of nature, formed on the example of numbers, in accor-

---

55   The earliest reference to this sign is from about a thousand years later – AD 600. See *Plato at the Googleplex* by Rebecca Goldstein, page 169 *fn.*

56   Some people think the *Epinomis* was influenced by the people who prepared this work for publication, but its mathematical mysticism is akin to the *Timaeus* and the *Laws.*

dance with the laws of harmony, is thoroughly Pythagorean .... It is not a sober natural science ... but a mystical surrender to the divine Creator of the disciple who has been initiated into the secrets of numbers and of harmony .... In this mystical region, everything flows together; one does no longer distinguish between musical intervals and the corresponding numerical ratios, nor between geometric and material bodies. The human soul communicates with the divine soul; *thinking is no longer human, it has become divine.* (B20, page 157. Emphasis added.)

Geometry led to spiritual ecstasy! The shadows cast on the wall of Plato's cave were geometrical shapes!

Sixth: Plato's *Dialogues* contain many criticisms of his "scientific" competitors, including the earth, air, fire, water and atomist folks. These criticisms expressed his keen "scientific" belief that their positions were wrong and that he, Plato, considered himself to be a scientist, not only a philosopher.

As said earlier, this mathematical core to Plato's thought is little mentioned. Plato is merely called a philosopher – which avoids the deeper flavors of his thought. Modern philosophers seem unaware of the science of measure or are embarrassed by it. For example, Bertrand Russell only said the following in *The Wisdom of the West*:

This side of the [Pythagorean] tradition is connected with a number of primitive tabus and rules of abstinence. (B38, page 21.)

Russell spared few chances to criticize Christianity – so he was not predisposed to weaken his case by mentioning the deep subjectivity in Greek "science."

Reincarnation facilitates "heavenly" communication. In his *Phaedrus*, Plato presented the case of a charioteer and his two horses:

When the soul comes into sight of a fair and beloved object, the wild horse rushes forward to satisfy his base lust, dragging along his mate ... and the driver. At first the driver and the better horse resist ineffectually; but of a sudden there comes to the driver *a remembrance of the pure external beauty he has beheld in a previous existence with the gods,* and, as it were, smitten by the vision, he himself is thrown backwards ... (B36, pages 129-130. *Phaedrus* 253c – 254e. Emphasis added.)

From this mistaking of reincarnation for conscience, several writers have reluctantly commented upon the next step:

In a general way we may say this: that the conception of ideas runs parallel in Plato's mind with the mythology of a vaguely personal deity. (B36, page 226.)

Plato justified acceptance of the axioms [of geometry] by his theory of recollection or *anamnesis* .... Humans had experience as souls in another world before coming to earth, and the soul had but to be *stimulated to recall its prior existence* in order to know that the axioms of geometry were truths. (B11, page 20. Emphasis added.)

Geometry was a phone line to heaven. Geometric truths were, indeed, "manna from heaven," communicated through *anamnesis*[57] (remembrance? or mental

---

57   *"Amnesia" is one word derived from anamnesis.* To forget your whole personality is so drastic an effect that it is more than a lack of remembrance. *Anamnesis conveyed the idea of*

"transport?") – or "taught" by descended souls or *daimonions*. While *anamnesis* is not really an "out of body experience," it certainly was a trip for the "mind's eye."

Plato promoted the so-called Socratic method[58] to prove that others could also recall geometric truths, with "prompting." These "recollections," he claimed, proved reason discovered preexisting knowledge, not invented understanding.

To Plato, knowledge is possible since we have in the [many times reincarnated] soul an original intuition of the truth [due to the repeated sojourns with the gods]:

> Seeing that the soul is immortal and has been born many times, and has beheld all things both in this world and in the nether realms, she has acquired knowledge of all and everything; so that it is no wonder that she should be able to recollect all that she knew before about virtue and other things. (B29, page 118. *Meno* 81C.)

This truth is part of his mathematical superstructure (Mathematic's Word). *Thus the certainty of "pure intuition."* Was this Platonic truth or rational mumbo jumbo?

Plato frequently used the word "*logos*," which, to him, meant truth as numerical ratio, the essence of geometry. Yet, this *logos* (geometry) could not be clearly discerned on the earth. He used his heavenly geometry to anchor thought. Plato considered the earth to be an arena of imperfect or obscured forms. Unveiling these forms became the challenge. Greek thinkers began to look at the cosmos with a penetrating "mind's eye" – enlightened by number and geometry.

But where does Plato say pure geometry resides? According to his hints, the pure geometric (and arithmetical) forms existed in ... an ethereal heaven. "Immanent" forms were earthly manifestations of this heavenly geometry. For Plato, *reason was divine, a communication from heaven, with the message written in geometry!*

Of that place *beyond the heavens* none of our earthly poets has yet sung, and

---

communicating (or connecting to) an important, but missing, part of your existence or of reality. It was not mumbo-jumbo!

In contrast, *mnemonic* is the Greek tongue-twister for com-mon remembering.

58   Socratic Method: A question and answer procedure recommended by Plato supposedly showing the ability of people to "recollect" from their past lives or intervals in "heaven." See Plato's example in the *Meno*. The example is not rigorous. Bertrand Russell wrote:

> "When ... in the *Meno*, [Plato] applies his method to geometrical problems, he has to ask leading questions which any judge would disallow." (B14, page 101.)

The believability of the process requires belief in prior existence with the gods and includes sojourns in the "heavens" between trips back to earth. Therefore, *the Socratic method did not "teach;" it "stimulated" the remembrance (anamnesis) of facts from a prior existence in another world.* (Is this where *a priori* originated? A prior existence resembles intuition – innate truth – as private knowledge.) See also the above note on *anamnesis*.

Plato insisted that evil resulted from a bad education, not from evil in the soul. People today sentimentally accept Plato's account of the origin of evil and the promise of education. However, I doubt few accept his entire theory as he further said in his *Timaeus* that *when bad men die, they are reincarnated as women.* If consistently or really bad, one later returns as an animal, lastly descending to a fish or a worm. (B28, pages 1171, 1206, 1210-1211.)

As a good student of Plato, Aristotle reportedly said about the physics of reincarnation embedded in the science of their day, "Woman may be said to be an inferior man." Greek rational thought seemed to say: "Man is a man, woman is a failed (recidivist) man returned to the earth for another chance." So much for a woman's dignity or family life!

none shall sing worthily …. *It is there that truth dwells*, without color or shape, that cannot be touched; *reason alone*, the soul's pilot, can behold it, and *all true knowledge is knowledge thereof*. (B28, page 494. *Phaedrus* 247c – d. Emphasis added.)

Scholarly disputes erupt(ed) as thinkers tried (and still try) to decipher what Pythagoras or Plato or Alétheia meant by pure numbers. *Anamnesis* pointed to an otherworldly encounter – certainly far from the footsteps of humans. Penrose referred to the "externally existing Platonic world." In this Platonic heaven there was a "place." Plato did not say if it was a temple or a museum or a palace or a cosmic bureau of standards.

This "Place" contained the *pure* reality ... and this *pure* form was *pure* number or geometry! (Actually written with "marked" letters of the Greek alphabet.) Numbers exist there as a "physical" reality. Importantly, these numbers were perfect in *all* respects. They could be extrapolated – with no margin of error! (1.000, not 0.999… or 1.001…)

Even so, there was difficulty in conveying the precise numbers to earth. Pythagoras had had a great idea about number being things ... until he met irrational numbers.

Thus, we arrive at pure Platonism – which also included the pure geometric forms. (After Aristotle and the Stoics, among others, criticized – or amended – it, neoplatonism arose – as the return to the "pure" sources.)

As a writer commented a century ago:

Wisely, therefore, does Plato assert that the philosopher ought not to descend below species, and that he should be solely employed in the contemplation of *wholes* and *universals*. (B39, page xxxi. Emphasis in original.)

Highlighting this, Aristotle said in his *Prior Analytics*:

... it is not possible to establish universal statements by means of particulars ... (B40, page 68.)

Plato grounded his universal rationalism with the top-down mental transport associated with reincarnation and *anamnesis,* thereby leading back to the unshakable foundation in the heavenly pure numbers. *Anamnesis* took him far from the footsteps of humans – far from his critics. If he had relied on the physical world, he feared being trapped by the welter of inconclusive bottom-up sense appearances. (So, this becomes another protective mystical rationalization for his superstructure.) He would have also lost his best argument against polytheism! Nonetheless, philosophers were justly suspected of being entranced by their own well-reasoning – and afraid of getting their hands dirty. They preferred the Universal Connectedness of Mathematic's Word to the messiness of reality.

This use of the mind's eye sheds light upon Plato's views on political leadership. He advocated rule by "philosopher-kings," perhaps by such as himself. Such "rational" people, trained under the highest category of Universal Connected Knowledge and therefore, "free" from subjectivity or worldly influences, could guarantee successful leadership of the *polis*!

Plato desired to construct a geometrical world. In his *Laws*, the ideal city had specific dimensions, and was populated with 5,040 households, *etc.* (i.e.: $1 \cdot 2 \cdot 3 \cdot 4 \cdot 5 \cdot 6 \cdot 7 = 5{,}040$. B37, page 96.) Achieving geometric perfection furthered Plato's utopian vision of heaven on earth; it was not mumbo jumbo!

Plato, wealthy and of aristocratic blood, disdained manual labor. In his utopian

Republic, he argued that manual labor was for the slaves (human cattle).[59] He considered it unlawful for a free man to engage in manual labor. Experimenting (physical investigation) was beneath a free man's dignity. It showed disrespect for the geometric source of truth and the few "penetrating glances" required to reveal cosmic truth.

For people brought up among pagan sacrifices, oracles, and a chaotic poly-theism, these mathematical "truths" – and the ability of *anamnesis* to put seekers in touch with the geometric heaven – could cause a conversion experience. The resulting ecstasy often instilled missionary zeal.

"Obviously," geometry fulfilled the lure of objective truth. Nature became an *intellectual challenge*. The Pythagoreans had seen arithmetic in nature and Platon-ists saw *geometry in nature. People still do!* (Euclidean) geometry did shadow – and still does – many features of experience. How do we interpret this shadowing (or modeling) ... or extend its applicability[60]? We will return to this.

Greek "science" drew a sharp distinction between astronomy and physics, and was preoccupied with finding causes – understood as the *reduction of phenomena to geometry. Scientia*, when looking at the starry vault overhead, could see (roughly) circular motion:

Plato lays down the principle that the heavenly bodies' motion is circular, uni-form and constantly regular. Thereupon he sets the mathematicians the following problem: What circular motions, uniform and perfectly regular, are to be admitted as hypotheses so that it might be possible to save the appearances presented by the planets. (B42, page 5. *Laws*, x, 898a – c says close to the same.)

Circular motion did not need a physical cause.[61] As shown earlier, it was the

---

59   Plato's opinion of the mental capability of the common man was low. He did not believe the human cattle could even master two trades. Adding more irony, Plato said this within the memory of the great Pericles ... the champion of democracy. Perhaps Plato's view reflected a "reincarnational hierarchy?"

(Reading Plato's *Republic* is not for the democracy inclined! Popper, for one, said that Plato despised democracy and tried to subvert it. His ultimate aim was to install a "scientific" Republic. See *The Open Society and Its Enemies,* Volume 1, B41.)

60   Some examples are the geometric structure of crystals; the Fibonacci series in sea shells; the honeycomb structure of bee hive cells. It is not surprising they found geometry in (an orderly) nature – an orderly designed nature. Once you exactly determine the relations of objects, geometric forms result. This led to detailed study of variants of the circle, such as the work on conic sections.

61   Ptolemy (*fl.* A.D. 127-151) or Aristotle is often blamed for the infatuation with the circular motion of geocentric astronomy! However, as seen here and a few pages earlier, Plato first mandated the circle as the perfect motion (natural motion) of geometry – and gave the earth a special "heavy" triangle to account for its central position in the cosmos. This fixation with circular motion dominated astronomy for some 2,000 years. Circular motion was "perfect;" it implied perpetual motion, and as such, no "gravity" was required to "cause" its movement! Actually, the *Timaeus* states that uniform objects (spheres) had no motion and circles exemplified this.

Many centuries later, Johannes Kepler illustrates the circular outlook; he tried to fit Tycho Brahe's observational data into circular orbits. He finally gave up and tried the "inelegant" ellipse. But once he had the ellipse, he needed a cause for the new-found "violent" or "forced" motion. It was no longer sufficient to say it moves because of geometry.

natural motion. No wonder Plato sharply criticized the prevailing opinion regarding the planets:

> The fact is, my friends, that the belief that sun, moon, and other heavenly bodies are 'wandering stars'[62] of any sort is not true. (B28, pages 1391 - 1392. *Laws*, VII, 822a.)

The observational discovery that planetary motion can be (approximately) systematized with geometry "confirmed" the intellectual adventure for them.[63] Eudoxus, mentioned earlier, gave the first formulation of the use of circles to account for planetary motion. (And Aristotle gave a physical model, with shells and rollers.) Centuries later, Ptolemy of Alexandria refined Eudoxus' system. *Astronomy exhibited Platonic form made concrete in circular motion.* To Platonic philosophers, this was not well-reasoned storytelling or mere saving the appearances. *It was truth, based on the science of incarnate geometry!* Therein mathematically processed thought triumphed[64] – and beckoned toward a lot of accompanying mumbo-jumbo seen only with the mind's eye. As Plato said:

> And he [god] gave to the world the figure which was suitable and also natural. Now to the animal [planet] which was to comprehend all animals, that figure would be suitable which comprehends within itself all other figures. Wherefore he made the world in the form of a globe, round as from a lathe, having its extremes in every direction *equidistant from the center*, the most perfect and the most like itself of all figures, for he considered that the like is infinitely fairer than the unlike. (B28, page 1164. *Timaeus* 33b. Emphasis added.)

The sharp distinction between (successful) astronomy and (unsuccessful) physics arose because circular motion (and geometric forms) was hard to discern in earthly processes. Yet, geometric *Scientia* demanded that earthly processes (physics) also yield geometric causes.

Alas, an Achilles' heel was present; it is obvious that no experiments were involved with the planets. True causes and motions were not derived, at least within the time span of records available to them. Their observation of the heavens did confirm that historical nature is orderly, but the mathematical explanation they developed was saving (some of) the appearances, not science. Geometry is not incarnate as matter. As later refined by Ptolemy of Alexandria, epicycles saved the "directional" appearances, but introduced unbelievable distance effects.

(It should be noted that Plato viewed the planets as gods – containing soul and body and of an aetherial constitution.)

---

62   *Planet* is a Greek word meaning "the wanderer." Plato objected to this misnomer because a wandering object doesn't follow a mathematically described path. For Plato, this meant a circular path. In view of atheorism, what would have been the result if Plato had advocated elliptical orbits? (Would such also save the appearances, but without needing epicycles?)

63   Histories of science spend many pages dwelling on the battle up through the Enlightenment against astrology and reincarnation. It would be an instructive study to determine to what extent the founding fathers of Greek "science" wittingly or unwittingly increased the allure of the selfsame astrology, especially through their belief in reincarnation, the planets being rational gods and the need for planetary navigational skills!

64   After reading many histories of ancient science, I am continually amazed that none credit Plato with mandating geocentricity or "natural" circular motion. They blame Aristotle or Ptolemy – but Plato is serenely unscathed! This blindness in the modern mind's eye needs de-sedimentation!

Alfred North Whitehead, in his 1927-28 Gifford Lecture, had mentioned the "philosophy of the epoch." Here we meet such an unstated item. Which is: *astronomy, like mathematics, is ahistorical.* Thus the heavens have natural motions, eternal stability and an infinite age.

So what was the science therein that was to "defeat" Christianity? *Philosopher's minds can see to the Good (One). Our "unaided" intellect, "aided" by mathematics and our pure and unadulterated rational thought, can grasp truth! Our theory is a clear intuition, buttressed with deductive proof. Matter is incarnate mathematics (of the 1.000 variety)!* Mathematic's Word, incarnated!

Dear reader, do you think that Greek thought has made you assent to this as truth? Can you join them in soaring, as on the wings of eagles, as recorded in Reason 101:1, and consider yourself thereby practicing unbiased rational thought?

Nonetheless, this "rational thought" summarized the philosophy of the epoch. Yet, if matter is not Pythagorean arithmetic or Platonic / Euclidean geometry, then their philosophy and natural philosophy were adrift on oceans of mathematics! The important question was whether matter or mathematics came first! Platonists opted for the primacy of top-down mathematics. The Bible revealed (and Aristotle independently agreed) that matter came first – but understandable only as a created fact.

Thus, the orderly *ex nihilo* creation is the superior view. Thinkers should consider the epistemological caution about saving the appearances, but this was a bitter pill to swallow. As the centuries rolled by, they buttressed their position with layered potpourri, but truth still eluded them. In fact, science has little to do with astronomy.

Reflection shows that even astrology, whatever merit it might have, did say the heavens were orderly. Horoscopes had no meaning without some orderliness. The Bible says the heavens are orderly; they are for signs and seasons. Platonic storytelling in astronomy was not a serious criticism of either, yet mathematical methodology was a great boon to empirical science, engineering and technology.

Greek thinkers showed that planetary directional positions could be mathematically predicted – but that organizing fact revealed no origin or distance "facts." But to these mathematical enthusiasts, the direct fact and the organizing "fact" *were* related! Really, their incarnate mathematics was a calculating fiction.

Commingling puzzle solving and storytelling is not healthy. Recollect their view of science mentioned on page 32.

To the Platonist, geometrical incarnation was knowledge. Indeed, for over 2,000 years, Greek geometry was considered synonymous with deductive proof, and a rational understanding of matter and man was systematically erected upon it.

Plato went further than the Pythagoreans in that he wished not merely to understand nature through mathematics but to substitute mathematics for nature herself. *He believed that a few penetrating glances at the physical world would suggest basic truths with which reason could then carry on unaided.*[65] From that point on

---

65   Considering Plato's abhorrence of infinity, some may note the apparent contradiction in his affirmation of grandiose extrapolation. Several comments can be made:

there would be just mathematics. Mathematics would substitute for physical investigation. (B11, pages 16-17. Emphasis added.)

The earliest known systematization of this geometric tool and worldview was the celebrated *Elements* of Euclid, (*fl. c*300 B.C.), a later student of Plato's Academy.[66]

Considering mathematics to be *physical* gave it a unique flavor. In fact, for over 2,000 years – until around A.D. 1850 – mathematics (based on Euclidean geometry) was not only synonymous with deductive proof but was called the *science of measure*[67] (the science of quantity). Admittedly, this mathematical outlook sounds strange to us (except perhaps to theoretical physicists and cosmologists). Today, mathematics is predominantly viewed as a collection of powerful and useful abstractions.

For centuries, the resulting "discoveries" about material stuff were *rigorously defended as truth.* As the "science" validating these finally lost its hold, some "truths" became museum curios ... and more should be! Nonetheless, much valid knowledge was derived.

Now that we have learned more about reason's trophies, we can better understand reason:

Reason 101: 1–2:
The fear of mathematics is the beginning of knowledge.
Our "all-seeing" mind's eye thus soars as on the wings of eagles.

Verily, our mind's eye is allowed to see great things.
The ahistorical mathematical line we give so experimenters know how to work.

Pythagorean reincarnation and Platonic preexistent life with the gods established mathematics, which in turn produced monotruth and thereby anchored reason – and truth, goodness and beauty. While still theistic, this rationalism bypassed pagan altars, divinations from animal organs, and various oracles.

In spite of this mystical foundation of Plato's intellectual adventure, after his death, atheism, materialism, and meaninglessness gained control of it.

We need a break to ask some important questions. What relevance does all this have to the Christian church? Well, first of all, the next chapter will complete the ancient history lesson.

The vast majority of what we have studied – and that information in the next chapter – was lost to Europe due to the hard times associated with the fall of the Western Roman Empire in A.D. 476. Around A.D. 1200, this information began to flow back into Europe. By then, this information was jumbled together – and yet

---

First, to extrapolate to the uttermost does not postulate infinity, only the uttermost. Plato's cosmos was indefinite, but large. Second, Plato's geometry was physical. Thus geometric grandiose extrapolation did not need special pleading. Today, geometry is an abstraction, not a part of reality. Grandiose extrapolation now requires a different justification.
66   Popper maintains the *Elements* was not a geometry textbook, but a handbook to begin the study of the main problems of Plato's revised Pythagorean worldview.
67   Plato named it the "science of mensuration."

considered absolute truth. So Europe was in for an intellectual headache trying to harmonize this material. They, and us, still suffer from it.

Trying to interpret Plato was hard work even in his day. As a quick overview, changes followed – and quickly.

Plato's pupil, Aristotle, proposed a new system. In close succession to this had risen Stoicism and Cynicism – plus the old Sophist, Atomist and naturalist positions were not totally dormant. Then Plato's successor as head of his Academy made major changes. History books refer to the "Old Academy," then "Middle Platonism." (Some add that there also was the Third Academy of Caneades, and a Fourth Academy of Philo of Larissa. Lastly, there was a Fifth Academy under Antiochus of Ascalan. See the Introduction to Cicero's *The Nature of the Gods*, pages 48-51.) Soon after that, the Academy's destruction was wrought by the Roman general Sulla when he captured Athens in 86 B.C.

Then neopythagoreanism and neoplatonism arose about 300 years later, around A.D. 270. Both seem to have originated in Alexandria, Egypt. Alexandria had earlier birthed gnosticism and hermeticism. All these were to later make their way into Europe.

Finally, these were put into a pot and stirred. Out of it came "Greek Knowledge." (The modern world also knows how to be eclectic and nonjudgmental!) Greek knowledge came to Europe via various routes. By then Athens was, itself, in decline. Rome passed on very little. Byzantium, the capital of the Eastern Roman Empire, passed on much material, but with a Platonic slant. The Arab, and then Moslem world, passed on material, but with an Aristotelian slant. The translated works in all of these may not have been that different from each other, but each was accompanied by commentaries, and their explanations had accents.

All of these shared an important characteristic. They each presented truth – the others were in error! (And the "staying power" of each of these systems was short.)

So, the ancient history review will conclude with the next chapter. But there will still be some not-so-old history to walk through. The "between-years" both preserved thoughts and incubated thoughts!

Whatever the allegations of the Greek natural scientists, none of their theses have survived or proved firm, as everything they created was invariably destroyed by their successors; consequently, it is superfluous to contradict them. They destroyed each other. And because they were ignorant of God, they could not agree that an omniscient cause directed the creation of the world. And yet they chose as firm ground this very uncertainty about the origin of things; each construc-ted his conclusions for himself.
St. Basil (A.D. 330 – 379)

The criticism the contemporary Sophist, Cynic, Stoic,[1] and the succeeding neo's made of Plato's physics and philosophy weakened the edifice. Materialist criticism came from the Stoics and Atomists.[2]

Atomists needed an infinite void for their atoms to move in. Random motions caused collisions and thus "created" the four elements of earth, air, fire and water. Atoms were a pure form, functioning like Pythagorean number or Platonic geom-etry. Democritus was one of the formulators of this understanding. He also postu-lated "soul atoms," which dissolved at death. Thus atheism was deduced.

Atheism shocked Greek peoples. Whether pagan, Pythagorean, or Platonic, the heavens were full of gods and other life. Atheism made the heavens truly barren! Atomists lived almost a "quarantined" existence among their countrymen. (Atomism was an undercurrent of dissent through the ages.[3])

Plato's doctrines were weakened by his successors as head of his Academy. The first, Speusippus, was either his sister's son or his sister's daughter's husband. He dismantled part of Plato's ladder. (We do not know why he made these changes. Perhaps it was a partial reaction to Aristotle's criticism and departure from Plato's Academy.) His successor, in turn, Xenocrates, made additional changes. And then there were the later neo's, discussed in this chapter.

Perhaps concurrently, Plato's systematization was weakened by Aristotle, who criticized much of Plato's work, even though he was Plato's most famous pupil.[4]

---

1   Stoic: A school of philosophy teaching that one should be unaffected by the world or emo-tions. The founder, Zeno of Citium, was actually trained in Plato's Academy. In addition, they had an Aristotelian-leaning "physics." See *The Physics of the Stoics,* B6, by S. Sambursky.
2   The name survives today to do yeoman's duty as atomic theory.
3   The early church at various times critiqued Atomism. See examples later in the chapter.
4   The surviving writings of Aristotle are more extensive than those of Plato. Aristotle's writing are not polished texts, but seem more like lecture notes. (Judging by the number of titles of Aristotle's works that have no copies available, writers conclude that an equivalent amount of Aristotle's writings are lost. A flood has been mentioned.) Aristotle's writing is noted

Aristotle spent twenty years at Plato's Academy and was 37 years old when Plato died. Aristotle was a master mathematician, yet he rejected the reverential attitude towards mathematics – and other-worldliness. (Aristotle agreed that there was a God, but that man could learn nothing about Him or other inaccessible objects. It was thus futile to find knowledge with a top-down viewpoint.) As quoted earlier, Aristotle, with his bottom-up attitude, did not want to search "far from the footsteps of humans."

> For [Aristotle], knowledge is not conditioned exclusively by mathematics .... It follows that the science of numbers and figures has only a restricted function, and that the conceptual rationalization of the universe cannot be obtained by the progressive mathematization of our knowledge .... For one thing, Plato was unable to show how number and magnitude generate *qualities*[5] .... Indeed, [Plato] was unable to establish mathematics as a universal method of knowledge... (B24, pages 156 -157. Emphasis added.)

Aristotle considered mathematics to be an invention of the mind, therefore subordinate to physical investigation and logical categories. This inductive approach removed a core section of Plato's ladder. *Aristotle maintained that our knowledge comes through our five senses. Rudimentary arithmetic and geometry can be learned from playing with marbles and drawing figures in the sand[6]. Advanced mathematics was built on subsequent thinking about rudimentary mathematics.* He advocated a more logical, observational finite approach.

> Aristotle in a way did for logic what Euclid was shortly going to do for geometry. Aristotelian logic has reigned supreme until the nineteenth century. (B38, page 87.)

For good measure, Aristotle's system began with an unmoved prime mover.[7] Yet neither competing system could handle *ex nihilo* creation – that created fact.

As a later Platonist defended Plato:

> However, the value of Aristotle's physics was limited.... Proclus considered Aristotle's writings in physics to be defective imitations, produced in a spirit of rivalry, of Platonic physics as revealed in particular in the *Timaeus*. A measure of Aristotle's heretical inclinations is to be found in the criticism he makes of the *Timaeus* ... (B13, page 179.)

Aristotle emphasized physical investigation of the "here and now," a bottom-up search for knowledge. It was proto-empiricism. Perhaps now you can realize why

---

for its extensiveness, attention to detail, and cohesiveness. It was *the* veritable encyclopedia of ancient knowledge.

5   Qualities have a long history of arguments. They may also be called accidents or secondary phenomena. Qualities are part of Aristotle's thought. They are such as color, occupation, location, and action. An object's color, a person's particular occupation, where he is living or what he is doing are Platonically considered nonessential. (And Plato's numbers and magnitudes could not "see" them.) While non-computable, they are essential to who you are. Further, how do you describe beauty, love, hate, courage, fear, *etc.*? These are essential parts of existence, but outside of mathematics!

6   I cannot recollect the source of this sentence.

7   Unmoved prime mover: Aristotle's logic warned people that an infinite regress (of cause and effect relationships) could not be foundational. His system was grounded upon an undefined unmoved prime mover, which (who?) in turn, was integral with Aristotle's concentric sphere model of the cosmos.

Aristotle, a master mathematician, did not like the number mysticism of his teacher. Aristotle had no need for *anamnesis*. He saw that Plato's rational methodology required belief, not analysis, to arrive at truth. Aristotle talked about numbers as one, two, three, *etc.* It has been said that reading an ancient book on mathematics showed Aristotelian inclinations if it so used one, two, three, *etc.*, instead of one thing, two things, three things, *etc.* Aristotle was very observant, his eyesight was remarkably keen to see some of the details he reported. He wrote on subjects as diverse as biology and physics – and founded logic and dialectics. He also tutored the future Alexander the Great. (This teaching experience was bumpy. At one point, Alexander locked Aristotle in a cage.)

Aristotle further wrote that:

> The minute accuracy of mathematics is not to be demanded in all cases, but only in those which have no matter. Therefore its method is not that of natural science; for presumably all nature has matter. (B40, Volume 2, page 1572.)

(The last assertion of Aristotle may not stand, for matter is charge and fields.)

> Although Aristotle's surviving treatises are not always clear, they are packed with huge amounts of profound thought about almost every subject imaginable. Aristotle practically originated the discipline of natural history…. The subject matter of one of his greatest books was so novel that no one even knew what to call it. *Metaphysics* got its name because it followed *Physics* in the standard list of Aristotle's works, and "meta" is ancient Greek for "after." Up until Aristotle's time, this subject did not have a name because he had not yet invented it. (B43, page 72.)

Aristotle's problem seemed to be that he was too good as a biologist. Actually, some of this work was not superseded until the eighteenth century A.D. (B38, page 80.) He drew the (unfortunate) conclusion that inanimate objects also had the same categories, including teleology.

To contrast the two: Plato was mathematically deductive – starting on a cosmic scale; Aristotle was logically inductive – starting from the "here and now." As Aristotle logically extrapolated to the "unmoved prime mover," his system did not mesh with the geometric outlook of the mind's eye. He undermined the science of measure.

Plato treated his mathematical cosmos as an exciting voyage of discovery. Aristotle considered Plato's cosmos an abstraction – mental entities – or a voyage of invention and storytelling.

> Aristotle never wants to withdraw from nature; rather he investigates even what transcends nature in terms of its relation to nature. Conversely, Plato, following the Pythagorean manner, investigates natural things insofar as they participate in what transcends nature. (B26, pages xxiii – xxiv.)

> Aristotle has heavily criticized, it is true, the doctrine of the Principles and the doctrine of the Ideas and in addition went on to deny the existence of the One-Good and all the transcendent Ideas or Forms. Nevertheless … he did not in any way intend to deny that some *supersensible realities* existed. He, in fact, wanted instead to demonstrate that the *supersensible did not have the nature that Plato conceived it to have*…. (B29, page 254. Emphasis in original.)

When Pythagoras and Plato said matter was mathematics, then matter began as endowed with universal mathematical characteristics (nondeformable – infinite hardness, infinite precision and no attenuation). Yet, it begged the question of how mathematics became incarnate as matter.

Conversely, when Aristotle said that basic mathematics came from doodling in the sand or playing with marbles, *he recognized that matter had no prior defined characteristics. One could not reasonably begin by extrapolating matter or reading mathematics into matter.* He did say that arithmetical and geometrical relations between particles of matter could be determined – and thus bottom-up mathematics began. T*his left matter to be investigated to find out what it was!* Was it big, little, round, square, soft, hard, hollow, solid, *etc*. Aristotle's view assumed that matter was "created," as a separate question.

Their disagreement over the priority of mathematics or matter impacts the believability of Universal Natural Law and its Universal Connected Knowledge. With Aristotle, mathematics is a shadow bottom-up phenomenon. No wonder Platonists and Aristotelians dislike(d) each other.

The painting by Raphael in 1510 is part of a larger painting, *The School of Athens.* (www.commons.wikimedia.org/wiki/image: Sanzio_01_Plato_Aristotle.jpg.) Plato is on the left pointing upward, and carrying his book, the *Timaeus*. Aristotle is on the right pointing horizontally in disagreement and carrying his book, *Ethics*. (We don't know if it is his *Nicomachean Ethics* or *Eudemian Ethics*.) The painting witnesses that their disagreement about the source of truth was

understood in the Middle Ages.[8] (I don't think this dispute drags in other particulars of their systems of thought.)

Regarding that troublesome ahistorical mathematical line, you could say that Plato proclaimed its reality and Aristotle knelt down, touched the earth and wondered if he felt vibrations in it!

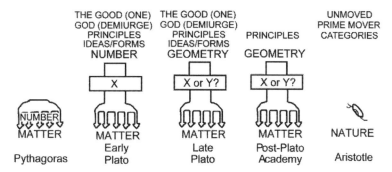

THE GOOD (ONE)   THE GOOD (ONE)   UNMOVED
GOD (DEMIURGE)   GOD (DEMIURGE)   PRIME MOVER
PRINCIPLES   PRINCIPLES   PRINCIPLES   CATEGORIES
IDEAS/FORMS   IDEAS/FORMS
NUMBER   GEOMETRY   GEOMETRY

X   X or Y?   X or Y?

NUMBER
MATTER   MATTER   MATTER   MATTER   NATURE
                  Early   Late   Post-Plato
Pythagoras   Plato   Plato   Academy   Aristotle

The "divine" Plato and the "immortal" Aristotle, like their competitors, were smart people. But smart people are not error-free, they can make big mistakes. Both, undoubtedly, had visions of what reality ultimately was, but events and discontinuity were beyond their grasp.

An important happening in that era was "Hellenism," the spread of Greek ideas throughout the remnants of Alexander the Great's empire. What exactly was spread seems to depend upon which authority you consult.

Also, emerging in the late B.C. to early A.D. period was an enthusiasm for "improving" Greek thought and "reconciling" it with Christianity, probably started in Alexandria, Egypt. The initial manifestations of this were gnosticism and hermeticism. Later was the Jewish Kabbalist movement – mysticism regarding Biblical numbers.

The land of Palestine had several theaters and sporting venues on the Greek model, introduced about 170 B.C. – including that athletes competed naked. We get some idea of the stress all this put on the Jewish faith when we consider the Maccabbean Revolt and the later strife between the Sadducees and the Pharisees.

Neopythagoreanism was born in the first and second centuries A.D. It re-emphasized number and introduced (reemphasized) magic and demons. Some say this was a partial reaction to the growing Christianity; neopythagoreans wanted to show that paganism had a coherent view of reality. They were ascetic, harmonized the old masters, yet emphasized astrology. Leaders were such as Nicomachus of Gersa and Numenius of Apamea.

Neoplatonism was born around A.D. 270. It was founded by Ammonius Saccas in Alexandria, but the written works came through Plotinus, Porphyry (and his *Enneads*), Iamblichus and Proclus. Neoplatonism harmonized the old masters, added the names of the pagan Greek gods, allowed astrology and magic, accepted an infinite cosmos, commended Plato's geocentric cosmos, reincarnation, was against Atomism and Christianity. (See also B44, pages 48-49.)

Neoplatonism was fascinated with the Greek translation of the Hebrew Bible, the *Septuagint*, particularly of the book of *Genesis,* and tried to reconcile it with Plato's *Timaeus*. (The event of ex *nihilo* creation could not be reconciled to the eventless ahistorical mathematical line and the subsequent "sightseeing.")

Both of these neo's originated in Alexandria, Egypt. Interestingly, Plotinus, as a student of Saccus, had as a fellow student, Origin, an early church Father.

Some historians point out that **Alexandrian** *mathematics* was different from **Athenian** *mathematics*. As the previous chapter showed, Plato forbade zero, negative, fractions and irrational numbers and emphasized rigorous geometrical proofs. Thus, they emphasized geometry – and arithmetic and algebra were discouraged. Yet, Alexandria made few advances in geometry, but advanced algebra and started trigonometry. *Both of these relied heavily on irrational numbers.*

Could this change in emphasis have been an impact due to Aristotle's influence? This shift in Alexandrian emphasis may be a witness to a rational shock among mathematicians due to Aristotle's reasonable unbelief of many Platonic concepts.

For some, rigorous geometric proof gradually shifted their rational view of geometry. It became "nature's inherent *geometric necessity*," rather than "manna from heaven." The deductions could be supported without Plato's geometric heaven, particularly with the publication of increasing numbers of geometry works. Mathematics supposedly emancipated reason from polytheism, but Greek thinkers predominantly clung to a foundationless mathematical vision (subjectivity).

Rationalists promoted Plato to a figurehead status. Without his *anamnesis,* reason became self-evident, no longer needing manna from heaven. Despite a flurry of fine words, mathematics and reason are *unanchored* concepts. Reason cannot prove reason; using itself to prove itself is a circular argument. Plato avoided this circular argument by his *anamnesis,* but his materialist successors abandoned it. These later Greek rationalists believed reason pointed to geometry and geometry pointed back to reason. This rational thought was a circular argument about abstractions, if one cared to notice. So it was an act of faith to "assent" to it as incarnate in matter! (Only time would tell if people would continue to see reason as objective, or just a tool at the disposal of mankind's private understandings.)

Rationalists rallied around arithmetic, geometry and logical categories. There were enough hints in Plato and Aristotle to "justify" this move. Foundational subjectivity and mathematical abstractions allowed grandiose extrapolation.

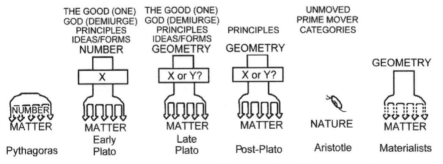

Rationalists, unlike Pythagoras or Plato or Aristotle, were no longer proto-atheist, but atheist. Their cosmos was not perforated, not even by philosopher's gods. Geometry, like number, was a self-existing entity whose perforation of reality was "given." *For materialists, geometry existed!* It was the interpretive key to the unperforated cosmos! Even if matter is no longer incarnate geometry, matter is, at the least, *ruled* by geometry. Matter did not precede mathematics; perhaps they are coeternal. Anyhow, gods are excluded because matter is infinite. With this "slight"

change to Platonic rational thought, these newer rationalists inherited all previous science and went on to systematize all data.

A few rationalists or fact gatherers cannot be connected to these schools of philosophy, such as Archimedes, Ptolemy of Egypt and Euclid.

A lasting result of Greek thought was Euclid's *Elements* (of number and geometry). This work highlighted the earlier progress in mathematics. The *Elements* transmitted to later ages the belief in the orderly and mathematical design of the cosmos. (This was deterministic design, not created design.) Indeed, it was the closest they could get to the "mind of god." It held out the hope that mankind, "aided" by mathematics, can transcend their earthly limitations and acquire knowledge about everything. "Aided" revealed truth should be unnecessary!

The *Elements* had a two-fold character. While it was formulated as an abstract subject, most of it was physically obvious. The exception was Euclid's "parallel postulate." It spoke about the inaccessible – do parallel lines meet at infinity? This non-empirical statement was important to astronomy but would be vulnerable several thousand years later. Perhaps empiricism is more important and the subject should be left unresolved.

Free and autonomous reason also acquired a deep distrust of history; it always went back to the gods. Whether presently active or on the horizon as creators or catastrophic shakers of events, deities were always there. Their irrationality and capriciousness were so historical and unmathematical – just like real people! Relegating the gods to superstition allowed thinkers to extrapolate ahistorically.

Following Greek "science's" deductive "proof" that physical reality is geometrical, the next question stemming from man's insatiable curiosity is: "How big is reality?" Reasonably, if matter is geometrical, if geometry is self-evident truth, and if deductive proof is impervious to criticism, *then what is the only rational answer?* In other words, how far does that ahistorical mathematical line extend, or what is the largest number one can count to? The science of measure became a self-fulfilling abstraction; *the universe is infinite.*

> The conception of the infinity of the universe, like everything else or nearly everything else, originates, of course, with the Greeks... (B45, page 1.)

The Greeks referred to are (inconsistent) contemporaries of Plato, for as we have seen, Zeno's paradoxes of motion reinforced Plato's aversion to infinity. Plato spoke about indeterminate dimensions; he avoided an actual infinity. Geometric purists were not so timid. One of these, Ocellus Lucanus, (variously given as fifth or second century B.C.), said:

> Further, it is credible that the universe is without a beginning, and without end, from its figure, motion, time and essence; and therefore it may be concluded that the world is unbegotten and incorruptible, *for its figure is circular, and as a circular figure is similar and equal on all sides, it is therefore without a beginning or end.* Circular is also the motion of the universe, but this motion is *stable and without*

transition.[9] Time, likewise, in which motion exists, is infinite, for neither had this a beginning .... From all these arguments, therefore, it is obviously credible that the world is unbegotten and incorruptible. (B35, page 205. Emphasis added. Footnote added.)

Rational thought "knew" astronomy was incarnate mathematics long before physics became so. Since the inception of "science," men have falsely drawn the conclusion that *astronomy proves that matter is infinite in age and extent, uncreated, eventless and determined. Ahistorical reason prohibits created facts. Reason therefore has no limit and its mathematics is the sole means of acquiring knowledge.* (The Atomists forthrightly believed in an infinite universe, without appeal to a geometric structure.) As a corollary, godlessness, materialism and meaninglessness are "necessary" deductions.

As at its birth in Greece, so at its rebirth in the "century of genius" [Italian Renaissance, A.D. 1450-1550] reason was not the free and irresponsible play of ideas but a radical and infrangible *conviction* that *in astronomical thought man was in contact with an absolute order of the cosmos*; it is truly a living faith in the illimitable power of the mind, but only in so far as it is admitted that *mathematical reasoning* releases a *transcendental* source of *certainty* which is more than our individual analytic power. (B46, page 5. Emphasis added.)

The science of measure – and its astronomy – is high metaphysics ... and "the" great fact! Grandiose extrapolation – astronomical extrapolation – was securely anchored. Science, falsely so-called, has always been identified by its close connection with mathematics, and mathematics with astronomy. Frequently, astronomy is referred to as the "queen of the sciences." (But what if mathematical reasoning does not produce certainty, but only wrestles with *rafts of data adrift on oceans of mathematics*? What if complex mathematics allows choices? What if acceptance requires belief in unseen paradigms, not "assent" to truth? What then?)

The science of measure revealed to its followers these "truths" about eternal, uncreated matter in its infinite cosmos – attributes once given to God. Granted, Plato, Aristotle and Euclid referred only to indeterminate dimensions due to their concern over Zeno's paradoxes and their aversion to atheism. (Although Aristotle gave it an infinite boundary, he considered it a potential infinite, not an actual infinite.) However, the adventure acquired belief in infinity and it grew with time. The Atomists believed it: Anaximander, Democritus, Epicurus, Diogenes Laertius and Lucretius. The neoplatonists generally believed it but quibbled over whether it was a potential or actual infinite.

It may be difficult for twenty-first century people to see what this ancient fuss over infinity and astronomy was about. If these are just about outer space, what is so important about that expanse of nothing? Well, after sacrificing to the gods or divining the future by reading animal organs, it comforted them to know "a lot of nothing" was all there was. The rigid nothingness of infinity provided a firm (and

---

9   Could this praising of the perfection of circular motion have influenced Copernicus and Galileo? Note also how "evolution" was unthinkable when the "deeper sciences" said reality is "stable and without transition."

comforting?) foundation by confirming the absence of the capricious gods.[10]

Some say that Plato's Academy in Athens lasted about 900 years, until closed by the Christian Eastern Roman Emperor Justinian in A.D. 529. (The Western Roman Empire had fallen to the barbarians fifty years earlier.) Actually, Plato's Academy was destroyed about 86 B.C. by the Romans when they conquered Athens. After a lapse of 500 years, in A.D. 410, a neoplatonic group formed a new Academy, which is what lasted until A.D. 529. But what would Plato have thought of the neoplatonic doctrine taught in his name? He might have been glad it was closed!

> The Academy [of Plato] and the Lyceum [of Aristotle] seem to have had continuous existence until the beginning of the first century B.C. (perhaps until the sack of Athens by the Roman general Sulla in 86 B.C.) ... Neo-platonists *refounded* the Academy in the fifth century A.D. and managed to keep it alive until about [AD] 560 or later; however, there was no institutional continuity between this and Plato's school. (B46, page 73. Emphasis in original.)

By then, Athens was in decline. Intellectually; it was replaced by Alexandria, Egypt. Politically, it was eclipsed by Rome and Constantinople.

Depending upon continent and era, history shows either Aristotle or Plato as favored. In the Middle Ages, part of Aristotle's system was incorporated into St. Thomas Aquinas's "Scholasticism." While this downgraded mathematics, the general desire for a cosmic perspective made it difficult to separate geometry from the Platonic strains and arithmetic from Pythagorean strains.[11]

Another factor causing doubt regarding which philosophical system was true centered on Plato's mandate that astronomers only use circles when explaining geocentric planetary motions. Two contradictory procedures were devised that both saved the appearances.

One came from Aristotle's school, involving crystalline spheres and rollers, a "physical" model centered on the earth. It was soon realized this scheme did not save all the appearances. Later, Ptolemy of Alexandria built on the work of Eudoxus and developed his mathematical treatise on the planets, the *Almagest*.[12] It utilized epicycles, but was neither physical nor exactly centered on the earth. Ptolemy's

---

10   Astronomers believed that the cosmos was bounded by the celestial sphere. Stellar parallax could not be detected, so they were, at the least, a long way away.

Considering atheorism, the then concern was how to explain geocentricity. Heliocentricity was then perhaps unknown, due to Plato's triangles and circular mandate. For all we know, there may be more than two ways to save the appearances of the ancient sky – and I am not championing any of them.

11   "True" Platonism did not last long, so the question arises: Did Plato actually believe in his theory of *anamnesis* for securing geometric truths? Sir Karl Popper, for one, in his *The Open Society and its Enemies* (B41), concludes that Plato was cynical and opportunistic. Yet, the either-or style of argumentation, the mathematical modeling pervading Plato's writing and his adherence to Pythagorean physical arithmetic lend weight to the belief that Plato was committed to his *anamnesis*.

12   The *Almagest* gave "line-of-sight" positions for heavenly bodies, using epicycles. This was its "damnable excellence," as some have said. When astronomy was asked to give more – such as distance or physical causes – the *Almagest's* shortcomings became apparent.

system was the more observationally accurate of the two – though less faithful to the science of measure. Conflicts between the two understandings were in the public arena and continued into the Middle Ages, exposing the nature of mathematics to fierce controversy. (See *To Save the Phenomena*, B42, by Pierre Duhem.)

As said earlier, this fierce controversy was not about science. Rarely was astronomy in the limited domain of science. The controversy also evidenced rational and reasonable failures!

C. S. Lewis, the English apologist, reports a modern example of the importance attached to this musty dusty history. He reports a conversation he once had:

"These are rather niggling points," said my friend. "You see, the real objection [to Christianity] goes far deeper. The whole picture of the universe which science has given us makes it such rot to believe that the Power at the back of it all could be interested in us tiny creatures crawling around on an unimportant planet! It was all so obviously invented by people who believed in a flat earth with the stars only a mile or two away." (B48, page 74.)

We will save Lewis' response until a later chapter, but between a couple of miles and infinity there is room for many systematizing models.

Despite contention in the ranks, and promoting Plato to a figurehead status, the "all-seeing" intellectual adventure initiated by Plato became, and remains, the ultimate, objective proof of atheism. When facing Christian criticism, the contending voices fall back and regroup around geometry. Deductive proof showed that reason can derive ahistorical monotruth (Universal Natural Law), thereby destroying the subjective world of polytheism – polytruth. Geometric relationships were found throughout nature, assuring them that knowledge was identified by its connection to a "physical" mathematics. *Geometry existed – and its physical incarnation or rule fulfilled the lure of objective truth! There was no need for alternative systematizations – or merely useful formulas – or radical doubt HERE.*

Thus nothing more was needed to explain reality? As monotruth thinkers, this justified their fierce antagonism to polytheism – and to Jewish or Christian monotheism! *Polytruth would also be the death of science, falsely so-called.* They defined two opposing sentences: religion is subjective (poly-opinion); "Science" is objective (mono-truth). "Public knowledge" showed that between these lay an unbridgeable chasm, commonly referred to as the reason versus faith dilemma. "Success" in unraveling nature's secrets made men of science (and of science, falsely so-called) realize they were involved in more than a dull search for facts. Their free and autonomous reason drew them into a love bond with boundless truth, goodness, and beauty! "Science" freed man from bias. Its truth trans-

The NEW Lawgiver

cended all labels, understandings, and creeds. This truth, this objectivity, this love would break down all barriers dividing men of goodwill! With a clear conscience, they "knew" it was their *duty* to bring others to this "knowledge." This simplistic epistemology was most intoxicating.

Materialism, meaninglessness, and godlessness are rational deductions implicit in the NEW lawgiver and the unperforated cosmos. These deductions also can be called secular or naturalistic. In truth, it may be hard to sort out their priority claims. Many think "history is bunk,"[13] so role reversals are possible.

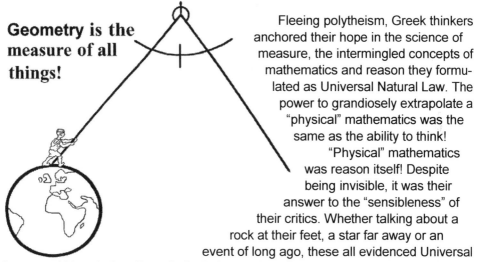

Geometry is the measure of all things!

Fleeing polytheism, Greek thinkers anchored their hope in the science of measure, the intermingled concepts of mathematics and reason they formulated as Universal Natural Law. The power to grandiosely extrapolate a "physical" mathematics was the same as the ability to think! "Physical" mathematics was reason itself! Despite being invisible, it was their answer to the "sensibleness" of their critics. Whether talking about a rock at their feet, a star far away or an event of long ago, these all evidenced Universal Connected Knowledge. From limited observation of geo-apparent natural regularities, rationalists used the science of measure to "prove" Universal Natural Law.

In the definitions in the opening chapter, we saw the challenge of determining the relationship of mathematical abstraction to reality. Their simplistic and "physical" mathematics *eliminated* this concern. Mathematics and reality were the same!

Rational thought of the day said science (falsely so-called) was truth. But that was shorthand to express, or hide, the "all-seeing" capability of *knosis*. *Scientia* (rationalism) in summary: *reason and objective truth and mathematics and grandiose extrapolation and monotruth and atheism are inseparable.*

Greek philosophers feared that doubting the science of measure would set in motion a chain of thought showing that "unaided" reason contains an admixture of subjectivity in its unseen mathematical "aids." They feared a collapse back into polytheism if the science of measure was not impervious to criticism.

How ironic, people today criticize various aspects of modern "science" – but not its unblushing use of Greek extrapolative infatuation.

This maturing storytelling knew the challenge. Polytheism – then Judaic and

---

13   History is bunk: A phrase I read somewhere. The idea that no guiding thoughts for "technological man" come from history. History diminishes in intelligibility when compared to modern intellectual achievements. The world's "messiness" contradicts the ahistorical mathematical line.

Christian theism – were their competitors. God and creation *ex nihilo* were their antithesis. Greek storytellers did not claim that a material cosmos was self-created. In harmony with their Science of Measure, the only rational alternative claim was for an infinite and eternally existing cosmos. This was in their mind's eye; this was the philosophy of the epoch.[14]

As this section draws to a close, we need to draw out the conclusion inherent in various references to mathematics and astronomy. To illustrate the "big picture," we use the words of Aristotle:

... For in the whole range of times past, so far as our inherited records reach, no change appears to have taken place in the whole scheme of the outermost heaven or in any of its proper parts. (B40, Vol. 1, page 451.)

The "outermost heaven" meant the region of the fixed stars, which "then" began just beyond the planets.

In good mathematical fashion, their timeline of history is infinite! "Unaided" mathematics easily affirms this.

Yet Plato had some qualms about the beginning, as he had talked about the "immature" stage of the basic triangles. In his *Timaeus*, he talked about Atlantis and its destruction, referred to a deluge(s) and to a "declination of the bodies moving in the heaven *around* the earth." [*Timaeus* 22a – 25d]. But mature triangles obeyed laws! Also, there was the memory of the violent earthquake and tsunami that centuries earlier had destroyed the Minoan civilization on the island of Crete.

In his *Statesman*, 269a and 272e – 273a, Plato talked about "the alteration in rising and setting of the sun and the other planets. The story tells us that on this famous occasion these all set where they now rise and rose where they now set." And that "a shudder passed through the world at the reversing of its rotation."

The (mature) planets were gods, (now) obeyed the laws, and were not wandering stars! So, these earlier reports were not considered mumbo jumbo, but historical reports from when the triangles were young! Thus the ahistorical mathematical line allowed some initial "events," but probably not in the outermost heaven.

But, getting back to Aristotle's comment, how far back did Greek "inherited records reach?" The blind poet, Homer, lived about 400 years earlier, around 800 B.C., but his epics weren't written down until later. Another early writer was Hesiod. Both writers presented a "war of the gods" as a backdrop to their histories. So written Greek records went back to no earlier than around 800 B.C. Greek poets preserved "stories" and they were also on pottery and statues. They do not uniformly show a lawful planetary system. More myth or more limitations to extrapolation(?).

Further, Pythagoras, among others, traveled in the Middle-East. Did they

14   As knowledge of reality and mathematics grew, this storytelling had repeated revisions.

encounter the same beliefs in these countries? Egyptians, Babylonians, Assyrians, and Persians had written records – on stone or clay tablets. Some recorded astronomical observations did not agree that the ancient sky was always harmonious.

Another criticism of Aristotle comes from Aristotle himself. In his *Meteorology*, he says: "Of the so-called Pythagoreans some say that this [the milky way] is the path of one of the stars that fell from heaven during the alleged destruction at the time of Phaethon. Others say that the sun used once to move in this circle." [B40, *Meteorology* 345, 13–16.] But Aristotle declared this to be impossible.

Aristotle also famously dismissed comets as real objects. He considered them as light phenomena in the sub-lunar region (below the orbit of the moon). This declaration preserved the unaltered constancy of the outermost heavens, in accordance with the nature of aether, the fifth element.

Greek astronomical records did not include the heavens over the southern hemisphere nor the data in such as ancient Chinese records. All-in-all, Aristotle's statement had limited Mediterranean area facts to support it. [15]

The most blatant departure from Greek views were in the Jewish Scriptures, and they dated back to many centuries earlier. Three incidents are highlighted: *ex nihilo* Creation (*ca.* 4,000 B.C.), the worldwide flood in Noah's time (*ca.* 2,500 B.C.) and the Exodus events, including Joshua's long day (*ca.* 1,450 B.C.).

So were Greek philosopher's statements about astronomy accurate? Anthropologists who study "primitive or de-civilized" people report that all have creation and universal flood accounts. The Babylonian Gilgamesh Epic is frequently mentioned.

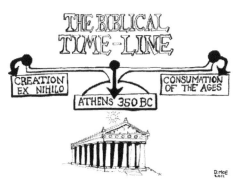

The Bible records "Joshua's long day" in Joshua 10: 11-14. I hope no one is surprised that this event cannot be reconciled with Greek ahistorical mathematical "science!" Does that mean the Joshua episode is myth? If you revere the Greek ahistorical mathematical line, it must be myth! But consider the following: If the sun stands still in the Middle East in the afternoon, what was that time in the rest of the world? In the Americas, it would have been a "long sunrise." In Asia, it would have been a "long sunset." Giving allowance for dating uncertainties, the ancient worldwide references have the requisite hour-shift to synchronize them with the Exodus account.

Ex Nihilo creation, Noah's flood and Joshua's long day violated the cherished ahistorical mathematical line! And these Biblical historical records overlap somewhat with some of the stories in such as Homer and Hesiod. It is possible to get to

---

15   In the *Annals of the World* by Bishop James Usshur [1581-1656] there is recorded an interesting note for 331 B.C. (due to either Josephus or Simplicius). Alexander the Great talked with the Chaldeans about "the movement of the heavenly bodies." Alexander forwarded to Aristotle their observations for 1903 years. Whether they influenced Aristotle is unknown as he was soon to leave Athens and die a few years later. I suppose those records are lost.

the other side of these events, but has the course of nature been deflected from the original straight line? *For what is "minor" in thousands of years is unwieldy in an infinite time frame!* Men do not merely assent to Reason 101! So we should look again at:

The fear of the Lord is the beginning of knowledge.

No wonder Greek "wisdom" did not conquer Biblical peoples.

Are these ancient accounts intercontinental synchronized myth-ology – with regular

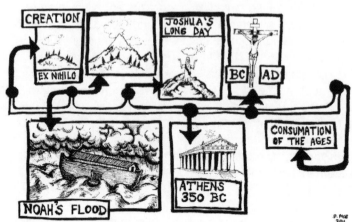

intercontinental mythology conferences? (Anyone ready for an exciting cross-ocean canoe ride?) The Greeks affirmed them to be mythological using mathematics or logic. They knew what Universal Connectedness required! So they could theorize – sightsee. Assuming that, in whole or part, historical reports are mythical, it was obvious that we live in an unperforated cosmos. Which is to say, they offered Reason 101: 1-2. (And we can't appeal to Isaac Newton, Albert Einstein or the Quantum Mechanics folks. They will speak later.)

What practical difference does it make? It is a major problem.

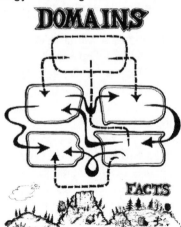

Is Greek cosmic incarnated mathematics a myth or is eyesight a myth? Was such mathematics story-telling or a Universal Natural Law – monotruth? No wonder astronomy was considered the "queen of the sciences." This "science" turned earlier historical reports into "myth" and allowed science to "prove" mathematical determinism! Yet, perhaps

saving the appearances in astronomy has to allow for periods of change, followed by a dampening down to quietude. The historical earthly tremors of earthquakes, volcanoes and tsunamis are further examples. (And later discontinuous physical processes were to be discovered. They cannot be grandiosely extrapolated. Thus, history trumps the ahistorical mathematical line contrary to what ancient rationalists said!) If a modern person used a time-machine to visit ancient Greece, would the Law "discovered" by geometrical circles-upon-circles, revealed via *anamnesis* from the heaven of Forms and Principles be story-telling or truth?

Neither Greek polytheism or Greek philosophy presented objective arguments. They both mingled strange ideas into their discourses.

(From later centuries, you probably have heard arguments from rationalists to the effect that "we cannot allow God to have a foot in the door." Many people agree that the supernatural *ex nihilo* creation threatens the ahistorical mathematical line – but *they overlook that the same threat comes from any discontinuity, such as earthquakes, volcanoes, or tsunamis!*)

We repeat the insightful quotation made in the last chapter by G. K. Chesterton, but with an additional section:

There comes a time in the routine of an ordered civilization when the man is tired [of] playing at mythology and pretending that a tree is a maiden or that the moon made love to a man. The effect of this staleness is the same everywhere; it is seen in all drugtaking and dram-drinking and every form of the tendency to increase the dose. Men seek stranger sins or more startling obscenities as stimulants to their jaded sense .... They try to stab their nerves to life .... All round the circle of the Mediterranean cities the people mourned for the loss of the gods and were consoled with gladiators. And meanwhile something similar was happening to the intellectual aristocracy of antiquity that had been walking about and talking at large ever since Socrates and Pythagoras. They began to betray to the world the fact that they were walking in a circle and saying the same thing over and over again. Philosophy began to be a joke; it also began to be a bore. That unnatural simplification of everything into one system or another ... revealed at once its finality and its futility. Everything was virtue or everything was happiness or everything was fate or everything was good or everything was bad; anyhow, everything was everything and there was no more to be said; so they said it. (B9, pages 164, 166.)

Imagine that several of these rationalists came together after a sleepless night. They were somewhat embarrassed, but finally talked about what bothered each of them. One said he had dreamed and had fallen into a conversation with some arithmeticians who tried to convince him that arithmetic was foundationless – or derived from playing with marbles. Actually, many had tried and, instead, came up with competing foundational theories. Then another reported that he had fallen in with a company of geometers in strange clothes and strange accents. He only remembered the names of Rieman and Lobatschewsky. They said they had invented / discovered geometries that contradicted what was soon to be called Euclidean geometry. Another reported that he had run into other strangers who said Aristotle's logic had flaws. Aristotle was not the only founder of a school of logic.

What could this all mean? Was rational thought killing itself? "Unaided" reason was being oversold! Revealed truth ("aided" reason) showed its superiority.

[Arithmetic, geometry and logic are not within rational proof. How can they refute the transcendent God of the Bible? If not at this beginning bookend of history, when does reason – or does it – acquire a rational basis for its grandiose extrapolations?]

As we reflect on this hidden, yet obvious, path that wends back through history, we note that *Greek thinkers did not prove:*
• the "incarnation" of mathematics or logic into matter. Both remain useful abstractions. Without this "incarnation," grandiose extrapolation was subjective and "origins" lost its Greek rationale.
• the impossibility of zero, negative, fractional or irrational numbers.
• the reality of a physical infinity.
• that a deterministic cosmos and its ahistorical mathematical line coexist with events or discontinuity – even of present realities such as earthquakes, volcanoes and tsunamis. *Ex nihilo* creation was the rational alternative.
• the irrationality of algebra and trigonometry.
• that they had found LAW or causality, rather than saving (some of) the appearances.
• natural motion is circular or that linear motion is forced.
• that "qualities" were unreal.
• that rationalists agree on reality.
• that reductionism is not an escape mechanism from flaws in the "all-seeing" eye or from inter-domain problems.

The Greek era greatly advanced mathematics and logic. They also began to learn many things about the playing field. But this empirical arena did not exclusively belong to them. Accessible reality and "inaccessible" reality remained unhelpful to each other. Yet, "unaided" reason remained so incensed with polytheism that they reflected little on the subjective nature of Mathematic's Word.

We must continue on our journey on that hidden, yet obvious, path …

We now move forward to the early interaction of Greek thought with Christianity. Conflict early arose. As we read part of *Genesis* chapter one, areas of conflict between Biblical revelation and Greek philosophy are evident:

In the *beginning* God *created* the heaven and the earth.
And the earth was without form, and *void*; and darkness was upon the face of the deep. And the *Spirit of God* moved upon the face of the waters.

> And God *said*, Let there be light: and there was light. (*Genesis* 1:1-3. Emphasis added.)

Which spoke for truth? Obedience to the Godly news of transcendent revelation? Or "unaided" reason, with the "aid" of mathematics, anchored far from the footsteps of mankind? The "unaided" faced an unpleasant choice: Christianity or intellectual adventure!

Why didn't the Lord inspire a few more lines of explanatory revelation about the origin of the cosmos? The answer is not given, but the early church Fathers can be instructive. Listen to Irenaeus:

> For [the Old Testament prophets] did not use *demonstration* in their treatises, seeing that they were *witnesses* to the truth above all demonstration. (B49, Volume 1, page 198. Emphasis added.)

The well-reasoned mindset of science, falsely so-called, in "fulfilling" the lure of objective truth, rejected the witness to the Gospel and the created fact. *Yet, an eyewitness to an "event" does not need "demonstration" to report truth! Acts* chapter 17 narrates St. Paul's encounter with such rationalists (and pagans) in Athens.

> Now, while Paul waited for [his companions] at Athens, his spirit was stirred in him, when he saw the city wholly given to idolatry …. Then certain philosophers of the Epicureans, and of the Stoicks, encountered him: and some said, What will this babbler say? Other some, He seemeth to be a setter forth of strange gods; because he preached unto them Jesus, and the resurrection …. (For all the Athenians, and strangers which were there, spent their time in nothing else, but either to tell, or to hear some new thing.) (*Acts* 18:16, 18, 21.)

Granted, St Paul in this visit to Athens, around A.D. 55, reveals that he encountered the Epicureans, who were atomists. But the Stoics were anti-Atomists! The followers of Plato and Aristotle are not mentioned; they were then in demise. Athen's thinkers were a quarrelsome crowd.

Such folk considered the following Biblical truths to be heretical and unscientific: The proclamation that God had *ex nihilo* created the cosmos; was interested in the cosmos; had visited the earth via His Spirit; then perforated the cosmos by sending His Son to earth; His dying on the cross and then raising Him from the dead.[16] A prelude to the Gospel was in order.

Pythagorean and Platonic thought saw the "god" eternally in heaven, noncommunicative, and attended by lesser souls who also never descended. The descended masters were definitely lower class but still exalted. As Plato stated:

---

16   In addition, the Pythagorean / Platonic viewpoint stipulated that "knowledge" was the key to an upward return to the best gods. Christianity says a repentant, cleansed heart is the criteria of salvation unto God. Also, Christianity stresses that salvation is open to both men *and* women – of all strata of life! "Scientists of the day" considered that contrary to sound reason. They *reasonably* excluded women because they needed to be reincarnated into the higher life form of animal man! This wasn't a sexist statement, because plain, animal man had to be, in turn, reincarnated as gnostic man/philosopher!

   Tertullian addresses some of the claims for reincarnation. While reincarnation began with an initial "oblivion," Pythagoras claimed to remember his past lives. Why only Pythagoras? Why not Plato? Why not me? And he discusses other problems. (B49, Volume III, pages 211-214.)

Now, when all of [the class of lesser gods], both those who visibly appear in their revolutions [as planets] as well as those other gods who are of a more retiring nature, had come into being, the creator of the universe addressed them in these words .... Three tribes of mortal beings remain to be created .... [I]f they were created by me and received life at my hands, they would be on an equality with the gods. In order then that they may be mortal, and that this universe may be truly universal, do ye, according to your natures, betake yourselves to the formation of animals, imitating the power which was shown by me in creating you....

Plato then elaborates on the reincarnational ladder:

If [the implanted souls in mortals] conquered these [feelings and passions] they would live righteously, and if they were conquered by them, unrighteously. He who lived well during his appointed time was to return and dwell in his native star... But if he failed in attaining this, at the second birth, he would pass into a woman, and if, when in that state of mind, he did not desist from evil, he would continually be changed into some brute who resembled him in the evil nature which he had acquired....

Plato next reveals the mathematical decay that intervened in "history:"

And [the lesser gods] did in fact at that time create a very great and mighty movement; uniting with the ever-flowing stream in stirring up and violently shaking the courses of the soul ... and they so disturbed the nature of the other or diverse that the three double intervals (that is, between 1, 2, 4, 8) and the three triple intervals (that is, between 1, 3, 9, 27), together with the mean terms and connecting links which are expressed by the ratios 3:2 and 4:3 and of 9:8 – these, although they cannot be wholly undone except by him who united them, were twisted by them in all sorts of ways, and the circles were broken.... (B28, pages 1171-1172. *Timaeus* 41a-c, 42b-c, 43c-e.)

This is not paganism or mumbo jumbo, but the sacred mathematical subjectivity of philosophers. They and their Æons became cultural barriers.

More of Plato's comments on the reincarnation of women are appropriate:

On the subject of animals, then, the following remarks may be offered. Of the men who came into the world, those who were cowards or who led unrighteous lives may with reason be supposed to have changed into the nature of women in the second generation. (B28. *Timaeus* 90e.)

Thus were created women and the female sex in general. But the race of birds was created out of innocent light-minded men .... The race of wild pedestrian animals, again, came from those who had no philosophy in any of their thoughts. (B28. *Timaeus* 91d-e.)

These are the laws by which all animals pass into one another, now, as in the beginning, changing as they lose or gain wisdom and folly. (B28.*Timaeus* 92c.)

Can you imagine "family life" between "enlightened" men and "recidivist" women within this intellectual view? (Plato seemed to assert that only men were in the original creation. Substandard males were reincarnated as women and others.)

Compared to such Greek "truths," New Testament writers reiterated events considered "foolish" to both pagan and well-reasoned Greeks, such as the fact that Jesus Christ was both True God and True Man; that He acknowledged no intellectual class distinctions; that His disciples had walked with Him and witnessed His miracles, death and resurrection.

Recall the admonition in 1 Timothy 6:20 "*avoiding science falsely so-called.*" Colossians 2:8 further admonished: "*Beware lest any man spoil you through philosophy and vain deceit, after the tradition of men, after the rudiments of the world, and not after Christ.*" Other New Testament references to myths and fables could likewise refer to science, falsely so-called.

Paradoxically, when atheism contacted the unfamiliar theism of Christianity (monotheism), these confident "scientists" were dumbfounded when some Christians [perhaps unwisely] quoted Plato, "God eternally geometricizes!" Applied to *Genesis*, order (geometric patterns) evidenced God's design. The cosmos, as God's *poema*, was a stable creation; it was not chaotic, unsystematic or eternal.

(Euclidean) geometry was thus no more than "thinking God's thoughts after Him." This throttled the atheistic thrust by pointing to the emerging facts within the "book of nature" as the imprint of the longstanding monotruth revealed in Scripture. Both witnessed to the transcendent God of Scripture's orderly creation.

"Universal" statements could avoid being dismissed as intellectual adventure only if validated by experience or infallible report. Man's "unaided" reason cannot provide validation, having no foundation independent from the selfsame creation. Nor could that rational abstraction, mathematics, reliably probe beyond history. *Only God can validate a cosmic perspective.* Scripture gives His transcendent revelation, "aided" reason, which rebuked the well-reasoned for their extrapolative infatuation, "aided" by their "all-seeing" mathematics.

This Biblical insight united the faith and reason of men of good will – particularly those converted from science, falsely so-called. Reason did not need a cosmic extrapolation for a foundation. The orderly playing field was to yield its secrets without recourse to godlessness, materialism, or meaninglessness. Accordingly, science flourished in the Christian perforated cosmos of design. Mathematicians, observers, philosophers and thinkers found creation's stability and order as reasons to rationally investigate the accessible, along with engineers, craftsmen and tinkerers. Monotheism provided the anchor, and monotruth proceeded therefrom.

Mankind remained the center of God's attention, and the earth remained the center of the finite cosmos. This allowed Greek geocentric astronomy to "harmonize" with Christianity. Objects in perfect circular orbits could be nowhere but where they were; evolution was not required to get them there. Causality[17] and the lure of objective truth were satisfied. It meant much the same as to say, "*In the beginning God created ...*" Whether Platonic or Aristotelian (in dimension) or Biblical, the cosmos was finite. (But the details change with time.)

(Jumping ahead momentarily, it was not until the Enlightenment that atheists

---

17   Causality: Effects have causes. This does not prove materialism – it could take an infinite regress to prove that God is not the first cause of the cosmos or to prove the cosmos is utterly large and unperforated. Rationalists need an infinite regress to obscure the fact that they had no knowledge about the original motion. Christians add that the word, *cosmos*, does not imply that a material cause initiates all motion or generates the original matter. The supernatural can create or intervene, this is miraculous and its out-of-the-ordinariness identifies these occurrences. Further, human minds can initiate local motion in our spheres of influence. The historical initiation of both of these causes is incalculable. The results, though, can be "sensed."

regained enough credibility and momentum to begin wresting intellectual leadership back from Christianity.)

As mentioned in the introduction, Biblical writers and the early church Fathers understood the intellectual climate in which they lived. Irenaeus, Justin Martyr, Tertullian, and Hippolytus show their concerns in the period from A.D. 150 to 220. They wrote treatises against heresies – derived from either paganism, philosophy or religion mingled with philosophy. These were necessary preludes to their Gospel presentations to seekers influenced by well-reasoned storytellers.

Hippolytus [*ca.* A.D. 170 - ca. 245], in his *The Refutation of all Heresies*, begins with what seems like a roll call of Greek philosophy:

Among natural philosophers may be enumerated Thales, Pythagoras, Empedocles, Heraclitus, Anaximander, Anaximenes, Anaxagoras, Archelaus, Parmenides, Leucippus, Democritus, Xenophanes, Ecphantus, Hippo.

Among moral philosophers are Socrates, pupil of Archelaus the physicist, (and) Plato the pupil of Socrates. This (speculator) combined three systems of philosophy.

Among logicians is Aristotle, pupil of Plato. He systematized the art of dialectics. Among the Stoic (logicians) were Chrysippus (and) Zeno. Epicurus, however, advanced an opinion almost contrary to all philosophers. Pyrrho was an Academic; this speculator taught the incomprehensibility of everything. The Brahmins among the Indians, and the Druids among the Celts, and Hesiod (devoted themselves to philosophic pursuits). (B49, Vol. 5, page 9.)

Hippolytus goes on to discuss details. The following excerpt about the contradictory answers provided gives the flavor of the times:

Hippasus of Metapontum and Heraclitus the Ephesian declared the origin *of things to be* from fire, whereas Anaximander from air, but Thales from water, and Xenophanes from earth .... But Empedocles *derives the universe* from four principles .... Oscellus, however, the Lucanian, and Aristotle, *derive the universe* from five *principles* .... The *followers*, however, of Anaxagoras of Clazomenae, and of Democritus, and of Epicurus, and multitudes of others, have given it as their opinion that the generation of the universe *proceeds* from infinite *numbers of atoms* .... But the *disciples* of Plato affirm that these *entities* are from three principles. (B49, Vol. 5, page 141. Emphasis added, italics in original.)

Schools of conflicting philosophy dotted the Mediterranean world. "Lovers of truth" were fragmented; polytruth was everywhere, just as St Basil was quoted at the beginning of the chapter!

In the *Hortatory Address to the Greeks* (once attributed to Justin Martyr, but now attributed to an anonymous source somewhat later), after reviewing a similar list of Greek philosophy, the author says:

You see, then, the confusion of those who are considered by you to have been wise men, whom you assert to be your teachers of religion .... How then, ye men of Greece, can it be safe for those who desire to be saved, to fancy that they can learn the true religion from these philosophers, who were neither able so to convince themselves as to prevent sectarian wrangling with one another, and not to appear definitely opposed to one another's opinions. (B49, Vol. 1, page 275.)

Tertullian, in *On Prescription Against Heretics*, (*c.a.*, 200 A.D.), made his famous comment about Athens and Jerusalem:

These [pagan philosophies] are "the doctrines" of men and "of demons" produced for itching ears of the spirit of this world's wisdom .... Indeed *heresies are themselves instigated from philosophy* .... The same subject-matter is discussed over and over again by the heretics and the philosophers; the same arguments are involved .... Unhappy Aristotle! who invented for these men dialectics, the art of building up and pulling down .... From all these, when the apostle would restrain us, he expressly names *philosophy* as that which he would have us be on our guard against. [St. Paul] had been at Athens, and had in his interviews (with its philosophers) become acquainted with that human wisdom which *pretends to know the truth, whilst it only corrupts it,* and is itself divided into its own manifold heresies, by the variety of its mutually repugnant sects. *What indeed has Athens to do with Jerusalem? What concord is there between the Academy and the Church?* .... Away with all attempts to produce a mottled Christianity of Stoic, Platonic and dialectic composition! We want no curious disputation after possessing Christ Jesus, no inquisition after enjoying the gospel! (B49, Vol. III, page 246. Emphasis added.)

Philosophers inspired theologians and vice versa. The frequency of their mention by the early church Fathers, and the many pages spent refuting them illustrates the philosophers allure and mortal challenge to truth. They falsely fulfilled the lure of objective truth, followed by a desire to "improve" or "explain" Scriptural revelation. The Fathers warned against the rewritten or truncated "Bibles" produced by heretics. Religion and philosophy agitate inquiring minds.[18]

As Tertullian[19] had emphasized, heresies are themselves instigated from philosophy. *Science, falsely so-called, is many times the prelude for a faith!* Not surprisingly, internal squabbles and obvious subjectivity brought these sciences of the day into disrepute or extinction. As said in the introduction, it would all be so easy if reason's accomplishments were obviously objective.

Lactantus (A.D. 260-330) was a late ante-Nicean father. He had read the philosophers extensively:

But since [philosophers] disagree among one another with great contention, and are for the most part at variance with themselves, it is evident that their path is by no means straightforward; since they have severally marked out distinct ways for themselves according to their own will, and have left great confusion to those who are seeking the truth.
...Philosophy appears to consist of two subjects, knowledge and conjecture, and of nothing more ... Philosophy has been divided into many sects ... In which do we place the truth? ... For each particular sect overturns all others, to confirm itself and its own *doctrines.* (B49, Vol VII, pages 10, 70-73. Emphasis in original.)

Lactantus's observation highlights the fragmented nature of philosophy. It was important to philosophers but how was it to be distinguished from mumbo jumbo?

---

18   The intent is not to castigate modern inquiry. After all, these Fathers themselves sometimes showed the influence of various "sciences of the day" or "common knowledge." The long dispute with grandiose speculations shows the false relations between Athens and Jerusalem – between science, intellectual adventure, and Christianity. The concern continues today.

19   Sadly, Tertullian ended his days estranged from the Church at large. The closing years of his life focused on an extreme asceticism and "New" Prophecy – yet this was the opposite spectrum from the philosophers.

The previous chapter discussed philosophy, physics and astronomy, but Greek writings also dealt with associated spiritual "baggage, including reincarnation, an impersonal world soul, an unknowable master "god," stating that good and evil should be relabeled as blind fate, listing of virtues of various gods, elevation of gnostic man, a devaluation of all "other" life, assertion of the impossibility of the Son of God dying on the cross and so on. To them, life did not cover a spectrum from a singular moral choice leading to heaven or hell, but repetitive worm to eighth sphere cycles of reincarnation.

The Pythagorean / Platonic sacred subjectivity (religion) included the cosmos! Plato's *Timaeus* is a central repository of this information. (The *Epinomous* also elaborates upon the nature and duties of the gods and demons.) Further information is contained in the writings of the neoplatonists, who consider that Plato (and even more the likes of Aristotle) purged many Pythagorean doctrines. Nonetheless, Plato's writings contain essential elements.

Plato's cosmos was circular but finite, with the earth at the center, due to its "heavy" triangles. This was within an enclosing shell – the Celestial Sphere.[20] The "fixed" stars were "lights," either close to or on the inner surface of the celestial sphere. The origin of this cosmic framework varied – sometimes a god created it; sometimes matter was uncreated, coeternal with this shell. Seven circles (spheres) were centered on the earth, and mandated by Plato. The seven planets (wandering stars) on these seven circles (spheres) were dwellings for various gods (or demons) – and also were themselves gods. Beyond the seven spheres was the eighth sphere – the ogdoad – the home of the unknown god. Fixed stars may have been dwellings for gods, depending upon who is the authoritative interpreter of Plato or Pythagoras. (Aristotle said something similar in his, *On the Universe*.) The philosopher's cosmos was well-populated, maybe even alive.

In Plato's *Timaeus*, this shadowy and unknown "god" above the planets and stars created the "lesser" gods – and perhaps also the celestial sphere. This unknowable "god" did not communicate with our earthly dungheap.[21] One could only make mathematical-like statements about "him." (An appeal to perforating revelation for knowledge about "him" contradicted their basic assumptions.) The "lesser" gods of at least the "neo" philosophers typically numbered 30 – the 30 Æons – specifically 8 + 10 + 12.[22] As quoted earlier, they were told to create life on earth. But, in the economy of reincarnation, at death, living things returned to their "native" stars. From there, later reincarnations sent most of them back to earth.

This was not necessarily an endless cycle. *Gnostic Men*, (not animals, men or recidivist women), who rose to "knowledge" during their sojourns on earth, went beyond the seventh sphere to the eighth sphere. This was the entry to a well-earned immortality – the region of the (fixed) stars – and god. *Gnostics did not fear death*, it was release from an evil enslavement.

---

20   The Celestial Sphere reminds me of modern space thrillers. When such folk get in trouble, they activate an "energy shield" or a "radiation shield."
21   Dungheap: A common name philosophers gave to the despised prison of the earth.
22   There were additional gods. They could be above, below, or simply confused as to where they should be.

Pythagorean (and perhaps Platonic) thought held out the prospect of acquiring the mathematical and astronomical knowledge required to successfully traverse the planetary obstacle course and triumphantly arrive at the eighth sphere. Incantations, rituals, magic, *etc.*, were sought as aids for the inevitable death journey. De Santillana reports:

> Men's spirits were thought to dwell in the Milky Way between incarnations. This conception has been handed down as an Orphic and Pythagorean tradition fitting into the frame of the migration of the soul .... [S]ouls ascend by way of Capricorn, and then, in order to be reborn, descend again through the "gate of cancer." (B33, page 242.)

In this mathematical world, motion was abhorrent; it shook the soul – the numbers and ratios got all jumbled up. Confused souls could then do evil. Plato wrote little on these details, but remember Plato's statement to the tyrant Dionysius that he never wrote down the "important" things. Enterprising thinkers mixed this vague recipe with Judeo-Christianity. Gnosticism was one of the results. It was a heady brew.

Gnosticism tried to reconcile eastern religions, Christianity and science, (whereas hermeticism emphasized Egyptian mystery religion). It was an eclectic movement, reeking of the sciences of the day. It attempted to "improve" Christianity in order to accommodate the philosopher's "science" and gods. Using Greek cosmology as the judge, the offenses in the Bible were many: the Lord, Jehovah, was too communicative with the dungheap, He did not show the proper "reserve." Furthermore, He even visited the despised and inferior earth. He should not demean His character by claiming to have *ex nihilo* created the earth and its inhabitants – or call it good! The Lord also did not acknowledge the 30 Æons. Accordingly, gnostics claimed the God of the Old Testament was a minor – almost outcast – god who did not understand the "big picture."

Regarding the New Testament, Jesus Christ could not be both True God and True Man. Gnostics knew Greek science showed "God" to be an absentee landlord, so an incarnation violated the ban on communication between heaven and the dungheap. If Jesus Christ was God, He couldn't have been here; or, at least He would not mingle with the dust of the earth – or suffer. If He was an animal man, He could not rise again or ascend to heaven. Accordingly, gnostics postulated that a "spirit" descended upon the man, Jesus. This "Christ Spirit" departed prior to the trial and crucifixion of Jesus, so only the man suffered, not the heavenly being. This "spirit" was a minor or a major god, depending upon which gnostic theory was believed.

This outlook is commonly called *dualism*: evil matter contrasted with good spirit. Yet, this outlook is far easier to understand as *subordination to the cosmic science of the day. It was life on the reincarnation treadmill.* (Starting in a preexistent heavenly perfection, mental oblivion, finding oneself in the earthly prison on a dungheap, with brief flashes of *anamnesis* for the gnostic few, then using mathematical and magical "knowledge" to navigate back to the higher stars ... then back again!) It was a dualism rationally mandated between gnostics and the ignorant lower life forms.

We can learn from this. How must Christianity be modified if evolution or the big bang were true? Reconciling Christianity and the science of the day still occurs. Too often, Christian authors concentrate on "faith," an "airy" contrast to the early church Fathers. Rarely do we today inquire if a "science of the day" has germinated a religious belief. *This is spiritual nichitis!* No wonder Christian young people fall away in droves while in college.

Irenaeus, bishop of Lyons, France, in his massive *Against Heresies*, written between A.D. 182-188 is an important witness to gnostic syncretism.[23] It is difficult and lengthy reading, partly due to the extinction of many of the heresies he describes. These heresies were full of mathematical mythology – such as we have been reviewing. The terminology is strange – the ogdoad, (the location of heaven), which is the number eight, is repeatedly mentioned. Yet this strange terminology was recognizable to those converted from the "science of the day."

Irenaeus took upon himself the thankless study required to understand such heresies. Let us now read some of his comments about gnostic syncretism:

1. They [Valentinians, perhaps the most popular form of gnosticism] maintain, then, that in the invisible and ineffable heights above there exists a certain perfect, preexistent Æon[24], whom they call Proarche, Propator, and Bythus, and describe as being invisible and incomprehensible. Eternal and unbegotten, he remained throughout innumerable cycles of ages in profound serenity and quiescence. There existed along with him Ennoea, whom they also call Charis and Sige.[25] At last this Bythus determined to send forth from himself the beginning of all things, and deposited this production (which he had resolved to bring forth) in his contemporary Sige, even as seed is deposited in the womb. She then ... gave birth to Nous ... This Nous they call also Monogenes, and Father, and the Beginning of all Things. Along with him was also produced Alétheia; *and these four constituted the first and first-begotten Pythagorean Tetrad*[26] which they also denominate the root of all things .... And Monogenes ... also himself sent forth Logos and Zoe, being the father of all those who were to come after him, and the beginning and fashioning of the entire Pleroma.[27] By the conjunction of Logos and Zoe were brought forth Anthropos and Ecclesia; and thus was *formed the first-begotten Ogdoad,*[28] the root and substance of all things....

2. ... Logos and Zoe, after producing Anthropos and Ecclesia, sent forth other ten Æons[29] ... They then add that Anthropos himself, along with Ecclesia, pro-

---

23   Irenaeus was martyred about A.D. 202.
24   Æon - A name for the philosophers' gods. We derive the word "eon" - ages - from this.
25   Sige, however, was no true consort to Bythus, who included in himself the ideas of male and female and was the only cause of all things ... [Footnote in reference text.]
26   Tetrad: Four, The base of the tetraktys. See page 63.
27   Pleroma: the dwelling of the unknown god, the eighth sphere.
28   Ogdoad: eight
29   A footnote in the text here adds: It may be well to give here the English equivalents of the names of these Æons and their authors. They are as follows: Bythus, *Profundity;* Proarche, *First-beginning;* Propator, *First-Father;* Ennoe, *Idea;* Charis, *Grace;* Sige, *Silence;* Nous, *Intelligence;* Alétheia, *truth;* Logos, *Word;* Zoe, *Life;* Anthropos, *Man;* Ecclesia, *Church;* Bythius, *Deep;* Mixis, *Mingling;* Ageratos, *Undecaying;* Henosis, *Union;* Autophyes, *Selfexistent;* Hedone, *Pleasure;* Acinetos, *Immoveable;* Syncrasis, *Blending;* Monogenes, *Only-Begotten;* Macaria, *Happiness;* Paracletus, *Advocate;* Pistis, *Faith;* Patricos, *Ancestral;* Elpis, *Hope;* Metricos, *Metrical;* Agape, *Love;* Ainos, *Praise;* Synesis, *Understanding;* Ecclesiaicus, *Ecclesiastical;* Macariotes, *Felicity;*

duced twelve [more] Æons....

3. *Such are the thirty Æons* in the erroneous system of these men; and they are described as being wrapped up, so to speak, in silence, and known to none [except these professing {gnostic} teachers]. *Moreover, they declare that this invisible and spiritual Pleroma of theirs is tripartite, being divided into an Ogdoad, a Decad, and a Duodecad.*[30] And for this reason they affirm it was that the "Savior"[31] – for they do not please to call Him "Lord"[32] – did no work in public during the space of thirty years, thus setting forth the mystery of these Æons.... [Gnostics] maintain that these are great, and wonderful, and hitherto unspeakable mysteries which it is their special function to develop; and so they proceed when they find anything in the multitude of things contained in the Scriptures which they can adopt and accommodate to their baseless speculations.

... 6. ... Then, out of gratitude for the great benefit which had been conferred on them, the whole Pleroma of the æons, with one design and desire, and with the concurrence of Christ and the Holy Spirit, their Father also setting the seal of His approval on their conduct, brought together whatever each one had in himself of the greatest beauty and preciousness; and uniting all these contributions so as skillfully to blend the whole, they produced, to the honor and glory of Bythus, a being of most perfect beauty, the very star of the Pleroma, and the perfect fruit [of it], namely Jesus.[33] ....

... 2. They affirm, therefore, that he [the Demiurge[34]] was constituted the Father and God of everything *outside* of the Pleroma, being the creator of all animal and material substances .... He created also seven heavens, above which they say that he, the Demiurge, exists. And on this account *they term him Hebdomas,*[35] and his mother Achamoth Ogdoads ... They affirm, moreover, that these seven heavens [planets] are intelligent, and speak of them as being angels, while they refer to the Demiurge himself as being an angel bearing a likeness to God....

3. They go on to say that the Demiurge *imagined* that he created all these things of himself, while he in reality made them in conjunction with the productive power of Achamoth. *He formed the heavens, yet was ignorant of the heavens; he fashioned man, yet knew not man; he brought to light the earth, yet had no acquaintance with the earth....*

... 1. ... They further hold that the consummation of all things will take place when all that is spiritual has been formed and perfected by Gnosis (knowledge)... *And they represent themselves to be these persons.*

2. Animal men, again, are instructed in animal things ... while they have not perfect knowledge. *We of the Church, they say, are these persons....*

... 2. ... For, summing up his statements respecting the Word previously mentioned by him, he further declares, "And the Word was made flesh, and dwelt among us." But, according to their hypothesis, the Word did not become flesh at all, inasmuch as He never went outside of the Pleroma, but that Savior [became flesh]

Theletos, *Desiderated*; Sophia, *Wisdom*. [These names are found in Greek writings, but their elevation to "gods" may have been due to neoplatonists or the gnostics.]

30   *i.e.*, 8 + 10 + 12 = 30. 12 is a duodecad.

31   This is an early example of false teachers adopting Christian terms, but with "new" meanings.

32   To call the Savior, Lord, was to confuse the distinctions between the Æons and the unknowable god.

33   This evidences the gnostic prohibition against Jesus Christ as being both True God and True Man. Gnostics held that Jesus and Christ were separate entities.

34   Demiurge: a less-than-flattering name for God as revealed in the Old Testament. Greek cosmic science forced gnostics to maintain that Yahweh was a subordinate lesser god.

35   Hebdomas: the number seven.

who was formed by a special dispensation [out of all the Æons], and was of later date than the Word.... (B49, Volume I, pages 316-317, 318-319, 322-323, 324, 326, 329. Emphasis added.)

Such is a lengthy example of the (inconsistent) gnosticism the early church successfully battled. It is *syncretism* – the blending of the science of the day and Christianity. Irenaeus describes additional variations of gnosticism. As Tertullian had said, heresies are themselves instigated from philosophy.

Gnostics edited and clipped the Bible in order to arrive at an acceptable residue.[36] Their layered potpourri was alien to the Word of God. Gnosticism's appeal: it was the religion compatible with the science of the day.

A further section from Book II of Irenaeus becomes more pointed on the sources of the gnostic inspiration:

2... *[T]hey also bring together the things which have been said by all those who were ignorant of God, and who are termed philosophers; and sewing together, as it were, a motley garment out of a heap of miserable rags,* they have, by their subtle manner of expression, furnished themselves with a cloak which is really not their own....

3. Again, adopting the [ideas of] shade and vacuity from Democritus and Epicurus, they have fitted these to their own views .... In like manner, these men call those things which are within the Pleroma real existences, just as those philosophers did the atoms; while they maintain that those which are without the Pleroma have no true existence, even as those did respecting the vacuum .... Again, when they maintain that these things [below] are images of those which have a true existence [above], they again most manifestly rehearse the doctrine of Democritus and Plato....

4. This opinion, too, that they hold that the Creator formed the world out of previously existing matter, both Anaxagoras, Empedocles, and Plato expressed before them ... [That God is the slave of this necessity, so that He cannot impart immortality to what is mortal, or bestow incorruption on what is corruptible, but every one passes into a substance similar in nature to itself, both those who are named Stoics from the portico and indeed all that are ignorant of God, poets and historians alike, make the same affirmation....[37]]

5 .... They also strive to transfer to [the treatment of matters of] faith that *hairsplitting and subtle mode of handling questions which is, in fact, a copying of Aristotle.*

6. Again, as to the desire they exhibit to refer this whole universe to numbers, they have learned it from the *Pythagoreans* .... [H]e simply sets forth the Tetrad of Pythagoras as the originating principle and mother of all things.

7. ... *Thus, then, by a complete perversion of language, they style ignorance of the truth knowledge: and Paul well says [of them,] that [they make use of]* "novel-

---

36   Some of these have survived to this day. When Biblical "scholars" treat these as equivalent to Scripture, confusion reigns. The English-speaking world is awash in Bible versions. Some, like a feminist or a "gender neutral" version show Scriptural tampering – for scientific compatibility. Gnostic texts exhibited such tampering.

37   Note in reference text. [Our author's demonstration of the essential harmony of gnosticism with the old mythologies, and the philosophies of the heathen, explains the hold it seems to have gained among nominal converts to Christianity, and also the necessity for a painstaking refutation of what seem to us mere absurdities. The great merit of Irenaeus is thus illustrated: he gave the deathblow to heathenism in extirpating heresy.]

ties of words of false knowledge" .... (I Timothy 6:20) (B49, Volume I, pages 376-378. Emphasis added.)

"Novelties of words of false knowledge" is also translated as "science falsely so-called."

Tertullian intimated in his earlier quote that St. Paul understood Greek philosophy. Several other times, Tertullian warns against the philosopher's gods. He applies St. Paul's admonition in 1 Timothy 1:4 to the philosophers' gods; beware of "fables and endless genealogies:"

Let, however, any man approach the subject from a knowledge of the faith which he has otherwise learned, as soon as he finds so many names of Æons, so many marriages, so many offsprings, so many exits, so many issues, felicities *and* infelicities of a dispersed and mutilated deity, will that man hesitate at once to pronounce that these are "the fables and endless genealogies" which the inspired apostle by anticipation condemned, whilst these seeds of heresy were even shooting forth. (B49, Vol. III, page 505. Emphasis in original.)

Further, Irenaeus makes the same connection between the Æons and endless genealogies.

During the second to third centuries A.D., a popular strain of mysticism was born, authors unknown, called the *Hermetic Tradition*. (The name derives from the Egyptian god, Thoth, otherwise known as Hermes Trismegistus – the thrice great Hermes. We shall encounter its revival in the next chapter.) With dissension among "scientists" so rampant, it was time to try another recipe![38]

A cautious summary ... is as follows: "These [Hermetic] writings are chiefly the product of Egyptian NeoPlatonists who were greatly influenced by Stoicism, Judaism, Persian theology and possibly by native Egyptian beliefs, as well as, of course, Plato, especially the *Timaeus*." (B50, page 3, footnote.)

As Antione Faivre, a sympathetic historian, noted about the resulting body of doctrine:

The theoretical and doctrinal coherence of which is scarcely perceptible. (B51, page 55.)

Everything was acceptable. Another interpretive babble was born.

Because of their doctrine of reincarnation – and interplanetary travel – gnostic writings discussed the magical influence of the stars and provided elaborate descriptions of the angels and demons associated with the zodiac and the planets. They called this "magic," not astrology. Magic was for accessing God ... for penetrating through the seven spheres. Astrology, in contrast, gave the influence of the planets on (unenlightened) mankind while still on earth:

Next came a process the Hermeticists shared with Gnostics and with the later-surfacing Kabbalists. It is known as the progress through the Hebdomad. [Seven planetary spheres.] The seven sacred planets of the ancient world were viewed as the symbolic guardians of earthly life. Through these regions the soul descends into earthly manifestation and through them again it must ascend to freedom and

---

38 Greek philosophers also resented the gnostic mixing of ideas. Plotinus, a neoplatonist, for one, criticized gnostics for misunderstanding Plato. Talk about the pot calling the kettle black!

light .... Having overcome the seven spheres, and with them the limiting influences of the cosmos, the initiate was now ready to enter the "Brotherhood of the Og-doad." This step is symbolized by entry into the eighth sphere [Ogdoad], beyond the cosmic prisonhouse of the seven .... The tone of this experience is quite *ecstatic*, that is, characterized by a very much *altered consciousness*. (B52, pages 14-16. Emphasis added.)

Hermeticism died out along with the other schools bordering the Mediterra-nean, but it was revived when Hermetic writings were rediscovered during the Italian Renaissance.[39]

As a disciple from the Renaissance, Giordano Bruno, put it (or inflated it) in his *Essays on Magic*:

Magicians take it as axiomatic that in all the panorama before our eyes, God acts on the gods, the gods act on the celestial or astral bodies, which are divine bodies; these act on the spirits [demons], who reside in and control the stars,[40] one of which is the earth; the spirit acts on the elements, the elements to the compound, the compounds on the senses; the senses on the soul, and the soul on the whole animal. This is the descending scale. (B53, page 108. Footnote added.)

Related to Hermetic thought was the Jewish Kabbal literature. Formulated around A.D. 500, it also fell into obscurity for centuries, and then flared up again about the time of the Renaissance. It was heavy in magic and numerology – as a mediator between God and creation.

In Acts 19:19 we read: "*Many of them also which used curious arts [magic], brought their books together, and burned them before all men: and they counted the price of them, and found it fifty thousand pieces of silver.*" *Magic was not a circus sideshow, but a scholarly pursuit, for many, an adjunct to philosophy!* Simon the sorcerer, mentioned in Acts 8:13, may have been in this "profession."

Fifty thousand pieces of silver bought – not comic books – but expensive works of magic or astrological "scholarship!" This also witnessed to a large number of conversions among educated people!

In critiquing gnosticism, atomism was not overlooked. Hippolytus of Portus, around A.D. 230 composed, *The Refutation of All Heresies*. In it we find the follow-ing statement about atomism:

Epicurus ... supposed, as originating principles of all things, atoms and vacuity. He considered vacuity as the place that would contain the things that will exist, and atoms the matter out of which all things could be formed; and that from the concourse of atoms both the Deity derived existence, and all the elements, and all things inherent in them, as well as animals and other (creatures); so that nothing was generated or existed, unless it be from atoms. And he affirmed that these atoms were composed of extremely small particles, in which there could not exist either a point or a sign, or any division; wherefore also he called them atoms. Acknowledging the Deity to be eternal and incorruptible, he says that God has providential care for nothing, and that there is no such thing as providence or fate,

---

39   Renaissance thinkers (humanists) believed that the oldest writings were the purest. The mythical Hermes was older than the Greeks ... so Hermetic tradition would be better than Greek tradition.

40   In this quote, meanings are not present-day meanings. Celestial or astral bodies are stars. Wandering stars are planets.

but that all things are made by chance. (B49, Vol. V, page 21.)

The *Recognitions of Clement* may have been written before A.D. 200, or it may be a later work attributed to Clement. It also contains a critique of atomism:

"But you will say, according to the opinion of Epicurus, that successions of atoms coming in a ceaseless course, and mixing with one another, and conglomerating through unlimited and endless periods of time, are made solid bodies ... For they say that those corpuscles, which they call atoms, are of different qualities: that some are moist, and therefore heavy, and tending downwards; others dry and earthy, and therefore still heavy; but others fiery, and therefore always pushing upwards; others cold and inert, and always remaining in the middle. Since then some, as being fiery, always tend upward, and others, as being moist and dry, always downwards, and others keep a middle and unequal course, how could they meet together and form body?

... And this also I ask: If this expanse of heaven which we see constructed by the gradual concurrence of atoms, how did it not collapse while it was in construction? ... And so I go on asking, until the answer comes to nothing and vacuity! (B49, Vol. VIII, page 170.)

Plato criticized atomism. Note the following: the basic building blocks of matter were triangles (*Timaeus* 56) – not atoms; the perfection and orderliness of planetary motion contradicts the random motions of atomism (*Epinomous* 982c – 983d); and soul precedes body in the stars (thus intelligence, not chance, determines nature's necessity (*Laws* X, 899). Whether these are good arguments is for the reader to consider.

Some early Christian thinkers considered the science of the day to be complimentary to *Genesis* – but to be read with caution. By now, Greek thought was a cross-pollinated eclectic mixture. Lactantus (third century) and St. Augustine (fourth century) both mention Hermes as if a real person. Some looked on Hermes as a Gentile seer who dimly foresaw some of the Christian truths of revelation. St. Augustine did warn readers about Hermes' obvious pagan statements. Later, some sacred art depicted such as Plato, Aristotle and Hermes conversing with Moses or Abraham or Jesus. While we today may think it obvious they should have avoided this association, remember the strength of the science of measure. Also, think again about today's struggle against the "objective truthfulness" of such adventures as the big bang.

(And remember that very little other pagan literature showed much rational order. Further, familiarity with Greek philosophical writings was necessary in order to communicate with many people.)

Yet, to consider Greek thought to be important, "relevant" Christians modified Christian thought. Yet the Demiurge was not Yahweh. Further, due to reincarnation, women were not a worthy object of love, and such as Plato's *Symposium* was avoided or unknown. Love in the *Symposium* is primarily "Man and his boy."

In one respect the early church Fathers had it easy – there were so many schools of Greek philosophy. Obviously, they all could not be true. This ease meant that a close scrutiny of Parmenides' claim, "far from the footsteps of man ...", did not have to be made.

In reading this history, some may impatiently ask for the "great principles" that others write about. Many thinkers who avoided mathematical mysticism made lasting contributions. And God knows numbers, but reality is not number. Did "something" design and create with numbers – or does physical stuff have numerical patterns as a consequence of *ex nihilo* creation?

The true meaning of mathematics remained obscure. Pagans and Aristotle had their proto-empiricism, which used bottom-up mathematics without grandiose purposes. Mathematics could be a tool of God, even though an unseen concept.

Geometry is helpful in activities such as construction, surveying and navigation. This it always has been – *anamnesis* did not make it more useful. Circles were circles – they conveyed no extrapolated knowledge about the cosmos. The cosmos could be orderly due to mathematical essence or created design! Arithmetic was useful, but number must cover the spectrum from bankruptcy (negative accounts) through to positive values. Disregarding Parmenides' claims, the cosmos revealed God's handiwork – created, orderly and finite.

We cannot laugh at those Greek philosophers and mathematicians, in spite of their manifest subjectvity. Reading books on the history of mathematics or of mathematicians is exciting, but doesn't transform their work from sightseeing to truth.

Indeed, they developed many useful mathematical tools, "rafts" of data and devices. Euclid's *Elements*, Archimedes' work on statics, mechanical advantage, burning mirrors, and buoyancy, Ptolemy's work on astronomy and geography, the work on conic sections, the calculation of the diameter of the earth and the sun, Galen's work in medicine, Aristotle's work in anatomy, biological classification and logic are only a few. These apply to both abstractions and mundane problem solving. Mathematics has useful formulas to reasonably investigate nature but didn't sanction rational extrapolative infatuation.

Further, when people today make grandiose claims for Euclidean geometry as a Universal Natural Law, they contradict our present-day enthusiasm for non-Euclidean geometry.[41] Nor must we be lulled into forgetting what mathematical disasters Morris Kline was referring to and which we have yet to encounter.

Stripped of the grandiose, the residue was useful mathematics – in harmony with the *ex nihilo* creation of Genesis 1:1. *Some may retort that "You are putting limits upon 'unaided' reason." Rather, they champion an "all-seeing," unproven cosmic rationalism, "aided" by Mathematic.* Their emphasis on free and autonomous reason is a blindness in the mind's eye which atheorism shows has a long history of unreasonableness. Universal Natural Laws have been repeatedly postulated, and just as repeatedly, proven wrong. Atheism, materialism, and meaninglessness remain subjective failures. Revealed truth ("aided" reason) had not been proved wrong.

To say the usefulness of mathematics follows from God's design is not to shirk

---

41   It is inconsistent to honor both. It seems the practice is to honor Euclid until a post-Christian environment is created, and then turn to non-Euclidean "truths" to then celebrate that all is now relative.

Before they celebrate too much, they should spend time playing with marbles or drawing in the sand – and contemplating events!

our investigative desires. It is the solution to the broad aspects of the puzzle, not the stymieing of the search for knowledge.

Greek thinkers were a quarrelsome lot! Bottom-up mathematics was useful; the top-down ahistorical mathematical line was unproved!

A great mystery remains regarding mathematics' uncanny ability to model the world – or provide surprising insights. Thinkers still wrestle with this puzzle. *What is mathematics without the accompanying baggage of science, falsely so-called?*

The Mediterranean world mainly focused on the mystical and cosmic baggage that grounded Greek philosophy. Also, there was little economic benefit even from the practical side of Greek thought. These benefits would have to await the guild societies and the expanding commercial and industrial world of Medieval Europe.

Greek philosophers had not satisfied the lure of objective truth. Number and geometry cannot grasp the universal; only God can. The Biblical worldview – and its revealed truth ("aided" reason) of the *ex nihilo* creation account – was reasonable and won out against the interpretive babble of the Greek philosophical schools and their "neo," hermetic, gnostic, kabbalist synthesizers. Additionally, the Biblical account put the individual in center stage. Philosophers, in contrast, had little interest in simple folk – animal man. Such human cattle, at the least, must await a better reincarnation. Nobility and grand ideas – the guides on death journeys – were what philosophers talked about!

From the early zenith of Greek philosophy and science, falsely so-called, these ideas lost the lure of objective truth. As St Basil and others had said, thinkers were not in harmony. They could not conquer either paganism, astrology, alternative adventures, sophistry or appeal to the masses. Oriental beliefs are also immune to this intellectual adventure and attract defectors from Greek ideals. This illustrates the foundational subjectivity of theories about the inaccessible.

Science, falsely so-called, was meaningless to the emerging Christianity, wherein monotheism undergirded reason. In a matter of centuries, much of this commingling of fact and speculation was rejected and lost. Also of significance was the moral decadence associated with most philosophical schools.

The intellectual aristocracy of antiquity presents a parallel to the modern pathos, for their layered potpourri, satiated feeling *and intellect* made the world ready for the Incarnation. Then and today, Christianity speaks to a wide variety of sins, from those of well-reasoned storytellers (who we focus on), to mystery cults, to legalists, to simple evils accessible to everyone. Christian faith and reason were then in harmony.

The world is not divine; it bears the scars of man's fall, and the devil is not the negative side of our personality. Well-reasoned mythology has engulfed the science of measure and its vision.

If we had the luxury of a time machine, how would our prelude *now* view this early history of science? Is it objective knowledge? Rather, might we be tempted to call it a myth, a background, an intellectual adventure, a program, a worldview, a paradigm, science, falsely so-called, well-reasoned storytelling ... or just a saddening babble? This certainly sounds like modern sophistry!

But now reflection gets uncomfortable. If we are embarrassed over the assertion that "fractions and negative numbers do not exist," "geometry is a phone line to heaven" or "geometry exists," how are these cosmic speculations better than the Biblical way of understanding the data (after *ex nihilo* creation) by viewing force as the cause of motion, modeled by bottom-up formulas, rather than resulting from top-down Natural Law? What is the proof of atheism, rationalism or meaninglessness? If grandiose extrapolation is mathematized storytelling, not puzzle solving, why prefer rationalism over Biblical *ex nihilo* creation?

Force or Law

The Bible warns us not to be tossed too and fro by the winds of human wisdom. (I Timothy 6:20.) The early church Fathers still offer useful insights. Irenaeus, (*ca.* A.D. 200), for example, said:

Is it a meaningless and accidental thing, that the positions of names, and the election of apostles, and the working of the Lord, and the arrangement of created things, are what they are? – we answer them: Certainly not; but with great wisdom and diligence, all things have clearly been made by God, fitted and prepared [for their special purposes];.... [Mankind's attempts at explanation present] an *uncertain* mode of proceeding, on account of their *varied and diverse* systems, and because every sort of hypothesis may at the present day be, in like manner, devised by any one; so that they can derive arguments against the truth from these very theories, inasmuch as they may be *turned in many different directions*.... For system does not spring out of numbers, but *numbers from a system*; nor does God derive His being from things made, but things made from God. (B49 Volume 1, page 396. Emphasis added.)

Such old advice is relevant and up-to-date. Christians could reason with their contemporaries. The ante-Nicean Fathers witnessed to their scholarly neighbors – and, in reaction, neopythagoreanism, neoplatonism and hermeticism tried to revamp their edifices. But their cosmic thoughts did not stand on a firm foundation. Playing with marbles or drawing in the sand is a sensible reasonable beginning for understanding the playing field. They teach rudimentary mathematics and illustrate Irenaeus' comment – followed up centuries later by science's view of forces and matter. Useful formulas are great for curve fitting, but mathematics and laws cause nothing; they shadow reality.

Revelation or mathematical derivation! Are 1 + 1 = 2 and associates really the key to top-down cosmic truth? Objective proof has not been offered that requires Christianity to "theologize away" a conflict with science, falsely so-called! Certainly so if you stood on the shore of the Mediterranean from A.D. 100 and onwards. Biblical *ex nihilo* creation was more credible than Greek science, falsely so-called.

(We mentioned in an earlier chapter that one should read books from a sampling of disciplines. We may be tempted to take the shortcut and consult the Internet. The results only add to the multiple voices!)

This being so, why is the data in astronomy, *etc.*, systematized in a manner consistent with rationalism's grandiose outlook. Atheorism raises this question; it is uncomfortable with extrapolative infatuation, knowing it tries to lead us away from the playing field – far from the footsteps of humans.

And we can expect that those with radical doubt will run for cover and practice their usual un-desedimented radical silence.

Back then, the consequences of these early searchers for truth were as follows:

Paganism: The moon made love to a man. The Olympian gods were nonsensical, immoral, human, and not interested in the simple folk. Followers were ... nothing. Debauchery and immorality were the typical accompaniments to "worship."

Pre-Socratic Philosophers: Knowledge of earth, air, fire, and water was foundational, in some order or combination.

Atomists: Infinitely divisible atoms in ceaseless random motion explains the origin of everything. It was comforting, too large to comprehend, and implied atheism. Existence was pragmatic activities while awaiting a pleasant extinction.

Pythagoreans: Matter is number – the simple ones, that is. Mathematics and reincarnation – the great rational trek. Life was a prison on a dungheap. Individual personality was muted. Philosophers were a law unto themselves. Others had to await a better reincarnation.

Sophists: Listen to everything people say and don't believe anything people say. And use it to your advantage.

Platonists: The first mature rationalists. Matter is geometry – Euclidean, that is, but valuing the Pythagorean heritage. Mathematical Law is a voyage of discovery.

Aristotelians: Nature needs to be investigated by observation and logic. Reasonably, mathematics is an invention.

Cynics: Live free from desires. Reality is deterministic. Live modestly.

Stoics: Reality is deterministic. Logic, ethics, physics. Elite people follow us.

Materialists: "Mature" Platonists, alone in a vast and empty cosmos. Geometry and reason were their delight. Rational thinking was honored – at least in name – and no competitors allowed.

Gnostics: All science can be harmonized with the distilled core of all religion.

Neopythagoreans: Number is supreme. Pagan mysticism and astrology lead the way.

Neoplatonists: Platonism, Pythagoreanism, Aristotleanism, and Stoicism "informed" by esoteric knowledge.

Hermeticists: Like gnostics and neoplatonists, but with an Egyptian flavor.

Science: A backwater to this discussion. Learning about the accessible. Geometry, logic, and arithmetic were servants.

Christianity: Life in a meaningful, good cosmos created *ex nihilo* by God. Mankind has a specific purpose and design. Events follow, but mankind had transgressed and fallen into sin. The cure of the cross of Jesus Christ condemned individuals with its judgment – and uplifted individuals with its cleansing. Redeemed life has meaning and a destiny of choice.

Thoughtful followers of the adventure may say, "Yes, our ancestors were sub-jective, but not us! It is regrettably true that "unaided" reason failed to deliver mono-truth. Our ancestors were deceived by their mind's eye, not by their senses. They *prematurely* insisted the cosmos was unperforated and ruled by godlessness, materialism, and meaninglessness. However, we *know* later events *absolutely* prove the *correctness* of the adventure's assumptions, as elaborated and refined by modern 'science'". But that is getting ahead of the history ...

By 100 B.C. the center of action had transferred from Athens to Rome. Romans were not interested in philosophy, but in fortifications, roads, city archi-tecture and aqueducts. There was a period of peace, the *pax Romana*. Evangelism in the Empire was also facilitated by the common languages of Latin and Greek.

Soon, the Roman Empire became too large and unmanageable, so it was split in two and the western portion [Roman] collapsed around A.D. 476. (The eastern portion [Byzantium] lasted for almost another one thousand years.) Most historians agree the Western collapse was due to moral decay, which stymied the battle against invading barbarians who were ... barbaric! Over some centuries, the Empire had become increasingly a slave kingdom. (Farmers and artisans were no longer free.) The only social safety net became the extended family.

Citizens could see that moral decay was somehow connected with the pagan and philosophical traditions. The masses were "entertained" with gladiators in the coliseums. As Chesterton said, boredom followed and some tried to stab their nerves back to life.

As the Empire was dying, the later emperor, Constantine, converted to Christi-anity. One of his acts was to allow church courts. This was in reaction to the dysfunctional state legal system. What civility and scholarship that survived did so under the protection of the growing Christianity:

> Christians quickly recognized that if the Bible was to be read, literacy would have to be encouraged; and in the long run Christianity became the major patron of European education and a major borrower from the classical intellectual tradition .... If .... we compare the support given to the study of nature by the early church with the support available from any other contemporary social institution, it will become apparent that the church was one of the major patrons – perhaps *the* major patron – of scientific learning. (B47, pages 150-151. Italics in original.)

Christianity appealed to both the well-educated – and the illiterate. Subsistence living was predominant. Literacy did survive among a low percentage of the popu-lation, but few could pursue scholarly activities. Some Christians fled from the barbarian onslaught to places like Ireland from whence they later returned and led a revival in these lands. After many centuries rolled by, prosperity began to recover.

As this early history draws to a close, the challenge to God's perforated cos-mos can be summarized as: *The well-reasoned had "unaided" rational proof of an infinite, unperforated and mathematical cosmos – the arena of beautiful top-down mathematics, clear extrapolations, blind fate and an event-less ahistorical mathe-matical line. It left no room for the revealed truth ("aided" reason) about the "exter-nal" heaven where God dwells; for monotheists to even say, "God eternally geo-*

metricizes;" for appreciating the drama of historical events or for simple folk to exercise moral control. All that remained was geometry.[42]

Philosophers have always said God could not exist within the cosmos – that would be pantheism. Now, as then, it is irrational to believe in both God and a physical infinity – or its unbounded stand-in. Infinity – that extrapolation to the uttermost – does not allow God a place in which to reign sovereign as the almighty God. These products of rationalism are assumptions. All too often they are blindly accepted fabrications, the result of a deliberate attempt to replace God's deity and divine authority as Creator![43]

Few thinkers realized it was rational all along to paraphrase *Genesis* 1-3: "God designed and created an orderly, complex, inorganic, event-filled finite playing field upon which He created life." The children of Israel did not have to engage in mathematical storytelling to know the ultimate order of things – or who orders them. God is outside of His cosmos and has spoken about Himself, the earth's creation and teleology through His perforating revelation, the Bible. God also acts in history. The Israelites had the record of Noah's flood, had walked through the Red Sea, had seen Jericho's walls fall; the list is extensive. *Biblical revealed truth has many historical avenues for confirmation.*

This history points to the natural, visited by the supernatural! *The cosmos is reasonable, perforated and event-filled!* Knowing His Word and world do not conflict, Christians later took the Greek intellectual adventures, stripped away (some/all of?) the mystical elements and built science therewith.

Judeo-Christianity could intellectually harmonize with this adventure before increasing realization about what an infinite cosmos meant. Undoubtedly, Plato's moral tone was attractive. But wherever theistic thinkers accepted the adventure and its science of measure, Christianity began to retreat from history and the playing field into "spiritual niches." *These warm, vague understandings masked their new niche status: spokesmen for secondary phenomena.*[44] The uneducated would not long be safe from well-reasoned nonsense, nor carnality be restrained.

Science, falsely so-called, started amidst ancient Greek polytheism and science matured in a monotheistic milieu. As such, the Christian mind could potentially question whether each of the terms of the "*scientia* in summary" satisfied the lure of objective truth, and if a necessary connection existed between science and the concepts of godlessness, materialism, and meaninglessness. Would the redeemed sons and daughters of Adam and Eve carry out this questioning?

Indeed, this questioning was carried out over many generations. The resulting confidence evident in changed lives is impossible to accomplish without supernatural assistance by the indwelling energizing Holy Spirit. As Tertullian said, "the blood of the martyrs is the seed of the church." Christians gave strong witness and

---

42   At least this is the majority consensus. But, as we have seen, others of the ancient rationalists said otherwise. What about atoms or arithmetic or logic or cynicism?

43   Thanks to my daughter for an insightful edit of this paragraph.

44   Secondary phenomena: Explanations at least a level removed from the essential nature of things. Secondary phenomena and saving the appearances are not as good as science. As such, they can be dismissed once knowledge of the deeper causes arise.

compassion. Their actions of adopting orphans, caring for the destitute, founding hospitals and indifference to threatened death showed that they were different. Their neighbors said, "see how they love one another."

Christianity critiqued and conquered many polytheisms, but the adventure required infinity to shut out monotheism. Not surprisingly, monotheism would not accept the "definition" that it was only another polytheism. Christians hurled back the challenge: "Look at history and nature and see the hand of God." Such advice was empirical – the opposite to "walking far from the footsteps of humans." This foundational challenge to the extrapolative infatuation of the ahistorical mathematical line generated an intense hatred of monotheism among well-reasoned folk. If, as monotheists said, monotruth is grounded on monotheism, then there is an irrational admixture implied in "unaided" rational thought and its science, falsely so-called. Rationalists realized that to shut out but not conquer monotheism left it as the only rational threat to science, falsely so-called. Revealed truth ("aided" reason) frightened them!

In allegory and truth, atheism is much like 1 + 1. Now our walk on the obvious, yet hidden, path leads into the time of Renaissance, Enlightenment and Reformation.

Their eyes saw what their minds permitted them to see.
Kline

Hardcore rationalists continued to celebrate their supposedly objective victory over theism and guarded the presumed unbridgeable chasm separating reason and faith. However, it is better to remain open to the lure of objective truth. Crucial elements of their ancient science, falsely so-called, are embarrassing today. The early church Fathers encountered such subjectivity via Sadducees, Hellenism, gnosticism, hermeticism, neoplatonism and the later Kabballah. Some of the inherent subjectivity we have seen. Further hints reside in abstruse books on philosophy or the history of science.

This chapter approaches to around A.D. 1800, but with a focus on philosophical matters. The next chapter covers the same time period, but with a focus on mathematics and empirical science.

As the long slow march of history continued beyond the collapse of the Western Roman Empire in A.D. 476, many centuries passed before European prosperity began to recover. These were traumatic times with famines, plagues, invasions, poverty, and migrations. Christianity survived the fall of the Western Roman Empire; but its growing acceptance brought a new challenge, hinted at in the last chapter. People wanted Christianity to mirror the "best" of Roman and Greek culture. Through many centuries, there was artwork showing Moses, Abraham, St. Paul, and Jesus alongside Plato or Aristotle or Hermes or Virgil. (National pride overrode concerns about subjectivity.) In parts of Europe, the Church was even "forced" to sanction dueling. This "enculturation" tended to downgrade the Christian emphasis on "all" believers – and Christian apologetics tended to sound philosophical. There was also some jealousy towards the Eastern Roman Empire (Byzantium). It had thrived, not collapsed, and was trying to "Easternize" the "Western" world and "Western" Christianity.

Almost as a timeout, we must realize that (inaccessible) science was not responsible for the rising standard of living occurring throughout the European world. Science – expressed in astronomy and mathematical abstractions – made little contribution to living. This is contrary to the implied centrality of science to everything – including rising standards of living. Many say that "engineering is applied science!" It is more accurate to say that engineering is creative thought in action. Therefore, *engineering and technology stimulate science.* In these centuries, there were no applicable sciences. Native ingenuity and engineering dexterity were the engines of progress. In later centuries, these distinctions may be harder to discern.

In the Middle Ages, technology and engineering did not owe anything to natural philosophers. The relationship was the other way around. Technical advances gave natural philosophers clues about how the world worked as well as providing equipment that they needed to investigate it. (B43, page 340.)

Following is a list of major innovations made between the fall of the Western Roman Empire and A.D. 1500. These accounted for the rising standard of living. Some were not invented in Europe, but their improvement occurred in Europe.

They were: iron ploughs, nailed horseshoes, stirrups (for saddles), 3-crop agricultural rotation, horse collar, whippletree (to harness two horses to a wagon), watermill, windmill, pointed arch, rib vaulting, flying buttresses, alchemists inadvertently discovering chemicals, many metals and glass apparatus, trebuchet (siege catapult), gunpowder, cannon, spectacles, clock escapement mechanism, blast furnace, paper, moveable type printing, human dissection (to escape from excessive theory), compass, telescope. Useless? Unreal? But unscientific! (B43, B47, B54 and B55.) Later in the chapter, more examples of this progress are added.

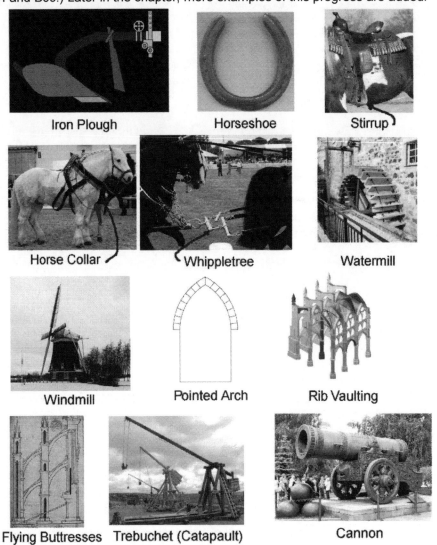

Iron Plough   Horseshoe   Stirrup

Horse Collar   Whippletree   Watermill

Windmill   Pointed Arch   Rib Vaulting

Flying Buttresses   Trebuchet (Catapault)   Cannon

(Those illustrated here and on the previous page are from www. wikipedia.com.)

Clock Escapement   Blast Furnace   Moveable
Mechanism   Type Printing

There were other items invented, such as cams, springs, treadle, cranks, connecting rods, governors, water pumps, even the humble wheel-barrow! The book, *Engineering and the Mind's Eye* (B92), has lots of old drawings. See also, *The Story of Inventions*, by Fred P Bachman, which adds the spinning wheel and the power loom. These devices came years before Nobel Prizes, but they fed, employed, defended and educated the European peoples!

Nor should we overlook that Christian missionary efforts converted the many European and invading tribes from paganism and barbarianism. The destruction of the Western Roman Empire had been a traumatic and impoverishing event!

Prosperity and then scholarship began to revive after A.D. 1000, universities were founded, and the later invention of the printing press was to rapidly spread the written word. Duhem showed, in the early twentieth century, that science was alive during the Christian Middle Ages; the Renaissance did not reawaken it. Renaissance spokesmen derogatively called the Middle Ages the "Dark Ages" to make themselves more attractive.[1]

About A.D. 1300, the Middle Ages drew to a close and intellectual ferment grew in Europe. The fabric of life – and preludes – looked less and less like they sprang from prevailing monotruths.

The traumas Medieval Europe underwent meant they retained very little of the writings of Greek thinkers and mathematicians. They also no longer read Greek; summaries or poor Latin translations of selected works were all that remained in Europe. (Plato's *Timaeus* and Porphyry's *Eosagoge*, a commentary on Aristotle's categories, had been translated into Latin by Boethius around A.D. 400.) Some documents did survive in a neglected manner in monastery attics and private libraries. There was a tendency to favor Plato due to St Augustine's writings. Yet, the "divine Plato" and the "immortal Aristotle" were thought to substantially agree with each other.

Greek writings survived in the Greek-speaking Eastern Roman Empire – the Byzantine Empire in Constantinople (modern Istanbul, Turkey) with an emphasis on Plato. These works filtered into the Arab world. With the rise of Islam, these works

---

1   See *The Beginnings of Western Science* (B47) by David Lindberg, chapter 14.

were preserved and extended, but with an emphasis on Aristotle. (The dry climate in the southern Mediterranean area assisted preservation.)

This time was intellectually challenging and dangerous, as we have seen. Additionally, there were religious wars, rival Popes, threats from Viking, Islamic and barbarian attacks, disruptions due to various crusades, the arrival of scholars and unknown Greek manuscripts from Constantinople, discovery of eastern and southern lands, even later the discovery of new worlds – and that to be revealed by the microscope and the telescope, strange fossils, and newly invented mechanical contraptions. Machiavelli questioned whether political conduct had a moral foundation. Uncertainty and some doubt of the truthfulness of Christianity emerged.

As European prosperity recovered, long-absent Greek thought began to reenter Europe. Some of Plato's writings came first. Later, there was a deluge of Aristotle's works, which came through Islamic North Africa and the then Islamic Spain. Trade and travelers also reawakened contact and interest. Many Europeans felt a "Golden Age" was being recovered. Fledgling European universities began to absorb these and develop them further.[2]

There was a brief and beautiful Renaissance of Pythagorean thought at the cathedral school at Chartres in France during the 12th century, due in large part to a Latin translation of Plato's *Timaeus*, and of course there was renewed interest in Pythagorean thought with the rediscovery of classical writings during the rebirth of learning in Renaissance Italy. (B35, page 43.)

This renewal of Greek ideas first excited Thierry of Chartres [*c.a.*, A.D. 1100-1146], one of the foremost scholars in France. He wrote in a speculative style, enamored by this recovered Pythagorean thought. His influence on Nicholas of Cusa will be seen later.

Most of this recontact was through neoplatonic writings, now biased towards Aristotle, but which had harmonized the various "masters." Athenian sources favored Plato – and a rational mathematical rigorous system of "proof." Alexandrian sources favored Aristotle – and reflected his bottom-up pragmatic view of mathematics. For a long time, European scholars did not realize the contradictory nature of what they were recovering:

But Bacon [*c.a.* 1214-1294] (like many of his generation) was convinced that all of the ancient and Islamic authorities were in fundamental agreement. (B47, page 313.)

Yet, Bacon was more Aristotelean than Platonic:

Bacon ... advocated a purely empirical, experimental method which, starting from observations of particular things and events, would move towards wider and wider generalizations ... *The understanding must not therefore be supplied with wings, but rather hung with weights, to keep it from leaping and flying.* (B56,

---

2   An example slightly out of sequence was the problem of map making. As sailors ventured into the Atlantic Ocean and down the West coast of Africa, the need for accurate maps grew. European thinkers could not draw a map of a curved earth upon a sheet of paper. Then Ptolemy's long-lost *Geography* was recovered. Step-by-step, this thousand-plus-year-old text explained the intricate mathematical requirements. Occurrences such as these astonished European thinkers. They truly looked back on a lost "Golden Age" of antiquity.

pages 20 and 28. Emphasis added.)

This reflects Aristotle's bottom-up (shadow formulas) mathematics, not Plato's top-down (causal Natural Law) mathematics. Yet, both hobbled efforts to understand reality. When thinkers then used the word, "experiment," they typically really meant "experience" or "observation."

> The distinction [between experiment and experience] is very important and follows from the common belief among ancient and medieval philosophers that *natural phenomena could not be expected to perform in a laboratory in the same way as they did in the world.* (B43, page 144. Emphasis added.)

> Bacon's novel advocacy of an examination of nature "out of its normal course" contravened a standard Aristotelian assumption that a distinction was to be maintained between "natural" and "violent" motion. On this view, observations made under the conditions imposed by experimental protocols would not assist in the understanding of how nature operates when free of such human involvement. *Interfering in the ordinary operations of nature would render the motions studied "violent" rather than "natural."* ... [Years later,] in *Observations on Experimental Philosophy* (1666), Margaret Cavendish – probably the only woman of her era to have directly witnessed experiments being performed by fellows of the Royal Society – was to argue that experimentation produced "*Hermaphroditical Effects,*" *that is, experimentalists were not studying nature at all, but a monstrous creation that was partly their own fabrication.* (B57, page 182. Emphasis added.)

[The "standard Aristotelian assumption" actually came from the astronomical concerns of his teacher, Plato!]

Part of Margaret Cavendish's concern had to do with magnifying devices (microscopes and telescopes). It would be years before viewing oddities would be resolved. (See her book, edited by Eileen O'Neil in 2001, pages 40–53, 99, 105.) In other respects, she was entangled in conflicting Greek thoughts, but her book is instructive about "scientific" thought in these decades before Sir Isaac Newton.

So the "divine" Plato and the "immortal" Aristotle shared a major mistake about matter and motion – perhaps the largest impediment to the advancement of knowledge. Aristotle then made another error about the cause of motion. The choice then was to turn back to Plato and his belief that truth was only to be found in top-down abstractions. More bad choices!

Another exception to the Platonic "all-seeing" belief was St Thomas Aquinas [1225-1274]. (He probably thought the ante-Nicean church Fathers had relevant warnings.) Aquinas favored a careful use of Aristotle's writings, except his belief in an infinite age for the cosmos. I suppose Aquinas was aware of Aristotle's view of the "sense" origin of mathematics, rather than through *anamnesis*. With this critical use of Aristotle, Aquinas advanced rigorous thinking. His work developed into the movement known as "Scholasticism." So, for some centuries, Platonism faded.

Up to this time, Aristotle had been known in Europe through only a few books. Now Europeans were beginning to sense the enormous volume of writing becoming available to them. Plato's writings comprise about 1,600 pages and scholars are reasonably sure they have copies of all his writings. Aristotle's writings, in contrast, comprise about 2,400 pages and scholars are reasonably sure that this represents maybe half of his total writings! Many others were lost in a flood.

Recovered Greek writings stimulated European scholars. The sheer volume of the writings was overwhelming and Aristotle's works were in the majority.[3] Name the subject and Aristotle had probably written an insightful book on it.

> ... [Aristotle's] powerful influence in late antiquity and his dominance from the thirteenth century through the Renaissance resulted not from intellectual subservience on the part of scholars during those periods or from interference on the part of the church, but from the overwhelming explanatory power of his philosophical and scientific system. Aristotle prevailed through persuasion, not coercion. (B47, page 68.)

Aristotle certainly knew how to observe, systematize data, and develop a worldview.

Numerous mathematical treatises began to be recovered. The scope of recovered Greek scholarship far overshadowed the little that Europeans had preserved – or developed on their own.

Aristotle's ideas were still the most influential. For example, William of Ockham (? - 1349) said:

> ... [O]nly individuals exist, rather than [Platonic] supra-rational universals, essences, or forms and that [Aristotelian] universals are products of abstraction from individuals by the human mind and have no extramental existence. (www.en.wikipedia.org/wiki/William_of_Ockham)

Around 1400, further works of Plato began to be available. This first occurred through Pletho, from Constantinople, who attended a church council in Florence, Italy. There he met and influenced the wealthy Cosimo de' Medici to have these works translated into Latin. Later, more Greek thought came directly from Constantinople when scholars fled before its conquest by Islamic forces in A.D. 1453. It became difficult to reconcile the Greek thinkers with each other or with Christianity. The challenge was to separate the empirically useful from cosmic speculations – or the Æons – or even the Pythagorean *akousmatikoi.* Actually, Pletho gave the alarming report that the "divine" Plato and the "immortal" Aristotle contradicted each other! This clash between the reasonable and the rational created scholarly turmoil.

To repeat, a new hazard appeared which the early church Fathers rarely faced. Earlier, the science of measure had been used against Biblical revelation. Now, recovered portions of the selfsame science of measure were considered by many to be God's creative tools. It would become difficult to maintain one's Biblical balance if the science of measure purported to show "how" God worked.

Accommodation was part of this desire to patch the "best" of Roman and Greek culture onto Christianity. This domestication was evident in discussing "creation" according to the Greek concept of the inaccessible unknowable "master" god, creation being a numerical affair, the earth being a dirty evil arena of creation,

---

3   Additional turmoil resulted because Aristotle's works initially came via the Arabic translation of Averroes of (the then Islamic) Spain. Averroes advocated the heresy of Monophysitism. Only later would better translations be available. Most of the (non-mystical) mathematical treatises came much later. For example, Archimedes' writings were not translated until almost the time of Galileo.

the nobility of dueling, the necessity of slavery for the simple folk, *etc.* God commu-
ned with philosophers and spoke to the priestly class. Interest in the vital Christianity
evident up through the ante-Nicean Fathers had not died out – but was generally
relegated to mystics, certain religious orders or simple folk.

In this atmosphere, (roughly identified as the Renaissance, A.D. 1350-1600),
some thinkers struggled with the contrasting outlooks and methodologies of the
"divine" Plato and the "immortal" Aristotle – in spite of the compromising attitudes of
the "neo's." Those leaning to Plato had an increased interest in the mathematical
and cosmic speculations buried in many of these recovered works, instead of Scripture. They expounded upon ethics, philosophy, *etc.* without reference to the Bible.

Once again, it became fashionable to side with Plato and understand knowledge as top-down mathematics. Such thinkers considered their minds to be
independent, freely judging nature and God. *But their free and autonomous minds
were chained to the science of measure.* An ancient Platonic voice beckoned,
"Hear, oh you who thirst for truth, all is geometry." Aristotle, beware!

> The intellectual framework of Medieval theories of motion is a conceptual
> jungle, suitable only for hardened veterans and certainly no place for daytrips
> from the twentieth century. (B47, page 291.)

This preference for the "pure" ancient sources from the lost Golden Age of
Greece was a facet of *Humanism.* But were the "truths" in those ancient documents
really true? When speaking about mathematics, physics, ethics or astronomy, were
they only presenting "facts?" Or were they entangled with the rational storytelling
that had fallen apart centuries before among the circle of Mediterranean cities?
Enlightened men, like their ancestors, lacked an anchor for objective truth or, rather,
had to choose which anchor to hang unto. Humanists resented the confining
Aristotle; they had an all-seeing Platonic bias.

> Sometime between 1535 and 1558, Oxford University [in England] contrived
> to loose every single manuscript in its collection and even sold off the bookcases
> .... In traditional histories, the rise of humanism is usually portrayed as "a good
> thing," but the truth is that the humanists almost managed to destroy 300 years of
> progress in natural philosophy. (B43, page 219.)

It would take the work of Pierre Duhem, around A.D.1900, to begin the re-
recognition of fragments of this lost work.

As part of this humanistic trend, in A.D. 1440, Cardinal Nicholas of Cusa [1401-
1464] published his *On Learned Ignorance.* His interest in the recovered Pythagorean arithmetic and geometry led him to conceptualize an infinite cosmos. To him,
learned ignorance meant that man, learned as he may be, is ignorant when facing a
mathematical or infinite cosmos. Rather, mankind has much nearer reasons for
learned ignorance – facing the incredible complexity of the playing field.

To give a flavor of his thought, consider the following extract:

> I maintain .... that if there were an infinite line, it would be a straight line, a tri-
> angle, a circle, and a sphere [all at the same time] .... And since there cannot be
> more than one infinite thing, you understand transcendentally that an infinite
> triangle cannot be composed of a plurality of lines .... it will be necessary that the

one infinite line be three lines .... Nor will this maximum triangle be composed of sides and angles; rather, the infinite line and the [infinite] angle are one and the same thing....

[After further reasoning] .... Therefore, the infinite line, which is a triangle, is also a circle .... Now, since an infinite line is indivisible and one, it is present as a whole in each finite line....

Now, an infinite diameter has an infinite middle. But the middle is the center. Therefore, it is evident that the center, the diameter, and the circumference are the same thing. (B58, pages 65, 66, 69, 76.)

Such use of the mind's eye covers the first third of the book. His elaborate use of infinity was, of course, against the wishes of Pythagoras and Plato. (His arithmetic, undoubtedly, started with two, had no fractions, zero, or negative numbers, and he counted one thing, two things, three things...)

He used this "knowledge" to write on theology. It seems that, whenever his "science" fog lifts, he sounds orthodox. He did recommend that science should "weigh and measure." Nicholas of Cusa reconciled Scripture to the science of the day, which, in turn, was quite old. 1 + 1 = 2 and associates were very real to him.

He drew on a deep heritage:

Nicholas of Cusa borrowed passages *verbatim* from Thierry [of Chartres] for his *De Docta Ignorantia*. (B59, page 110. Emphasis in original.)

We next encounter Regiomantanus (1436-1476), a mathematician, astronomer, astrologer and translator of Greek works. He had his own printing business also.

He was followed by Ficino (1433-1499) and Pico Della Mirandola (1463-1493), important translators of ancient texts. Ficino worked for the renowned Cosimo de' Medici of Florence, Italy, mentioned earlier. Ficino translated the *Pimander*, (about 1460), a part of the long lost Hermetic Tradition from Egypt. Ficino produced it in a severely edited form. It was thought to be a very ancient document – perhaps as old as Moses. If Greek ideas had allowed their minds to soar as on the wings of eagles, this "new" and older Egyptian truth would reveal to the mind's eye more transcendent truth! It implied the "Golden Age" of the Greeks was only a pale copy of older, hence better, Egyptian lore. The translation was popular but subject to criticism due to the magic and astrology in it.

Pico then translated for Cosimo de' Medici all the works of Plato and of the leading neoplatonists. Florence became the center of Platonic thought in Europe. He next translated the books of the Jewish Kaballah. He advocated it for its magical knowledge – how to penetrate past the heavenly spheres and approach God! Pico is well-known for his *Oration on the Dignity of Man*, of about A.D. 1487. This oration – a challenge to debate with Christian scholars – is rife with Pythagorean mysticism, Hermetic magic, Kaballah – even a touch of Zoroaster. This does not raise the dignity of man! The following gives a flavor of his wisdom:

And that celebrated exclamation of Hermes Trismegistus, "What a great miracle is man...."

[God] had already adorned the supercelestial region with intelligences, infused the heavenly globes with the life of immortal souls and set the fermenting dungheap of the inferior world teeming with every form of animal life....

Who would not wish to be so inspired by those Socratic frenzies which Plato sings in the *Phaedrus* that, swiftly fleeing this place, that is, this world fixed in evil ... Then the leader of the Muses, Bacchus, revealing to us in our moments of philosophy, through his mysteries, that is, the visible signs of nature, the invisible things of God, will make us drunk with the richness of the house of God....

Consider carefully and with full attention, oh Fathers, what these deliverances of Zoroaster might mean....

Philosophy has taught me to rely on my own convictions....

Among the Arabians, there is in Averroes something solid and unshaken....

[I] have proposed for disputation many points of the early theology of Hermes Trismegistus, many theses drawn from the teaching of the Chaldeans and the Pythagoreans, from the occult mysteries of the Hebrews .... We have proposed a harmony between Plato and Aristotle....

I have, in addition, introduced a new method of philosophizing on the basis of number. This method is, in fact, very old....

I have also proposed certain theses concerning magic, in which I have indicated that magic has two forms....

I have wanted to make clear in this disputation, not only that I know a great many things, but also that I know a great many things which others do not know. (B60, pages 3, 5, 26-27, 32, 36, 45, 49, 51, 53, and 69.)

This is early humanism – the most ancient authors sing the praises of mathematics, which is the most reliable guide to truth. Nonetheless, Pico ended his days as a Christian monk. The enigmatic monk, Savonarola, was not impressed with his systematizations and had converted him to Christianity.

As a similar warning about misplaced enthusiasm, their contemporary, Leonardo da Vinci, (1452-1519), the great artist, thinker, tinkerer and mechanical inventor, was more Aristotelian:

"Mental things which have not gone in through the senses are vain and bring forth no truth except detrimental." *What is detrimental are the universal statements which close our mind to reality* ... This [Leonardo's] use of mathematics is essentially different from that of *the Greeks, which had led them to organize a world of abstract entities fit only for contemplation,* and to geometricize the heavens into a system of eternal and uniform circles. (B61, pages 69-70. Emphasis added. First quote from Leonardo, the rest from the book editor.)

Only a thinker and tinkerer like Leonardo could have been so attuned to reality and everyone agrees that he was successful in many areas of inquiry. Thus, he recommends Aristotle's bottom-up outlook.

(This picture is a larger portion of Raphael's 1510 *The School of Athens* that was used earlier. From

In contrast, Paracelsus (1493-1541), a colorful figure from that era, typified the learned mindset:

> Paracelsus held a natural affinity with the Hermetic, neo-platonic, and Pythagorean philosophies central to the Renaissance, a worldview exemplified by Marsilio Ficino and Pico della Mirandola ... Astrology was a very important part of Paracelsus' medicine, and he was a practicing astrologer – as were many university-trained physicians... (www.en.wikipedia.org/wiki/paracelsus)

In spite of da Vinci's earlier caution, into this turbulent background a long obscure book was published in 1543, the *Book of the Revolutions of the Heavenly Spheres*,[4] by Nicholas Copernicus (1473-1543). As a geometrical purist, and following ancient references to Philolaus[5] (*ca* 470 - *ca* 385 B.C.) and Aristarchus of Samos[6] (310-230 B.C.), he rejected Ptolemy's addition of the equant[7] to the existing epicycles in his circular planetary orbits. Equants displaced the cosmos from revolving around the exact center of the earth. Copernicus thought this Ptolemaic imperfection justified moving the center of the planet's circular orbits from the earth to the sun's neighborhood.[8]

As Koestler points out, Copernicus thought he could reduce the required number of epicycles from Ptolemaic astronomy's 39-40 down to 34, but he actually increased the number to 48.[9] The science of measure certainly appreciated geometry as a top-down law, not as a bottom-up explanation for motion. The book was obscure for more than a century. "Circles upon circles" was an attempt at "saving the appearances," not science.

Visible change in the heavens next caught people's attention. Between the times of Copernicus and Galileo, there was the "new star" of 1572, (now called a

---

4   It is one of the few famous books that never sold out the first edition.

5   The mention of Philolaus is rather interesting. He was a leading Pythagorean of the second generation. The comment by Aristotle back on page 67 seems to be aimed at Philolaus. From that quote, we further learn that Philolaus postulated a "fire-centric" universe. This central fire was surrounded with bodies in the following order: (invisible) counter-earth, earth, moon, sun and then the other planets. (Whether this model only reflected Pythagorean number theory or was a veiled reference to a previous planetary arrangement is unknown.) See www.wikipedia.org/wiki/philolaus and www.plato.stanford.edu/entries/philolaus/.

6   Philolaus and Aristarchus have not been mentioned earlier. Other writers lament the ancient neglect of, at least, Aristarchus' ideas and are puzzled by this lack of interest.
     The irony is that Plato was responsible for this slighting of heliocentricity, as shown in an earlier chapter, as he discussed the earth's heavy triangles. Yet, humanists used Plato to criticize Aristotle, so their mind's eye could not see that Plato – their hero – was the culprit!
     Copernicus's book, *On the Revolutions ....,* sidesteps the issue. In Book 1, Chapter 7, he refers to "ancient philosophers" without naming Plato and his *Timaeus*. He also has few references to Aristotle, but many to Ptolemy. It's hard to think that Copernicus mistook Ptolemy for a disciple of Aristotle rather than of Plato!

7   Copernicus also used the equant, but never highlighted it. Equants caused planetary orbits to swing enough to hit neighboring spheres. This detracted from the believability of even Copernicus' own heliocentric, circular, epicyclic astronomy.

8   Copernicus' book does not evidence Hermetic astrology and magic.

9   See *The Sleepwalkers* (B62), by Arthur Koestler.

supernova explosion). It showed change among the supposedly unchangeable stars. This was followed by the comet of 1577 seen all over Europe. The eccentric Danish astronomer, Tycho Brahe, quickly proved the comet entered within the planetary orbits, meaning it was moving *through* the layers of the so-called crystal-line spheres, thus contradicting Aristotle. Further, Galileo's telescopic observations were to soon reveal similarities between planetary bodies (ethereal, so-called) and the earth. Aristotle and Ptolemy, your competing saving the appearances of Plato's worldview are in trouble!

Tycho Brahe, just mentioned, was troubled by some of the same planetary problems that Copernicus was. Tycho developed a planetary model which retained the central earth, but the other planets revolved around the sun, which, in turn, revolved around the central earth. The Tychonian model saved the appearances as well as any other systematization. It was a serious contender for several centuries. Some say it still is! At least relativists have difficulty making absolute criticisms of his method for saving the appearances.

Kepler preferred Copernicus' system but scrapped the circles in favor of inelegant ellipses.[10] He then began a quest for a "force" to replace the self-explana-tory circles – whose philosophical importance went back to Plato. Galileo preferred Copernicus' epicyclic and circular geometry over Kepler's ellipses, Tycho's system or Ptolemy's. Heavenly "appearances" are easy to understand but difficult to know.

Mathematics was regaining its powerful influence. Cassirer reports that the Renaissance mind knew that:

> Although nature is simple inexhaustible and infinite, we are nevertheless cer-tain that it is the infinity of ... mathematics. And although we can never encompass their entire extension, we nevertheless can grasp their ultimate foundations, their principles. *The ideality of mathematics lifts the mind to its greatest heights and brings it to true perfection....* [As Galileo said,] [t]o be sure, the divine intellect knows the mathematical truths in infinitely greater fullness than does ours, for it knows them all; but of the few which the human intellect grasps, I believe that the knowledge of them is *equal to divine knowledge in objective certainty since man can see their necessity*, and there can be no higher degree of certainty than that. (B63, pages 162-163. Second emphasis added.)

This is more ahistorical metaphysics! Copernicus' and Galileo's circles were a Platonic "necessity" which "saw" into the "mind of God!" Grandiose extrapolation – to the infinite – received more approval. The "ideality of mathematics" is rational code that shows that Universal Connected Knowledge banished myth – including discontinuous historical events such as creation *ex nihilo*, Noah's flood and Joshua's long day. Does God prefer the same mathematical dialect? Astronomy has caused many investigators to come to grief![11]

---

10   Some mathematicians and astronomers have pointed out that if Plato had mandated ellipses in astronomy, then Ptolemy's or Brahe's geocentric astronomies would have been as simple as Copernicus' heliocentric astronomy.

11   Much is made of the fact that Galileo's laws of motion played havoc with Aristotelian physics. The mathematical formulation of these laws of motion also irritated the Platonic science of measure. And Galileo was caustic in his relations with fellow members of academia; *he had the "gift" of making enemies*. Astronomy remains a battlefield where adventurous egos clash. The

Reflecting back on the last two chapters, "orthodox science" had initially accepted a potential infinity but had banished an actual infinity. Now an actual infinity bursts out all over the place – "proved" by the lack of parallax seen for the stars. Previously, the infinity of the cosmos was not openly expressed. Out of "deference" to God and His infinite attributes, many referred to the cosmos as *indefinite.*

The conspicuous exceptions to this deference were Sir Thomas Digges (1546-1595), Giordano Bruno (1548-1600) – and perhaps Robert Fludd (1574-1637). The first mention of the use of the Copernican theory to support the infinity of the cosmos was in 1576 in a book by Sir Thomas Digges. Giordano Bruno followed in 1584 with his *The Ash Wednesday Supper.*

Prior to this time, the Atomists (non-mathematically) promoted an infinite cosmos. Others, like Oscellus Lucanus, previously mentioned, promoted infinity due to the perfection of the circle. And Cardinal Nicholas of Cusa, as we have seen, promoted the infinite cosmos.

Giordano Bruno felt a New Age was dawning. He apparently added many of his own ideas to the mystical and reincarnational tradition, including ideas on demons, magic, talismans, alchemy, and astrology. He wanted to traverse the cosmos and reach the divine! (See his book, *On Magic.*) To his mind's eye, a sun-centered infinite cosmos, populated with an infinite number of inhabited stars, was objective truth. Bruno thought the work of Tycho Brahe, in destroying Aristotle's crystalline spheres, definitely aided the up and down movement of spirits and demons. He praised Copernicus for his "science." Unhinged from Biblical and astronomical absolutes, Bruno considered heliocentricity and infinity as the "omens" of the New Age of cosmic understanding.

> Bruno was an out-and-out magician, an "Egyptian" and Hermeticist of the deepest dye, for whom the Copernican Heliocentricity heralded the return of magical religion .... [His] aim was to achieve Hermetic gnosis, to reflect the world in the *mens* [divine intellect, divine knowledge] by magical means ... and so become a great Magus and miracle-working religious leader. (B50, page 450-451.)

Giordano Bruno thought Hermes Trismegistus predated all known religious sources – and Greek science. Bruno was knowledgeable on Aristotle and heavily criticized him. (He does not seem to have been aware that he should also criticize Plato.) Bruno had a Messianic mission to usher in the New Age. The Catholic Church disagreed! And:

> Many of Bruno's own mathematical applications savor rather of Neopythagorean mysticism than of the spirit of modern science, and his geometry was far from Euclidean....
> In the scheme not only do the Ideas of Plato, the numbers of Pythagoras, the Forms of Aristotle, find a place, but also all the Gods of the Greek mythology, of the Egyptian religion, of the Babylonian and Hebrew esoteric cults. The same

---

scholar, Cardinal Robert Bellarmine, cut through Galileo's thicket of words and found the saving of appearances – not knowledge. So report a number of "frank" historians of astronomical details.

character is to be found in the writings of the so-called Hermes or Mercurius Trismegistus, to whom Bruno constantly appeals.

Foremost of all, however, of the influences which directed Bruno's thought was that of the Cardinal Nicolaus of Cusa....

The three characteristics of the universe as a mirror of God which Bruno sought to drive home to the minds of men were its infinite extent, the infinite number of its parts, or the similarity of its constituent elements throughout its whole extent. His illustrations and his arguments would in many cases cause a smile if they were put forward seriously at the present day....

Neither body nor space can be thought of the one apart from the other. Granted the infinity of space, that of matter necessarily follows by an inverse of the principle of sufficient reason: – for there is no reason, according to Bruno, why this small part alone of space, where our earth is, should be filled; the eternal operation is not distinct from the eternal power, *nor could it be the will of God to cramp nature, which is the hand of the all-powerful .... There is then in truth an infinite universe, such as our imagination demands.* (B64, pages 124, 129, 141, 182, 184. Emphasis added.)

For various and contradictory reasons, men like Digges and Bruno laid great stress on the "knowledge" revealed in geometry and infinity. They used the Copernican geometric understanding of the solar system to justify the infinite cosmos they already believed in.[12] Simple mathematics and grandiose extrapolation supported the adventurer's rational quest for an infinite cosmos.[13]

Such thinkers treated "the infinity of the cosmos" as rational proof that Biblical faith conflicted with "unaided" reason – and inferior to reason. In those centuries, (much like the modern New Age philosophy), common "knowledge" agreed that this astronomical adventure "proved" inhabited planets surrounded other stars. Scholarly books were based on this "fact" in the Renaissance, such as *On the Infinity of Worlds*, by Giordano Bruno. (Promotion of this "truth" is one of the reasons Bruno was burned at the stake in A.D. 1600.[14])

---

12   Richard Tarnas, in his, *The Passion of the Western Mind*, claims that most of the early enthusiasts for the Copernican understanding were influenced by hermeticism. (1990, page 295.)

13   This took at least two centuries before being accepted, but textbooks may imply otherwise. It is unclear if the Copernican "watershed" with Christianity was due to the planetary model or to the *subsequent* extension of it to "prove" the cosmos was infinite – as some rationalists had always maintained. In either case, as Feyerabend said, "Everyone agrees that *Copernicus' hypothesis* was a big step forward, but hardly anyone can give a halfway decent account of it, let alone enumerate the reasons for its excellence." (B4, page 202. Emphasis in original.) See also the discussion in chapters 6 and 7. This weakness, in the face of praise, makes us respect atheorism.

Have you noticed how Copernicus' mathematical treatment *proved* heliocentricity? Methinks it takes more than top-down mathematics to secure a proof. Did Copernicus merely find another way to save the appearances? This is another reason to question whether astronomy is a part of science.

(I have always thought it odd that people believe that science is synonymous with the laboratory and the experimental method, yet simultaneously call Copernicus a great scientist! That is a grammatical and logical disconnect. He was a renowned thinker and model builder, but he was not a scientist!)

14   Many historians refer enthusiastically to Bruno as a "martyr of science." Infrequently is the substance of his writings referred to. Some, though, are surprised his superstition and magic merit attention. Bruno wrote extensively on mnemonics – the art of remembering. His belief in reincarnation and the migration of souls meant that remembering myriad magical details was an invaluable navigational aid.

Not surprisingly, it became increasingly difficult to view astronomy as a "value-free" endeavor. *Principles* and *necessities* notwithstanding, atheorism remains skeptical of astronomical adventures.

"Official" Hermeticism ended suddenly. It is instructive as to how quickly non-critically accepted ideas can be exposed. In A.D. 1614, just 14 years after Bruno was burned at the stake, Isaac Casaubon published a book showing the Hermetic text to be a second century A.D. document. He showed how it quoted from Platonic and Pythagorean sources, yet these Greek documents never mentioned Hermes.[15]

Some say that Hermetic flavors live on in some secret societies, such as the Rosicrucians and (speculative) Freemasonry. Another reaction to this Hermetic debacle was a revulsion against ancient books. Many Christian groups still avoid old non-Biblical books.

How did Copernicus, Brahe, Kepler, and Galileo view the Hermetic tradition? Their writings show scant similarity to that of Hermetic enthusiasts. Kepler, though, could write in a mystical style. Once, he did tangle with a Hermeticist. He complained that "you use geometry like a Pythagorean, not as an astronomer."

The popularity of infinity continued to grow. Maybe people thought they were safe from subjectivity now that magic was gone, but they retained a major subjectivity – the Platonic science of measure.

Throughout these centuries, the commingling of understanding and knowledge caused a sense of unease and impending change due to the truthfulness accorded to the science of measure. Cosmic adventures were overriding the proto-empiricism of the budding European economy. As these systematic understandings grew in objective stature in the minds of European thinkers, their souls began to face the Greek dilemma of materialism, meaninglessness and atheism. As the crystalline spheres of Aristotelian astronomy crumbled, the well-reasoned grew angry at their prior "cramped" life. No longer bound by a restraining Aristotelian or Biblical cosmos, they could soar to infinity.[16] Their "all-seeing" mind's eye soared and *the earth shrank into an insignificant speck of dust in a cold impersonal infinite cosmos.* God, as revealed in Scripture, became a myth. Biblical historical truth that once had comforted became burdensome.[17] The Greek ahistorical intellectual adventure was again creating conflict in men's souls.

The submerged magic of many European peasants possibly added to the turmoil of the times. Pockets of paganism apparently remained in Europe until a century or so ago.[18]

---

15   Recent studies have identified some links between Egyptian mystery cults and Pythagorean mysticism. See *Ancient Philosophy, Mystery, and Magic*, by Peter Kingsley.

16   Due to the infallibility of geometry and the Renaissance hatred of Aristotle, Plato escaped criticism and Aristotle took the blame. Yet, reflect back on what Plato said in his *Timaeus* regarding the triangular proofs of geocentricity. (Of course, those with radical doubt continue their radical silence.)

17   It would be worthwhile to study if the combination of the science of measure and the Copernican understanding spurred on vociferous anti-Christians such as Spinoza, Voltaire, Diderot, Hobbes or Hume. Also, what affect did this combination have on Christian thinkers of the time ... as they either established "reformed" churches or "cleansed" from within the Roman Catholic Church? Maybe people have said and believed too much!

18   B59, early chapters.

Being sucked into an infinite cosmos excited some thinkers. Just think, all this "truth" without the need for powerful telescope or space travel.[19] The "all-seeing" power of reason was truly awesome. Other people were generally not so pleased.

Reasoning without limitations led to these conclusions, which many people unwisely accepted as fact. Rational thought had power! Supposed Universal Natural Laws transcended models limited to accessible geo-apparent natural regularities. Astronomy (and mysticism) were pivotal in advertising the materialism implicit in the science of measure and was a catalyst for other thinkers. Indeed, we in the twenty-first century are also guilty of pronouncing certainty upon what we wish to believe.

Such thinkers became freed from the "cramping effect" of Biblical authority, but chained to Universal Natural Law; $1 + 1 = 2$ and associates being foundational to the science of the day. An infinite cosmos models the ahistorical mathematical line; it is unperforated by definition, hence incompatible with *ex nihilo* creation. Thus, Biblical truths began to retreat into "concepts" or "matters of faith."

Not surprisingly, this time period initiated modern philosophy. With the re-emerging *ahistorical* Universal Natural Laws – and their handmaiden, astronomy – undermining the *historical* Biblical cosmos, at least among an increasing number of thinkers, most everything in the cosmos needed new explanations! (Including some mathematical puzzles of the Greeks, thanks to the work of such as Valla and Cardano, who were surprised to be able to solve some previously unsolved Greek puzzles. Perhaps they could solve more!) Some wanted to merely rethink Christian philosophy. Strict rationalists wanted to jettison everything – but their various new philosophies became potpourri. All were excited, but none could agree on how to proceed.

But was the science of measure, itself, in error? Had anyone considered that possibility? Not only should the question be "how to proceed" but how to retreat![20]

---

19   Jaki reports that planetary "life" was accepted among astronomers until about one hundred years ago. See *Cosmos and Creator*. Sir William Herschel (1738-1822) populated the sun, and Lambert (d. 1777) populated even comets. Not surprisingly, Nicholas of Cusa and Giordano Bruno also accepted such life. Likewise, Christiaan Huygens and Immanuel Kant.

20   As rational thinkers paused to take inventory of their ideas, they saw the following: God and His finite *ex nihilo* creation remained proven "wrong" by the Science of Measure – and its ahistorical mathematical line. Yet, for the cosmos to create itself remained absurd. Infinity was still

By about A.D. 1600, and under the onslaught of supposedly unbiased reason, Natural Law, and new philosophy, some Christian thinkers gave up the fight and became atheists. Others retreated into philosopher's gods or Deism – or into sophist indifference. Some retained Biblical truth through the camouflage of a duality of "two books." (The book of Science / Mathematics and the book of Religion, which did not overlap.)

For some, if Christianity was no longer based on the personal God who lovingly watched over His creation, then a "lawcode" Christianity was proper, in imitation of the science of measure. Still others opted for warm, vague words; promoting themselves to an airy existential niche. More uncertainty appeared!

In this emotionally and intellectually charged atmosphere, the paradoxical position of Galileo can be appreciated. In this atmosphere of assertive rationalists, yet tinged with astrology, magic, kabballah, causes, hermeticism as well as just plain Plato versus Aristotle, Galileo took a startling step. As Galileo developed his concepts of motion, he said science can only explain "how" things happen, not "why" – and thus experiments have priority over mathematics. This was part of Galileo's disdain for "worlds on paper," which bypasses many of the above quarrels; it was proto-atheorism![21] No wonder so many thinkers, including Descartes, wanted to ignore him, because they "knew" "science" had a big picture.

> The whole history of science perhaps cannot point to a single figure about whom opinions differ so widely as about Galileo. No one indeed is prepared to challenge his scientific greatness or to deny that he was perhaps the man who made the greatest contribution to the growth of classical science. But on the question of what precisely his contribution was and wherein his greatness essentially lay there seems to be no unanimity at all. (B44, page 333.)

In this confusing atmosphere of disunity among the well-reasoned, the cosmic explanations in the new philosophy of Descartes (1596-1650) exercised great influence, but he tinkered with the science of measure. His development of coordinate geometry revitalized *algebra* by reintroducing taboo mathematical concepts. It allowed representation of zero, negative and irrational numbers.

What did "number" really mean? His use of algebra warned of future disasters.

---

the only rational alternative. Although astronomy was poorly understood, further research would surely clear up the confusion! These deliberations were nurtured by the extrapolative infatuation sanctioned by the Science of Measure. Hopefully, it would remain untarnished, so that these conclusions would not have to be reexamined.

21   This does not harmonize with his advocacy of Copernicanism. A letter written late in his life reflects upon this inconsistency between his physics and astronomy. Part of this is as follows:

> "The falsity of the Copernican system must not on any account be doubted, especially to us Catholics ... And just as I deem inadequate the Copernican observations and conjectures, so I judge, equally and more, fallacious and erroneous those of Ptolemy, Aristotle and their followers." [As the author, Drake, then commented], yet there was nothing hypocritical in Galileo's saying that all science, including astronomy, is a fiction to the extent that it lies beyond the range of practical observations; indeed, *astronomy as Copernicus left it could not be reconciled with many actually observed facts known to Galileo.* (B65, pages 417-419.)

[Note that Galileo does not blame Plato for geocentricity! Note also that the translator, Drake, extended Galileo's comments to all of science.]

His new philosophy gave prestige to *atomism*. His terms, matter and object, were deceptive. Although implying substance, they reduced matter to point particles (the rebirth of the atomism of Democritus). With his point particles, Descartes left out the real world, and animate nature was assumed to be the same as inanimate nature. To "prevent" the soul from being likewise nonexistent, Descartes postulated "spiritual atoms" and a dualism. They were not accepted for long.

> [Descartes] insisted that the most fundamental and reliable properties of matter are *shape, extension, and motion* in space and time, all of which are mathematically describable .... The real world is the totality of mathematically expressible motions of objects in space and time and the entire universe is a great, harmonious, and mathematically designed machine. (B11, page 44. Emphasis added.)

Note that Descartes did not have to wonder if earth-based facts were "modulated" elsewhere in the cosmos. The infinite hardness of matter and the infinite precision of mathematics "affirmed" that such caution was unneeded. Note also that "shape, extension, and motion" referred to the

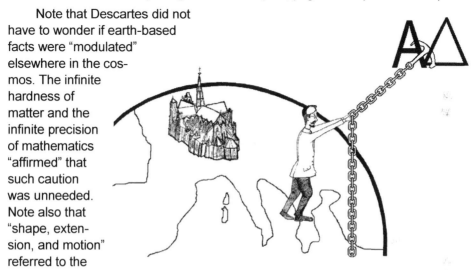

effects of matter but not with matter itself. That important unmathematical "sense" subject was ignored – as was the reality of qualities ignored.

> When Proclus' *Commentary on the Parmenides* [of Plato] became available in Latin to Nicholas of Cusa, he would use it extensively in the development of his profound theories of the philosophical importance of mathematics with regard, in particular, to the divine. One might mention furthermore the great interest taken by mathematicians in the Renaissance in Iamblichus' philosophy of mathematics as reformulated in Proclus' prologues to Euclid, an interest expressed in the idea of a *mathesis universalis* that can be traced up to Descartes and beyond. (B23, page 211.)

Cartesian atomism was the rage of Europe for some time, (except in England). Matter and extension of atoms explained everything – until his new philosophy was eclipsed.

> It is strange that in the vast body of writing about Descartes accumulated in three centuries, that almost no one seems to have called attention to this bizarre misfit – Euclidean geometry boldly advertised in the *Method* and shamelessly ditched in the *Geometry* .... Maybe philosophers don't read the *Geometry*, and mathematicians don't read the *Method*. (B14, page 113.)

A contemporary English physicist and chemist, Robert Boyle, (1627-1691) provided other criticism of atomism and its ancient roots:

The [ancient philosophers] had accepted a number of premises which Boyle did not find justified – that matter is eternal; that from eternity it has been divided into atoms; that the number of atoms is infinite; that they have infinite space to move in; that they are endowed with a great variety of shapes; that they have been in motion from eternity .... *With justice Boyle claimed that [ancient philosophers] had assumed everything that had to be proved.* (B66, page 112. Emphasis added.)

None of these atomist assumptions are public knowledge.

Baruch Spinoza (1632-1677) may have been a target of Boyle's criticism, for this Dutch philosopher "pushed" thought in the direction of mathematics. He praised infinity and said ".... Remember only mathematics." In troubling times, this was his source of comfort. Everything else, including a "factual" Bible, were expendable. He further said:

At the highest level of knowledge, where the mind moves solely among eternal truths, applicable to the universe as a whole, we are *free from the influence of particular things around us*. (B56, page 131. Emphasis added.)

This is faithful to the Pythagorean / Platonic rationalism. Spinoza's books are liberally sprinkled with the word infinity. As Moses Mendelssom, his contemporary, said of Spinoza, "He is drunk with infinity."

Through Descartes, an important cliché entered Western thought. He is noted for saying, "I doubt, I think, therefore I am." [22] Many thinkers welcomed this cliché because it affirmed their disconnection from the increasingly discredited *ex nihilo* creation. [23] Truth was again to be discovered and extrapolated without any appeal to authority – *except the authority of mathematics*.

(Much earlier, St Augustine had said, "If I err, I exist!")

The then recently challenged Christian cosmos is a created fact. It has design, order, rationality, finiteness, and a God-ward centered rational thought – thanks to its Creator. As Pierre Duhem pointed out, the rationality of creation allowed science to proceed in Europe, whereas in other cultures, science was always stillborn. As such, it was more realistic to replace Descartes' cliché with "God thinks and has created; therefore I, as His rational creation, can also think and be ..."

But the "new" philosophies wanted to forget the alternative that creation is not the best of all possible worlds, that it is the only world. Yet the created fact is a marvelous specific thing. Interest in things sounds similar to Aristotle's methodology, which emphasized the study of things, rather than of mathematics. Little wonder that St. Thomas Aquinas had earlier employed many Aristotelian concepts.

Things lead our thoughts back to a specific creation – the finite playing field. Such thinking undercut the new trend to emphasize infinity, or re-elevating mathematics to a position of supremacy or searching "far from the footsteps of humans."

People like Descartes had mathematics in their mind's eye, not Biblical truth or sense experience. He followed Pythagoras, Parmenides and Plato. With the "clear" intuition of inerrant mathematics as an all-seeing guide, they sought cosmic prizes, perhaps expecting to be the "next Aristotle." The "new" Copernican truth meant they

---

22   Spinoza's quote of Descartes includes the "I doubt" clause. *The Essential Spinoza*, Michael L Morgan, page 225.

23   Dr. Stanley Jaki, S.J., in his *Cosmos and Creator,* calls attention to this change in perspective.

no longer relied on Biblical revelation and its finite, *ex nihilo* creation. (Descartes reportedly formulated his new philosophy after a period of intense introspection ... and perhaps of ecstasy. Perhaps he had studied the Brotherhood of the Ogdoad!) God was receding from view, along with *Genesis* 1:1. Reason 101 was strengthened!

Without Descarte's cliché for support, cosmic-minded thinkers lacked a good verbal starting point with which to explain the new "face" of the cosmos, much less explain their own existence. Atheism and materialism were unwise ideas to expound upon within the still generally accepted Christian cosmos. But the self-createdness implied in "I doubt, I think, therefore I am" sounded somewhat neutral – but "open" to mathematics.

Yet, many creative thinkers (mathematicians, composers or artists), could not consistently believe in the resulting materialism. This conclusion of the new philosophy was too cold and impersonal. More importantly, it denied their own creativity; ideas (information) are not materialistic! Writers and composers would capture this tension in the following centuries as thinkers – bound by a restricting materialism – bounced between various alternative new philosophies.

Descartes created a new "phone line to ... ?" This abstraction strengthened rationalism, but his slogan was intuitively no better than "God thinks and has created. I am thus created; therefore I can think and investigate God's *ex nihilo* creation."

Here we are!!! ... On an insignificant spec of dust, in a corner of the immense cosmos, whirling about for who knows why. What is that Bible-thumper trying to say!!!!

Before we move on, Descartes deserves some criticism. His doubts did not extend to mathematics.

"Above all I enjoyed mathematics, because of its certainty and self-evidence of its reasoning, (page 31) ... I took to be tantamount to false everything which was merely probable, (page 32) ... I believed I would have sufficient [precepts] in the four following rules: (page 40) ... The first was to never accept any thing as true that I did not know to be evidently so ... The second, to divide the difficulties that I was examining into as many parts as might be possible[24] ... The third, to conduct my thoughts in an orderly way, beginning with the simplest objects ... And the last, everywhere to make such complete enumerations and such general reviews

---

24   This seems to be an example of the peril of reductionism. See footnote 35, page 45.

that I would be sure to have omitted nothing ... *Only the mathematicians have been able to arrive at any proofs* (page 41) ... [*Therefore,*] I doubt, I think, therefore I am! (Page 58) (B67. Emphasis added. Footnote added.)

Morris Kline then summarizes a lot of Descartes' following words:

A perfect God would not deceive us, and so our intuition can be trusted to furnish some truths .... *God would not allow us to reason falsely.* (B68, page 93. Emphasis added.)

Nonetheless, could Descartes deceive himself? Had he determined that God used the same limited mathematics as he did? Had he determined that God's cosmos was ahistorical? (Surely not with historical events like the Bible describes!) Had he considered if a "clear intuition" could be untrue? His "unaided" reason, "aided" by Mathematic's Word, did not sufficiently save the appearances. And we haven't even come to the mathematical disasters mentioned by Morris Kline.

Reacting to this emerging confusion, in 1659, John Wallis had complained about the rationalist charge against Christianity:

The Christian world had no sound knowledge ... and as though man could not understand religion if they did not understand philosophy, nor philosophy unless they know mathematics. (B66, page 109.)

Wallis, in the years just prior to Newton, was the leading mathematician in England. He also had a long-running quarrel with the geometry-mesmerized utopianist Thomas Hobbes. (See *Infinitesimal*, by Amir Alexander.)

Listen also to Descartes critic, the philosopher and more mature atheist/deist, Voltaire: "*Descartes, born to uncover the errors of antiquity, and to substitute his own!*" But in some respects, Voltaire was less than truthful in promoting his idea of truth:

But [Voltaire] was less [truthful] on seashells, like those which had been found – in fossilized form – on the top of the highest mountains. Horrified that such evidence might lend credence to the story of the Flood, he stoutly maintained the theory that such shells had been dropped along the way by pilgrims ... And what about the reindeer and hippopotamus fossils found at Étampes just south of Paris? A collector must have mislaid them.... (B69, pages 325-6.)

Infinity was the popular intuition of the well-reasoned. It implied necessity, intellectual power, mathematical vindication, freedom, atheism and intellectual "up-to-dateness!" The well-reasoned were sucked into an infinite cosmos.

Infinity became a *mathematical fact*, crucial for interpreting *data*:

We have already seen that the invisibility for the human eye of the fixed stars discovered by Galileo, and, accordingly, the role of his *perspicillum* [telescope] in revealing them, could be interpreted in two different ways: it could be explained by their being (a) too small to be seen, or (b) [large but] too far away .... As a matter of fact both interpretations fit the optical data equally well and a man of that period had no scientific, but only philosophical, reasons for choosing between them. And it was for *philosophical reasons* that the prevailing trend of seventeenth century thinking rejected the first interpretation and adopted the second. (B45, page 94. Emphasis added.)

Notwithstanding these "expanding" horizons, the typical man of "science" in the 1500s and 1600s still considered himself to be a Christian – or at least a man of

"God." Not everyone took the ancient "scientific authorities" at face value – or realized their incompatibility with Christianity. Sir Isaac Newton, for one, was too pragmatic. But he and his contemporaries generally assumed that they were only thinking God's thoughts after him as they sought to see His order (mathematically) imprinted upon nature.

Next on stage was Sir Isaac Newton and his gravitational understanding, and it astounded people. His universal gravitation was the supreme example of *Universal Natural Law!* While Newton remained Christian and scientifically pragmatic, many folk who read his works tended to see the universe as an unperforated self-governing machine. Where then was the need for God?

However, as another hint of looming mathematical problems, Sir Isaac Newton's renowned *Mathematical Principles of Natural Philosophy* was double-minded regarding mathematics. It is filled with drawings of geometric proofs, even though Newton was already known for his dexterity in algebra and calculus. His scholarly contemporaries looked down on algebra and his calculus, so Newton laboriously constructed those geometric equivalents to his algebraic proofs.

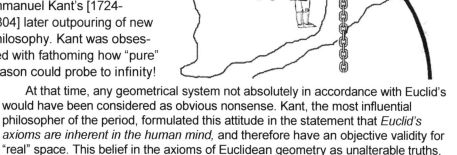

Newtonian gravity overwhelmed Cartesian atomism. Newton's "universal" laws of gravitation stimulated Immanuel Kant's [1724-1804] later outpouring of new philosophy. Kant was obsessed with fathoming how "pure" reason could probe to infinity!

At that time, any geometrical system not absolutely in accordance with Euclid's would have been considered as obvious nonsense. Kant, the most influential philosopher of the period, formulated this attitude in the statement that *Euclid's axioms are inherent in the human mind,* and therefore have an objective validity for "real" space. This belief in the axioms of Euclidean geometry as unalterable truths, existing in the realm of *pure intuition,* was one of the *basic tenets of Kant's philosophy.* (B73, page 219. Emphasis added.)

Note the parallel between "pure intuition" and Plato's *anamnesis.* Unhinged from the Bible, the search was still ongoing for Plato and Parmenides' firm foundation "far from the footsteps of humans." New philosophies abounded, unblushingly using conflicting rational grandiose extrapolations to escape from the created fact.

Some people may quote the English philosopher David Hume's (1711-1776) argument against the supernatural:

A miracle is a violation of the laws of nature; and as a firm and unalterable experience has established laws, the proof against a miracle, from the very nature of the fact, is as entire as any argument from experience can possibly be imagined. (B70, page 128.)

Hume wrote this as a pleasant atheist and a firm believer in Universal Natural Law, new philosophy, and the Science of Measure. As C. S. Lewis said, a miracle is *not* a violation of the laws of nature. How many of the "laws" confirmed by Hume's "firm and unalterable" experience are still held in good report? Undoubtedly, non-Euclidean geometry, zero and negative numbers, foundational schools of mathematics (and debris) and logic were unknown to him. This is another reason to go back to the beginning: ancient Athens and Jerusalem.

As C. S. Lewis further points out, David Hume was inconsistent here in relation to his other writings:

The odd thing is that no man knew this [the unknowable status of the Uniformity of Nature] better than Hume. His essay on *Miracles* is quite inconsistent with the more radical, and honourable, skepticism of his main work.
The question, "Do miracles occur?" and the question, "Is the course of Nature absolutely uniform?" are the same question asked in two different ways. Hume, by sleight of hand, treats them as two different questions. (B71, page 103.)

Hume says, in effect, miracles cannot happen, even though we do not know the uniformity of nature. C. S. Lewis is referring to Hume's statement:

There can be no *demonstrative* arguments to prove *that those instances of which we have had no experience resemble those of which we have had experience* ... Upon the whole, necessity is something that exists in the mind, not the object. (B72, pages 201 & 214. Emphasis in original.)

Hume is trapped by his "soaring" logic. And so, in spite of great bluster to the contrary, David Hume cannot rule out the miraculous, event-filled historical reports in the Bible – or later event-filled lives. When confronted with Christianity, he spuriously makes his claim. The rest of the time he returns to skepticism.

Under the glory of the science of measure, God's providence, miracles, and sanctification became awkward to talk about. The tendency was to "promote" God to the position of the "Great Watchmaker."[25] But as an absentee landlord, God could not remain the personal God present in Sacrament, nor changing men's lives through the indwelling Holy Spirit. *As the cosmos became mathematized, it became ahistorical, unperforated and uneventful!*

Thinkers of that day might have said they "banished" continuing miracles due to a study of Scripture, but many rather meditated upon the science of measure – and *then* reinterpreted Scripture. Humanism was advancing beyond editing ancient manuscripts to facing the moral conclusions ingrained in the science of measure.

This milieu of mathematical monotruth commingled understanding and knowledge, so Boyle's criticism fought a losing battle against cosmic systematizations. By the time the Renaissance gave birth to the eighteenth century Enlightenment, infinity joined geometry to undergird reason, much as Plato's *anamnesis* had at an

---

25   Watchmaker Universe: An idealization after the time of Newton, built upon the writings of William Paley. It praised the harmonious perfection of the cosmos and in the eternality of matter implied in the laws of conservation of matter and energy. The universe was visualized as a perpetual motion machine – without need for God, except perhaps to wind it up at the beginning.

earlier time. The well-reasoned had thrown out history, along with the gods on Mars Hill. All that remained was the endless determinism of monotruth. The Biblical record of beginnings and catastrophe became indecipherable to them.

A latent tension existed because algebra was not completely subordinate to geometry, nor was the calculus understood. And what about one apple, two apples, three apples ...? Physical number had been distorted, but it still existed. Uneasiness arose: Were mathematized thinkers puzzle solvers or storytellers?

As said earlier, men such as Plato and Aristotle did not accept an actual infinity, and likewise Copernicus, Kepler, and Galileo, for they rejected or ignored infinity. Sir Isaac Newton is attributed with a one-dimensional infinity: an infinite space containing a finite material universe, extending back in time no further than 4004 B.C.

Nicholas of Cusa had marked a return to old ideas that was to grow among broad-minded thinkers. Approaching the modern era, we find some influential thinkers, in addition to Descartes, endorsing infinity enthusiastically. Men such as Henry More (1478-1535), William Gilbert (1544-1603), the father of magnetic research, Giordano Bruno, Baruch Spinoza, Immanuel Kant, Pierre LaPlace (1749-1827), Voltaire and others believed in the infinite cosmos.

Hermeticism was dead, but the infinite outlook lived on! Cassirer captured the feeling well:

Infinite space is required as the vehicle of infinite power; and this; in turn; is nothing but an expression of the infinite life of the universe .... We grasp the infinite with the same organ with which we grasp our own spiritual being and essence: ... the ego.... Whoever does not find within himself the heroic fervor of self-assertion and of limitless unfolding will always remain blind to the cosmos and its infinity .... *The Ego can face the infinite cosmos inasmuch as it finds within itself the principles by which it knows that the cosmos is infinite.* (B63, pages 187-191. Emphasis added.)

The ego's "clear intuition" of "principles" is private "knowledge" substituting for *anamnesis* – far from the footsteps of humans. Most of the above quote is attributed to Giordano Bruno – the Hermetic "scientist." Such thinkers thought they were merely giving assent to "principles" of truth, rather than acting on a belief. They "rationally" saw that Biblical revelation ("aided" reason) does not exist!

The science of measure was not immune to criticism, even though it under-girded the new philosophies. Confusion regarding reason continued. For example, we look back to Descartes, who stated:

Let us now declare the means whereby our understanding can rise to knowl-edge *without fear of error* ... [Intuition][26] is the conception of an *attentive mind* so distinct and so clear that *no doubt remains* to it with regard to that which it com-prehends; or, what amounts to the same thing, the self-evidencing conception of a sound and attentive mind, a conception that springs from the *light of reason alone*,

---

26   Intuition: Supposed ability of the mind's eye to directly "see" truths, without the mediation of mathematics or other aids. Whether from Descartes or Kant or Husserl or Brouwer, it has parallels to Plato's *anamnesis*. Such thinkers tried to be of service to "god," but always tripped over their "clear" allegiance to ahistorical infinity.

and is more certain, because more simple, than deduction itself, although as we have noted above the human mind *cannot err* in deduction either. Thus everyone can see by intuition that he exists, that he thinks, that a triangle is bounded by only three lines.... (B11, page 230. Emphasis added.)

(Descartes' intuition only contemplated Ideas – about nondeformable matter. He does not critique grandiose extrapolation applied to physics nor address events.)

Anamnesis was the original guarantee for mathematical truth, proving that frequent reincarnations made one conversant with mathematical truth. Yet, "clear" intuitions tried to substitute for the original, while too embarrassed to acknowledge the frailty of assent to truth. Both appealed to the all-seeing capability of the mind's eye – which is not public knowledge.

The word intuition, as mathematicians use it, carries a heavy load of mystery and ambiguity. Sometimes it's a dangerous, illegitimate substitute for rigorous proof. Sometimes it's a flash of insight that tells the happy few what others learn with great effort. (B14, page 61.)

Doubts about inductive or deductive proof indicate that little progress had been made over viewing reason as "manna from heaven" – or alternatively, a faculty the God of the Bible gave to mankind. Understanding and knowledge remained com-mingled, protecting grandiose extrapolation from criticism, because the science of measure was SCIENCE. Little alarm was forthcoming; the mind's eye was still considered rational, thus infallible.

Others of the Greek thinkers' simplistic understandings have been discarded, but not the long reigning clear intuition of Universal Natural Law. It haunts the modern world. Philosophical, historical, and atheistic books overflow with this "reason!" To use a modern example, the late "objective" and mystical Aristotelian rationalist, Ayn Rand [1905-1982] said:

> To grasp the axiom that *existence exists*, means to grasp the fact that nature, *i.e.*, the universe as a whole, cannot be created or annihilated, that it cannot come into or go out of existence. Whether its basic constituent elements are atoms, or subatomic particles, or some yet undiscovered forms of energy, it is not ruled by a consciousness or by will or by chance, but by the Law of Identity. All the countless forms, motions, combinations and dissolutions of elements within the universe – from a floating speck of dust to the formation of a galaxy to the emergence of life – are caused and determined by the identity of the elements involved. Nature is the *metaphysically given* – *i.e.*, the nature of nature is outside the power of any volition. (B74, page 30. Second emphasis in original.)

Ayn Rand was in a continuing line of unsuccessful extrapolative thinkers. Yes, they think, and "see" clear intuitions with their mind's eye. This acceptance of infinity was long lasting, to deny it was to betray reason:

> As late as 1938 a Nobel-laureate physicist still rejected calculations of the age of the universe from radioactivity on the basis that infinity was the very foundation of science. (B75, page 269.)

Indeed, only in the last century have astronomy-minded folk retreated from their cherished infinite universe into an unbounded, expanding and curved space. The loss is mourned, but they accept the prodding from the adventure of relativity.

Like their earlier counterparts, what would happen if they suspected that their love for truth was bound to subjective mathematical hopes and dreams? *The irony remains; critical freethinkers unblushingly binding themselves to extrapolative infatuation.*

In my reading, I have noticed that historians have a reluctance to use the word, "infinite," to describe astronomy before A.D.1900. A frequent substitute word used is "stable" or "static."

To delve deeper into the well-reasoned mindset, we return to the concept of motion. A mild example was gradual change. Some denied that change ever occurred. Parmenides had said: "What is, is!" Others said reality was slowly cyclic, such that in a life span the portion seen "appeared" as change. *A real rate of change was feared, because, as said earlier, given enough time, mathematical impossibilities arise.*

For example, assume it is correct that measurement indicates the earth's "secular" orbital (or rotational) speed is slowing, increasing the length of the year by one second per decade. As there are about 32 million seconds in a year, a change of *one second per decade* seems laughably insignificant and irrelevant. However, *a mere billion years ago,* 100 million decades have passed, so the earth's orbital speed would have been (much) faster than now.[27] And this would change the dis-

---

27   This assumes a linear decrease in rotation. Recent articles state that "leap seconds" are being

tance between the earth and the moon, which compounds the dynamical problems. (See the next paragraph.) This change in speed suggests short ages, which limits ~~grandiose~~ extrapolation to ages not acceptable to the well-reasoned, for their ahistorical mind's eye "sees" that the earth has been here much longer. The well-reasoned therefore teach men of goodwill that measurable change, in major physical constants, is an intolerable affront to rational thought! Discontinuity, such as Noah's flood, was even more improbable!

Again, around 1970, the Apollo astronauts placed mirrors on the moon's surface. Subsequent bouncing of laser beams off these mirrors show that the moon is receding from the earth about 1.5 inches per year! *Again,* a ridiculously small amount. *But,* a billion years ago, the moon would have been 1.5 billion inches closer! (That would be about 23,000 miles – or 10% closer! Actually, much closer because the force of gravity increases as the square of the distance reduces.) And in the hypothesized 4.6 billion year age of the earth and moon – Yikes! Well, we had better drastically revise astronomy! Or is it that the speed of light is changing?

Anyhow, as **Reason 101: 1 – 2** previously proclaimed:

The fear of mathematics is the beginning of knowledge.
Our "all-seeing" mind's eye thus soars as on the wings of eagles.

Verily, our mind's eye is allowed to see great things!
Our ahistorical mathematical line tells experimenters how to work.

In spite of their science of measure, the ancient Greeks lived in the real world. The greatest problems in science involved motion and change. Their science of measure created this dilemma, which they tried to solve using the same science.

There is another fallout from the science of measure: *evolution could not occur!* The stable cosmos of the ahistorical mathematical line prohibits cosmic change. Evolution is change; circular or cyclic motion is unchanging. Further, the science of measure knew that "1" was a true constant, not growing to 1.01 or even to 1.000000000001. (Nor could it diminish to 0.99999999! Natural Laws – written with numbers – could not evolve. If everything is top-down mathematics, only the steady state cosmos harmonizes with simple natural law.[28]

There is no sign of any idea of a running down of the universe, of any precursor to the concept of entropy, in the whole scientific thought of Greek antiquity before the intervention of Christianity in the later writings of Philoponus [*c.a.* A.D. 640]. (B76, page 16.)

Philoponus expressed his "running down" in criticizing Aristotle's advocacy of an infinite age for the cosmos. Philoponus also showed a mathematical contradiction involved in talking about an infinite age; this criticism stood for a thousand years.

But, later thinkers began to talk about evolution because of strange fossils – in strange places. Also, after rejecting *ex nihilo* creation, they slowly realized that man

---

added every two or three years, not once per decade.
28   This made life difficult for cosmic thinkers. Many a rationalist declared allegiance to a steady state cosmos, even though, today, other ideas are more paradigmatic.

was too complex to suddenly, materialistically, appear. To account for man's appearance, they had to evade science and use sufficiently vague terminology.[29]

Such is the tyranny of the science of measure: change is absurd. With mathematics limited to Euclidean geometry and arithmetic to whole numbers above two, and with "measure" and "quantity" considered interchangeable, accepting even gradual change required the universe to have either a catastrophic breakdown or develop multiple infinities. Multiple infinities were impossible and reinforced the absurdity of change. A mathematical argument against the infinite age of the cosmos existed back in the Middle Ages. It said that while the sun goes around the (geocentric) earth an infinite number of times in an infinite time, the moon would also go around the earth an infinite number of times, but an infinity 29 times larger! But... multiple infinities were impossible.

(Various articles in astronomy magazines help readers appreciate why hints of measurable change cause such editorial furor. Change falsifies the science of measure.)

Almost with an apology, we return again to the earlier discussion on the engine of progress: native ingenuity, engineering and technology – or was it actually (inaccessible) science? Here are some later examples of what was going on in empirical science, for "theoretical" science prefers an event-less contemplation. For while we have been discussing theoreticians up to this point, one could get the impression that they, indeed, were responsible for all the improving standards of living.

Philosophers of science constantly discuss theories and representation of reality, but say almost nothing about experiment, technology, or the use of knowledge to alter the world .... History of the natural sciences is now almost always written as a history of theory. (B77, page 149. I believe Paul Feyerabend recommended this book in his *The Tyranny of Science*.)

Experimenters, engineers, technicians, craftsmen and tinkerers need further mention. Consider the following examples, primarily from the chapters on Experiment and Observation in *Representing and Intervening* (B77):

• Humphrey Davy (1778-1829) was a notable theoretician and chemist, yet he discovered oxygen (or photosynthesis) just due to curiosity. In a pond near his house he noticed that ferns below the water surface had bubbles on their surface. Davy put a jar over these, (presumably he constructed a stand and waited several days) and collected these bubbles. When he inserted a candle, the flame flared up greatly. Thus Davy discovered oxygen.

• The invention of the steam engine in the 1700s was due to tinkerers and engineers. First was the "atmospheric engine" of Newcomen in 1712. This was vastly improved by Watt's "condensing engine." Finally, Trevithick's 1804 "high-pressure engine" completed the development. The puzzle was that they could not

---

29   This continues even today. That which is amenable to mathematics, such as genetics or microbiology, causes great difficulty. Such as reported by the late Nobel laureate Jacques Monod (*Chance and Necessity*), who believed in evolution. Yet in his genetic specialty he could not see how evolution could occur, so he had to rely on astronomers to tell him "how to work." [We would say he could not recognize intelligent design.] The Intelligent Design movement, grouped around the *Discovery Institute*, has elaborated on the dilemma.

explain the improved fuel economy of Trevithick's engine. Thus the thermodynami-
cist, Sadi Carnot (1796-1832), was called on to explain the result. So today, we
have the "Carnot cycle."

Carnot's became the first scientific investigation of the steam engine. By the
time Carnot wrote, steam engines had been in use for more than 100 years, and
the Industrial Revolution, propelled in large part by the application of steam
power, was well under way in Europe. The case is precisely the opposite of the
cliché of technology as applied science. Carnot's analysis of the steam engine
provides the paradigm case, rather, of technology setting the agenda for scientific
research. (B54, page 305.)

 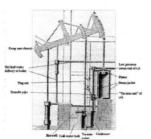 

| Newcomen Atmosphereic Engine | Watt's Condensing Engine | Trevithick's High-Pressure Engine |

From this came the steam locomotive and the steamboat.

(Drawings above and on next page from www.wikipedia.com.)

• William Herschel, the noted astronomer, in 1800 discovered radiant heat by
his attention to detail. He had been using colored filters in his telescope and when
he handled the filters he noticed that some of them felt warm to the touch. Why?

• Chemistry is indebted to alchemists. Granted, alchemists wasted a lot of time
and resources on strange ideas.

• In 1824, Thomas Telford completed the world's first suspension bridge across
the Menai Straits in England, a span of about 600 feet. The bridge is still in use.

(Drawing from the Scottish Engineering Hall of Fame.)

He used cast iron chain links to support the suspended structure. (Wire rope
was not yet developed. As recounted in B54, pages 292 to 294, engineers and
builders had no references with which to judge such a novel structure. So a government commission solicited suggestions from engineers and scientists. The engineers
provided some suggestions. The astronomers and mathematicians had silly suggestions. The author goes on to note:

To their credit, some of the theoreticians on the committee recognized that
science was not yet prepared to minister to technology. Isaac Milner, the Lucasian

Professor of Mathematics at Cambridge (Newton's professorship), observed that theory would be useless in such applications until it was *combined with practical knowledge. The theoretician, he observed, "may … appear learned, by producing long and intricate Calculations, founded upon imaginary Hypothesis, and both the Symbols and the Numbers may all be perfectly right to the smallest fraction, and **the bridge be still unsafe**." (B54, page 294. Bold in original. Emphasis added.)*

The author also mentions Thomas Edison, and his "invention without science" at his Menlo Park laboratory. (Page 167.) Edison did not fear "hermaphroditical effects!"

Otto Gas Engine
(later version)

• Nicholaus Otto (1832 – 1891) was a commercial traveler in the grocery business. He became interested at age 29 in the gas engine. He perfected some earlier contraptions in 1866. (B55, page 342.)

• I suppose myriads of contraptions were developed with no inkling of any theoretical science. "The gunners, foundrymen, smiths, shipbuilders, engineers, and navigators all did their work and made their inventions and improvements with the aid of nothing more (and nothing less) than experience, skill, intuition, rules of thumb, and daring." (B54, page 200.) Qualities bless mankind!

Concurrently, there were developed the cotton gin, batteries, sewing machine, grain reaper, electromagnet, generator and electric motor, phonograph, motion pictures, telegraph, telephone, automobile, vacuum tube, transistors and rockets. Few of the inventors of these things had much education. Keen eyes and alert minds were the needed ingredients. (See again *The Story of Inventions* by Frank B Bachman.)

So what is meant by science, engineering and technology? Buried beneath the rhetoric is the ongoing conflict between those who want to grandiosely extrapolate (Platonism) and those content to experiment (Aristotelianism.) Confusion results when "explainers" ignore the hidden, yet obvious, path wending up from ancient Greece!

Returning to "theoretical science," we close this chapter by reflecting upon people who considered themselves eminently reasonable and objective, but who often were the most bullheaded, blind believers in rationalism. They could not see the beauty and design of God's world because their mind's eye would not permit it.

There is an interesting point to ponder regarding the mathematician, De Moivre (1667-1754):

There is often told a story of his death, to the effect that he had declared it to be necessary to sleep a quarter of an hour longer each day than on the preceding one. If he was sleeping six hours a day when he began this series, it is evident that the first day thereafter he would sleep [six and one fourth] hours, and on the 73rd day he would reach the limit. [He died in his sleep the following day.] (B78, Vol. 1, page 451.)

Mathematics can be hypnotic! It is such a clear intuition!

In 1794, Thomas Paine published his *The Age of Reason*. Nestled amongst his criticisms of Christianity is his beacon of light: The infinity of space, the plurality of worlds, and the eternal divisibility of matter:

> From whence then could arise the solitary and strange conceit that the Almighty, who had *millions of worlds* equally dependent on his protection, should quit the care of all the rest, and come to die in our world, because, they say, one man and one woman had eaten an apple.
>
> I know, however, but of one ancient book that authoritatively challenges universal consent and belief; and that is "Euclid's *Elements of Geometry*;" and the reason is, because it is a book of *self-evident demonstration, entirely independent of its author, and of everything relating to time, place, and circumstance*. ... But it is quite otherwise with respect to the books ascribed to Moses, to Joshua, to Samuel, &c. (B79, pages 59 and 79.)

These physical "fruits" of the abstract ahistorical mathematical line or science, falsely so-called, rendered Christianity impossible for him and he was in-step with the well-reasoned tradition. Paine understood self-evident Greek science! (And we have yet to encounter the mathematical disasters mentioned by Kline.)

Consider also the eminent French mathematician Pierre Laplace, who coauthored the Kant-Laplace Nebular Hypothesis of the natural – mathematical – origin of the cosmos (over fifty years before Darwin). When Napoleon asked him where God fit into the Nebular Hypothesis, he replied with *sincere* objectivity and disdain, "Sir, I have no need for that hypothesis."[30]

Yes, intellectual adventurers whole-heartedly pursued the lure of objective truth and fell in love with "truth." These staunch defenders of "knowledge" are extolled in word and song. They saw freedom and truth (and an appreciation for goodness and beauty) flowering everywhere! The extrapolative certainty of "self-evident scientific truths," such as infinity, materialism, godlessness, and meaninglessness readily exposed the *irrational crime of*

How quaint! Earth is the only place in the whole cosmos where (frequent) unmathematical motion occurs.

Christianity: believing in a mathematically impossible history and possessing an non-extrapolatable measure of matter and man!

Rational extrapolative folk looked back at their rational ahistorical effort and then boldly said: *Let the Christian mystics rage. We do not see through a glass*

---

30   There seems to be some doubt about how to understand this remark. Did Laplace say this as an atheist or as one who believed in the philosopher's god?

darkly. We possess an all-seeing rationalism that reveals the error of their short story. The cosmos and mathematics are interchangeable. God – if He exists – will also be lawful!

Mathematicians who take 1 + 1 = 2 and associates seriously hold, live, and die by strange beliefs, intuitions and certainties. Their cherished infinite cosmos was a mathematical construct. It is sometimes forgotten that during this period, deductive proof reigned supreme and geometry was KNOWLEDGE, not a mere Euclidean systematization. Inductive thought or empirical proof were not needed and generally anathema.

While it is true that conceptual thought would be impossible without either inductive or deductive methodology, three flaws are apparent when using them to transform understanding into knowledge. *First,* understandings may be based on "deceptive" intuitions; *second,* unwarranted extrapolations may be subjectively utilized; and *third,* mathematics may have an unappreciated flexibility. All these can lead to an inaccurate portrait of reality. In their day, however, no scholarly way existed to limit the science of measure's extrapolations, short of absurdity. Atheorism was absent from intellectual arsenals!

This prelude illustrates the Biblical warnings against science, falsely so-called. Try to visualize the communication barrier that arose when the scattered brethren – witnesses to Christ's miracles, crucifixion and resurrection, beholders of transformed lives, infused with the Holy Ghost – encountered "scientists" proclaiming, "Hear, oh you who thirst for objective truth, *all is geometry!*" The ahistorical mathematical philosophy of the epoch was a communication barrier.

Too often, we forget that such as the gnosticism of the first several centuries after Christ was not just philosophy or religion. It harmonized Christianity with the science of the day (*i.e.,* the secret "soaring" knowledge of number and harmony)! Throughout history the mistake of commingling "new" understandings with knowledge is repeated. It "objectively" reconciled faith to another "reason:"

To the Gnostic myth the cosmogony of Plato's *Timaeus* and the first chapters of *Genesis* contributed in almost equal proportions. (B80, pages 36-37.)

Throughout the whole Middle Ages, [the "divine" Plato's] *Timaeus* was considered one of the fundamental works of philosophy. (B63, pages 125-126.)

Sadly, but not surprisingly, some Christian theologians also found geometry irresistible. They wrote theology in the style of geometric deductive proof. Some even struggled with whether Jesus Christ was a geometrical being!

The school of Chartres [France] was Western Europe's elementary school of speculation. All the cosmologies of the twelfth to eighteenth centuries, as well as magical-naturalist humanism and rational theology were first worked out there .... The Breton brothers, William and Thierry, founded this NeoPlatonist school of cosmic interpretation, which virtually reduced God to numbers and geometrical figures, and creation to an automatic process .... The being of the Son was a geometrical polygon .... The object of this was ... a clear, rational construction according to the archetype of [divine] numbers and the pattern of arithmetic and geometry. (B59, pages 108-109.)

Edward Herbert (1581-1648), the father of Deism, wrote *The Ancient Religion of the Gentiles,* which was posthumously published in 1705. In it he had urged a quick and permanent abandonment of the idea that God intervened supernaturally in man's world in any way. Nonetheless, he was somewhat out-of-step with his contemporaries:

> [U]nless according to the Copernican System you will have the Earth move; which seems improbable, in regard this sluggish terrestrial weight, so unfit for motion, would double exceed the velocity of the cannonball before mentioned. Tycho Brahe proves, that the fixed stars do not only move in longitude from the vernal division of the zodiac, but in latitude also... (B81, page 82.)

Likewise:

> [Leibnitz, 1646-1716] wrote [that] God, the geometrician and mathematician, created the cosmos, as the Psalm says[31], according to measure, number and weight, and therefore the universe plays God's game on earth out of its own force and wisdom .... Leibnitz's basic ideas came from the geometric mysticism of the middle ages, from Chartres in the twelfth century up to Nicholas of Cusa. God as an infinite sphere whose centre is everywhere and circumference is nowhere had first been conceived ... at the end of the twelfth century. (B59, page 417.)

Such hymns to mathematical incarnation are, nonetheless, a shameful display! Yet, consider the attractive *reasonableness* of the *physical* mathematics embodied in the science of measure. Because irrational originally meant mathematically impossible, *thus* also physically impossible, belief in the science of measure conflicted with belief in discontinuities, much less in a created world – personal accountability to the Creator – or anyone's need for a Savior. You really had to walk closely with Him to keep the faith! Today, many people question whether sin should be redefined as a disease, showing that some still treat Christianity as an adventurous myth, not as a living relationship.

As reasoners considered their achievements, they were able to comprehend the full introduction to knowledge: "The fear of mathematics is the beginning of knowledge. Verily, our mind's eye is allowed to see great things." **Reason 101: 1a & 2a**.

Reacting to these "exciting" geometrical advances in the appreciation of truth, goodness, and beauty, the reformer, Dr. Martin Luther (*c.a.*, A.D. 1525) had said it as only he would dare, *"Reason is a devilish whore!"*[32]

---

31   The actual reference is not to the *Psalms*, but to the Apocryphal *Wisdom of Solomon*, 11:20.
32   Freidrich Heer, in his *The Intellectual History of Europe*, B59, page 223, disparages this conclusion of Luther – his "monstrous distrust of reason." Luther's use of this phrase is from his *Bondage of the Will*, written against Erasmus of Rotterdam. Their conflict regarded whether individuals could use their "free will" to come to God, with help from their reason. The conflict was not over the use of the will in such things as choosing what to eat. Erasmus, in his *Enchiridion*, seemingly placed no limits on reason. He also preferred Plato and Pythagoras to Aristotle.

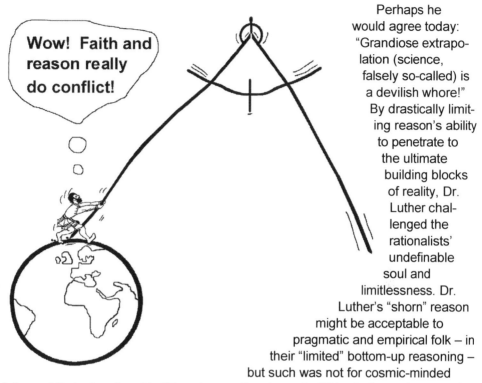

Perhaps he would agree today: "Grandiose extrapolation (science, falsely so-called) is a devilish whore!" By drastically limiting reason's ability to penetrate to the ultimate building blocks of reality, Dr. Luther challenged the rationalists' undefinable soul and limitlessness. Dr. Luther's "shorn" reason might be acceptable to pragmatic and empirical folk – in their "limited" bottom-up reasoning – but such was not for cosmic-minded folks and their clear "unaided" top-down rational proofs. If his challenge is accurate, is the "free and autonomous reason" of the mind's eye a reasonable guide in the search for truth, goodness, and beauty?

Interestingly, Dr. Luther can be so quoted, as can the early church Fathers, without criticism about being anti-science, only in the context of the history of the science of measure. Christians cannot effectively critique the mindset of scientific rationalism when restricting themselves to geology, biology or "spiritual things" – a spiritual "nichitis" that avoids the hidden yet obvious path of the between-years. Such an attitude reasons its way to its own aridness or nonsense.

Are twenty-first century Christians willing to articulate their prelude? Then they can confront promiscuous reason and its shameless flitting from one rational "truth" to another. It is not enough to dismiss the need to confront promiscuous reason by saying this discussion is about non-current rational thoughts. If that were really true, how are materialism, godlessness, and ultimate meaninglessness now justified?

Yet again, rationalists had not proven that:

■ empirical science, engineering and technology need guidance by grandiosely extrapolative "science."

■ the universe is infinite.

■ historical measured rates of change are an illusion.

■ histories of knowledge advancement can ignore engineering, technology and tinkerers.

■ reason is *not* a devilish whore, when top-down rationalism is divorced from empirical science.

We have seen that rationalism's "progress" was treading a bumpy road. As we continue on that obvious, yet hidden, path, the next chapter goes forward and backward. That chapter introduces us to an increasingly bumpy road, thanks to the initial mathematical encounters with perplexity, confusion and disasters!

In "Praise" of Extrapolative Infatuation

Let humans be free and master the infinite cosmos.
No longer enslaved by sense, opinion, faith or events,
Nor content with myth, magic, or appearances;
Let reason reveal Natural Law's cleansing power
        via the purity of self-evident mathematics.

Understand Universal Connected Knowledge:
"Science's" Genesis among the Greek masters;
"Science's" value-free mathematical language;
"Science's" power of grandiose extrapolation;
"Science's" myth-shattering Universal Natural Law.

Confidently reap the harvest thereby nurtured:
Be not afraid of the unknown
Identify, measure and rationally explain it!
Combat evil (non-"sense") with pure reason
Create good by altruistic allegiance to truth.

We can make quite suitable use of mathematical signs because of their incorruptible certainty.
Nicholas of Cusa

For as Positio [the line, First Power] refers to a line, quadratum [the square, Second Power] to a surface, and cubum [the cube, Third Power] to a solid body, it would be very foolish for us to go beyond this point. Nature does not permit it.
Girolamo Cardano

Salviato: "Now, Simplicio, you must know that astronomers and mathematicians have discovered infallible rules of geometry and arithmetic."
Galileo Galilei

It is important to be clear about the fact that modern mathematics is guided from the outset by cosmological – astronomical interests. This is true not only of Vieta, but of Kepler, Descartes, Barrow, Newton, etc.
Jacob Klein

Life is not an illogicality; yet it is a trap for logicians. It looks just a little more mathematical and regular than it is; its exactitude is obvious, but its inexactitude is hidden; its wildness lies in wait.
G K Chesterton

The universe is all there is, all there ever was, and all there ever will be.
Carl Sagan

Reason grounded extrapolative infatuation upon transcendent mathematical truths taught via the *anamnesis* of the mind's eye. This made sense from the Pythagorean and Platonic viewpoints. Previous chapters reviewed peculiarities in the resulting science of measure.

As rationalism now controlled the adventure, mathematics must be self-evident truth. No longer grounded in the Garden of Eden or accessible via reincarnation, mathematics now stood alone – or on infinity. Reason and its mathematical extrapolations valiantly strove to remain the objective foundation for knowledge of an unperforated cosmos. The alternative remained; rationalism is merely the storytelling vestments of philosophers and mystics.

This pre-modern view was still a minority view among the general population, but in this chapter we see mathematical puzzles arising even then among rationalists. (The dominant view was the Christian *ex nihilo* worldview.)

As we ponder the history of science, a sense of bewilderment and embarrassment often occurs. Surely learned people never believed those mathematic things. *But they did* and it taints the "scientific" truths "known" then, both of the playing field and elsewhere! Were they produced serendipitously or by sleepwalkers, as Koestler said? Are they merely popular myths?

Further, are there theological ramifications? The "scientific" principles of atheism, materialism, infinity, the science of measure, *etc.*, were self-evident truths to those believing that simplistic mathematics meant Universal Natural Laws, not useful formulas. However, "Geometry exists," viewed atheoristically, points to a stable, finite, complex and perforated creation having discernible geometric patterns. *No wonder ex nihilo creation remained the reasonable outlook in A.D. 1700!*

Thoughtful followers of the intellectual adventure still remind us; "Yes, *then* we were subjective, but not now! Later events prove the correctness of the adventure's assumptions about the unperforated cosmos – as elaborated and refined by modern 'science' and its revealing of the universe's 'vast distances and long ages.'"
They hoped that disowning Hermeticism had purged rational thought of the subjective. They hoped the subjective resided in the impulsiveness of the utopianists, not in the mathematical principles of the mind's eye. *They were mistaken.*

When thinkers ignore the wisdom of the Bible, the study of nature yet leads to the limiting conclusion cited by St. Paul in Romans 1:20:

> *For the invisible things of Him from the creation of the world are clearly seen, being understood by the things that are made, even His eternal power and Godhead; so that they are without excuse:*

At first inspection, studying (inanimate) nature using the science of measure seemingly avoided such limitation. Yet the science of measure both helps and muddles our reasoning! Examining more scientific history unveils in-house tools showing this. *Meanwhile,* reasoning about the inaccessible remained invincible, not full of pitfalls, leading a charmed existence – preeminently objective, incarnate in the science of measure, and sanctifying grandiose extrapolation.
Not surprisingly, histories about the growth of science and science, falsely so-called, review astronomy and various investigative fields, but say little about the material reviewed in this chapter. Nonetheless, emphasis gradually shifts to the new ways thinkers grappled with fact and truth. "Unaided" reason, invincible yet undefined, showed increasing incomprehensibility.

Entropy, attenuation and secular events, plus Biblical events such as Creation *ex nihilo* or the Fall in the Garden of Eden, remained incomprehensible to rationalists. Lack of appreciation for the unmathematical phenomenon of thinking allowed rationalists to also crudely catalog man (and other animate life) together with inanimate material stuff. Man's spirit and God's Spirit were difficult to reconcile with the intellectual adventure. Increasingly, God's miracles and comforting presence were explained away as "unreasonable."[1]
The science of measure receives little direct discussion in typical histories, yet endless references to "immutable Natural Law," "the clockwork universe," or "reason" attest to its deterministic presence. Book titles, before they were truncated,

---

1   Science and theology books up to the Middle Ages referred to miracles both in Biblical times and within the later Christian community. They accepted a perforated cosmos. It might be interesting to study when both types of miracles disappeared from rational discourse. Yet, for those of us who are Catholic (or Nicean), the "visibly(?)" miraculous has not disappeared – either from Holy Communion or from various healing sites. For some other brethren, the miraculous remains evident in healings and answered prayer.

also evidenced it. Spinoza's *Ethics* (*c.a.* A.D. 1675) was originally called *Ethics Demonstrated in Geometrical Order*. Today, no one objects to an argument just because of the manner of presentation. But in that era, the geometric method of presentation transformed it into objective truth.

In spite of this euphoria over the inaccessible, progress in the accessible realm was primarily due to empirical science (experiment, engineering and technology), craftsmen and tinkerers. We have seen the caution about Platonic expansiveness that men such as Roger Bacon and Leonardo da Vinci expressed. In the 1600 and 1700s, Christianity set the pace for scientific advances.

This outlook was summarized as the **First Principles of science**, in the first chapter, page 9, partially repeated here:

A. The universe is real. Its origin is *ex nihilo*; the created fact.
B. The universe is reasonable (orderly), witnessing to the "mind of the Maker."
C. The human mind can understand much about the accessible universe because the mind is a major feature of being "created in the image of God."
D. After the *ex nihilo* creation event, material actions proceed due to cause and effect relationships – with few exceptions. Events occur; laws may not acknowledge them, but nothing happens because of definitions.
E. There is unity in the cosmos. One God and His common laws govern the universe.
F. Sense observation uncovers direct facts. Open eyes and creative minds, in all walks of life, were successfully improving living standards and knowledge. Experimental rigor was gradually recognized as needed to help distinguish between storytelling, saving the appearances and cause and effect relationships. Knowledge was expressed mathematically to limit ambiguity.
G. Mathematics reflects the rational design of reality.

These First Principles reflected Christian belief as well as various Greek principles of logic and mathematics. Creation *ex nihilo* implies that a reasonable mind can explore an event-filled, yet orderly, unified, rational, finite universe. Cause and effect rejected belief in strange causes of motion, astrological "spirits" or "essences" directing physical processes. But First Principles do not come from science; they frame science. Principles reflect belief, with evidence.

Unfortunately, geometry was threatened by the continuing failure to find a rigorous derivation of Euclid's parallel postulate. It was gradually realized that *Euclid's was not a physical geometry; but one of many abstract geometries!*

Looking back 2,000 years, Euclid's 5th postulate says that parallel lines do not meet when extended to infinity. In the accessible world, there is no way to deny this. In the inaccessible world, Euclid's statements had appeared to be correct, although worded in an indirect manner.

Many later geometers spent years trying to provide a better definition for the 5th postulate. Finally, in the mid-1800s, several geometers tried to prove Euclid's parallel postulate by postulating incorrect ideas (reduction to absurdity), and thus their falsity would, by default, prove Euclid's parallel postulate correct.

They were in for a surprise! They postulated that parallel lines do meet (or cross) at infinity – and they could find no faulty reasoning involved in the non-Euclidean geometries that resulted. More versions were developed later, the point of departure for all being a rewording of Euclid's "parallel postulate."[2] From the 1850s to around 1900, the consistency of non-Euclidean geometries was grudgingly accepted, but believed to have no physical applicability.

A version of non-Euclidean geometry is called "hyperbolic," meaning lines on the surface of a sphere. This has applicability – intercontinental air travel routes fly the "great circle," instead of a straight line. Sometime in this process, someone even measured a large triangle – measured between various mountain peaks. To the limits of instrumental accuracy, the three angles totaled 180 degrees. Thus, in the physical world, Euclidean geometry is the valid geometry.

But ... what about in the macro-world of astronomy? What can be a yardstick in space? The only possible one is a light beam. Is a light-years-long beam of light straight or of constant velocity? That was sure to cause arguments.

In this macro-world, "proof" for non-Euclidean geometry comes from believing it and then framing explanations consistent with it. But that is circular reasoning supported by a consensus of learned participants. Einstein would use it to mold his relativistic mathematics to save the appearances.

If "Geometry exists," do *"Geometries exist?"* Poincaré (1854-1923) was somewhat perplexed by the possibilities:

> We are led to a series of theorems even stranger than those of Lobatschewsky [1793-1856] and Riemann [1826-1866], but equally free from contradiction. I shall give you only one of these theorems .... A real straight line may be perpendicular to itself. (B84, page 46.)[3]

The famous mathematician Karl Friedrich Gauss (1777-1855), had earlier prudently decided to remain silent regarding his pioneering investigation of non-Euclidean geometry:

> He said in his letter to Bessel that he probably would never publish his findings on this subject because he feared ridicule or, as he put it, he feared the clamor of the Boeotians, a reference to the proverbially dullwitted Greek tribe. One must remember that ... the intellectual world at large was still dominated by the conviction that Euclidean geometry was the only possible geometry. (B11, page 83.)

Today, non-Euclidean geometry is hailed as a triumph of thought; a necessary prelude to the adventure of relativity. That was not the attitude of nineteenth century mathematicians! A further dilemma was the *multiplicity* of non-Euclidean geometries. Later mathematicians, such as Minkowsky, gave prominence to only one of

---

2   In retrospect, Euclid had been also uneasy. His "parallel postulate" was not formulated as an independent axiom.

3   Euclidean geometry stipulates that the sum of the three angles of a triangle is 180 degrees. Lobatschewsky and Polyai, instead, said the sum of these three angles was slightly more – or less – than 180 degrees. (Very long) curved "lines" are thus possible – and Reiman and some others provided even more formulations.

these – and only one of its many solutions. This eclectic attitude did not sit well with those committed to the lure of objective truth.

This failure to prove Euclid's parallel postulate threatened arithmetic – for good reasons. Contrary to the rationalist's assent to "all-seeing" mathematical Universal Natural Laws; experimenters, thinkers, observers and mathematicians were in for some surprises. Their empiricism, their concentration on mechanics – and inter-action with the swelling number of craftsmen and tinkerers – instead of astronomers (on whom the Platonists focused) led to these surprises.

This new exploration of nature revealed an increasing complexity; "taboo" mathematics crept into the resulting explanations. Experimenters, thinkers, observers and mathematicians "created" increasingly esoteric, but powerful, mathematical tools to understand complex phenomena. Heat flow, ocean waves, violin strings, tides, gravity, *etc.*, in complicated situations required these new mathematical tools for successful modeling. (Examples follow later in the chapter.) This successful physical problem solving initially muted concern about violation of taboos; or incon-sistencies in the mathematical and logical foundations for these tools; or whether all tools yielded compatible results, or required atheism, materialism, and meaningless-ness! Consequently, inductive proof and empiricism crept into prominence,[4] but could not justify grandiose extrapolation either.

Mathematical purists ignored experimental science, with its clutter of appara-tus, rules of thumb, design safety margins or *ad hoc* mathematical tweaks. Today, most people tend to laugh at the purist's ivory-tower approach. Yet, if "science is a seamless garment,"[5] to accept empirical results and their seemingly innocent, but limited, mathematical conclusions and tools threatened the rationality of the then hallowed ahistorical science of measure. If it had defects, illuminated by its irrele-vance to the expanding Industrial Revolution, why was the science of measure so admirably suited to measure beyond the known? (To doubt its truth made rational-ists seethe with indignation!) Its greatest deduction was the supposed determination that the cosmos is infinite – the fruit of extrapolative infatuation!

So we now can appreciate more of **Reason 101: 1 – 3:**

The fear of mathematics is the beginning of knowledge.
Our "all-seeing" mind's eye thus soars as on the wings of eagles.

Verily, our mind's eye is allowed to see great things!
Our ahistorical mathematical line shows experimenters what to do.

Do we understand our new mathematical knowledge?
Can our mind's eye deceive us? What is all this noise?

A problem was looming because the success of experimenters, engineers, technicians, craftsmen, and tinkerers, with their (sometime) pragmatic use of mathe-matics were beginning to threaten mathematical objectivity. This success and the continuing presence of seemingly innocent taboo concepts made some thinkers

---

4   This pragmatic muting of rigorous concerns about mathematical theory allowed Christian men of science to flourish and remain dominant.
5   I do not remember the source of this phrase.

nervous about mathematics' rational (*i.e.*, physical) foundation. These newer mathematical concepts were to join the longstanding list of the dubious: discontinuity,
change, negative numbers, fractions, irrationals and even the humble zero. Jointly,
these threatened to separate the adventure of "extrapolative science" from the lure
of objective truth.

Accordingly, nervous mathematicians in the eighteenth and nineteenth centuries attempted something long overdue. They tried to (re)construct the objective
basis of arithmetic and incorporate these *newer* mathematical concepts, with their
new-fangled and scandalous infinitesimals, imaginaries, and multiple solutions.

These mathematicians failed. In their attempt to reconstruct arithmetic's
foundation, they, instead, discovered several consistent ways to explain arithmetic.
Typically, over the time period from about 1880 to 1930, *four competing foundational schools of arithmetic were gradually recognized: logicist, formalist, intuitionist,
and set-theoretic.*[6] Thus, the sum total of (admittedly useful) mathematical tools
form a competitive agglomeration, not a unified system.

The introduction to a book on mathematical logic has the following revealing
comment:

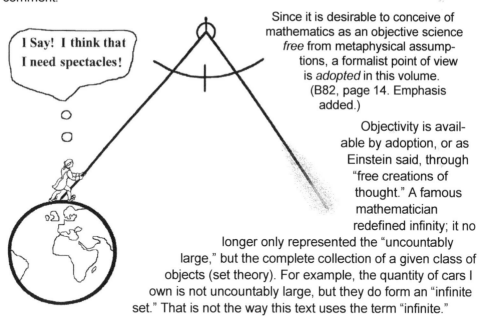

Since it is desirable to conceive of
mathematics as an objective science
free from metaphysical assumptions, a formalist point of view
is *adopted* in this volume.
(B82, page 14. Emphasis
added.)

Objectivity is avail-
able by adoption, or as
Einstein said, through
"free creations of
thought." A famous
mathematician
redefined infinity; it no
longer only represented the "uncountably
large," but the complete collection of a given class of
objects (set theory). For example, the quantity of cars I
own is not uncountably large, but they do form an "infinite
set." That is not the way this text uses the term "infinite."

---

6   These are the names per Morris Kline in *Mathematics, the Loss of Certainty* (B11). Roger
Penrose, in *The Emperor's New Mind* (B83), labels them as: Platonist, Formalist, Intuitionist and
Finitist. Reuben Hersh, in *What is Mathematics, Really?* (B14), gives a similar list.
      Logicist: (Finitist) Mathematics is a subdivision of logic.
      Formalist: Mathematics is a set of abstract rules, having no inherent meaning. It is a
calculating game.
      Intuitionist: Accepts intuition, but denies reality of infinite sets.
      Platonist (set-theoretic): Mathematics is a real entity existing somewhere that our minds can
discover or communicate with. It is not invention. Infinite sets exist. (This last item would be non-
Platonic.)

Despite self-censorship, well-reasoned men of the late nineteenth century failed to find any extrapolative comfort in multiple geometries and multiple foundations for arithmetic. Disaster loomed!

This confidence that truths would be discovered in all fields was shattered by the recognition that *there is no truth in mathematics .... Mathematics offered to the world proof that man can acquire truths and then destroyed the proof ....* [As a result], man lost his intellectual center, his frame of reference, the established authority for all thought. (B11, page 99. Emphasis added.)

Almost with a spirit of sarcasm, Bertrand Russell famously said:

Mathematics may be defined as the subject in which we never know what we are talking about, nor whether what we are saying is true. (*Mathematics and the Metaphysician.*)

If scientific results were not mathematical monotruth, then truth hadn't been found! Top-down mathematics was thereby measured and found wanting. A mathematical proof was not enough to guarantee a grandiose statement's applicability to the real world. Galileo and Newton's work had pragmatically highlighted this caution, as their emphasis on experimentation showed the inadequacy of a deceptive mathematical rigor. Their attitude was an unwelcome cleavage of mathematical beauty from physical truth, throwing a cloud of doubt over grandiose extrapolation.

Doubt – or at least perplexity – was increased due to the increasing development of algebra[7], trigonometry, calculus and other new disciplines.

Mathematics changed from 1600 to 1900. It entered as *mono-mathematics*; relatively simple concepts that could be physically modeled and easily accommodated to Euclid's *Elements*. It exited as *poly-mathematics* – with all the democratic pitfalls that implied.

Modern mathematics, with its various foundational schools and layered rational accounts, is not the science of measure that Plato or even Galileo knew. When Galileo read the mathematical book of nature evident in the playing field, he *knew* that he was discovering knowledge, not doing mathematical storytelling. With many of the "infallible" rules of geometry and arithmetic which Galileo believed in reduced to consensus agreements of "learned" participants, are the "discoveries" supported by new philosophy, but unsupported by experiment, merely further storytelling?

Adherents of the science of measure had not distinguished between abstractions and reality, between mathematics and matter. This flowed from their unreasonable assent to the science of measure's clear intuition that mathematics and the cosmos are interchangeable. The finite alternatives, Creation *ex nihilo* or bottom-up mathematics, did not fit their simplistic mathematics! Lacking atheorism, they fled to extrapolated absurdities – the consequence of mathematical absurdities.

Well-reasoned man, with his free and autonomous reason, seemed to have confronted Romans 1:20. At the least, atheism, materialism, and meaninglessness were inadequately grounded. Cosmic thinking saved (some of) the appearances; it

---

7   As pointed out earlier, algebra had been generally ignored since Greek times. It seemed to be an indirect way to solve physical problems and its methodology incorporated strange features.

was not public knowledge. Causality was inferred, not proven! This was the established authority for grandiose extrapolations, including atheism. Surely this dead end for rational thought was not what the lure of objective truth intended!

Remarkably, the kingdom of the Science of Measure had lasted over 2,000 years.[8] Its demise destroyed "physical" mathematics. Its destruction in the late nineteenth century was a scandalous insult to "unaided" reason, a betrayal of "science" and rationalism. "Sure, sure," adventurers thought, "fledgling experimental science could continue unhindered, but what protected it from chaos ... or creation *ex nihilo* ... if mathematics and astronomy were understandings, not knowledge?"

And empiricists thought, in turn, "Experiments free us from your top-down mathematical enchantment. Experiments slap our hands if we don't behave. Our bottom-up reasonable empirical attitude doesn't need astronomy. Why, perhaps Aristotle was right; mathematical concepts arise through our senses – stimulated by drawing in the sand or playing with marbles."

Geo-apparent natural regularities don't allow measurement of an infinite universe with a polytruth yardstick! This defeat mocked Plato and Euclid and tore asunder the seamless mantle of "science." Purists chafed at the thought that simple folk would continue to laugh at their admonition that the source of truth was "far from the footsteps of humans." If rationalists had not objectively transcended science's playing field, were they merely well-reasoned storytellers? Were monotheism, atheorism and creation *ex nihilo* the reasonable alternative foundation – but sanctioning only playing field systematizations?[9] The adventurer's knowledge of the basic building blocks of the cosmos was reduced to abstract words. Words – or equations – never seem to say it just right. *"Unaided" reason had failed ... again!*

Reason 101: 1 – 4 now has a quandary:

The fear of mathematics is the beginning of knowledge.
Our "all-seeing" mind's eye thus soars as on the wings of eagles.

Verily, our mind's eye is allowed to see great things!

---

8   The best insight on this history of mathematics is *Mathematics: The Loss of Certainty* (B11), by Morris Kline, but without much said on the Greek mysticism. Other works covering similar ground are *What is Mathematics, Really?* (B14), by Reuben Hersh, and *Proofs and Refutations*, by Imre Lakatos, (but set as a classroom discussion of mathematical confusions).
9   This certainly was a plausible conclusion to draw in A.D. 1850. But the response from the Christian community seemed muted. Perhaps theologians were now overawed by the science of measure or no longer concerned about science and, thus, weren't watching this unfolding drama. Also, mathematics by then was becoming an arcane and complicated specialty. Many people were more agitated by Charles Darwin and "evolution."

Some theologians may have been writing sermons on "God as the Great Mathematician." The destruction of a "physical mathematics" was an embarrassment to that effort! So such theologians shifted their attention to something else. Perhaps they should have written a sermon on "Does mathematics truthfully understand the world?"

Our ahistorical mathematical line shows experimenters what to do.

Do we understand our new mathematical knowledge?
Can our mind's eye deceive us? What is all this noise?

Is our mind's eye bipolar or poly-polar?
Is it our imagination that soars as on the wings of eagles?

But some thinkers came to the rescue of "unaided" reason! They said mathematics is a subdivision of logic, logic is self-evident, and so the "all-seeing" edifice would remain. *Logic exists*; so *Scientia* remains: reason and objective truth and logic (and a subordinated mathematics) and grandiose extrapolation and monotruth and atheism remained inseparable. This "firm" logical foundation for rational thought anchored mathematics and astronomy. It renewed the zeal of the well-reasoned, assured once again that they held no systematic errors of ancient origin. Thus we have the above-mentioned logicist school of mathematics, admirably defended by Alfred North Whitehead and Bertrand Russell in their massive *Principia Mathematica*, published in 1910. As an example of their "new" knowledge, they defined the number 1 as: $\hat{\alpha}\{\exists x \cdot \alpha = \iota^{\prime}x\}$[10]. (B93, page 1198.)

Logic is identified with Aristotle, so his philosophy enjoyed some return to respectability. Many thought the destruction of the science

of measure was due to carelessly framed postulates in the basic logical syllogisms.[11] "Define, define, define" became the password to "scientific" truth. However, this viewpoint forced each thinker to view even himself as simply "undefinable neural reactions" peering out of a physical shell. They could not define their mind into existence, even though these wrote their award-winning books! These thinkers became existential, unreal. In contrast, Christianity and most Greek thinkers had agreed that a real, external world existed.

Logicism was a difficult endeavor:

In *My Philosophical Development* [1959], [Bertrand] Russell confessed, *"The splendid certainty which I had always hoped to find in mathematics was lost in a bewildering maze .... It is truly a complicated conceptual labyrinth."*[12] (B11, page

---

10   Their contemporary, Poincare, said sarcastically that this was an admirable definition to give to people who never heard of the number 1. (B93, page 1198.)
11   Syllogism: A statement of three parts. The first two are statements about purported facts. From this, a conclusion is drawn. It is the old Aristotelian IF ... IF .... THEREFORE.
12   Nonetheless, Bertrand Russell confessed: "Only within the scaffolding of these [rationalist] truths, only in the firm foundation of unyielding despair, can the soul's habitation henceforth be safely built." (*A Free Man's Worship.*)

230. Emphasis added.)

Russell was discovering that the beautiful garden of their mathematical "aid" had no way out – it was a labyrinth. A recent mathematician, David Berlinski, calls it an "immense inferential trail." (Nothing proven, just high probability – unredeemed Promissory IFs – which, nonetheless, provide a THEREFORE.) A co-laborer of Russell, Gottlieb Frege, earlier had a similar unpleasant surprise:

> Frege was about to publish a monumental work in which arithmetic was reconstructed on the foundation of set theory. His hope was shattered in one of the most poignant episodes in the history of philosophy. Russell found a contradiction in the notion of set as he and Frege used it....
> Frege added this postscript to his treatise: "A scientist can hardly meet with anything more undesirable than to have the foundations give way just as the work is finished. In this position I was put by a letter from Mr. Bertrand Russell, as the work was nearly through the press." (B14, page 148.)

A fellow mathematician, David Hilbert, around 1920, boasted of his own work:

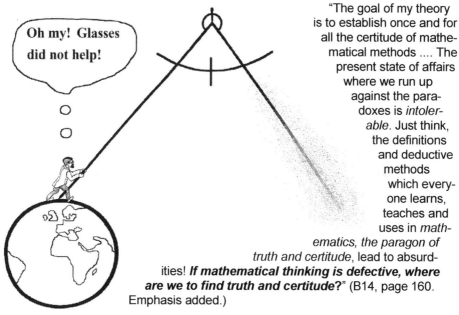

"The goal of my theory is to establish once and for all the certitude of mathematical methods .... The present state of affairs where we run up against the paradoxes is *intolerable*. Just think, the definitions and deductive methods which everyone learns, teaches and uses in *mathematics, the paragon of truth and certitude*, lead to absurdities! ***If mathematical thinking is defective, where are we to find truth and certitude?***" (B14, page 160. Emphasis added.)

Mathematical thinking defective? Wasn't it enough to smother your work in 1 + 1 = 2 and associates: Arithmetic, geometry, and logic – and then all argument was to cease? Is there false confidence based on clear intuitions? Intellectual disasters in the mind's eye? Can these alarms be correct?

Indeed, alarm was in order, for logicism was soon challenged. David Hilbert's boast did not last long. In 1931, Kurt Gödel published his "incompleteness theorem" in his *On Formally Undecideable Propositions of Principia Mathematica and Related Systems*. (The *Principia Mathematica* is the 1910 edifice of Russell and Whitehead.) Gödel showed that nontrivial mathematical or logical systems are incomplete. Mathematics, logic, or the cosmos are not self-explanatory, thus not in rational thought!

(However, this was of little concern to empirical science. Only extrapolative "sciences" felt a real threat to their "accomplishments.")

There are now many schools of logic:

> *There are many different logics.*... This means that no single logic is strong enough to support the total construction of human knowledge. But it also means that, when all the logics are taken together, they are *not sufficiently coherent with one another* to serve as the foundation for human knowledge.... (B85, page 42. Emphasis added.)

The rescuers only lasting result is an undefinable angst (paralysis affecting the well-reasoned), resulting from *unrepentus intellectus mistakus* about cosmic thoughts, mathematics, clear intuitions and reason. Words – or equations – never seem to say it just right. *Free and autonomous reason had failed ... again!*

For the well-reasoned, these double defeats (of mathematics and logic) meant all coherence and ultimate meaning were gone. It was almost like a perverse play-back of what John Donne had said centuries before at the demise of the Ptolemaic universe following Galileo:

> And new Philosophy calls all in doubt ...
> 'Tis all in peeces, all cohaerence gone
> All just supply, and all Relation
> (B45, page 29.)

These defeats can be dated to the end of the nineteenth century and the first decades of the twentieth.

In sum, rationalism was on a bumpy road!

Parallel to the demise of Euclidean geometry and the suspicions about arithmetic, mathematicians were becoming uneasy. Many began to suspect that mathematics had no foundation. "Cohaerence" was lost. THEREFORE, a major concern was to reground mathematics – and to start this by saying what a ONE was!

ONE had been understandable as a Pythagorean unit of matter. Geometry had been understandable as Platonic matter. But what could they say about ONE *now*? The existence of ONE was missing; was it the Existent One that they were avoiding? They feared the truth in saying that "God is the Great Mathematician."

Understanding the ONE was no easy task – and they splintered into quarrelling groups in the process. The challenge of defining ONE was that to do so meant to account for DISCONTUITY! This remained a feared concept. How to go from nothing (zero) to something! They were reluctant to say that THE *ex nihilo* ONE did it. Instead, their explanations became metaphysical – or subjective.

ZERO ONE

Under Plato, it had been easy to see ONE as incarnate in matter. But now, logicians said the number 1 was $\hat{\alpha}\{\exists x \cdot \alpha = \iota'x\}$. Others looked to infinity, additional axioms and set theory to explain the ONE. "The grand abstract universal set structure ... with its set of all sets of sets of sets of empty sets." (B14, page 284.) Others were content to say, "Mathematics is!" Others said that "repeated addition" proved the ONE.

Perhaps we now see why William of Ockham had earlier said "that the mind is to be hung with weights." A recent mathematician penned a short statement: "For

Zeus's sake," asks Socrates, "is it not mysterious that one can know more about things which do not exist than about things which do exist?" (B14, page 218.)

Mathematicians began to split into two camps. *PURE mathematicians and APPLIED mathematicians.* Pure mathematicians ended up with four competing explanations, as said earlier. Nonetheless:

> Godfrey H Hardy (1877-1947) ... is reported to have made the toast: "Here's to pure mathematics! May it never have any use." Leonard Eugene Dickson (1874-1954) ... used to say: "Thank God that number theory is unsullied by any applications." (B11, page 295.)

Rationalism was peeping through! Hardy was also famous for his allergic reaction to Christianity! PURE mathematicians were unsuited for real things, so employment was generally restricted to institutions of "higher" learning. Presumably they didn't worry about taxpayers having to pay their salaries!

APPLIED mathematicians stopped talking about "foundations." They preferred to stay in the laboratory. Later, more has to be said on what experiments mean in relation to causality, as opposed to just saving the appearances.

"Physicists don't need infinite sets, and they don't need to compare infinities." (B14, page 175.) The two camps no longer understand each other.

Approaching A.D. 1900, in a parallel manner to mathematics' increasing dilemma, advances and turmoil appeared in science. Rational thinkers unfairly took credit for all achievements of the previous centuries, even though rational mathematics was in serious doubt. **Intermediate First Principles in Science** were introduced, (see pages 10 and 11). Finding Direct Facts happened less and less because so much had already been found:

A. The universe is real.
B. The universe is rational (orderly), not chaotic.
C. The human mind can understand the universe because of its mathematical structure.
D. Activity proceeds due to cause and effect relationships.
E. There is unity in the cosmos. One set of natural laws governs the infinite universe.
F. Scientific experiments and observations uncover facts. Scientific rigor distinguishes between storytelling, saving the appearances and cause and effect relationships. Observations in astronomy approach the objective standards of experimental science. Scientific results are expressed mathematically to limit ambiguity.
G. Mathematics reflects the ahistorical rational order in nature; *mathematical law* is a science.
H. Rational thought can safely extrapolate into the inaccessible.

These austere Intermediate First Principles now had minimal Christian guidance. The question of origins was either ignored or thought to be answered within geology and biology. Common Notions of that day rejected supernatural or historical restrictions to ahistorical physical processes – thus opting for infinity.

Subsequently, many cultured Christians began to talk less about God's action in historical events and more about "principles." The intellectual trauma within *pure* mathematics received little recognition because of the euphoria over *applied* mathematics, technological, engineering and experimental advances and new philosophy. Few were aware of a crisis of confidence developing that exposed the gap between empirical science and extrapolative "science." More crises would follow.

Cultured Christian folk were then withering on the vine under the glare of rationalism's identification with scientific conquests. But forced apologetics gave rise to Fundamentalism. Its vocal lack of enthusiasm for rationalism's *consequent* attacks on the Word of God brought renewed vigor to Biblical scholarship and evangelism. However, it seems they were not aware of the century-by-century history of conflict between rationalism and faith. They did not formulate any analysis of the foundation of rationalism in grandiose extrapolation – in the science of measure.

This remarkable silence deserves more study. Diverse sections of the Christian community accept the infinite (or unbounded) cosmos that grounds the "long ages" viewpoint. Such folk then relegate *ex nihilo* creation to the subjects of geology and biology or to the "gaps" in "scientific" knowledge.

Later crises in "science" must wait awhile. We pause in this study of history to examine closer the troublesome new-fangled mathematical tools mentioned earlier in this chapter. Then these and later crises can be better appreciated.

[I suppose pure mathematicians still say top-down mathematics existed before matter. Others may say mathematics rules matter – leaving unaddressed how mathematics creates matter. But neither rational variation overrules the reasonable belief that matter came first – created *ex nihilo* – and implying that useful bottom-up mathematical formulas result from relations between units of matter.

Scientific and technological knowledge now began an enormous advance. Yet, nagging uncertainty grew. As this advance yielded direct facts, could rationalists immersed in "all-seeing" systems of layered facts – or layered potpourri – step back and find universal truth in this knowledge?]

We now begin to encounter more of the *mathematical disasters* that Morris Kline referred to that were scattered across many years.

As mentioned earlier, the Greek adventure had forbidden equations of the fourth or higher powers because they had no geometrical significance. Nonetheless, physicists discovered their usefulness when modeling various complex phenomena. Higher order equations could not remain taboo. For example, the pressure loss of gas flowing through a length of pipe is given by the equation:

$$\text{Pressure Loss} = \frac{\text{Pipe Length x Gas Density x Gas Flow}^2}{\text{K (constant) x Pipe Diameter}^5}$$

What physical meaning is there to the diameter of a pipe to the fifth power? Or its roots? Such equations highlighted the need to resolve a nagging problem when using algebra to solve quadratic equations (to the second power), instead of with the Greek preference for a geometric solution via the "completing the square" methodology.

A general algebraic solution took a long time to formulate, partly because mathematicians did not want to recognize that quadratics had two mathematical solutions! (See page 82.) Ironically, the demon of polytruth had snaked its way into the very sanctuary of (mono-truth) mathematics! The mathematical icon for mono-truth had a forked tongue! Poetic justice! How could their love of truth remain altruistic? Where was rational thought when one needed its cleansing power to *eliminate thinking about mathematical choices?*

Suppose we have a cubical vessel whose volume is 8 cubic feet, and we wish to find the length of one of its edges .... We can solve the problem by mathematics. We let x be the required length, and all we have to do is to solve the [cubic] equation, $x^3 = 8$. *But this equation has three solutions, viz.* 2, $\sqrt{-3} - 1$, $-\sqrt{-3} - 1$, *– all having the same mathematical validity.* But we know that the only one of these solutions that can possibly correspond to the reading of measuring rods is 2 .... So we ignore two of the mathematical solutions, and quite overlook the significance of the fact – namely, that *in the language of mathematics we can tell lies as well as truths, and within the scope of mathematics itself there is no possible way of telling one from the other.* (B86, pages 32-33. Emphasis added.)

As shown above, multiple solutions offer an added dose of bitterness; they usually add a mysterious entity, the square root of a negative one, ($\sqrt{-1}$). With number and matter interchangeable in the science of measure, no number when multiplied by itself could yield a negative product (quantity). (Refer back to Joseph Ray's comment on page 65.) Nonetheless, because positive roots worked, solutions containing the $\sqrt{-1}$ could not be ignored.

(Appendix B goes into more detail on the step-by-step process involved in deriving multiple algebraic solutions.)

After years of *violent* arguments,[13] negative roots were made respectable by defining the square root of -1 as $i1$. i is an abstract symbol, $i1^2 = -1$. Algebraic expressions that included imaginary numbers are also called complex numbers.

In the early 1800s, William Rowen Hamilton further "clarified" negative numbers with his "quaternions."

The introduction of quaternions was another shock to mathematicians. Here was a physically useful algebra which failed to possess a fundamental property of all real and complex numbers, namely, that $ab = ba$. (B11, page 91.)

Complex numbers are sometimes still called imaginary numbers in deference to "physical" mathematics. But more was to come:

Not long after Hamilton created quaternions, mathematicians working in other domains introduced even stranger algebras .... Arthur Cayley introduced matrices ... Quaternions and matrices were but the forerunners of a host of new algebras with stranger and stranger properties. Hermann Grassman created a variety of such algebras. (B11, page 91.)

---

13   Somewhere I recollect reading that more than one mathematician was physically injured in these "arguments."

The end result was "hypernumbers!" Algebra was demanding attention after more than two thousand years of neglect, but the following quotation shows additional reasons why early Greek mathematicians discouraged interest in algebra:

> Though Diophantus [third century A.D.] is notable for his use of algebra, he *accepted* only positive rational roots and *ignored* all others. Even when a quadratic equation in one unknown had two positive rational roots, he gave only one, the larger one. When an equation clearly led to two negative roots, or irrational or imaginary roots, he *rejected* the equation and said it was not solvable. In the case of irrational roots, he *retraced* his steps and showed how by *altering* the equation he could get a new one which had rational roots. (B11, pages 108-109. Emphasis added.)

Is his freedom of choice and altering of equations an example of "unaided" reason fulfilling the lure of objective truth? What textbook definition of science rationally applies here? At the least, 1 + 1 = 2 and associates are sorely compromised in actual practice! See Appendix B for details.

Later mathematicians faced a similar problem, due also to the $\sqrt{-1}$:

> [Nineteenth century] mathematicians were in a dilemma. If mathematics was the science of quantity, then these "impossible numbers" must be quantities; *but "negative" and "imaginary quantities" were simply nonsense, incompatible with all previous definitions of quantity.* On the other hand, these "impossible numbers" were the logical consequences of using certain general and powerful methods for solving equations; and the queer numbers could not be banished without calling to an abrupt halt the gradual perfecting of mathematical techniques. *"Impossible numbers," absurd as they were, were undeniably useful.* (B19, page 169. Emphasis added.)

In conclusion, quadratic equations (and those to higher powers) have multiple solutions and some contain negative and imaginary numbers.[14] The passage of time showed that $i1$ can model such things as the direction of a magnetic field. $i1$ remains somewhat mysterious because electromagnetism has a tinge of mystery. Applied mathematicians were comfortable with

---

14   Experimenters can avoid multiple solutions by working forward from an equation to solve a physical problem rather than backwards from a solution to a general equation. A property is cubed, rather than taking the cube root.

this abstract result, but not "pure" mathematicians; they remembered their ancient rallying cry that polytruth is the death of science!

Before these discoveries, **mathematics means (had meant) monotruth!** Solutions to equations *always* yielded one answer. Therefore subjectivity was (thought to be) absent from the mind's eye when engaged in mathematical thinking. An earlier chapter hinted at a looming problem where "completing the square" was demonstrated. Geometric problem solving gives only one answer; algebra is more generous. *There are as many solutions as the equation has powers.* (For example; equations with X^4 have 4 solutions, and so on. Tensor calculus, which is used in relativity, has X^{10} and string theory has X^{26}!)

The philosopher Nancy Cartwright points out:

The use of certain mathematical devices, such as complex numbers, *will generate excess terms* which we do not expect to have any physical significance. (B87, page 121. Emphasis added.)

Later, she refers to these excess terms as **mathematical debris!**

An article in *Sky and Telescope* supports this concern. While discussing "space-time," Sten Odenwald mentions the following:

And it's worth remembering that mathematics can sometimes introduce concepts that are only a means to an end and *have no independent reality. In the abstract world of mathematical symbolism, it isn't always clear what is real and what's not* .... Particle physicists often have to deal with *"ghost fields"* that are simply *temporary scaffolding* used for calculations, and that *vanish* when the calculations are complete. *Nonphysical devices* such as negative probability and faster-than-light tachyon particles are *grudgingly tolerated* so long as they *disappear before the final answer.* (B88. Emphasis added.)

As we advance beyond arithmetic and geometry, we have encountered algebra. (See Appendix B.) It manipulates "quantities" that are squared, cubed – or even higher. When the gears of algebra begin to grind towards a solution, an object is first replaced with a mathematical point! Next, "temporary scaffolding" (intruding mathematical objects) may appear at various levels. Then we arrive at the solutions – yes, multiple answers, some of which incorporate $\sqrt{-1}$. Is this what actually happens within matter as solutions become evident? Next we discard inconvenient excess algebraic results. With the mathematical debris cleared away, the object magically reverts away from a mathematical point. This process is saving the appearances, not an exercise in cause and effect!

In reading various histories of mathematics, you frequently encounter words like, "the solution to this ___xxx___ mathematical puzzle took years to resolve." The algebraic meatgrinder was a daunting challenge!

Pierre Duhem earlier gave a similar warning:

Between the concrete facts, as the physicist observes them, and the numerical symbols by which these facts are represented in the calculations of the theorist, there is an extremely great difference. (B89, page 133.)

Here were challenges earlier thinkers did not face! How could the lure of objective truth be fulfilled within this new and strange territory populated with new-fangled constructs, choices, and debris? How do our abstractions relate to reality? The simple textbook definition of science is no longer adequate to distinguish between puzzle solving and storytelling. (But we will wait until the next chapter to describe the full descent into paradigms.) And "mathematical facts" will not lead to monotruth if reasoners courageously list all possible solutions, including the reasons for selecting such-and-such solution.

Freedom of choice is hidden in plain view! So today, thinkers ponder the inaccessible with consensus agreements among colleagues to "get around" this loss of monotruth. We may laugh at these examples or consider them quaint artifacts of history, but if seventeen hundred years earlier, Diophantus could not "see" multiple solutions, maybe thinkers today cannot "see" things that violate cherished postulates of our "science of our day."[15]

Reason 101 was becoming more convoluted, **Reason 101: 1 - 5:**

The fear of mathematics is the beginning of knowledge.
Our "all-seeing" mind's eye thus soars as on the wings of eagles.

Verily, our mind's eye is allowed to see great things!
Our ahistorical mathematical line shows experimenters what to do.

Do we understand our new mathematical knowledge?
Can our mind's eye deceive us? What is all this noise?

Is our mind's eye bipolar or poly-polar?
Is it our imagination that soars as on the wings of eagles?

How then can we objectively fulfill our leadership destiny?
Does knowledge come thru the senses?

Talk about the "divine" Plato versus the "immortal" Aristotle!

Looking back to a somewhat earlier time, we now better appreciate how the success of Sir Isaac Newton's systematic understanding of gravity had been initially a great challenge to mathematical purists. They called gravity an *uncommon unintelligibility*! In fact, they accused Newton (and Liebnitz) of introducing occult qualities with the calculus (fluxions). As mentioned in chapter three, in his published

---

15   The relationship of mathematical abstractions and reality will come into better focus after we better appreciate the scope of the disaster.

results Newton recast everything into Euclidean geometry to minimize controversy.

Contemporary mathematicians abhorred his calculus because it did two strange things: It introduced "points" and put zero to strange uses! To calculate the path of a planet (moving under the influence of "gravity"), he first pragmatically reduced the gigantic planet to a mathematical point, moving along a curve. To plot the path of this curve accurately, the moving point's position required frequent re-calculation. For utmost accuracy, his fluxions required the distance between positions to be infinitesimally small. (An infinitesimal distance is one divided by infinity. Not quite zero ... and manipulated by infinity. Both were taboo to the science of measure!)

> The non-mathematician is apt to believe that the mathematician is in possession of a set of *infallible principles of reasoning* which enables him to reach truth *without ever going astray. For a long time this belief was universally held.* But when, with the invention of the calculus, mathematicians began to work with queer sorts of notions like that of the infinitesimal – a paradoxical entity that was sometimes zero and sometimes not zero at the convenience of the calculator – faith in the infallibility of mathematical reasoning began to wane. (B90, page 271. Emphasis added.)

The science of measure, knowing that matter and top-down mathematics are infallibly interchangeable, could not comprehend Newton's *idealization* of a planet reduced to a mathematical point![16] Contemporary mathematicians did not accept zero or negative numbers, so one can imagine their quandary when, going even farther, Newton replaced a whole (physical) planet with an infinitesimally small (mathematical) point. They still counted by one apple, two apples... No wonder contemporary mathematicians accused Newton of occultism!

There were flaws involved in Newton's idealization, and later work made some apparent. Newton's mathematics assumed that all influences upon an object act "as if" the object can be replaced by a mathematical point.[17] This is technically incorrect because most objects are not perfectly round or of uniform composition. Such non-spherical objects are said to have "oblateness," which covers influences such as surface effects (friction, rotation, collision), internal structure (elasticity, non-uniform matter), and non-gravitational effects (magnetic fields, electric charge, *etc.*). Some were unknown in Newton's day. Anyhow, such cannot

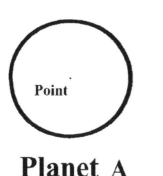

Point

Planet A

Planet B

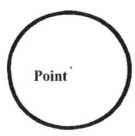

Point

---

16   Incidentally, the calculus was used for well over one hundred years before decent sense could be made of its theoretical meaning.

17   That was safe to assume if gravity is the only possible force affecting planetary motions. Yet Newton was well aware of the earth's "flattening of the poles" and equatorial bulge.

occur within or upon a point-like object.[18]

Golfers know the inaccuracies due to worn or "trick" golf balls. Also, spacecraft traveling near the moon have encountered "mascons" (**mass con**centrations).[19]

The eminent British mathematician, Roger Penrose, points out another problem that occurs when mathematical points represent objects very close to each other:

> There is *indeterminism* whenever exact triple collisions occur! If we like, we can simply *rule out* exact triple or higher-order collisions as "infinitely improbable" .... This is a little unsatisfactory, and we may prefer a picture in terms of *point* particles. But in order to avoid certain theoretical difficulties raised by the point-particle model (infinite forces and infinite energies, when particles come towards coincidence), one must make other assumptions .... (This also allows us to avoid the problem of deciding how point particles are supposed to *behave* when they collide!) (B83, page 169. Emphasis in original.)

The realm of mathematical points precludes rigorous (and believable) mathematical modeling of reality. The calculus works when the objects under analysis cannot collide (or have other surface effects). The calculus cannot incorporate an object's actual diameter. When close dimensions become influential, calculus is "at the limit" and the object must revert to normal size.

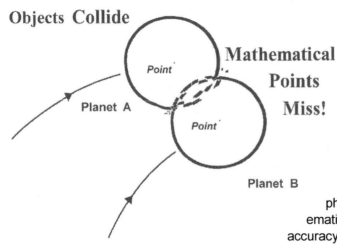

To illustrate the contrast that this drawing makes about the difference between physical objects and mathematical points, what is the accuracy required to throw a mathematical point with the intent of striking another mathematical point? Likewise, can a ball the size of a mathematical point *roll* down an inclined plane? (Try to draw the force diagram.) In fact, consider a riddle: If a mathematical point lies on a table with a surface as flat as a geometric line, to what angle must the table be tilted before the point will roll?

It is true that the calculus is an approximation, but there is the tacit assumption that it is of very high approximation. Such is the impression usually made, but *ad*

---

18   Surface effects and internal structure have to be "defined" properties of point-like objects. *"Points," having no dimensions, have no "interior volume" to account for physical characteristics; such must be a matter of definition.* This is a continuing weakness of reducing an object to a point-particle idealization. Dr. Charles Lucas, jr. has insistently pointed this out. Perhaps earlier, Pierre Duhem said the same.
19   The distance these spacecraft fly above the moon's surface "bobs" up and down in response to unknown sources of high gravitational attraction, over certain distinct areas of the moon. A recent pair of spacecraft was sent to the moon by NASA (the GRAIL mission) to study these gravitational variations.

hoc experimental fine tuning (adjusting constants) is sometimes required to achieve conformance to reality.

Not without cause, the philosopher and theologian, Bishop George Berkeley, (1685-1753), had objected to the new ideas in the calculus. He called the infinitesimal the "ghost of departed quantity" because a metaphysical concept was replacing physical objects. Obviously, within the framework of the Platonic science of measure, he was correct. His criticism could be overcome only by divorcing mathematics from matter – which divorce caused other problems for the abstract basis for rationalism. Anyhow, as we shall see, ignoring surface effects and internal structure creates discrepancies between prediction and observation.

Despite these cautions, the predictive success of Newton's equations ran roughshod over the accusation of occultism. The cosmos became populated with gravitating mathematical points.

For good measure, another example of surface effects occurs when a baseball pitcher throws a curve ball and strikes out the batter ... and also pure mathematicians. The ball curves due to surface effects caused by its rapid spinning.

Also, when non-spherical spacecraft begin to tumble due to the drag of the outer reaches of the earth's atmosphere, watch out! They are no longer reducible to a point-like idealization and thereafter the calculus cannot accurately predict their reentry.

[Rationalists had to bite their tongues, for their dilemma was intensified. On the one hand, the calculus was successful in the playing field, and was interpreted to support rationalism. If, on the other hand, mathematics was just a calculating fiction to assist in saving (some of) the appearances, how could they objectively defend their cherished – and mathematically deduced – infinite cosmos against alternate systematizations? They could only hope for the best future outcome for their adventure. They asked the philosophers of science to comfort them![20]]

---

20   Yes, thinkers were a little nervous as they reviewed the inventory of their ideas. It certainly was not the clear intellectual landscape they had previously envisioned. Their favorite weapons of extrapolation would need, at the least, a transformation. Nonetheless:
    - The *original* proposal of God and his *ex nihilo* creation was still wrong. Newtonian gravity, mathematical monotruth, the ahistorical mathematical line, the infinite cosmos and the algebraic meatgrinder ruled it out – even though all these were layered assumptions, not direct facts.
    - For the universe to create itself was still absurd.

And someone added verse 6 to **Reason 101**.

The fear of mathematics is the beginning of knowledge.
Our "all-seeing" mind's eye thus soars as on the wings of eagles.

Verily, our mind's eye is allowed to see great things!
Our ahistorical mathematical line shows experimenters what to do.

Do we understand our new mathematical knowledge?
Can our mind's eye deceive us? What is all this noise?

Is our mind's eye bipolar or poly-polar?
Is it our imagination that soars as on the wings of eagles?

How then can we objectively fulfill our leadership destiny?
Does knowledge come thru the senses?

Oh well! Perhaps we can no longer assent to causal truth.
At least we can assent to consensus layers of saving the appearances.

Nonetheless, as time passed, the aforementioned surface effects and internal structure caused discrepancies between observation and planetary theory. This was in addition to the still unresolved three-body problem.[21] Unable to replace or improve the (differential and integral) calculus, these cyclic discrepancies required the invention of *perturbation theory,* empirical fudge factors tacked onto the calculus. Hidden in plain view was the fact that perturbation theory rendered the whole analysis remarkably similar to the epicycles and equants used by Ptolemy in his long-abandoned geocentric theory[22]. In other words, the calculus "baseline" models a perfect curve of motion, and imposing circles thereon (perturbations) made it possible to "modify" the curves in order to save the (cyclic) appearances, much as Ptolemy's equants and epicycles had:

In calculating these perturbations [of planetary motions] the mathematician is forced to adopt the old device of Hipparchus, the discredited and discarded epicycle. It is true that the name, epicycle, is no

Epicycle   Real & Fourier Orbit

- The infinite gravitating cosmos was still the only *rational* answer. But could we prove it any longer? With mathematics having obvious subjectivity, was our reason up to the challenge?

21   Influence of the various planets upon one another presents an understandably complex equation. Laplace provided a detailed analysis in the early 1800s and the results still seem subject to dispute. The contention involves whether Laplace proved that "eternal" orbital stability exists versus the existence of "secular" uncertainties that limited confidence in mathematical extrapolations to thousands of years. Perhaps the cosmos is not always ahistorical or tranquil.

Laplace is famous for this mathematical treatise proving the planetary orbital stability inherent in Newtonian gravity. But some have pointed out that Laplace's analysis replaced Newton's geometric proof with his own calculus version. So, what did his analysis prove?

22   Perturbation theory: cyclical correction factors added to the main mathematical treatment of motion. Perturbation models the cyclic deviation of an object in motion from a mathematically predicted path.

longer used .... The physicist and mathematician now speak of harmonic motion, of Fourier's series, of the development of a function into a series of sines and cosines. (B91, pages 132-133.)

This shows that top-down (causal) Natural Law mathematics is not reflecting reality. Will bottom-up (shadow) formulas do any better?

But one may properly ask, can incorrect theories actually work? Consider the dilemma of aeronautical engineers: Americans use Bernoulli's principle of lift to design asymmetrical airplane wings. Europeans use the Newtonian principle of lift to design symmetrical airplane wings.[23] With appropriate mathematics, most theories can be made to "work."

Another discovery, made by Weierstrass late in the nineteenth century, was that curves generated by plotting out certain equations were discontinuous. (There are points on their surface to which no tangent can be drawn.) It dumbfounded rationalists to ponder curves to which Greek geometry was inapplicable.[24]

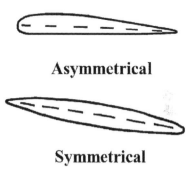

Asymmetrical

Symmetrical

Recently, experimenters have forced the recognition of nonlinear dynamics. Chaos theory, fractals, and the chemical works of Prigogine capture the dilemma. Such systems are non-integrable; *they are not ahistorical.* (The equations modeling their actions cannot be extrapolated to + or - infinity!) Prigogine referred to bifurcation points. Chaos theory refers to "sensitive dependence on initial conditions" or the more mundane hysteresis phenomena. Small errors do not stay small, (Kellert).

The increasing dexterity of tools like the electron microscope reveals previously unknown details in microbiological structures. These structures – and their independent, but ingrained, information codes – are so ordered and complex that fresh doubt is cast on their being anything but engineered for what they are. They have irreducible complexity, as introduced by Michael Behe in *Darwin's Black Box.*

These surprises, due to "unaided" reason's trust in mathematics, gave credibility to the warnings of experimenters, whose work had already encountered limitations. As a result, *new terms entered our vocabulary, such as: equilibrium, limit, instability, resonance, phase transition, boundary conditions, nonlinear dynamics, critical ratio, singularity, bifurcation point, catastrophe, sensitive dependence, irreducible complexity, hysteresis, temporary scaffolding and mathematical debris.*

---

23   American aeronautical engineers abandon Bernoulli's principle of lift when designing supersonic aircraft. Further, if you look at aircraft imported into the United States, notice the symmetrical wing shape.

24   We have dwelt on the problem that surfaced regarding non-Euclidean geometry. But there were other "unsolved" problems inherited from antiquity. They were: squaring the circle, trisecting the angle and doubling the cube. (These had to be solved with straight edge ruler and compass.) In 1882, Lindemann proved all three were impossible to solve because they required an "unnatural" number, known as "transcendental." Nonetheless, for centuries, great effort had been expended on trying to solve these.

Most physical systems possess "potential" instabilities that are unleashed under the proper conditions. For example, an opera singer holds a certain high note – and shatters a crystal goblet!

Or, have you watched a marching band "break rank" to walk across a suspension bridge? Their rhythmic foot-stomping might match the bridge's natural frequency, (like the vocalist's pitch matched the goblet's), causing the bridge to collapse. Likewise, pulsing air currents made the famed "Galloping Gertie" suspension bridge, Tacoma Narrows, collapse in 1940, months after its completion.

> ("[T]he collapse of the Tacoma Narrows suspension bridge in 1940 [led to] the "major lesson" of .... "the unwisdom of allowing a particular profession to become too inward looking and so screened from relevant knowledge growing up in other fields around it." Had the engineers of the Tacoma Narrows Bridge known more of aerodynamics .... The collapse might have been averted. (B92, pages 191-192.)

(Technically, the bridge's "natural frequency" was matched by the oscillation period of pulsating air currents in the narrow valley of the bridge. The aerodynamic effect is called "aeroelastic flutter." Flutter is puff, puff, puff – at the right frequency – and Galloping Gertie falls down! AND ... the engineer's mathematically correct calculations emulated rational scientists in this oversight! See page 161 on the bridge across the Menai Straits.)

People began to wonder how immutable Universal Natural Law, that unstoppable dissector of the vast ahistorical cosmos, which Law is so solid, so unshakable, so grandiosely extrapolatable ... but yet, almost as with a puff of air, its products can be shattered. Could a deep, subtle misunderstanding of ancient origin, a continued imposing of abstract top-down mathematical order upon geo-apparent natural regularities and complexities, still exist?

We have repeatedly mentioned the idealizations of infinite hardness, infinite precision, event-lessness and the multiplication of probabilities. For example, what is the gap between the hardness of a diamond and infinite hardness? The gap is still infinite! The Platonic deductive idealization of mathematical matter is misleading.

Science's reach was shrinking as it matured. Thinkers began to recognize the *"complexity of nature's simplicity."* (Kline) Some also point out that certain "sciences" are nothing but mathematics and theory – fact-free science.[25] Considering this history, pause and consider whether a conceptual housecleaning is in order.

Likewise, those involved with manufacturing high technology products live an apparent paradox. On the one hand, they spend vast sums on computers, computer simulations, and laboratory testing, but on the other hand, possessing all these models and data, they are loathe to extrapolate. Sometimes they will not even inter-polate. The "complexity of nature's simplicity" is a formidable barrier.

This accumulating list forces a great change from the grandiose beliefs of people like Laplace, famous for using the science of measure to advocate mathematical determinism. For him, reality was like an infinite pool table. The position of all the balls thereon, at any time, could be precisely calculated – but no hys-teresis, triple collisions, mathemati-cal debris, cloth imperfections, resonances or non-homogeneous or elastic pool balls, please.

The pool table becomes an inappro-priate illustration because its edges represent discontinuities. The balls and cue stick in the adventure operate without restraint or limit in an infinite cosmic abstraction! Infinity – that ancient subjectivity – forces rationalists to assume that "one chunk of space is as good as any other." (The center is everywhere and the circumference is nowhere, per Cardinal Nicholas of Cusanus! Page 140.) This is the sacred cosmological principle, *censoring* out discontinuities – which were inconceivable to "pure" mathematicians anyhow.

In this atmosphere of clear intuitions, it was hoped precise local measurement and exact mathematics would unravel all of reality's mysteries – as Plato had de-creed. But no mortal actually knows if a limit resulting from *attenuation* occurs due to other laws interacting "out there," the locations of centers, the appropriateness of the mathematical models or even if discontinuous events occur. Rather, one must be there to verify whether the equations need fine-tuning or replacing!

For example, the Voyager spacecrafts are a great disappointment, (as well as a great engineering feat), as they travel beyond the planets. After 35-some years, (and 2 milli-light years [0.002 light years] of travel distance), they are finally at the boundary between the solar wind and "space." Will the Voyagers later encounter another "medium?" Such attenuation spoils grandiose models and extensions. Physics is finite. Then one must comprehend organic life, reacting and/or thinking.

Working out the equations of the pool table cosmos was hard enough. Such thinkers could not afford to be distracted by birds flying around searching for food, butterflies choosing flowers, children playing games, or even themselves in the act

---

25   I read this phrase somewhere.

of thinking or falling in love! For the sake of the "larger picture" presented by the "all-seeing" deterministic "science of measure," thinking was glossed over, or the thinkers assumed that *their* minds became brains and merely reacted, like a machine.

With top-down mathematics no longer a guarantee for monotruth, rational thought faltered. To re-secure monotruth, they could only agree on ways to look at things. Science began to splinter into various specialized paradigms – consensus agreements of learned participants. (Outsiders, of course, were not learned.) *Thus, scientific paradigms were born – and monotruth became a figurehead!*

Yet again, rationalists had not proven that:
▲ algebra, arithmetic, geometry, calculus and trigonometry are a unity;
▲ mathematics is not a labyrinth;
▲ algebra is not a meat-grinder;
▲ reality has almost "infinite" stability;
▲ mathematics retains an objective "connection" to reality;
▲ an observation and an experiment provide the same mathematical certainty;
▲ all of the solutions to an algebraic equation can be used.

Studying the history of science, from bookend-to-bookend, can make one dizzy. Universal Natural Laws – with their Universal Connectedness – had looked so steady. Were they only inflated useful formulas?

But diverting your gaze to the present, we see dynamic actions occurring. Then looking back once again at those Laws, one gets the impression that they are shimmering or unsteady. It reminds me of Alice in *Alice in Wonderland* where she meets the Cheshire cat. But then she is left with only the "grin of the Cheshire cat."

The disagreement between Plato and Aristotle is still present – universal laws versus accessible complexity! (Those two thinkers must have had some interesting conversations!) Dynamic complexity mandates *ad hoc* modifications for Laws – but then the Laws are no longer Laws, but useful formulas, maybe only algorithms. In computer speak, IF ....; THEN ....; ELSE .... That is not causality!

Perhaps Laws are icons and all we have are bottom-up useful formulas!

As a Nobel laureate physicist was quoted by Morris Kline:

Percy W. Bridgman [said] "[M]athematics is a human invention." Theoretical science is a game of mathematical make-believe. (B11, page 325.)

(The new mineral, Bridgemanite, has recently (2014) been named after him. Elsewhere, someone reported that when Bridgman was told that he had received the Nobel prize, he did not even look up from his laboratory work as he said: "Tell them that I'll believe it when I see it.")

History is a setback to our "Pure" Universal Connected Knowledge but clarifies our "applied" saving (some of) the appearances!

And this is not the full extent of the mathematical disasters that Morris Kline and others talked about. The following chapters report on these. And yes, we will plow some of this ground over again! Empirical (applied) science and extrapolative (pure) science are beginning to look estranged from each other!

Logic is the art of going wrong with confidence.
(Anonymous)

Mathematics is invention, not discovery.
Ludwig Wittgenstein

Fundamental equations do not govern objects in reality; they only govern objects in models.
Nancy Cartwright

Whoever says they understand Quantum Mechanics does not understand Quantum Mechanics.
Niels Bohr

Modern physics has definitely decided in favor of Plato. In fact the smallest units of matter are not physical objects in the ordinary sense; they are forms, ideas which can be expressed unambiguously only in mathematical language.
Werner Heisenberg

Plato was a Pythagorean. The thread from Pythagoras to Hilbert to Gödel is unbroken.
Reuben Hersh

Physics is not like geometry; in physics there are no definitions and no axioms.
Rudolph Carnap

Experimental science, engineering and technology were having great success, but realities finer details were getting complicated. Puzzlement over the meaning of science increased. Inaccessible science increased in visibility, helped by the increasing usefulness of poly-mathematics.

In earlier centuries men had literally "stepped to the stars" with geometry. As their mind's eye journeyed into space, no discontinuity limited their extrapolations. They considered this to be the first "giant leap for mankind."

Rational men of "science" now knew that a rock at their feet, a distant star, or an event of long ago were all accessible. Objections to grandiose extrapolation were *irrational;* objectors were derided for insisting that, while $1 + 1 = 2$, "scientists" should not therefore assume that (physically) $1,000,000,000,000 + 1 = 1,000,000,000,001$. Nonetheless, objectors were concerned about supposed things beyond experience by a huge factor, like 1,000,000,000,000. This objection was based on an appeal to look at our event-filled history and nature's complexity and see the hand of God. "Scientists" laughingly derided this as *catastrophism*[1], for the "all-seeing" science of measure had revealed all discontinuity and limitations mathematically absurd – in spite of historical instances to the contrary.

Even if Biblical events were dismissed as mythical catastrophism, event-less Universal Natural Laws were encountering data that detracted from the believability of such laws. They might even be revealed to be saving the appearances.

Slowly, the data explosions generated by the increasing precision and sophistication of experimental, observational, and mathematical techniques forced an unwelcome realization. No *one* mathematical law describes, much less rules, the cosmos. Other laws, some unknown, can *intersect,* thereby weakening or deflecting what "universal" natural laws would otherwise predict. Aeronautical engineers even coined the phrase, "unk-unks;" unknown-unknowns.

This limiting process is attenuation.[2]

Galileo's perspiculium (telescope) illustrates attenuation. He finally achieved about 33 power magnification. Pointed out to sea, it could spot approaching enemy warships two hours sooner than the keenest eye. Such demonstrations showed its value.

Assumptions are hidden behind this demonstrated value. For example, consider a mirage "lake" on a hot summer day. Heat changes the air's index of refraction sufficiently so that when looking at the distant ground one actually sees the blue sky overhead. What would Galileo's telescope reveal ... sky or land? Such attenuation does not violate the telescope's "natural laws," but there is the unspoken assumption: the air between telescope and object is of normal refractive index.

---

1   Catastrophyism: Historically, the defense of the Biblical record of the earth's early history that flows from the created fact. Vast geologic changes (mega-discontinuity) witnessed to Biblically recorded catastrophe, rather than uniformitarian (gradual) processes extrapolated to explain the same appearances, but postulating longer time periods. Recognizing catastrophism causes awareness of the fragility of many natural processes – and awareness of the pent-up natural forces held in balance. This does not preclude supernatural intervention in the cosmos, but it highlights the forces available for "unleashing."

2   Attenuation: The gradual weakening or distortion of a phenomena due to imprecision or interference from other phenomena. Attenuation sums the effects of complex interactions. It hints at the negation of that pleasant assumption; *all else remains constant or insignificant.* For example, is there "tired light?" Grandiose extrapolation invites increasing error.

Like Galileo, the telescope is next pointed skyward.[3] After compensating for the earth's atmosphere, is one viewing stars through a rarified aether or the void of space, using Galileo's "infallible rules of geometry and arithmetic?" Remember that the solar wind is a recent discovery. Is there a wind beyond the solar system? What about magnetic fields, electric charges or currents in space? Nor should we neglect the unk-unks. All these can require major adjustments to the appropriate (shadow) formulas. With due respect to intellectual adventures in astronomy, atheorism makes one suspend commitment, smiling condescendingly at astronomy textbooks.

The little that is certain about complex relationships warns that Universal Natural Laws are subjective. *Grandiose extrapolation is not public knowledge;* it subjectively requires the assumption "all else remains equal (insignificant, constant)." Attenuation points to Natural Law *without* that assumption. However, they have sufficient accuracy in the playing field to serve as models, yet shorn of Universal Natural Law.

Reason Awry! Maybe Wisdom is needed after all!

The above cosmic drawing of intersecting laws is messy. Instead, mathematicians "capture" the perturbating and attenuating interference between formulas and refer to *convergence* as a limit, when the rate of change diminishes towards zero.

At other times, the interference refers to *divergence* as a limit, when the rate of change increases towards infinity.

---

3   Galileo's early telescopes had grinding imperfections. Some of his contemporaries declined to look through his telescopes, but not because they hated the "new astronomy." Many times, you had to believe before you could see. (Telescopes and microscopes had a long-lasting challenge to explain "where" the image resided.)

Margaret Cavendish, referred to in an earlier chapter, was also puzzled by similar questions. Look also at some of Galileo's sketches of his planetary observations. William Sheehan, in *Planets and Perception*, dwells on the later "certainty" with which astronomers could "see" canals and vegetation on various planets.

Divergence is a polite way of saying that infinity appears within a formula, thereby stopping the calculation.

Divergence is unwelcome.[4] A complex playing field needs complex mathematics to tentatively model its complex regularities! Even catastrophes can be partially analyzed. (Chaos theory – the modeling of unstable interactions, but not valid on a grandiose [ahistorical] scale.)

Many thinkers now realize scientific laws are abstractions; they model "idealized" processes, not even the machinery providing the process. The model is not a comprehensive portrait of reality. As examples, consider the following:

• Airplane wings provide lift, but their physical construction is not within the model that calculates this lift.

• A vacuum tube (or transistor) does wonderful electronic things, but its physical details are not in the model of how electrons move within it.

• The internal combustion engine produces power, but its physical details are absent from power models.

A model is a portrait of a thin slice of reality. There is no "large" model integrating all the systems, as Cartwright pointed out.

Attenuation implies more than complexity, perturbation, or catastrophe. Utilizing complex mathematics to understand complexity (or the inaccessible) allows the investigator a beguiling freedom to sightsee, choose constants or solutions with which to form patterns (free creations of the mind) to fit the regularity observed within thin slices of reality. Meshing multiple portraits of thin slices of reality allows additional ahistorical modeling freedom.

Astronomy exemplifies the lack of public knowledge. Consider how distance is "measured" in space. Consult a textbook or various Web-sites and you discover that it takes numerous pages to explain the rational ladder of assumptions. This is not necessarily bad but it does raise the caution of atheorism about saving the appearances.

---

4   Divergence was not clearly recognized until the early 1800s. The story is told of a famous mathematician who hurriedly went home from a lecture on divergence. Once home he checked the proof sheets of his forthcoming book and discovered that major equations therein diverged. He still published the book, but with a page added pointing out the fundamental error in his work!

In 1826, another mathematician, Abel, said: "The divergent series are the invention of the devil, and it is a shame to base on them any demonstrations whatsoever. By using them, one may draw any conclusions he pleases...." (Yet he concluded that they surprisingly "seem" to work.) (B93, page 973-974.)

The astronomical assumptions and "measurements" rise in multiple steps, beginning with:
- The universe is of a natural origin.
- Planets form naturally.
- The solar system is heliocentric.
- The universe is extremely large, because there is little stellar aberration.
- There is no preferred place in space (cosmological principle).
- Space is empty – or at least doesn't distort what we see.
- Gravity is a well-understood constant.
- Stars are like the sun.
- The sun is a thermonuclear generator.
- Distant starlight travels in a straight line at constant speed.
- Red or blue light indicates velocity
- Pure top-down Universal Natural Law guarantees these.

BUT:

- Satellites probe the planets and "near" space and provide empirical correct-ions about the accessible heavens. Theory without empirical correction is rarely useful!
- Leap seconds are being added to the year.
- Apollo moon landing instruments indicate the moon is receding.
- Voyager I and II are not where they are supposed to be.
- Mid-course corrections are always required.
- Instruments have gone only 0.002 light-years from the earth. (See next page.)

THUS:

- Bottom-up empiricism is needed in milli-light-year environment. Therefore, it will be more needed in "mega"-light-year region!
- Atheorism needs to be respected.
- Unknown – unknowns are real.

And on into deep space?

- On to star cluster motions.
- Galaxy motions.
- Interpretations of star color.
- Influences of relativity and quantum mechanics.

This is quite a ladder, but is it a reasonable ladder of laws or of rational assumptions to access the inaccessible? And the "philosophy of the epoch" may shelter other assumptions. By the end of this chapter, other assumed ideas may reveal a tinge of doubt – such as the physics of gravity, atomic structure and fields. Astronomy has few direct facts – it is the realm of layered facts, and hopefully, not layered potpourri.

Also, do not forget to determine overall probability by multiplication of the individual probabilities!

And be careful how we pat ourselves on the back. We wow ourselves as we say the sun is 93 million miles away, which means a satellite on the other side of the sun would be 186 million miles away. An enormous distance! But, with the speed of light at 186,000 miles per second, that is only 16.7 minutes away. Expressed in light years, it is only 31.7 micro-light years away, (31.7 millionth of a light year, 0.0000317 light years). The planet Mars, where sophisticated instruments have been for some years now, is an average of 0.000023 light years away –or 134 million miles! (12 light-minutes.)

The Voyager I and II spacecraft, launched more than 35 years ago, are about 123 AUs from the earth. That is 17.2 hours away, or 11.5 billion miles away – a long distance! Yet, on a different measurement scale, it is a mere 2 milli-light years away (0.002 light year). And they are slightly off their expected locations. Yet astronomers confidently assert that they can determine the distances to stars millions of light years away! *Wow! That is buzzillions of extrapolation from the known!*

With proper humility, atheorism shows that data from stars "millions of light years" away utilize many assumptions and much grandiose extrapolation to be credible knowledge, instead of mere saving (some of) the appearances. Indeed, grandiose thinkers are artists, deftly modifying paradigms as they systematize. Atheorism brings us back to our senses; complex and grandiose systematizations may only save some appearances.

A distasteful thought loomed: Mathematics is too fruitful! Man has "progressed" from thinking God's thoughts after Him to calculating reality with beautiful mathematics and then on to thinking our own thoughts after ourselves. Perhaps mathematics can perform like a kaleidoscope, which does not appeal to men of good will.

The NEWER Lawgiver

We can conclude that *there is no tree of mathematics*, like there is no tree of evolutionary life! In both cases, a garden of bushes exists. There is no deterministic explanation of reality that allows one to stand-to-the-side and watch ONE equation gloriously unfold reality. Instead, mathematical "laws" have *ad hoc* empirical correction factors tacked on. Indeed, they can be useful formulas!

Most assume that astronomy and mathematics explain the heavens, but we overlook a vital ingredient! *There always has to be a mathematician active in the process!* He must select from an empirical arsenal of mathematical inventions that which is needful at the moment and then on to another artifact from his arsenal for the next phase. These "artifacts" are appended to the image of (mono-)mathematics; they are like Manhattan beads – trinkets to make the storytelling credible. He is a Dr Ad Hoc, sculpting the mathematics to "illuminate" the inaccessible. That is a choice, not determinism!

Dr Ad Hoc, in the empirical realm, is a realist. But he is like the Wizard of Oz in the inaccessible realm; a rational mathematician searching for Universal Connected Knowledge! There he is a man of faith, not an atheorist! If he were, he would be a bottom-up mathematician – perhaps even a respected pragmatic tinkerer!

As Dr. Martin Luther said, "Reason is a devilish whore." Tertullian, before him, had asked; "What indeed has Athens to do with Jerusalem?" Today we may ask, *"What indeed has rational paradigm to do with reasonable science or revelation?"*[5]

Five things add up to a turning point in evaluating rationalism: the distinction between mathematics and reality; mathematical choices; models as partial portraits of reality; attenuation and events. *These support atheorism; the reasonable disbelief of grandiose extrapolation.* Thinkers, experimenters, mathematicians, engineers, technologists, craftsmen, tinkerers and observers operate within a complex web of interacting models. (*There is no "pure" top-down mathematics in the accessible world. Progress in living standards is indebted to empirical innovations or corrections!*) These *ad hoc* corrections do not support Parmenides ancient advice to search "far from the footsteps of humans." Atheorism remains; only God has a complete knowledge of physics and mathematics, plus He provides a transcendent report ... which debunks adventures. Well-reasoned people forgot to enquire if their mind's eye understands, even darkly, the mind of God.

The science of measure – or its successor, logic – possessed a *flexible yardstick,* easily calibrated by the assumptions of the day. Grudgingly, this dawning appreciation for the "complexity of nature's simplicity" not only made grandiose extrapolation vulnerable; it also made thinkers wonder what exactly mathematics is! Most concluded that *mathematics is an abstraction or symbolism having many forms, which allows short descriptive intersections with matter, but not interchangeability therewith.*

Data explosions destroyed mathematics' interchangeability myth. They precipitated the previously mentioned improvements in experimental, mathematical and observational tools. The result is described by Kline:

> But gradually and unwittingly mathematicians began to introduce *concepts that had little or no direct physical meaning.* Of these, negative and complex numbers were the most troublesome. It was because these two types of numbers had no "reality" in nature that they were still suspect at the beginning of the nineteenth century, even though freely utilized by them .... But then the introduction of quaternions, non-Euclidean geometry, complex elements in geometry, n-dimensional geometry, bizarre functions, and transfinite numbers *forced the recognition of the artificiality of mathematics.* (B93, Vol. 3, page 1029. Emphasis added.)

Yes, science is finite, very finite, and the garden of mathematics is not causal. Man's understandings outrun his knowledge. We have acquired data and useful formulas, not Universal Natural Laws! Indeed, as said earlier, paradigms are easy to

---

5   Remember the context in which those committed to the science of measure worked. They had a sense of freedom, but they were not free thinkers. Top-down Universal Natural Law cast the shadows on the Platonic cave wall they watched. For example, with creation *ex nihilo* taboo to them, planetary motion could not have started by design, recently. They wondered if they could think of a way for the planets to get there, and similar questions. What a tangled web is woven when people begin to believe the philosophy of the epoch justifies their own extrapolations.

understand but difficult to know. They impose a grandiose outlook.

The well-reasoned found little comfort in realizing that abstract mathematics could continue to be grandiosely extrapolated. This orphans mathematics and disconnects rationalism from an "objective" backbone. For, *if anyone heeded atheorism,* this thin slice of reality might approximate totality better than the utterly large cosmos most people blissfully keep right on paradigming. *Objectively, no mortal knows more!*

Extrapolative infatuation is loyal to something other than public knowledge. So how then is the Biblical created fact refuted? (This specter recurs later.)

Technically, it is no longer proper to say that "the underlying structure of physical reality is mathematical." All that can be said is that inorganic matter (whatever that is) can be fleetingly systematized with various mathematical models. Confusion was beginning to replace certainty. Consider the confession of the eminent mathematician, Bertrand Russell:

> We arrive at the mathematical laws of the physical world. Physics is mathematical, not because we know so much about the physical world, but because we know so little: it is only its mathematical properties that we can discover. (B94 page 163.)

Could this witness to saving (some of) the appearances? With your mind's eye, try to visualize the dilemma Bertrand Russell refers to. It is easy to visualize planets moving in serene orbits. But, with the calculus, only mathematical points are moving "out there." Where did the big physical planets go? Are we actually looking at the ghost of departed quantity? Does the planet move for the same reason that the shepherding mathematics moves points?

Russell most likely was puzzled by what actually is gravity, fields and atomic structure. As we shall soon see, the triumph of mathematical point "particles" means physics "understands" matter with equations; fundamental physical properties can no longer exist.

Hindsight is clearer than foresight, yet the triumph of materialism did require some "simplifying" assumptions. As recounted by Burtt:

Infinity, Materialism, Determinism, Atheism, ... Complexity - Atheorism??? Do I know all that I believe???

> How could the world of physical matter be reduced to exact mathematical formulae by anybody as long as his geometrical concentration was distracted by the supposition that physical nature is full of colors and sounds and feelings and final causes as well as mathematical units and relations? (B95, page 305.)

They concentrated on abstract mathematics' measure of matter, but not matters complex substance or unmeasurable qualities.

Whitehead also commented on the absence of attenuation:[6]

> The concergent effect of the new power of scientific advance ... transformed

---

6   Whitehead said this as criticism of Newtonian Rationalists. Whitehead did not apply this criticism to his own promotion of the adventure of relativity.

the middle period of the [nineteenth] century into an orgy of scientific advance. Clearsighted men, of the sort who are so clearly wrong, now proclaimed that the secrets of the physical universe were finally disclosed. *If only you ignored every-thing which refused to come into line, your powers of explanation were unlimited.* (B96, page 101. Emphasis added.)

Some thinkers began to suspect that subjectivity tainted the cosmos "discovered" in the great quest. When did subjectivity enter science? Look to the distant past, not the present or even recent past, nor blame it on that recent giant among thinkers and experimenters, Sir Isaac Newton (1642-1727), for he was pragmatic – and Christian.

It is obvious to the most cursory student of Newton that he was as thorough-going an empiricist as he was a consummate mathematician .... For Newton there was absolutely no *a priori* certainty, such as Kepler, Galileo, and preeminently Descartes believed in, that the world is through and through mathematical, still less that its secrets can be fully unlocked by the mathematical methods already perfect-ed .... *[For Newton], there is a distinct difference between mathematical truths and physical truths.* (B95, pages 212-213. Emphasis added.)

This sounds like atheorism, not rationalism! Newton and his contemporaries engaged in systematic investigations to explore God's created world. Perhaps Newton saw astronomy as *rafts of data adrift on oceans of mathematics.*

Newton is well remembered for his "gravity," yet he also upset his contemporar-ies by championing inductive logic, which favored the experimental method. This was at the expense of deductive logic and its *apriori* Universal Natural Laws and their Universal Connectedness. (Plato versus Aristotle appeared once again.)

Newton's Universal Law of Gravitation left gravity as a result without a cause and understood without experiments. Newton was indeed pragmatic! (Refer to the next several pages.) As such, his celebrated fluxions (calculus) upset mathematical purists. The calculus replaced astronomical objects with mathematical points. New-ton was accused of occultism!

His contemporaries and later generations tended to view mathematics as a top-down "incarnating" causal phenomenon. They could then easily "explain" why $F = G \cdot M_1 \cdot M_2 / r^2$, whereas Newton could not! This progressive attitude, in turn, foster-ed thoughts re-espousing determinism and atheism.

Blaise Pascal (1623-1662) had warned that "the heart has more reasons than reason is aware of." Inversely, "mathematics and logic have more answers than reality is capable of."

Atheorism notes a long-running similarity in astronomical theories. Plato said that circles are the center of geocentric astronomy. Ptolemy of Alexandria postulat-ed epicycles and circles to save the appearances of Plato's geocentricity. Coperni-cus postulated epicycles and circles to save the appearances with heliocentricity. Kepler finessed heliocentricity with ellipses. Newton finessed it with the quantity of matter. In the absence of experimentation, many inferences (to the "best" expla-nation – abduction) are made – but are these the only inferences possible? Ortho-dox and heterodox astronomers are prolific authors. Their arguing does not appear to be tapering off. It's almost a relief to realize that *astronomy remains outside of the domain of science.*

In Newton's day, matter had no structure below the gross level. There were no atoms or subatomic phenomena – only "mass," the totality of matter. At best, matter was viewed as inert little marbles. Further, space only contained the aether, a mysterious "substance" that required a Promissory IF. Nor were electric and magnetic fields, charges, currents or unk-unks in their mind's eye. So Newton was properly cautious due to the missing physics of gravity.

(Newton also accepted that the cosmos was about 6,000 years old.)

Subsequent investigations also failed. Rationalists considered all postulated physical causes of gravity to have a fatal defect: "running down" in thousands or millions of years. They knew drastic attenuation was impossible ... especially historically measurable change ... *so further analysis of these proposed "causes" was not needed!*[7]

Soon after, Sir Henry Cavendish developed the Cavendish Balance, an ingenious and sensitive instrument to measure the force of "gravity" between large metal balls. The results correlated well with the value Newton had calculated, but considering that the planets had not been weighed, was this correlation a coincidence or a causal fact?

It may not be apparent, but Newtonian gravity carries on the grandiose extrapolation of an infinite cosmos. To see why, in your mind's eye, travel to the edge of an assumed finite, stable but unbounded cosmos. The outermost stars are not equally surrounded by other stars. Therefore, a gravitational imbalance exists – and these stars will be attracted inwards. Thus, a finite stable unbounded cosmos collapses with Newtonian gravity – so, Newton *assumed* an infinite cosmos. The advent of relativity supposedly remedies this collapse "defect" by *postulating* an outward expansion of a finite but unbounded cosmos.

It seems a waste of time to point out that no thinker has actually been "far out" into space. As an exercise in atheorism, what assumptions are required in order to make gravity a fact?
- Gravity is a cosmic constant.
- Fields, charge or minute matter in space are insignificant.
- Matter causes gravity, physically by __?__ __?__ __?__ .
- There is no containing shell to the cosmos or suitable equations thereof.
- There are no significant unk-unks out there.
- The mass of planets and stars match gravitational expectations.
- Heliocentricity is correct for reasons better articulated than saying that Copernicus' circular epicyclic system proved a fact or that Galileo's "proofs" were indeed proofs!
- There is no historical evidence of planetary orbital instability.

Considering these Promissory IFs, did Newton discover gravity, after all? If

---

7   An 1890ish Encyclopedia Britannica's article on gravity reviewed a number of possible causes of gravity. All were rejected because they implied the universe was "running down," hence incompatible with extrapolative "science" and its infinite age for the universe.

science respects atheorism, then it is fair to say that, at the least, something is missing and may not be provided by relativity. Such thoughts cause some people to think the sky is falling in, but the sky will keep doing quite well whatever it does without our ideas to keep it working. Atheorism is skeptical – like Newton himself.

Contrary to Newton's hope and popular belief, no one has ever explained how gravity acts; the physical reality of this force has never been demonstrated .... *Gravitational force is merely a name for a mathematical symbol. Even the notion of mass is a fiction in Newtonian mechanics.* (B11, pages 56-57. Emphasis added.)

Why would the mathematician, Morris Kline, the source of the above quote, say this? Force and mass and inertia are not direct facts – they are mathematical facts. It is one thing to measure a force between metal balls in the Cavendish Balance, but how is a planet or the sun weighed? Great ingenuity is utilized in such determinations, but no absolute guarantee is given – and then what "is" the force?

This uncertainty is evident in modern discussions about some comets (called dirty snowballs) – or even the moons of Saturn. Why are such expected to be "icy?" Because that is the only way to explain their location or "cosmic" origin in a way that works in gravitational equations, explains the comet's tail or hopefully explains where the earth's water comes from. When satellites approach these objects, theoreticians frequently have indigestion! Perhaps "dark matter" or "dark energy" have the same tenuous existence. *Kline reports that in the centuries following Newton, gravity was referred to as an "uncommon unintelligibility."*

Stepping into a time machine enhances a rising sense of skepticism about gravitational certainty. Take the opportunity of observing Newton at work ... and listen to the advice modern thinkers give him. It is always possible to create another systematization of the utterly large cosmos. But that is just the problem with poly-truth – free will and esoteric mathematics have too much to choose from.

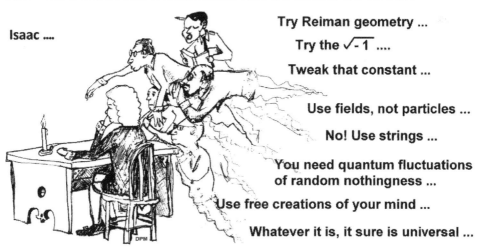

Isaac ....

Try Reiman geometry ...

Try the $\sqrt{-1}$ ....

Tweak that constant ...

Use fields, not particles ...

No! Use strings ...

You need quantum fluctuations of random nothingness ...

Use free creations of your mind ...

Whatever it is, it sure is universal ...

It is necessary to look closer at Sir Isaac Newton and his gravity with its "uncommon unintelligibility." *Paradoxically, Newton was one of the few that did not believe in Newtonian gravity!* In an oft-quoted remark, he said:

That gravity should be innate, inherent, and essential to matter, so that one body may act upon another, at a distance through a vacuum, without the mediation of anything else, by and through which their action and force may be conveyed from one to the other, is to me so great an absurdity, that I believe no man who has in philosophical matters a competent faculty of thinking can ever fall into it. (B62, page 339.)

In the very next sentence, Newton reveals his uncertainty:

Gravity must be caused by an agent acting constantly according to certain laws; but whether this agent be material or immaterial, I have left to the consideration of my readers.

In other writings, he identified the "agent" as the God of *ex nihilo* creation. (See below.) Newton searched for a physical cause of gravity (to complement his mathematical model), but failed. He respected the gulf between physical reality and mathematical symbols. He thus said, "I make no hypothesis" – at least regarding gravity. (On other subjects, he readily formed hypotheses.) His laws of gravitation saved the appearances very well – but not perfectly.

In light of Galileo's "how" and "why" distinctions, Newton modeled "how" gravity saves the appearances. He recognized that the "why" cannot be answered until a physical cause is found.[8]

Newton's elaborated on the puzzling nature of gravity in letters responding to questions posed by a Rev Dr Richard Bentley in 1693. In the letters, Newton insists that an "intelligent agent" has to be the cause of the planetary configuration. Most commentators dismiss Newton's comments as "due to his religious prejudices."

But that dismissive attitude shows that they haven't read Newton's letters. These writers make the assumption that the correctness of Newton's gravitational equations applied to whatever gravitational situation was hypothesized. Actually, Newton was responding to a specific transient dynamics question of Rev Bentley, who had asked if Plato had been correct:

... [in] affirming that the motion of the planets is such as if they had all of them been created by God in some region very remote from our system and let fall from thence toward the sun, and as soon as they arrived at their several orbs their motion of falling turned aside into a transverse one. And this is true, [Newton asserted] *supposing* the gravitational power of the sun was *double at that moment of time,* in which they all arrive at their several orbs; but that *the divine power is here required in a double respect*, namely, to turn the descending motions of the falling planets into a side motion, and, at the same time, to double the attractive power of the sun. So, then, *gravity may put the planets into motion, but without the divine power it could never put them into such a circulating motion as they have about the sun....*

You sometimes speak of gravity as essential and inherent to matter. Pray do not ascribe that notion to me, *for the cause of gravity is what I do not pretend to know...* (B97, page 216. Emphasis added.)

If you search the internet for "satellite capture" you find Newton's argument. Satellites from earth need "braking maneuvers" to achieve "orbital insertion" around planets. *Newton acknowledged that his "laws" did not accommodate whatever transient event brought the planets (or comets or asteroids) into their present order but*

---

8   Accepting this is not intended as a prelude to relativity.

only accounts for their present observed stability! Transient events are unmathematical historical discontinuities

Newton's analysis also did not apply if the planets sequentially arrived at the sun. (Then, the "variable" gravity would disturb the already orbiting planets!)

Why did later generations not heed Newton's analysis? Well, they did agree that full-size planets could not be captured – but perhaps dust size particles could evade his conclusion. They were not inclined to accept the *ex nihilo* alternative!

They were committed to infinity – even though our previous chapters showed that infinity is not an aspect of empirical science. They were compelled to rationally struggle towards a natural explanation for the origin of the universe – even though it has zero probability.

Newton applied this argument to his predecessor, Descartes, and his "vortex theory" of the origin of the solar system. (Incidentally, this shows Descartes as a "philosophical theist," not an event-accepting Biblical theist.)

Newton's successors tried to evade Newton's analysis by "explaining" planets as originating from rotating, collapsing dust clouds. (Not gas clouds as it was already then known that gas pressure's expansive effect was greater than, and opposed, gravity.) Such were the nebular hypothesis proposals of Immanuel Kant (in 1755) and Pierre Laplace (in 1796). At least the one by Laplace tried to evade these facts by assuming the dust cloud was already rotating. (See footnote 2 for http://creation.com/pierre-simon-laplace-the-nebular-hypothesis.)

Immanuel Kant is remembered as a philosopher, yet as the last paragraph says, in 1755, early in his career, he also tried to explain the cosmos in his *Universal Natural History and Theory of the Heavens.* Regarding his nebular hypothesis, he said:

> Matter, which organizes itself ... through a blind mechanical process ... [Their resulting motions] are nothing other than a free continuance of an impetus impressed upon them once .... [With the] fine particles sinking .... [they] will shift each other sideways from their vertical movement, and the straight linear descent will end up in orbital movements. (B98, pages 10, 15, 45.)

How convenient that all the "fine particles" know how to shift to one side only! *Kant offers no supporting physics or mathematics.*

Further, Immanuel Kant went on in his book to praise infinity:

> A constitution of the world which did not maintain itself without a miracle, has not the character of that stability which is the mark of the choice of God .... I find nothing which can raise the spirit of man to a nobler wonder, by the opening unto him a prospect into the infinite domain of omnipotence .... Millions and whole myriads of millions of centuries will flow on, during which always new worlds and systems of worlds will be formed after each other in the distant regions away from the center of nature, and will attain to perfection .... *Let us then accustom our eye to these terrible catastrophes as being the common way of providence, and regard them even with a sort of complacence* .... [T]hen the spirit which meditates upon all this sinks into profound astonishment .... All nature, which involves a universal harmonious relation to the self-satisfaction of the Deity, cannot but fill the rational creature with an everlasting satisfaction, when it finds itself united with this Primary Source of all perfection. (B97, pages 241, 242, 243, 246, 248, 249.

Emphasis added.)

Kant believed in IF .... IF .... THEREFORE we have Universal Connected Knowledge! He considered Newton to have made a mistake in admitting something that could not "organize" or "maintain" itself for an infinite time. Kant, like Descartes, was a philosophical theist, not an event-conscious theist of the Bible. Their enthusiasm for infinity was like that of Giordano Bruno. Also remember:

> Even the most skillful mechanic is unable to construct apparatus in which material objects move in consequence of their mutual gravitation, yet people quietly continued to designate the gravitational explanation of planetary motion as mechanistic. (B44, page 497.)

Kant mentions a book, *Cosmotheoros*, by Christiaan Huygens (1629-1695), published posthumously in 1698. Huygens does speculate in this book on life on other planets and solar systems, in an infinite universe. But he does conclude atheoristically:

> But indeed all the whole story [in Descartes vortex theory] of comets and planets, and the production of this world, is founded upon such *poor and trifling arguments*, that I have often wondered how an ingenious man could spend all that pains, in making such fancies hang together. For my part, I shall be very well contented, and shall count I have done a great matter, if I can but come to any knowledge of the nature of things, *as they now are*, never troubling myself about their beginning, or how they were made, knowing that to be *out of the reach of human knowledge,* or even conjecture. (B99, pages 122-123. Emphasis added.)

Certainty in inaccessible "knowledge" can only find "poor and trifling" arguments to support itself.

How quaint! Earth is the only place in the whole cosmos where (frequent) unmathematical motion occurs.

So, today, we face an easy choice! *One*, we can accept *ex nihilo* creation – a short time ago – but without a mathematical clue as to how "He did it!" (Sort of an acquiescence to Aristotle's observational realism.) *Two*, we can accept an infinite age for the cosmos – but also without a mathematical clue as to how "it" did it! (Sort of an acquiescence to Plato's mathematical enthusiasm.) Search the internet and there still is no agreement on how the planets materialistically come to be or to be where they now are. See www.en.wikipedia.org/wiki/Nebular_hypothesis for one example. Well-reasoned folk still believe it happened naturalistically, ignoring its "low" (or zero) probability, yet they continue to build on such "poor and trifling arguments" and go on to more remote mysteries, such as the Big Bang! This, they say, is science! They construct proof out of probabilities, contrary to Plato – who famously said that those "who construct proof out of probabilities are imposters!"

In the great game of baseball, it is not possible to score a run – or even a homerun – without touching all of the bases! In the great game of astronomy, first base would be the planetary system. And the "missing" nebular hypothesis is linked to the still-unresolved three-body problem, mentioned in a previous chapter. Listening to Plato, astronomers begin with a "homerun" and then "work back" to first base. Astronomy plays by subjective consensus rules. Atheorism is the better option!

People tend to forget that Newton had stated that he had only saved the appearances with his "useful formula" of gravitation. Then, very little was known about magnetic or electrical phenomenona. In the later 1800s, it was recognized that magnetism, electricity and gravity all contained an inverse-square relationship. This led to a fleeting hope that a relationship existed between them, but discoveries were occurring so quickly that this possibility was passed by. One gets the uncomfortable impression that gravity remains a well-understood uncommon unintelligibility. In contrast, atheorism and learned ignorance are wise attributes.

Presumably, gravity is a property of matter. Looking ahead, matter means atoms, which means electrons, protons, neutrons, charge, electric and magnetic fields. *If our knowledge of such is deficient, then the mechanics of gravity will also likely be deficient.*

If history is any guide, as mankind has now made some small milli-light-year steps into space, we should expect continuing space exploration embarrassments. Observatory-type instruments have yet to be positioned for long durations at significant distances from the earth.

Many hastily agree that Newton merely saved the appearances because, *now*, we work with the true reality: relativistic or quantum phenomena. They say this with conviction; they think we moderns have left subjective foundations behind. But it is not so. From Maxwell's equations, to Einstein's equations, to Bohr's equations – the ancient freedom of choice and faulty "clear" intuitions remain.

A little rain on the parade is welcome refreshment to those who prefer the lure of objective truth. (Refer back to pages 28 to 30, where the definitions of science are reviewed.) Newton's view was probably between the original Greek view and the current view (similar to the Christian view on page 51). He did not subscribe to the modern extrapolative view; his skepticism of mathematics was tied to his preference for experiments. So astronomy remains outside the domain of science.

We may want to shout, "No," but an interesting affirmation of atheorism comes from the writings of the Dutch historian, Dijksterhuis, referring to Pascal:

From this [criticism of hypothesis] we can also understand Pascal's extremely reserved attitude towards the Copernican system. In one of his most famous *Penses* he lets the sun revolve around the earth .... Though the so-called proofs which Galileo had advanced for the Copernican system had been perfectly convincing to their author, they by no means satisfied the very rigorous demands that

Pascal made on a scientific proof; in his eyes the theories of Ptolemy, Tycho Brahe, and Copernicus, all three of which are capable of explaining the phenomena of planetary motion, were entirely equivalent *opinions, fantasies,* or *caprices* .... There is thus no reason for the surprise bordering on indignation with which some of Pascal's biographers refer to his reserved attitude towards the Copernican system as a regrettable error. (B44, page 450. Emphasis in original.)

The "criticism of hypothesis" is discussed in the surrounding pages in the reference. The main point was *that a hypothesis is not a proof for a theory if other hypotheses' can also explain the phenomena!* Pascal also had a horror of hidden mechanisms. Remember also the page 145 footnote comment of the caustic philosopher Feyerabend regarding the Copernican hypothesis.

So, in a big sense, gravity remains an enigma, and mysteriously dependent upon whatever sense we can make of matter.

This leads to a review of the many advances in science and technology from the mid-1800s to the early twentieth century. These culminated in the relativistic and quantum understandings alluded to at various places. These "advances" were fertile grounds for interpretation by philosophers and even by some theologians.

Up through the middle of the nineteenth century, "life" was not fully integrated into the adventure. It had taken a long time to get much beyond the four elements of earth, air, fire, and water. "Flesh and bones" did not rigorously fit into these. With the advent of the periodic table of the elements, modern chemistry began. In 1770, Antoine-Laurent Lavoisier decomposed water into hydrogen and oxygen. This finally destroyed the old truth that everything is composed of earth, air, fire and water. It was soon discovered that flesh and bones were made of the same elements as everything else. True – it was complicated, but "further research" was thought to be able to solve everything. (Even today, cellular structure is shown to be too ordered and complex for anything but intelligent design and information processing – the hand of the *ex nihilo* creator.)

Darwin's adventure of evolution came about this time. While chemical elements were peripheral to that discussion, awareness of them may have stimulated his development of a new systematization, as most likely did the infinite cosmos.[9]

---

9   We have seen the ancient belief of Democritus and Ocellus Lucanus on infinity. This belief was carried on by the various neo's in the succeeding centuries. Yet, Plato and Aristotle dissented, using the concept of a potential infinity. Then on page 155, we mentioned the names of others who accepted the reality of infinity.

Books written by various leading intellectuals of the 1500s to the 1800s include sentences featuring the words "evolution" and "chance." The concepts were "in the air." I think this was due to the groundwork provided by these astronomers and mathematicians in arguing for infinity and rationalism. Consider the following additional dates:

1576 – Sir Thomas Digges expounds the infinite universe.

1590s – Giordano Bruno advocates an infinite age for the cosmos.

1698 – Christiaan Huygens assumes an infinite cosmos.

1730 – Bradley discovered stellar aberration for some stars.

1745 – Georges-Louis Leclerc, comte de Buffon, proposes that the earth was formed after a comet collided with the sun. In 1775, he said the earth is 75,000 years old.

1755 – Immanuel Kant wrote his *Universal Natural History and Theory of the Heavens*, (B98), where he postulates a nebular hypothesis and praises an infinite universe.

1785 – Hutton says the earth has an infinite age.

But, for this history, the major clash approached: the clash between Newton and Einstein. Besides systematizing gravity, Sir Isaac Newton developed a corpuscular theory of light. He assumed light to be small particles of excited matter – a ballistic phenomena. There had been attempts at an alternative wave theory of light, but it had fallen by the wayside.

In the following narrative, remember that an atom was initially conceived of as a hard, marble-like foundational unit of matter. A problem was approaching – this atom versus the "field."

Magnetism (and "magnetic fields") had been studied for some time – lodestones (natural magnets – from Magnesia, Turkey) had been known for thousands of years. Also, electricity was known through work on primitive batteries and static spark phenomena.

Before discussing the nature of the clash, we must review the development of magnetic and electrical laws.[10] (The clash occurred after the work of James Clerk Maxwell – and before knowledge of atomic structure.)

Ampere, Faraday, Oerstad and Ohm were early investigators in the early to mid-1800s, beginning with electrical current, mainly generated from primitive batteries. Batteries produced voltage and current. Investigators fumbled for years trying to understand them. Was "current" a newly discovered element of electrical fluid or was it a property of existing elements?

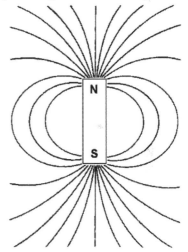

Magnets were investigated, and magnetic properties are displayed as fields, as first done by Michael Faraday in 1832. The patterns are often shown by sprinkling iron filings on a sheet of paper with a magnet underneath. The filings arrange themselves into the now familiar lines-of-force pattern. Magnetic fields or action cannot be visualized as a corpuscular (ballistic) phenomena

1796 – The mathematician, Pierre Simon Laplace, proposes his nebular hypothesis. In 1812, he further proposes that the universe is a vast machine. He did not need the "God" hypothesis.

1838 – The astronomer, Freiderich Besel, measures the first stellar parallax, of 61 Cygni, with an implied distance of 6 light years.

1841 – The lawyer, Charles Lyell, "estimates" that the age of the earth is 300 million years.

1856 – Helmholtz estimates the age of the sun at 20 million years.

1862 – Lord Kelvin estimates the earth's age at 20 to 400 million years.

It seems a reasonable assumption that Charles Darwin was acquainted with the "science of his day." Its "vast distances and long ages" gave "direction" to his storytelling about evolution, like it did for geologists. See *The Great Turning Point,* by Terry Mortenson, for additional details of the shift in geologic emphasis.

10   This trek through history will be conventional, but ends in confusion. We then will look for an understanding of what went wrong.

because they are too-finely graduated.[11]

It was soon discovered that electric current produces a magnetic field – an electromagnet. Then Faraday's discovery that relative motion between a magnetic field and a wire generates an electric current was another great puzzle.

Researchers also discovered that static electricity had a puzzling "voltage" field associated with it (electrostatic field). (Demonstrated by the "hair-raising" effect of a van der Graff static generator.)

Faraday, Ampere and others wrote empirical laws reporting on these phenomena. James Clerk Maxwell studied these laws and from them he formulated what are known as Maxwell's electromagnetic field equations, published in 1873. These are differential equations, using quaternion algebra with 4 imaginary dimensions, infinitesimal sized objects and the calculus. (Mathematical concepts – nonphysical.)

Maxwell used his equations to predict much of what is now taken for granted in electromagnetics. Signal propagation from an antenna and the finite speed of light being the most famous of his predictions. These predictions were fiercely resisted for some years. His electromagnetic field equations brought back the rejected idea of light as a wave. (When electric and magnetic fields radiate from a wire, they are combined into electromagnetism.)

Maxwell utilized the still surviving ancient concept of a (luminiferous) aether to be the medium that carries light from source to receiver. Additionally, Maxwell postulated that it was also the source of magnetic field energy, *because there was then no evidence of magnetism being a property of matter, excepting lodestones. Current flow was thought to "organize" a "stress" in the aether, from which magnetism was unleashed.* He also postulated a "displacement current" in trying to explain the phenomena of a charging capacitor. The aether and displacement current helped his explanation of how his equations saved the phenomena – but there was (and is?) no experimental confirmation of these.

For this reason, and because he displayed his results as 20(!) differential equations, written with the new abstract quaternion algebra of William Rowen Hamilton, his results mystified most contemporary experimenters. When a famous contemporary experimenter was asked to explain Maxwell's science of electromagnetism, he could only shrug his shoulders and say: "Maxwell's science is Maxwell's equations," (because few mathematicians understood the oddity of quaternion algebra!)

Maxwell was chastised for speaking where he had no experimental basis. It is commonly described as the first instance of the mathematician telling the experimenter what to do. (But Plato had long before told astronomers to use only circles in their work.) In 1887, Heinrich Hertz discovered electromagnetic signals in space, so arguments ceased, but understanding remained low. This is not to discount the pragmatic value of his work, but questions remain as to whether Maxwell's equations are a mix of saving the appearances and empirical knowledge.

---

11   Technically, it has not been experimentally possible to examine a field at the sub-sub-microscopic level to really say what is going on! Also, an ocean wave does not exist as a "thing in itself." It is a whole bunch of water molecules but it is too complicated to calculate the motions of zillions of molecules, so waves are a statistical simplification. Perhaps electric and magnetic fields are also a statistical simplification of "something."

The Common Sense Science group, like Pierre Duhem earlier hinted, points out that Maxwell's equations discarded some of the data in the empirical laws of Ampere, Faraday and others. His equations need point-particle idealizations for the motion of current particles. (Fields do not have this limitation.) Point-particles, having no size, cannot have inherent properties, but had been a harmless concept when applied by Newton to gigantic planets, because it was obvious that a transition to an abstract domain had been made.[12] But, "current," while a flow of small objects, is not "like" point particles. Minute analysis of current requires a shift back to real size particles.

The value of Maxwell's differential equations spread and the clash with Newton's corpuscular theory of light occurred. As Young's wave theory of light was reconsidered, an important need was to determine exactly how a wave of light moved through interplanetary space. (It had been somewhat easy to visualize a [self-contained] Newtonian corpuscle of light moving through space.) Light presumably needed to be transmitted through the luminiferous aether: the fifth Greek element.

(Invisible) electromagnetic radiation was energy, but (visible) light was also energy. Were the two the same? They are, but does Newton's corpuscular theory of light work for electromagnetism? *No!* (Electric and magnetic fields are not distributed particles.)[13]

It became urgent to better understand the aether! Several ingenious observational apparatus' were devised to measure an expected slight distortion in the propagation of light as the earth plowed through the (stationary and space-filling) luminiferous ether. The most elaborate of these was the apparatus that Michelson-Morley used in their observations of 1887.[14] *The apparatus was quite sensitive, but it detected very little distortion!* This created quite a shock. Newton's work had stood

---

12   Even well into the twentieth century, solving equations was incredibly time consuming. Kepler, even earlier, used reams of paper – and months of time – to do his computations on planetary motions. Later mathematicians developed logarithmic tables and "slide-rules," that sped up computations enormously – but not up to "computer standards."

Pragmatically, Newton's mathematical point idealization sped up orbital computations. Observed deviations called forth perturbation theory – which required adding *ad hoc* epicycles to the calculus.

The "pure" alternative would have been to calculate with a full size object – which requires adding many local calculations on a range of parameters – and then move the objects a small amount and then repeat the round of computations. Today, centuries later, this procedure is used to model reactions in molecular chemistry research. However, it may take a month of computer time to model less than a thousandth of a second's worth of atomic motion. Such computational accuracy a century ago was not even dreamed of.

So Newton and Maxwell can be "forgiven" for point idealizations as a tradeoff for computational speed. But their learned readers should not have forgotten that there were pitfalls associated with the tradeoff.

13   Quantum Electrodynamic Field Theory does quanticize fields. Is this saving the appearances or physical reality?

14   Slightly later were the observations and apparatuses of Gale, Sagnac, and Airy. However, all of these measurements were made before the discovery of the electron – or radioactive decay. So their puzzling results still may not be properly explained.

for two centuries, and now one of his pillars was in trouble. *Furthermore, there was an unexpected consequence:*

> To all appearances, the earth stood permanently at rest in the ether, while the sun and the whole of creation circled around it; the experiments seemed to bring back the geocentric universe of pre-Copernican days. Yet it was impossible that this should be the true interpretation, for the earth was known to be moving round the sun at a speed of nearly twenty miles a second, and the experiments were sensitive enough to detect a speed of one-hundredth part of this. (B100, pages 102-103.)

Geocentricity! Thanks to the stellar parallax measurements and their interpretation in "light" of the infinite cosmos, most people "knew" that Ptolemy and Tycho had been dispensed with some three hundred years earlier. Rationalists "knew" that if geocentricity was to be the result of criticizing the cosmos inherited from the waning Science of Measure, then the reliance on mathematics was undoubtedly correct. The alternative was unthinkable.

Yet, the doubting nature of atheorism is just a little curious about what were the 1887 *experimental (versus observational)* "proofs" that the earth was "known to be moving around the sun at a speed of nearly twenty miles a second." It was not enough to quote Galileo that "mathematicians and astronomers had discovered infallibles rules of geometry and arithmetic." Solar system motions are "explained" with mathematics, but not with causal physical answers. Thus, cautious thinkers later coined the word, paradigm! (Well – we just scientifically agree to look at phenomena in this way.)

On a supposedly unrelated subject, then came another big surprise! In 1897, Rutherford experimented with an early vacuum tube and he detected something flowing through it. The something was current and later named the electron. But the electron had to be a part of the "atom," but this meant that atoms were not hard marble-like bodies.

About the same time, x-rays were discovered by Roentgen, then the natural radioactivity of certain substances like radium and uranium by the Curies, then electron scattering experiments. Next came the spectroscopic analysis of starlight.

These additional blows to nineteenth century "knowledge" were dissolving Democtritus' hard, marble-like atom. A great search began to understand the components of the atom. And at the same time, the infallibility of arithmetic and Euclidean geometry had been shattered … and more mathematical paradoxes were being uncovered.

These mysteries in the atom and in mathematics impacted the ongoing efforts to explain the unwelcome results of the 1887 Michelson-Morley apparatus. Not surprisingly, for many years after the 1887 observation many mathematicians attacked the "aether" problem with furious and esoteric mathematical scribbling. Einstein's systematization was to triumph in 1905. His model banished the aether. He adopted the slightly earlier mathematical postulate of Heaviside / Lorenz that matter contracts slightly in the direction of motion – the speed of light modified by the $\sqrt{-1}$. (This "slight contraction" due to velocity negated the null result of the

Michelson-Morley observations.) Thus, we pay homage to relativity – and leave unanswered what is a wave in an aetherless space.[15]

To give a flavor of the mathematics relativity requires, consider the following "clarification" by Sir James Jeans:

And we shall not measure time in ordinary seconds, but in terms of a mysterious unit equal to a second multiplied by $\sqrt{-1}$ ... Mathematicians speak of $\sqrt{-1}$ as an "imaginary" number, because it has no existence outside of their imaginations, so that we are measuring time in a highly artificial manner. If we are asked why we adopt these weird methods of measurement, the answer is that they appear to be nature's own system of measurement.... (B100, page 131.)

Saving the appearances is the modern way to satisfy the lure of objective truth! Einstein's own description of the usefulness of $\sqrt{-1}$ is also instructive:

It must be clear even to the nonmathematician that, as a consequence of this purely formal addition to our knowledge [*i.e.* $\sqrt{-1}$], the theory per force gained clearness in no mean measure. (B101, page 57.)

Gravity as a force was banished – force being a metaphysical term. But the "new" gravitational creases are also metaphysical! So, the clash between Newton and Einstein involved the nature of light and gravity, the 1887 Michelson – Morely apparatus and illuminated by Maxwell's electrodynamic laws[16]. And matter (the atom) remained a mystery.

In a few years, relativity was "precisely confirmed" by the 1919 solar eclipse expedition of Sir Arthur Stanley Eddington. Yet his "precise" confirmation remains at 20% accuracy and plagued with problems:

The deflection of starlight by the sun [as predicted by Einstein and "confirmed" by Eddington in 1919], was such a success that it produced the 1919 media event. The measurements of the deflection ... from today's jaundiced viewpoint ... were only of 20 percent accuracy and were plagued by systematic errors .... Nearly a dozen eclipse measurements between 1919 and 1973 resulted in only small improvements in accuracy. (B102, page 295.)

In the spirit of atheorism, it is proper to again ask several questions that the astronomer Dr. Charles Lane Poor asked in 1922 in his *Gravitation versus Relativity*, (B91). First, what is the effect of the sun's atmosphere on the line-of-sight grazing angles involved in eclipse measurements? Second, how successfully does the adventure of relativity account for the perihelion precession (apsidal motion) of the *other* planets, besides Mercury? Also, Eddington discarded the data on many stars on his photographic plates. (These deletions probably helped "raise" the accuracy to the only 20 % accuracy result cited.)

As a contrarian, Thomas Edison long ago quipped when asked what he thought of Einstein's relativity: "I don't think about things that don't make sense!"

While most authorities continue to say Eddington's 1919 eclipse expedition

15   Einstein did not "see" that Maxwell's recasting of current carrying particles into point-particles led to large errors under high velocity conditions. (To be discussed later.)
16   Gravity cannot be measured independently – so, it was banished. Relativity also cannot be measured – it postulates that things like planets follow "creases" in a space-time continuum. As a consequence, data can only be interpreted in the consensus paradigmatic "light" of relativity.

"precisely confirmed" Einstein's adventure of relativity, some do acknowledge the truthfulness of the above 20 % quote. However, they typically quickly refer to today's cutting-edge science news. To stop epistemological questioning, they may point out that recent measurements with x-rays of planetary positions, as they pass behind the sun (occultation), confirm Einstein's adventure to within one per cent. But visual data is close to the predicted amount only when the eclipsed star is viewed through the sun's thin atmosphere, (like viewing space through the earth's atmosphere, near the horizon). Further away from the sun, no effect is observed. See www.extinctionshift.com/ and referenced sites. So, theory continues to trump (local) experiment (or observation)!

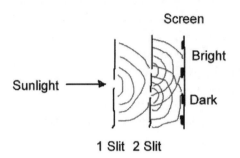

Screen

Bright

Sunlight →

Dark

1 Slit 2 Slit

Reverting back several years, there had been some ingenious experiments with dual-slit interferometers showing light and dark interference patterns of light, which only make sense if light is some sort of a wave. It does not seem possible to return to corpuscular light.

Meanwhile, additional mysteries impinged upon our cosmic understanding. One mystery was the discovery of "black-body" radiation. Heated bodies gave off energy in bursts of radiation at set frequencies. In 1900, Max Planck developed an equation that matched these quantized frequencies – but the why was not known.

Around 1911, out of all these experiments and others came a model of the atom, close to what is understood today: full of orbiting electrons around a central lump, known as the nucleus, and proposed by Rutherford.

Electrons whiz about the nucleus, like planets in orbit around the sun. At the time, it was known that the electron had charge; thus, it should continuously emit radiation due to the continuous centripetal acceleration from its being pulled away from a straight line by its orbital motion. The electron's fields were interacting with

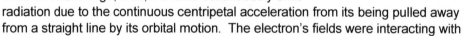

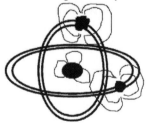

other charge centers. They were generating electricity and this takes power! This would cause the orbiting electrons to lose energy and then spiral into the nucleus of the atom – with the result that the atom collapses. In addition, the electron's internal electrostatic field and the resulting Coulomb force should blow the electron apart! (*The electrostatic field in an atom is 10^{39} stronger than gravity,* 1 followed by 39 zeros.)

How were these fatal defects to be solved? Answer: define the electron to be a mathematical point! In 1913, Niels Bohr, a major developer of quantum mechanics, did so to "solve" the defect[17]. The laws of physics were declared to be inapplicable to the sub-atomic realm! Nothing can act on a mathematical point as it is dimensionless. So the "properties" of his "new" model of the atom were applied by definition – values crafted to fit known characteristics. Such "intrinsic" properties of the point particle electron within the solar model of the atom were declared to be exempt from the laws that were applicable to the "larger" scales of reality. (For example, how can a "point" act as an antenna to transmit or receive energy?)

The nucleus of the atom was the next vulnerable item because investigators became aware of cosmic rays. These rays had properties that resembled the nucleus of some atoms. Cosmic ray collisions yielded debris and radiation. Shortly thereafter, atom smashers and associated detectors were developed. A torrent of data was unleashed, from which investigators assumed that the components of the nucleus had properties similar to that of the electron – more point-particles, but with different defined properties!

Bigger atom smashers and more sensitive detectors led to the surmise that the components of the nucleus were, themselves, being broken into smaller "things." To make sense of it all, the "Standard Model of the Atom," as understood within the Paradigm of Quantum Mechanics, was developed over many years. It has 61 components with names such as quarks, leptons, mesons, strong force, and others.

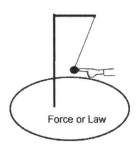

Force or Law

When these "properties" were proposed, they were lamented as the *Death of Science*. There no longer was a cause and effect relationship! *Thus was born Inaccessible Science Paradigms!*

How can an equation move an object? The mathematics used to express these concepts could not be related to physical properties, so to express criticism was to admit an ignorance of cutting-edge higher mathematics. This stifled some critics.

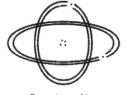

Force or Law

With the advent of the mathematical point model of the atom, what is there for a law to shadow? All of the atom's components have properties, but the mathematical point solar model of the atom no longer "allows" physical reasons for them. These measured values are indexed into mathematical data arrays for use by (matrix mechanics) equations. No wonder perplexed researchers considered this to be the death of science!

If your "mind's eye" is especially keen, you can see that each mathematical point is actually a "cloud" of top-down (causal) mathematics. Furthermore, according to

· = Mathematical Points

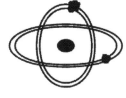

Rutherford Atom   Quantum Atom

---

17   Nonetheless, Hofstadter, in 1961, was awarded the Nobel Prize for measuring the diameter of the proton!

Quantum Mechanics, electromagnetic fields have also disappeared – replaced by more mathematical points, with "appropriate" equations.

Some developers of quantum mechanics candidly said that there is no model of the electron (or atom) that can be visualized – one can only save the appearances with complex equations – the ghost of departed quantity. First, Niels Bohr[18], then Werner Heisenberg, then P. A. M. Dirac:

> The quantum world does not actually exist. All we have is an abstract quantum description. It is a mistake to believe that the purpose of physics is to find out how nature is made. Physics is interested only in what we can say about nature. (B103, page 301.)

> [T]he elementary particles of modern physics are even more abstract than the atoms of the Greeks ... [I]t is not a material particle in space and time, but only, in some sense, a symbol whose introduction gave the laws of nature a particularly simple form. (B103, page 309.)

> We shall retain Maxwell's theory to describe the field right up to the point-singularity which represents our electron and shall try to get over the difficulties associated with the *infinite energy* by a process of *direct omission or subtraction of unwanted terms,* somewhat similar to what has been used in the theory of the positron. Our aim will not be so much to get a model of the electron as to get a simple scheme of equations which can be used to calculate all the results which can be obtained from experiment .... Provided these conditions are satisfied, it should not be considered an objection to the theory that it is not based on a model conforming to current physical ideas. (B104, page 3. Emphasis added.)

And as Niels Bohr elsewhere said; "Whoever says they understand quantum mechanics does not understand quantum mechanics."

Yet their contemporaries and successors said the quantum world was real. Rationalists actually enjoyed "assenting" to this as a fact. In a few years, it was discovered that the electron also had magnetic properties, but it would be a long time before that clue would be explored.

The time between 1870 and 1940 witnessed breathtaking discoveries occurring in fairly rapid succession, as we have reviewed: Maxwell's electromagnetic laws, the battle over the nature of light, the dissolution of the atom, new views on gravity, reconstruction of the atom with point particles and various mathematical debacles. It can make the head spin! One suspects that incomplete theories were used to "assist" other incomplete theories. The end result is what Bertrand Russell lamented: "It is only the mathematical properties of matter that we have discovered." Point particles allowed nothing else.

But was this "science" storytelling or puzzle solving? It is possible that these investigators over-relied on a flexible mathematics. Amusingly, Albert Einstein said the following about the beginning of quantum theory:

> Einstein appeared to have a similar opinion (of Heisenberg's 1925 paper) ... "The most interesting development produced lately is the Heisenberg-Born-Jordan theory of quantum states. The calculation is pure witchcraft, with infinite determin-

---

18 Niels Bohr was awarded a Noble Prize in physics in 1922 – a rapid acceptance of his 1913 paper on the quantum model of the atom, with the point-particled electron.

ants in place of Cartesian coordinates. It is most ingenious and, owing to its great complexity, safely protected against any attempt to prove it wrong." (B104, page 290.)

Quantum mechanics folk do pay attention to results of atom smashers. How-ever, new results were perplexing and distributed amongst 61 sub-components of the solar modeled atom. This led to gluing on to the already intricate mathematics additional *ad hoc* subroutines to be used, when needed.

Thus, quantum mechanics is guaranteed of successfully saving the appearances. Success is due to its being a bundle of equations, but unfortunately, these don't "flower" from a master equation. The trick is to know how to select which subequation (or data set) to use when. It takes great skill (by a modern

The NEWEST Lawgiver

Wizard of Oz) to make the proper choices – and thus prove determinism – by saving (some of) the appearances!

To understand the mounting confusion in modern science, we will further examine the mainstream efforts to understand subatomic reality with point particles – and defined properties.

To "understand" such complex and inaccessible phenomena, the mathematics of quantum mechanics is statistical, complex, esoteric and maybe even subjective. Contrary to textbooks, quantum mechanics is not an agreed fact, but an authoritative learned consensus known as the "Copenhagen Interpretation" of 1927. Amazingly:

> Quantum electrodynamics gives the most precise predictions of any physical theory. Yet physicists have known from its birth that it is self-contradictory. They make *ad hoc* rules for handling the inconsistencies. Divergent series of divergent terms are manipulated and massaged. (B14, page 31.)

There have always been alternative systematizations. Further, the divergent series required manipulation and massaging with "renormalization" – discussed shortly and also refer back to the illustration on page 186. Einstein never accepted the Copenhagen Interpretation because his relativity theory and Quantum Mechanics contradict each other.

I remember reading that Oriental philosophy influenced some contributors to the Copenhagen Interpretation. Additionally, there was instant fame waiting as a prize. Papers were hastily prepared for publication for fear of what someone else might be preparing. There was a desire to be the next Newton or Galileo.

Out of Quantum Mechanics came several things:
• Light is not the light of marbles or even of electrons. Light is photons – wave-

packets of energy. (Do not try to visualize a wave-packet. It is an abstract mathematical construct developed to save the appearances.) One result is the principle of "complementarity." Contrary to earlier beliefs, light is now said to be both wave and particle – depending upon which experiment is referred to. It has been jokingly called a "wavicle."

• Related to this is "indeterminateness." Not only are photons wavicles, but we are told that precise measurement cannot simultaneously determine position *and* velocity of a (point) particle. We don't know where the mathematical point is – within its cloud of equations!

• Less well known are some "quirky" ideas regarding how photons, *etc.*, move. Apologists seriously maintain that to go from location A to location B within an atom, the point-particle actually does not move from A to B. Instead, it is "annihilated" at A (*i.e., nihilo ex* – ceases existence) and "*ex nihilo* recreated" at B. (The technical literature refers to "creation" and "annihilation" operators. These "operators" are secular *ex nihilo* postulates!) In case this strikes you as odd, remember that this is said by rationalists who would be offended if you considered them to be subjective, metaphysical, well-reasoned storytellers, or occult. The (complex, top-down) equations demand (or allow) it!

• An outgrowth of this particle annihilation and creation are phrases such as: quantum fluctuations of random nothingness, or universes may pop into and out of existence depending upon their quantum operators!

Atheoristically, the quantum point atom has driven a frantic mathematical effort to save the appearances. These fundamental point particle equations diverge from commonsense – and extrapolated adventures cannot be stretched to rationally deal with the data. The theoretical physicist, Murray Gell-Mann, observes:

> We suppose that [quantum mechanics] is exactly correct. Nobody understands it, but we all know how to use it and how to apply it to problems, and so we have learned to live with the fact that nobody can understand it. (B105, page 229, note 2.)

The noted physicist Richard Feynman agrees: "I can safely say that nobody understands Quantum Mechanics."[19]

The missing understanding was due to the banishment of causal prediction. So, they learned to use the rules governing the sub-equations and data arrays, which saved (some of) the appearances and gave short-term predictability, but no one knew why this was so!

We face rafts of data adrift on oceans of mathematics! Does the relativistic / quantum confusion hint at layered potpourri? Modern science cannot handle this question, so a bleak reality looms; Mathematics is so fruitful that it can prove almost

---

19   *The Passion of the Western Mind*, by Richard Tarnas, page 489.

any viewpoint.

But participants find this a safe haven! Out in the unmathematical world, there are questions about the objective nature of mathematics, physical puzzles to solve, and old unanswered questions rearing their heads once again. For example, real objects can touch each other, whereas mathematical points rarely do. Di Francia reports:

> [Gas Law] is in good agreement with the result of experience for [unpressurized] *monoatomic* gases .... For other gases, however ... the theory often clashes with experience ...
>
> Let us consider a *point mass* ..... Its mechanical state is perfectly specified by giving its three coordinates [up-down, back-forward, and sideways]... and the three components ... of the velocity .... Free atoms ... behave ... as point masses.
>
> When the body has nonnegligible size, [*i.e.*, not a point particle], besides the translational degrees of freedom there are also rotational degrees of freedom [roll, pitch, and yaw] .... A diatomic molecule ... behaves approximately this way ... [and some] diatomic gases show conspicuous discrepancies. The situation for poly-atomic gases is even worse .... In most cases the theory is in flagrant disagreement with experience. (B106, pages 177-178. Emphasis in original.)

Bohm reports a similar problem:

> When one applies the existing quantum theory to the electrodynamics of "elementary" particles (such as electrons, protons, *etc.*), internal inconsistencies seem to arise in the theory .... Among the things that cause [this] ... one of the most important is the assumption, which seems to be an intrinsic part of current theories is that "elementary" particles ... are mathematical points in the sense that they occupy no space at all .... *No way has yet been found to incorporate consistently into the current quantum theory the assumption that the electron occupies a finite region of space.* (B107, page 121. Emphasis added.)

To calculate "actual" properties in a point-size object causes infinity to arise in the equations. This sounds similar to Penrose's comment, mentioned in an earlier chapter, about triple collisions of point particles and indeterminism.

Physical Object

Point Particle and "Field"

If the electron is actually larger than a mathematical point, then when physical electrons in a laboratory collide, it is imaginary point particles with an imaginary (short-range) effect – the strong force – that mathematicians model. This mathematical imagery can be easily confused in the literature with representing the actual laboratory objects or electromagnetic fields. Bishop Berkeley's criticism of the "ghost of departed matter" is still relevant. It also tempts one to challenge materialists – with their disdain for the metaphysical – to model atomic phenomena without metaphysical point particles as the "structure" with which to interpret related "cloud chamber" tracks.

Di Francia has another interesting observation:

> Nuclear forces are too strong to be studied with perturbation methods .... The successive perturbations do not diminish to the point of being negligible. On the

other hand, we do not know of an alternative mathematical way of dealing with the problem. The situation is really paradoxical. We do not know what to use as initial data in a problem that we would not know how to solve mathematically anyway! (B106, page 313.)

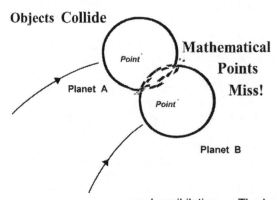

Objects Collide

Point

Planet A

Point

Mathematical

Points

Miss!

Planet B

A further vexing feature of quantum electrodynamics is that these point-particles cannot be chased from here to there. As stated a few pages back, they must be "annihilated" at Point A and "re-created" at Point B, rather like the manner in which the ancient impetus theory of motion explained the motion of arrows!

[A] central feature of quantum field theory is particle creation and annihilation .... The basic mechanism by which these creation and annihilation processes occur remains just as mysterious for these (massless) photons as it does, say, for massive mesons ...

[Q]uantum theory is 'the blackest of blackbox theories: a marvelous predictor but an incompetent explainer' .... Are [these later attempts at an explanation] anything more than a definitional move to paper over our ignorance with a new set of words?

The author goes on to mention the "divergent series of divergent terms" within quantum electrodynamics:

There appears to be no compelling reason to consider the infinities associated with the renormalization programme of quantum field theory as representing anything corresponding to physical reality. It is every bit as plausible that these infinities are an indication of the shortcomings of standard quantum field theories.

... The sense in which experimentalists "see" protons or electrons is only somewhat less tenuous than that in which they claim to "see" quarks. (B108, pages 26, 27, 31, 32.)

More than once the literature of science (and science, falsely so-called) mentions "small" objects. For example, the late Sir Herbert Dingle said:

We think we have reached velocities approaching the speed of light when we have, in fact, only inferred them theoretically as possessed by theoretically inferred particles. (B86, page 212.)

Those familiar with his *Science at the Crossroads* know that his concerns led to a profound difficulty with abdicating common sense to mathematics, particularly as evidenced in Einstein's adventures of relativity.

And another thinker comments:

The standard and most successful method to solve problems of interacting systems is by *perturbation* ... The method works only when the coupling energy is small compared to the energy of the free entities ... When quantum field theory was first formulated, the first-order results were quickly obtained for many quantities, and they agreed fairly well with experiments. However, when physicists pushed to the second-order terms, *the results blew up in their faces; they were all* infinities ... The solution to the problem of infinities is based on the *insight* that the bare electron, with which the theory starts, is *fictitious* ... In *renormalization*, all infinities are absorbed into the *fictitious* bare parameters, which are *replaced* by the real electron mass and charge as measured in experiments ... The theory is unable to specify the real parameters for the physically significant entities; finally it has to appeal to experiments. (B109, pages 191-193. First emphasis in original.)

More may be "fictitious" than the author realizes! Renormalization is a fancy name for an eraser! Rational mathematics provides modeling freedom.

Again, Feyerabend contributes his usual unwelcome comment, highlighting the "renormalization programme" mentioned above:

[T]he classical electrodynamics of Maxwell and Lorentz implies that the motion of a free particle is self-accelerated. Considering the self-energy of the electron one obtains divergent expressions [to infinity] for point-charges while charges of finite extension can be made to agree with relativity only by adding *untestable stresses and pressures inside the electron*. The problem reappears in quantum theory, though it is here partially covered up by *"renormalization."* This procedure consists in *crossing out the results of certain calculations* and replacing them by a description of what is actually observed. Thus one admits, implicitly, that the theory is in trouble while formulating it in a manner suggesting that a new principle has been discovered. *Small wonder when philosophically unsophisticated authors get the impression that "all evidence points with merciless definiteness in the ... direction ... [that] all the processes involving ... unknown interactions conform to the fundamental quantum law."* (B27, pages 60-61. Emphasis added.)

Even Stephen Hawkings, the eminent British mathematician, has reservations about Quantum Mechanics, due also to the process of renormalization:

...[R]enormalization involves canceling the infinities by introducing other infinities. Although this technique is rather dubious mathematically, it does *seem* to work in practice .... Renormalization, however, does have a serious *drawback* from the point of view of trying to find a complete theory, because it means that the actual values of the masses and strengths of the *forces cannot be predicted* from the theory, but have to be *chosen to fit* the observations. (B110, page 157. Emphasis added.)

His co-worker, Roger Penrose, said about the same thing:

However, it [quantum electrodynamics] is a rather untidy theory – and a not altogether consistent one – because it initially gives *nonsensical 'infinite' answers*. These have to be *removed* by a process known as 'renormalization.' ... However, this approach has additional infinities of its own, and one makes sense of it only via the introduction of *'mathematical tricks.'* Despite the undoubted power and impressive accuracy of quantum field theory *(in those few cases where the theory can be fully carried through)*, one is left with a feeling that deeper understandings are needed before one can be confident of any 'picture of physical reality' that it may seem to lead to. (B83, pages 289-290. Emphasis added.)

No wonder quantum mechanics, with its renormalization scheme, was lamented as the "death of science." Talk about a disconnect between theory and practice. Another reviewer of the status of atomic theory said:

As a compact summary of everything we know, the standard model [of the atom in quantum mechanics] has two major defects: one aesthetic, one concrete. Our aesthetic sense tells us there are too many particles [61], [and] too many forces ... The concrete problem is one of inconsistency. When the force-field theories, in impressive agreement with all the data, are asked to predict the result of experiments carried out at very high energies, *they churn out physical absurdities.*" (B103, page 347.)

Another researcher comments:

For all its usefulness, the standard model [of the quantum atom] has a big problem: It has a long list of *adjustable constants.*... [W]e must specify the values of the constants .... [T]he theory is mathematically consistent no matter which values we put in .... We have no idea why these numbers have the values they do; we simply determine them by experiments and then plug in the numbers .... *There are twenty such constants* .... *[It] is a tremendous embarrassment.* Each one represents some basic fact of which we are ignorant. (B111, pages 12-13. Emphasis added.)

Harken back to the high school definition of science and imagine doing a laboratory exercise and getting an excellent grade for utilizing "adjustable constants" via renormalization! No wonder 1 + 1 = 2 and associates are honored in name only. *No wonder quantum mechanics can be so precise – it gets to use an eraser (renormalization) to modify itself to match what is expected. In the process, unwanted infinities are removed!*

Another quotation relating to quantum mechanics shows the challenge of making mathematics objectively model reality:

Mathematics is capable of attacking problems where discontinuities are present, but the technical difficulties are very great; and this is the chief reason why the theory of numbers presents such obstacles. [See page 178.] On the other hand, where we are dealing with problems of continuity the mathematician feels more at ease; and that superb mathematical instrument known as the differential equation [calculus] becomes applicable. Incidentally we can understand why it was that Planck's discovery of quantum phenomena or discontinuous jumps in the processes of nature was such unwelcome news to theoretical physicists; the differential equation had lost its power. (B112, page 383.)

Investigations of close encounters between small objects reach a point where a mathematical point is, well, pointlessly inaccurate! Unfortunately, understandings in electrodynamics and atomic phenomena rely heavily upon mathematical point idealizations. To save the appearances does not explain the appearances. The ghost of departed quantity may have been reincarnated. Again, rationalists bit their tongues!

Math enthusiasts think they have crossed a watershed. They now close the book on the prior history of science. Their new science, "Modern science," is thought to be unconnected to older science. Physical causality has been replaced by top-down (causal) mathematics. Direct facts are submerged under layered potpourri and history becomes bunk. Nonetheless, subjectivity remains. Freedom of choice exists in esoteric mathematics when formulating complex systematizations. The results may be well-ordered, but still subjective. An eclectic attitude allows enthusiasts to pick and choose what segments of the new "science" to accept.[20]

20   I am troubled by parallels to the contemporary Christian scene. Books are written about the "*Scandal of the Evangelical Mind,*" but end up recommending the acceptance of extrapolative

These enthusiasts have led science to an unexpected U-turn. While science started with the assumption that the "divine" Plato's top-down (causal) mathematics came before matter – and derived Universal Natural Laws – later developments in science, and debacles in mathematics – pointed towards matter coming first – as modeled with ~~laws~~ useful equations – thanks to the "immortal" Aristotle instead. But the sub-atomic point particle "necessity" returned top-down (causal) mathematics to priority. (More accurately, what is now used should be called saving-the-appearances mathematics.) Their quantum world is a mathematical world – it is not about objects in reality. They consider Mathematic's Word the real world; the physical world is unreal! Pythagoras, Parmenides and Plato would be at home here.

After all these well-publicized developments, **Classical Science** was seen to be inadequate! A revolution in science had occurred and Dr Thomas Kuhn captured it with the word, "*paradigm*," in his *The Structure of Scientific Revolutions*. This shift was reviewed earlier, especially pages 11-13.

The main drivers of this shift in perspective were the rising mathematical uncertainty and the elusive natures of Relativity and Quantum Mechanics. Broad scientific agreements were no longer possible – at least not on an experimental basis and its cause and effect relationships. The best that could be hoped for was consensus agreement of learned participants.

The actual **Inaccessible Science Paradigms** are given on pages 13 and 14; and pitfalls follow on pages 14-15. *Now we can be thoroughly modern!* "General" consensus of learned participants reflects this catastrophic overhaul of science. In summary:

A. The universe is an illusion. Creation *ex nihilo* is unbelievable!
B. Micro-reality is not causal.
C. Classical science has died. Science is a game – with strict rules, paying homage to the non-causal quantum mechanics.
D. In spite of chaos, there is unity in the cosmos, but there is no TOE (Theory of Everything).
E. Experiment and observation uncover some facts.
F. *Mathematics is the Foundational science!*
G. *Consistent connected mathematical models display the unaided proof of the unity of the materialistic universe.*

This new outlook is the result of about sixty years of discovery, creativeness and innovation, which was essentially complete by 1940. However, like the proverbial genie who keeps popping out of a bottle, change appears periodically in "scientific" journals, with questions such as: Is the sun shrinking, thereby generating its energy, and dispensing with neutrinos, or is the earth's rotation slowing down? These rumors cause great uneasiness. *They indicate processes that cannot be*

---

infatuation. Unfortunately, one gets the impression that contemporary Christians and grandiose extrapolators have almost the same clear intuitions – or breathe the same adventurous "atmosphere"! The Paradigmer has his beautiful equations – and nothing else. The contemporary Christian also is ahistorical – the Bible and me – his and the church's history vanish, including any checks that allow discernment of "private interpretations." With this outlook, reality becomes unknown. This parallel deserves further study.

extrapolated for the billions of years required to keep the adventure credible.

For a modern touch, some astronomers now search for solar neutrinos (actual mathematical points) and, in the last few years, for actual geometric lines, a postulate of the superstring theory. Conceptual upheavals are fermenting:

> Physicists are particularly excited about the superstring theory because it forces us to revise our understanding of the nature of matter. Since the time of the Greeks, scientists have *assumed* that the ultimate building blocks of the universe were *tiny point particles*. Democritus coined the word *atomos* to describe these ultimate, indestructible units of matter.
>
> The superstring theory, however, *assumes* that the ultimate building blocks of nature consist of *tiny vibrating strings* .... According to the superstring theory, our world only *appears* to be made of point particles, because our measuring devices are too crude to see tiny strings. (B113, pages 4-5. Last emphasis in original.)

Considering that a point particle is no bigger than one divided by infinity, the author seems to suggest that "tiny strings" are even smaller, perhaps 0.00001 divided by infinity! String theory contains as many as 26 dimensions – and 26 solutions – of which most are "curled up" and can only be seen by the mind's eye! Actually, both strings and points are well-reasoned storytelling; they cannot be measured. Rationalists "assume" and generous layers of mathematics causes reality to "appear" to agree! Unfortunately, M-theory is trying to displace string theory before it is even born. Paradigms are such fun! The superstring theory also illustrates another phenomena: Defects in existing paradigms are not widely admitted until a replacement begins to promote its systematization. (Some say that String Theory is dying. Time will tell.)

Allegiance to mathematical idealizations blocks fruitful alternative inquiries into reality and squanders resources. The paradox of the new consensus paradigm "science" can be summed up in a poem:

> The Titans of intellectual adventure clashed:
> Newtonian gravity against Maxwell's electrodynamics,
>
> The triumphant electrodynamicists were generous,
> Praising Newtonian gravity as a "special case" of relativized gravity.
>
> After all, the explanations both overflowed with equations.
> But the explanations of the actual equations were opposite:
>
> Gravity utilizes force, relativity postulates space-time creases.
> Oh! Cavendish balance, do you measure creases or forces?
>
> Relativity was "precisely confirmed" in that solar eclipse expedition.
> Even though of 20 per cent accuracy, it is precise(!), and all is relative.
>
> Anyhow, "science" triumphs, proving that reason is objective.
> And as Sir Hoyle explained in his astronomy textbook:[21]

---

21   *Astronomy and Cosmology, A Modern Course*, B114, Sir Fred Hoyle. Pages 7-8, 416. Hoyle says, in part:
"In describing their *relative* motions, it makes no difference whether we consider the Earth to move around the Sun, or the Sun to move around the Earth .... We now know that the difference between a heliocentric theory and a geocentric theory is one of relative motion only, and that such a difference has no physical significance."

> Whether the earth goes around the sun or vice versa, has no physical
> significance!

> So, taking him at his word,
> And atheoristically viewing the 1887 Michelson-Morley observations!
> A stationary earth is confirmed by the null result.

> But we are told that it has no physical significance.
> Relativists face a big challenge,
> To be always or situationally relativistic![22]

Even in supposed basics, enigma abounds. Read the 7 or 8 or 9 respected authors who dwell at length on the "Galilean controversy" and try to find therein the same proof for Copernicus' circular epicyclic understanding.[23] Thinkers are still trying to agree on a non-mathematical explanation!

Additionally, philosophical reflections of famous men of science reveal continued puzzlement over gravity, mass, force, light, *etc.* For example, consider the musing of Henri Poincaré:

> There is no escape from the following definition, which is only a confession of failure. *Masses are coefficients which it is found convenient to introduce into calculations.* (B84, page 103. Emphasis in original.)

The *Focal Point* article by the astronomer, Goeffrey Burbidge, in the June 1990 *Sky and Telescope* magazine, is a dash of cold water on cherished astronomical extrapolations. It smacks of atheorism:

> We live in an era when it seems legitimate to try everything conceivable within the known laws of physics, particularly in the *absence* of data. However, in areas where there are significant problems stemming from observational data, there is complete *silence* ... [about such as] the nature of redshifts ... [and] the apparent instability of galaxy groups and clusters .... After all, while [the big bang] predicts the expansion and the microwave background, it also predicts a smooth universe with no galaxies, no stars, no planets, and no life. (B116, page 580. Emphasis added.)

Astronomy is not crucial to experimental science. What does atheorism notice about astronomy? (It is not necessary to follow Geoffery Burbidge into "deep space" to be concerned.) What about such things as:

- Observational evidence of historical changes of distance in the solar system.
- Newton's analysis of planetary capture theory.
- The discrepancy between the solar system's distribution of mass and angular

---

22   If you believe that there is no physical difference between Copernicus and Ptolemy, recalculate the results from Besel's 1838 determination of the parallax of 61 Cygni within a geocentric universe. Relativists are relative in their rational use of relativity!
23   *The Sleepwalkers*, (B62), Arthur Koestler.
Against Method, (B4), Paul Feyerabend.
The Crime of Galileo, Giorgio de Santillana.
Galileo at Work, Stillman Drake.
The Copernican Revolution, Thomas S. Kuhn.
Galileo, Science, and the Church, Jerome Langford.
The Galileo Connection, (B115), Charles E. Hummel.
To Save the Phenomena, (B42), Pierre Duhem.
The Mechanization of the World Picture, (B44), E. J. Dijksterhuis.

momentum.

    - If all is relative, what goes around what?

    - If all is relative, why is the earth's position in the sky seen to be "near" the center using quantized red-shift data, http://creation.com/our-galaxy-is-the-centre-of-the-universe-quantized-redshifts-show, or the cosmic background radiation data which indicates an embarrassing "axis of evil," http://creation.com/cmb-conundrums ? (These topics are hotly debated, so ....?)

    - What is an interstellar straight-line sighting when contending with solar atmosphere, solar wind, intergalactic medium, and unk-unks?

    - Which editorial review board has the last say on the value for the Hubbell constant?

    - What does the red shift of starlight really indicate?

    - Is there "tired light?"

    - If mathematics and reality are not interchangeable, and mathematical points and geometric strings are fighting for supremacy, why not suspect the presence of spreadsheet enamorment.

    - Why do astronomers, searching for monotruth, reach wildly divergent systematizations?

    : Could man be drunk, but not with wine? (Isaiah 29:9)

I suppose that each item in the above list is affirmed or denied by various consensus groups of experts. The name-calling over these is not always friendly. It is easy to be called a supporter of "crank science." All the previous chapters contain hints about what can retard an interest in an "open unbiased" attitude. Many times, it takes an "off the record" conversation with some members of Paradigm Science to be able to get their unguarded personal answers.

Atheorism and learned ignorance are the objective option. The gap between consensus understanding and knowledge is growing. The consensus of learned participants (paradigms) may yet be driven to contemplate the alternative systematization of *ex nihilo* creation. 1 + 1 = 2 and associates only have figurehead status.

Feyerabend again warns us:

> None of the theories which Carnap, Hempel, Nagel, Popper or even Lakatos want to use to rationalize scientific changes can be applied, and the one that *can* be applied, refutation, is greatly reduced in strength. *What remains are aesthetic judgments, judgments of taste, metaphysical prejudices, religious desires, in short, what remains are our subjective wishes*: science at its most advanced and general returns to the individual a freedom he seems to loose when entering its more pedestrian parts, and even its "third world" image, the development of its concepts, ceases to be "rational." (B4, pages 294-295. Emphasis in original.)

Such is a salute to the rational shock within the consensus of learned participants. Rational Universal Connected Knowledge may be adorned with *ad hoc* modifiers! Aye, it is a hard task to be loyal to the "all-seeing" adventure and also be objective. Thinkers may have axes to grind; dominant personalities have wide maneuvering room! Philosophers of science continually fail to show why many claimants to the name of science *are* not actually science, falsely so-called. Experimenters, thinkers, observers and mathematicians would do a great service to the

advancement of knowledge ... and its distinction from understanding if they published the following:
   - assumptions in astronomy (and other adventures)
   - criteria used to reject alternate solutions to high order equations
   - arbitrary constants
   - antinomies (contradictions, what refuses to conform)

   For example, when astronomers finally backed away from the infinite universe
that ruled from the time of the Greek masters to about 1930, the resulting dynamics
of the so-called expanding universe created at least one problem. Not enough mass
or energy was observed for their model of the universe to be stable. In fact, there
was only between one to ten per cent of the required amount! The consensus now
says that ninety-six percent of the universe's mass or energy is "invisible" – the
equations predict it! (*Astronomers sometimes need to be graded with a generous
bell curve.*) To the well-reasoned, astronomy is considered the purest "science," so,
they do not doubt that they are "all-seeing." They are, instead, looking at the
"emperor's new clothes," sewn with ultra-thin point particle fabric or watching the
Wizard of Oz (aka. Dr Ad Hoc) at work!
   In line with this, many times serious discussion in talk shows starts off somewhat like: "To understand science, we must start with the big bang." To accept that
premise, one must accept some accompanying baggage: Grandiose extrapolation
is valid; paradigm science is objective; and to know the accessible playing field,
mathematical stories about the inaccessible are crucial – far from the footsteps of
humans and empirical science! (Plato's preferred procedure!)

   As the astronomer Robert Jastrow pondered the big bang, he was forced to
conclude:
      For the scientist who has *lived by his faith in the power of reason*, the story
   ends like a bad dream. He has scaled the mountains of ignorance; he is about to
   conquer the highest peak; as he pulls himself over the final rock, he is greeted by a
   band of theologians who have been sitting there for centuries. (B117, pages 105-
   106. Emphasis added.)

   To paraphrase: astronomers extrapolate to the uttermost; use free creations of
the mind; ignore scaffolding, debris or details that refuse to come into line; sculpt the
mathematics to suit their free and autonomous reason; yet their "unaided" rational
efforts to systematize their paradigm cannot avoid a falsifying singularity: *ex nihilo*
creation.
   The only difference between a recent and a long ago creation is the acceptance of grandiose extrapolation ... and its baggage. *Ignoring that difference,
however, is a major concession to subjectivity!*
   We need wisdom! The more objective approach is to accept learned ignorance and hear the Word of the Lord regarding origins. No wonder the revealed truth
("aided" reason) of the recent *ex nihilo* creation is still the reasonable view of reality.

   Astronomy is such an exciting systematic understanding! Why then do so
many well-reasoned folk instead call this an intellectual adventure – a paradigm – a

science? Does the following comment by the astronomer, Narlikar (1982), now make sense?

> Gravity remains an enigma .... [There are] many interesting and fruitful ideas about gravity *outside the frameworks of Newton and Einstein.* Contrary to the view held by the conservative majority of astronomers, I feel that the last word on gravity has not yet been said and that some astronomical phenomena already warrant a fresh input of ideas. (B118, page vii. Emphasis added.)

Narlikar did not say what "fruitful ideas" he had in mind. Such may be unwise to discuss in "consensus" academia.

People avoid the obvious as they say, "Gravity has been proven accurate to one part in 10 million." Of course, this is true in the laboratory realm – several centuries of measurement and observation from the surface of the earth!

Not surprisingly though, laboratory measurements do show discrepancies, such as during eclipses. Also, in recent years, versions of the Cavendish balance have been taken underground into deep mines. Discrepancies in what the force of gravity should be, of the order of 0.25 percent, have been noted. Even the Voyager spacecraft are not where they are calculated to be. Like the previously discussed change of one second per decade in the orbital speed of the earth, these discrepancies over "short" distances threaten grandiose extrapolation.

Instead of saying the gravitational equation: "$F = G \cdot M_1 \cdot M_2 / r^2$ is not wrong," ask "What is the universal law of interaction between objects?"

Interaction = Mass Force + Surface Effects + Electric Force + Magnetic Force + Gas Force + Unk-Unks

With this *complex ~~Natural Law~~ (OOPS!) systematization*, the gravitation equation still has approximate applicability but is only one factor in the great mathematical spreadsheet attenuating in the sky! Realizing that a few observing instruments (not experiments) have been sent only about 0.002 light years into the solar system sea (Voyager I & II beyond Neptune), I face a problem when looking at the majestic night sky. I no longer "see" vast galaxies millions of light years away. Rather, I wonder why the purveyors of such "explanations" of the perceived, but inaccessible, electromagnetic phenomena set up in their mind's eye the constants, solutions, or mathematical models they do.

A surprising thought occurs while viewing images from the Hubble Space Telescope. In the images of the so-called "Eagles Nest" (Eagle Nebula, M16 in 1996), we see the Hubble's great light gathering power. Then we see images of the "nearby" ex-planet Pluto, which attests to the Hubble's great power of magnification. Which is it really? The Hubble Space Telescope or the Hubble Space Microscope? Now that is a philosophical question to ponder!

I even wonder if a computer program would operate ... one incorporating all the equations assumed to be valid and as culled from the most reputable astronomy textbooks. Further, if atheoristic folk dabbled with the reference framework utilized in programming the spreadsheet, would academics tolerate such heresy? Perhaps it is not that the universe has 96 % dark matter and dark energy, but that "unaided" reason has achieved only 4 % accuracy! A sad commentary on "unaided" reason!

Eight centuries ago, science had been helped, then hobbled, by *Aristotelian logical scholasticism*. We now live under a *Platonic mathematical scholasticism*. Are rationalists subjective – soaring – in their faith-commitment to well-reasoned story-telling and not merely "assenting" to fact? "Unaided" reason betrays bondage if it is afraid of history or revealed truth ("aided" reason), confirmed in our atheoristic understanding of the playing field.

The edifice of science contains "subjective" errors. The science of measure, its grandiose extrapolations and layered potpourri are the mischief makers.

Some rationalists may respond by saying, "Even if we admit that some of our truths are only saving the appearances, we must remember that layered facts are involved. Consistency between the layers gives the highest probability that this is scientific puzzle solving, not storytelling. We are not embarrassed by our need for paradigms!"

Others say science is "self-correcting." That is a Yes and No truth. No, (inaccessible) science does not show flexibility in its devotion to monotruth. Malleability and accommodation are not "law-like" actions. Yes, (inaccessible) science shatters periodically and then rigidly regroups around new paradigms.

Indeed, the history of science shows that new research results are resisted by those who have a loyalty – not to direct facts – but to a web of layered facts – or layered potpourri. This has happened many times throughout history; published "scientists" are rarely "self-correcting." The increasing precision and sophistication of experiment and observation continually pressures the "scientific" consensus.

A further problem relates to the "fluidity" of the equations used, including their constants, when facing uncomfortable facts:

> Scientists then complicate the theory, in a way that incorporates several adjustable constants. Finally, they adjust those constants to hide the missing pre-dicted phenomena, thus explaining why the unification, if true, has not resulted in any observations. But such maneuvering makes the theory hard to falsify, be-cause *you can always explain away any negative result by adjusting the constants.* (B111, page 69. Emphasis added.)

If the gravitational and electromagnetic "science" reviewed herein nonetheless is the "true" description of the appropriate phenomena, we can sympathize with those Christians (and others) who develop a tightly compartmentalized view of faith and reason. Christians can play in their sandbox; "unaided" reason can play in their sandbox; and never in the 'twain shall they meet!

But it becomes a tilted playing field, for God's action within redeemed individuals leads to observable results. Whose sandbox do these observable results belong in? So the compartmentalized life slides into the life of spiritual abstractions for many. For others, the compartmentalized life suggests a dead-end for reasoning along an event-less mathematical line. These can break free to encounter the "untamed" God.

This puts rational thought into a fine dilemma. Also consider Feyerabend's comment about the *ad hoc* in mathematics, page 31, Russell and Berlinski's comments about a "complicated conceptual labyrinth" and an "immense inferential trail," page 38, Feyerabend's later comment, page 226, on the freedom a theoretician gains in the more abstruse depth of theory and the comment on page 229 on how complex mathematics can hide problems. To correct these things, we must stop asking the rational "fox to guard the henhouse"!

Hope springs eternal! Our walk on the hidden, yet obvious, path reveals mankind's remarkable ability to let the wish father the facts! But some rationalists weep and turn aside to modern sophistry.

Our focus has been attracted to relativity theories, quantum mechanics and the big bang as we approach the end of the hidden, yet obvious, path. They climax the subjectivity clogging the cosmos "explained" with extrapolative infatuation. Rationalists are always looking for "fresh understandings" or content with endless tweaking.

Rationalists can still view electrodynamics as a part of materialism. *But this has become materialism with "supervisory" human intervention.* Everything is smothered with equations, but supervised equations are not blossoming flowers, thus inappropriate to replace *ex nihilo* creation!

My impression is that a substantial part of the problem swirling around gravity, electrodynamics and quantum phenomena centers around a false understanding of the atom. As said before, early laws were promulgated without knowing what current flow, the electron or the atom was. And when they were known, there was a remarkable tendency to assume that what had been said years earlier was fundamentally correct, not saving the appearances – so they contented themselves with *ad hoc* tweaking of existing models and equations.[24, 25]

The search for truth is obscured by a rational fog. Thinking about this pleasant labyrinth, I became aware of an alternative model of the atom. By implication, this leads to an alternative to relativity theories, quantum mechanics and the big bang. It indicates that "unaided" reason went astray before these three subjects appeared.

As electric and magnetic phenomena were initially investigated, the science of measure interfered with this effort. A flashback illustrates some irony in this situation. As science began in ancient Greece, thinkers opted for the grand idea: Mathematic's Word: Top-down (causal) mathematics and matter are interchangeable[26]. This enshrined the bewitching power of equations. Their power was still strong in Galileo's day. But Sir Isaac Newton, the empiricist, as said earlier, did not

---

24   This leaves an opening for research using the transformation information about the finite size charge elements that Maxwell (and Heaviside?) was not aware of, and later investigators could not fit into his (their?) differential equations. Also, the late Dr. Thomas Barnes' study of the electron's magnetic field led him to surmise that major changes were required in electromagnetic theory. See his books, *Space Medium*, and *Physics for the Future*. Mathematicians, start your engines! All hands on the spreadsheet!

Dr. Barnes' initial research has been extended by the Common Sense Science organization. Their results and continuing research can be viewed at www.commonsensescience.org.

25   Earlier science history showed how thinkers "patched up" Plato and Aristotle's work to allow them to endure for centuries. Problems only led to *ad hoc* modifications. Such a preference for *ad hoc* improvements of Newton or Maxwell or Rutherford are the modern equivalent.

26   As mentioned earlier, would this sentence make sense if said as: Top-down mathematics and fields are interchangeable? Matter – atoms – numbers – triangles have a "hard" similarity – but not to fields. Maybe something like "jello with a halo" is needed – to recognize the loss of infinite qualities!

believe in Newtonian gravity – action-at-a-distance. Newton's contemporaries and successors were not as empirical and pragmatic as he was. As the years went by, action-at-a-distance became a necessary component of gravitational astronomy – and part of the growing rationalism. Action-at-a-distance supposedly explained something important about matter[27] – but probably nothing about fields. They did not find gravity an uncommon unintelligibility. (In other words, *they understood but did not know!*)

One hundred years later, Michael Faraday began his investigations of electric and magnetic phenomena. (While Faraday was a brilliant experimenter, he was, as he himself said, not very good with mathematics.) With his efforts to understand magnetic "force," he faced a dilemma. Faraday disliked action-at-a-distance, so he explained magnetism as a field. We now refer to magnetic lines of force.

Current, itself, was poorly understood. Current and charge are related, but beyond that little was known. Current comes out of a battery and pushes something through wires.

James Clerk Maxwell, the mathematician, studied Faraday's, Ampere's and others experimental results and recast them into a broad mathematical structure. He corresponded with Faraday and it became apparent that they did not agree on "force." Faraday even wrote an addendum to his report to the Royal Society to make sure no one would doubt his views.

Maxwell formulated his mathematics of electromagnetism before there was knowledge of current, radiation, radioactivity, atoms, electrons and protons. (And the same had been true in Newton's day – who commendably was cautious!) *Also, except for lodestones, there was no evidence then of magnetism within the elements,* much less within the unheard of atoms – or electrons. Thus, the only place Maxwell could visualize as the source of electric and magnetic energy was a potential (voltage) "stress" in the surrounding "luminiferous" ether. This stress was activated by the battery voltage and acted upon current-carrying matter.

Maxwell used his potentials to recast Faraday's laws into a Newtonian action-at-a-distance formalism – while retaining Faraday's fields. This point-particle combination was to cause errors when later high velocity particle phenomena were encountered; the physics was later mathematically "corrected" by Einstein with his concept of relativity. At the time, it was not realized that the "physical" lagging fields associated with the toroidal ring model of the electron could physically account for the same phenomena[28].

The next surprise is that Maxwell's four laws of electromagnetism do not appear in his 1873 publication. As said earlier, Maxwell actually used 20 plus equa-

---

27   Because little was actually known about matter, the gravitational saving the appearances had little causal content.

28   Maxwell used 4 of the 5 empirical laws developed earlier by Ampere, Faraday, Gauss (2), Lenz, plus 1 later called the Lorentz law. Maxwell also used about 8 approximations or idealizations.

These were innocent at the time. But as new phenomena was uncovered, exceptions were noted, and probably more are accumulating. Extreme conditions many times lead to new discoveries. See *The Universal Force*, Volume 1, by Charles W Lucas, Jr. Pages 24 to 31.

tions with 20 unknowns; written with Hamilton's quaternion algebra that had been recently introduced – including four imaginary dimensions, *i, j, k, l*. (No wonder his equations mystified most of his contemporaries!) These are not the 4 equations Maxwell is famous for!

In response to criticism, Maxwell had begun revising and eliminating the quaternions, but illness slowed him down and he soon died. (With the computational tools then available, quaternions were extremely difficult to calculate with. It was too tedious to use for extensive analysis. Something quicker and less abstract was needed and Heaviside provided it.)

Here enters Oliver Heaviside into the story – whose limited schooling ended at age sixteen. Heaviside made many contributions to telegraphy, radio transmission, electrodynamic theory and he invented the operational calculus. Heaviside did not like Maxwell's use of "potentials" or his quaternions, so he replaced Maxwell's 20 quaternion equations with the now-familiar 4 differential equations – by, at the least, retaining the vector component of Maxwell's algebra. Heaviside also predated knowledge of atomic phenomena. (Some mathematicians still argue over whether he should have left Maxwell's quaternion equations alone.) Heaviside – famous in his day for not giving explanations – did say there were some situations where quaternion equations were useful. *He was known as Maxwell's prophet and Maxwell's apostate!*

Atomic problems arose once J J Thompson discovered the electron in 1897. Modeling of the atom began. The first attempt in 1902 had the electrons as "blobs of charge" surrounding a nucleus, (the plum pudding model). It was replaced in 1911 with the Rutherford planetary model, which seemed like a reasonable conclusion. The electrons were now "spheres of charge," like miniature planets orbiting around the nucleus.

· = Mathematical Points

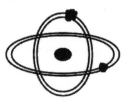
Rutherford Atom

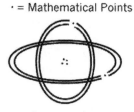
Quantum Atom

However, a small spherical electron would be blown apart by its enormous internal electrostatic repulsive force, the Coulomb force (10^{39} stronger than gravity). This repulsive force on a mathematical point electron should be even more likely to blow it apart. A great mystery!

(And the orbital motion would lead to an energy loss via radiation – and the collapse of the atom.) It was soon determined that the electron also has a magnetic field, in addition to an electrostatic field. But charge doesn't have magnetic effects until it is moving (in a circuit); before then, it only has the electrostatic field.

Around 1913, Niels Bohr, the mathematician, "solved" these difficulties by saying the electron is a mathematical point.[29] The resulting model of the atom was

29 I guess we have a choice about what to believe! Back on page 216 are quotes from Bohr and others, to the effect that their equations were only mathematical contrivances to save the appear-

mentioned earlier – a lumpy unit nucleus surrounded by orbiting mathematical points (electrons).

The point charge electron of quantum theory has the "virtue" that it cannot undergo the process of magnetic induction or radiation. In fact, points can't undergo anything or be anything! Thus their downside is that the properties of the electron – which have been measured – became matters of definition, not of physical reality (which is described with "cause and effect" happenings). Thus we have the lamented "Death of Science" and its replacement by paradigms.

Remember some of the earlier quotes about renormalization, fictitious bare electron or adjustable constants. These earlier quotes said that the electron as a mathematical point leads to absurdities – and subjective choices. The Wizard (an out-of-place Dr Ad Hoc), with Manhattan beads can save (some of) the appearances, but no more! This loss of cause and effect meant that reality has these absurd properties. Not a flattering compliment to mathematicians – or the Creator!

Note: RP + A = Refined Paradigms and Associates.

As said earlier, the nucleus soon revealed more of its complexity under increasingly powerful atom smashers and sensitive detectors. Depicted here is the first "electron-positron" cloud chamber track at the California Institute of Technology. Words can be misleading, are these the tracks of particles or debris? (www.twinkle_toes_engineering.home.comsat.net, article on electrons.)

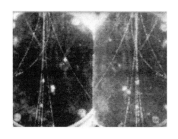

In the resulting Standard Model of the atom, detector tracks were important but

---

ances. Yet later, they and their followers are understood as saying that their mathematical models are "really real."

not the only thing involved. We have seen hints in renormalization (canceling out infinities), creation and annihilation operators, force carriers, adjustable constants, *etc*. Point particles had no inherent characteristics to build on.

Interpreting a detector track such as shown here (identified as a Baryon, in 1974, Brookhaven National Laboratories), was not for the faint of heart! But was the mathematics so complex by then that more strange mathematical properties were piled onto the existing assemblage? They valiantly tried to keep track of all the "data," but understand it with an incorrect paradigm.

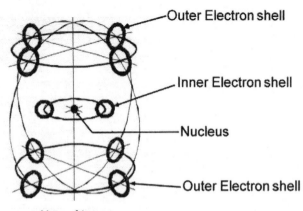

Outer Electron shell

Inner Electron shell

Nucleus

Outer Electron shell

Neon Atom.
Courtesy CommonSenseScience.org

However, research carried on by the Common Sense Science (CSS) organization has examined this dead end and is postulating a better alternative. See page 19 for additional information.

They first point out that in 1915 – when the nature of the electron and the atom were still being fiercely debated – a "ring" model of the electron was proposed by A. N. Parsons in his *A Magneton Theory of the Structure of the Atom*[30]. In 1918, H. S. Allen presented *The Case for a Ring Electron* to London's Royal Society. After that, Compton and Bostick performed experimental work supporting this theory.

This model of the atom is not a planetary model. Electrons are not in motion, nor a sphere, nor a point particle. *Rather, the electron is a small stationary located ring of charge, with the charge circulating around itself as a toroidal shape.*

The circulating charge (current) has associated electric and magnetic fields which cause the charge on each electron to circulate in a toroidal pattern around a "charge fiber." (The "charge fiber" is an artistic effect.)

Ring Electron

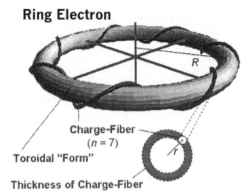

R

Charge-Fiber
$(n = 7)$

Toroidal "Form"

Thickness of Charge-Fiber

Courtesy CommonSenseScience.org

---

30   In the preceding years, there was some discussion of electrons being tiny magnets. A. N. Parsons, a graduate student in chemistry, was attracted to the ring model because it gave a good explanation of chemical bonding.

This circular current flow generates a stationary (DC) magnetic field (also called a standing wave). A rough visualization is that the electron is a ring magnet[31].

The toroidal ring electron is stationary in various positions around the nucleus and maintains its form due to a balance between its electric and magnetic field forces, which are evenly spread out over the circular charge. Individual electrons space themselves out in a balancing of their individual electric and magnetic fields. In relation to the atom's nucleus, the electrons are magnetically and electrostatically "locked" into various stationary positions. Thus, the electron's electric and magnetic fields are "at rest" in respect to the nucleus and thus not subject to the radiation losses associated with the Bohr mathematical-point solar model. In larger atoms, electrons are arranged in shells around the nucleus, accounting for the atoms stable electric and magnetic properties. It also explains the chemical bonding between atoms as a magnetic and electrostatic coupling.

This 1915 ring electron model suffered an early eclipse, partly due to errors made by its initial advocates. Probably, though, the Bohr mathematical-point solar modeled atom was so ununderstandable that it had to be accepted! (Even Einstein said that the complex mathematics in quantum mechanics protected it from refutation!) Also, there was the 1919 eclipse expedition of Eddington and Bohr's 1922 Nobel Prize that sort-of closed off further objections to either relativity or quantum mechanics. Further, as Parson was only a graduate student in chemistry, sophisticated mathematicians saw no need to listen to him?

The toroidal ring electron allows the return to a model of the electron based on physical principles, not on point-particle definitions. The model further means that the proton is a different version of a toroidal ring of charge.[32] As such, results of atom smashers and their detectors are interpreted differently than that using the Standard Model. Everything is now made of charge and fields. Point-particles and "things" like force fields are no longer useful. The data remains, but different conclusions result.

Full elaboration of the model includes the ability to derive atomic force laws, but without the need for mathematical point particles, hence no need to invoke relativistic or quantum notions. Importantly, the ring electron model is both a particle (the ring) and fields (waves). These two components negate the quantum duality of switchable existences

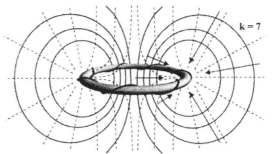

Toroidal Helicon Showing Its Electric and Magnetic Fields
(Not to Scale. Both Field and Force Lines are Shown.)
Courtesy CommonSenseScience.org

---

31   Is it any surprise that the diameter of the ring electron is "similar" to the diameter of the "strong force" surrounding the point particle electron in quantum theory?
32   The proton is a similar ring structure. The neutron has a ring proton in "suspension" within a ring electron.

between particle and wave "states!"

Additionally, the toroidal ring electron model shows how the high velocity distortion of electric and magnetic fields are understandable with a finite-sized object – the ring electron – without invoking mathematical points. A mathematical point cannot predict or model this characteristic.

Maxwell's quaternion equations did not model the then unknown subatomic electron, proton and neutron and their physical characteristics, including what happens under high velocity. The self-inductance of sub-atomic objects reacting back upon themselves would later loom in importance.

Only much later was it realized that current was the basic constituent of matter, charge and related electric and magnetic fields. These fields can be partially detach-ed from matter and cause electromagnetic behavior. The "home" of current is the electron and the proton.

The electron's magnetic field is circulating around the toroidal charge ring at the speed of light and maintained by the current flow in the rotating charge in the ring. When the electron is moving at close to the speed of light, the circulating fields have difficulty keeping up with the motion of its source charge. The fields lengthen out with this high speed movement. (This either "pinches" the charge ring or pro-duces cemf [counter electromotive force] in its own or adjacent charge rings.)

This high velocity elongation of the attached fields is illustrated below. We thus encounter "primitive" mass or inertia! Thus there is an implied shortcoming in at least applying Maxwell's electrodynamic equations to high velocity particles.

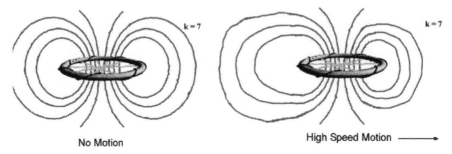

No Motion   High Speed Motion ——————▶

Toroidal Helicon Showing Its Electric and Magnetic Fields
(Not to Scale.)
Courtesy CommonSenseScience.org

When Maxwell wrote in the 1870s, there was no way to get a particle to move at close to the speed of light, so the concept could not then be investigated. Current flowed through wires, but wires were an innocuous "carrier."

The shortcoming of the fact that his calculus, any calculus, has to calculate with point particles was of no importance at the time. Maxwell did deal with large fields in motion – electromagnetic radiation. His calculations did reveal many facts about electromagnetic fields, but it was not realized that a point particle of matter in his calculus is not the source of the fields. Granted, the electron is very small, with a major diameter in the range of 3.8×10^{-13} meter, but the toroidal circulating charge element at its circumference is much smaller, in the range of 3.5×10^{-106} meter, both of which are very large compared to a mathematical point!

There are instruments that can measure down to about 10^{-11} meter – and they do not "see" the toroidal ring electron. Its major diameter is not of a disc of charge but locates the thin charge toroid at the electron's extremity, at 10^{-106} meter. No instrument can see that finely.

The ring model also explains the other subatomic experimental results, including the quantum jumps of blackbody radiation. (Quantum theory "explains" these as electrons jumping to different orbits when energy is absorbed or radiated – using "creation" and "annihilation" operators.) In contrast, the toroidal ring electron model reasonably explains it as changes in the number of turns the charge makes as it wraps around the "charge fiber" at various energy levels.

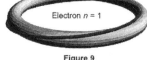

Figure 9
Electron Fundamental or Ground State

All of these ring phenomena are calculable from standard electrical engineering formulas. Yet, some may wonder why a mathematical point is different from a ring electron. Well, the point-particle electron has defined properties – including its "strong force." (This is not called a "strong field," because it does not obey

Figure 10
Electron 1st Harmonic or Excited State

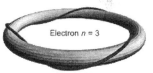

Figure 11
Electron 2nd Harmonic or Excited State

Courtesy: Common Sense Science

field laws.) This "strong force" is a theoretical entity of short range – approximating the diameter of the ring electron. This leads to complicated mathe-matics, which isn't required with the toroidal ring electron concept.

Comparison of the two models of the atom shows why quantum mechanics has to be complicated. It has individual point-particle electrons whizzing through their orbits, while the toroidal ring finite-size electrons are stationary.

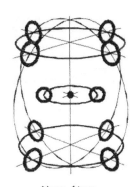

Neon Atom.
Courtesy CommonSenseScience.org

· = Mathematical Points

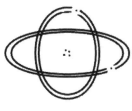

Quantum Atom

Perhaps this is why quantum mechanics says position and velocity cannot both be measured simultaneously. To make a measurement, a "wave collapse" must occur to the point-particle.

If the solar modeled atom is believed, you must enter the world of relativity, quantum mechanics and the Big Bang to explain phenomena. If the toroidal ring model of the atom is believed, you remain in the world of electrical engineering!

So, the toroidal ring electron has much simpler mathematics while the solar model of the atom is all an infinitesimal blur! All material is atomic and the atomic is all charge and electromagnetic fields. Technically, there is no matter surrounded by fields. Rather, charge and fields are organized into structures that are "matter."

With the atom being an electromagnetic phenomenon, a toroidal ring electron explains gravity in electromagnetic terms. Electric and magnetic field forces are 39 orders of magnitude stronger than the force of gravity, so gravity is a residual interplay between the various charges within each atom. An atomic bomb or a nuclear reactor utilize these charge forces, 10^{39} stronger than gravity.

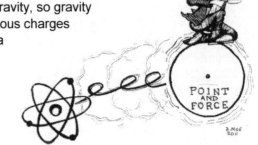

(Granted, Quantum Mechanics invokes "gravitons" to explain gravity, but, as definitions for mathematical convenience, they are dependent on the point-particle concept, so easily seen as strings of Manhattan beads.) In retrospect, note that the Cavendish balance, used to measure gravity, has to have its components electrically neutral to get accurate results. Is that hinting at the electrical source of gravity? (What would happen if these two large field intensities could be channeled such that they had more localized intense interplanetary effects?)

The proper approach to critiquing Relativity and Quantum Mechanics is to focus on the electron and the model of the atom! *There is no need to enter the quantum point-particle labyrinth!* Details and ramifications of the ring model are spelled out in the publications of the Common Sense Science group. See www.commonsensescience.org/resources, especially volume 9 issues #2, 3, 4 and volume 10, issue #1 for these articles in the Focus on Science Volumes.

This work is now beginning to appear in book form. The first of four projected volumes is now available; *The Universal Force*, volume 1, by Dr Charles W "Bill" Lucas, jr. Other authors will likely be publishing also. All of these discuss additional factors that got overlooked by Maxwell and subsequent investigators. The mathematics in all of these is much simplified and tied to electrical engineering principles. This is not to say that electricity is simple at the atomic level – it isn't!

From the perspective of this book, science walked into the dead end of relativity, quantum mechanics and the big bang because of the respect shown to those ancient Promissory IFs: *mathematics and reality are interchangeable and reality is an ahistorical mathematical line.* As results were published in line with these assumptions, later researchers tended to "fall-in-line" and provided *ad hoc* tweaks to existing equations, as reality was shown to be more complicated. It took unusually strong souls to examine if the tweaked equations faithfully modeled physical reality. If the first bookend and between-years are forgotten, objections to the existing confusion fails to sound a clear note.

Mathematic's Word favors the "point" of arithmetic as the electron's model. The toroidal ring model was too warped a circle – it is considered mathematically inelegant. Empiricism was not asked to comment on the dilemma.

We look with great interest at the continuing work of the Common Sense Science group. Appendix C provides information on the timeline of science regarding electromagnetic discoveries.

Another group of investigators is delving into a related area, that of plasma physics in astronomy. This is based on the work of the Nobel laureate, Dr. Hannes Alfven, who called attention to the effects of current flow in space – "*plasma physics.*" This assumes an electromagnetic effect – either in addition to or as a replacement for conventional gravity. This group, under the umbrella of "the electric universe," (www.holoscience.com), is feasting on the results of the increasingly powerful instruments sent into the solar system in recent decades. Their work has developed a view of stars as "electric discharge phenomena" (along the "power lines" of the universe) instead of as nuclear fusion machines. Their plasma "gravity" has not been mathematically rigorized, but it will probably mesh with the work of CSS in the future.

The electric universe folks also inherit the mantle of the late Dr Immanuel Velikovsky, so they philosophically suffer from the dilemma of postulating significant and sometimes catastrophic gravitational effects, while yet believing in an otherwise unremitting materialism. Some housecleaning is to be expected.

There is also the continuing work of the exiled astronomer, the late Dr. Halton C Arp. His work shows the errors in assuming that stellar red-shift is a distance indicator.

All three of these investigations confront the "philosophy of the epoch" on the sub-atomic front. Recollect the ancient timeline of history – the Biblical timeline has the discontinuities of Creation *ex nihilo*, Noah's flood and Joshua's long day. With the force of gravity being so weak – 39 orders of magnitude smaller than electric and magnetic forces – these discontinuities are especially miraculous. However, talk of

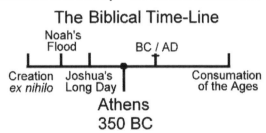

The Biblical Time-Line

"plasma" may open the door to astronomical instances of electric and magnetic forces having significant force levels, and being made available for unleashing.

The work of these three groups of investigators climaxes another change in science; it faces another unexpected U-turn! Matter and force regain primacy over top-down (saving the appearances) mathematics! These investigators work with properties of matter – albeit properties of charge and fields – and use bottom-up mathematics to apply measured engineering principles. We can expect "revolutions" to occur in astronomy and elsewhere.

Rational thought now moves from **Classical Science** and **Inaccessible Science Paradigms** to **Empirical Science**. The primary difference is a reluctance to use grandiose extrapolation because matter no longer has infinite hardness or infinite precision. The basic units of matter are now charge and fields. These have an admitted flexibility! It is no longer reasonable to be a rationalist!
Beware of the labyrinthine nature of poly-mathematics!
Empirical Science adheres to the cause and effect criteria, centered around a rejection of unseen entities and undue trust that mathematical constructions exhaustively reproduce the real. Empiricists accuse the paradigmers of accepting saving the appearances instead of the more rigorous cause and effect criteria.
Nonetheless, empirical science is unable to explain electromagnetic and sub-atomic phenomena without utilizing the toroidal ring electron concept. Empiricists want to avoid mathematical infatuation! Platonic Mathematical scholasticism is dead. We must retreat from its ethereal mathematical heaven and replant our feet in the intermediate real-world and its empirical equations.
Empirical science recognizes that it is not alone in addressing the needs of humanity. The worldwide rising living standards largely came about without credit to science. For that, thank native ingenuity of laypeople, craftsmen, engineers, tech-nologists and tinkerers.

The accessible portion of Classical Science did not die, but became **Empirical Science**! (See pages 18-19.)
  A. What can be manipulated and measured is our domain. Other studies we cannot comment upon; perhaps some are scholarly disciplines. Theory has limited realistic extension, such as the Periodic Table of the elements. Science is one of the ways to acquire knowledge.
  B. Experimental science is orderly. Well – mostly! Natural or manmade objects can exhibit resonances or other instabilities.
  C. The human mind can understand processes. But understanding utilizes a toolbox. A toolbox witnesses to pragmatism – not to rational determinism.
  D. Activity proceeds due to cause and effect relationships. We "see" but do not "see into" these relationships. Qualities, mystery and beauty abound.
  E. There is unity among phenomena, but distinctions and unique characteris-tics remain. We cannot follow this unity into the inaccessible. Science is performed "now" – not as a "stand-in" for elsewhere or other times. Be wary of extrapolative infatuation!

F. Facts are owned by no model or procedure. "Anything goes" in the search for facts! Keen eyes and agile minds are a blessing. *Observation and experimental interrogation are not the same.*
G. Mathematics is a tool, but its plurality highlights an ingenuous garden of choice, not a tree of determinism. Mathematics provides useful formulas.
H. Rational thought, to avoid disasters, should not extrapolate with pliable mathematical dice! Nor have allegiance to paradigms.

Empirical science has developed amazing tools, but cautiously explores such as the sub-atomic. That popular paradigm labyrinth witnesses to the alternative need for a believable, robust model of the atom. Empirical science will recast the entire landscape of rational thought, including astronomy and sub-atomic studies.

Several chapters ago, we mentioned the confidence of experimental science – that experiments would slap their hands if they went astray. This view now requires some modification. Back then, experimental work rarely ventured below the molecular level. Now, it routinely enters the subatomic realm. In this realm, unless experimenters are strongly empirical, they have to rely on relativity and quantum mechanics to "tell them" what they "really" see! Therefore, "hand slaps" are no longer independent!

Such is the specter of attenuation. No wonder arenas such as mainstream astronomy exhibit more storytelling than puzzle solving. The revealed truth ("aided" reason) evident in *ex nihilo* creation is quite compatible with atheoristic science! The "all-seeing" "unaided" vision of rationalism is not in rational proof!

Yet again, rationalists had not proven that:
♦ History or reality are infinite.
♦ Mathematics reliably models physical causes.
♦ Mathematics is scientific discovery, not *ad hoc* invention.
♦ Grandiose extrapolation is objective.
♦ Observation is as valid as experiment.
♦ Planetary formation/capture is a deterministic fact.
♦ The Standard Model of the point-particled atom is objective.
♦ Paradigm science overrides empirical science. Theoretical "facts" trump empirical facts.
♦ "Dark" matter and "invisible" energy are not 96 % in error.

But our journey on the hidden, yet obvious, path is not quite completed.

In praise of (playing field) science

Let mankind be free of *manmade* limitations:
Avoid subjective dreams and utopias;
Use the tools of reason
Be not hypnotized by science's language
Nor mesmerized by extrapolation or adventure.

Understand scientific procedure:
It's tentative view of the inaccessible
It's puzzle solving limits due to reality's complexity,
It's caution over its equational limitations.
Doubt extrapolative infatuation.

Reap the harvest thereby grown:
Be not afraid of the unknown;
Investigate, but respect, its mystery;
Combat evil, guided by wisdom – found elsewhere.
Nurture good by first admitting atheorism.

Avoid the allure of storyteller's "science:"
Let facts trump extrapolative infatuation;
Have more than mathematics as your guide;
Respect data invalidating simple natural law;
Seek wisdom; respect the larger reality beyond science.

R is for reason, a primitive god.
G. K. Chesterton

The subtle analysis of the obvious has produced a spiral of never ending complications.
Morris Kline

Simmias: "I am aware that those who make proof out of probabilities are impostors."
Plato

If any one offers conjectures about the truth of things from the mere possibility of hypothesis, I do not see how anything certain can be determined in any science; for it is always possible to contrive hypothesis, one after another, which are found rich in new tribulations.
Sir Isaac Newton

Reason is not a source of theories, it is an arbiter of mistakes.
Julienne Ford

The world, including the world of science, is a complex and scattered entity that cannot be captured by theories and simple rules.
Paul Feyerabend

There is no rigorous definition of rigor.
Morris Kline

If mathematical thinking is defective, where are we to find truth and certitude.
David Hilbert

In the nineteenth century whole philosophical dynasties rise and fall within a few brief years, and the technical jargon of one school becomes the gibberish of the next.
Henry Aiken

The definitive study of the herd instinct of astronomers has yet to be written.
J Daniel Fernie

Of all the forces we know, there is none stronger than a paradigm.
Robert Stirniman

Martin Luther was correct; we confront a heretical fact: *Reason is "rational" only when shorn of grandiose extrapolation.* Knowledge and understanding of the accessible playing field show why atheorism is operative: *Complexity attenuates extension into the inaccessible, while a soaring mind's eye sees extension where none exists!* Experimenters, observers, mathematicians, engineers, technologists, craftsmen, tinkerers and thinkers face an eleventh commandment: *Thou shall not grandiosely extrapolate.* This reflects Luther's dictum: "Reason is a devilish whore." Intellectual adventures, even when useful, are not science. Indiscriminate use of the label "science" makes scholarly pursuits offensive to men of good will.

Surprisingly, *free will, operative in mathematical choices, justifies rationalism!* Social understanderers contemplating freewill versus determinism should study mathematicians, their equations, and their debris – not monkeys or artfully crafted "social situations."

Another heretical fact looms: Science's domain is not the universe, but that *portion of the universe* amenable to experimentation. Attenuation, mathematical profundities, and freewill so warn us. Atheorism highlights investigators at work in, with, and towards knowledge of the finite playing field, and not through understanding a hypothesized utterly large cosmos. Only in the finite playing field can reason have optimum freedom.

We seem dangerously close to the situation where the accessible is the domain of investigators – including empirical scientists – and the "ivory-tower" is the domain of theoretical science. The art of science shows how relentless grappling with accessible complexity differs from extrapolative infatuation. Grandiose extrapolators develop false conclusions about the inaccessible by banishing attenuation and adjusting, but otherwise ignoring, mathematical profundities. They smugly boast that they are objective! That unbridgeable chasm is not between reason and faith, but between reason and their rational subjectivity.

Another heretical conclusion is that the cosmos is not mathematical, yet mathematics can provide snapshots of thin slices of reality. Laplace's grand equation of the pool-table cosmos does not exist. No one "untended" equation flowers out to explain reality. The Wizard of Oz remains fully employed in saving the appearances!

The well-reasoned do not acknowledge their subjectivity. Their rush to affirm the extrapolative sciences, falsely so-called, compromises their objectivity. They prefer well-reasoned nonsense to learned ignorance. René Descartes used the science of measure and said matter and extension are all that exists. In contrast, G. K. Chesterton rose to the pinnacle of heresy and doubted the well-reasoned doubters of Christianity. (And how is their angst today? Fine, thank you!)

Unfortunately, many visualize science that avoids grandiose extrapolation as a deadend, certainly not a paradigm driven consensus of learned participants! With childlike naiveté, many still affirm, "Science is objective, unbiased. Science is experimental and avoids unwarranted extrapolations." But after a frown and recollection of "science's" cosmic dimensions, they compromise themselves as they quickly add, "Oh yes, astronomy is also scientific even though it is not experimental."[1]

Even Galileo was criticized by the trendsetting intellectual community for his views:

> Galileo selected certain well-defined and very restricted areas of inquiry within which mathematical analysis could clearly advance physics .... Most historians of science ... strive to look behind Galileo's work in physics and find there some grand speculative scheme of the universe, though it was precisely the absence of anything of the sort that was to cause Galileo to be so quickly forgotten .... [This absence caused] Descartes ... [to] flatly [reject] Galileo's physics as having been built without foundation. (B119, page xxi.)

---

1   I was startled to hear something like this on a radio interview a long time ago.

As that historian points out, Galileo's focus on "how" ignored the desires of science, falsely so-called's, to be "all-seeing" and grasp Universal Connected Knowledge. This led to severe criticism by "scientists" of the day. "Extrapolative scientists" criticize empirical scientists. Once again, "science" is an overused word.

Laplace claimed, "I have no need for that [God] hypothesis," Nietzsche said with self-acclaimed objectivity, "God is dead," and Hume, "Commit those books to the flames." In reality, grandiose extrapolation is not public knowledge, but faith in "unaided" rational thought ("aided" by mathematics, logic and the desire to be all-seeing). Therefore, when the well-reasoned try to indict Christianity for its so-called crimes, do not let them call it "*faith against reason*" but recognize it to be "*faith against extrapolative infatuation.*"

Seeking clearly identified understandings is not ignoble, but no matter how scholarly they appear, they must be content with consistency – and hopefully avoid being well-reasoned nonsense. Reason is not a part of this spectrum, but a tool to help comprehend it.

Avoid false compromises. Some thinkers may imply that evolution is bad if applied to biology and geology, but okay if applied to the sum of totality – the cosmos. In effect, they say, "In the (recent) beginning, God *ex nihilo* created an infinite or unbounded cosmos," or, "cosmic evolution; biological creation." While God in His omnipotence certainly could create a very large cosmos, proof has to be sought in revelation or science, not in rationalism.

Because astronomy is a grandiose enterprise, accepting grandiose extrapolation leaves these creationists logically vulnerable when facing evolutionary-minded geologists and biologists. Such claim to be merely applying the (uniformitarian) *extrapolative principles sanctioned by astronomy;* systematizing details confirming that the utterly large applies to both time and distance. Creationists do, however, draw attention to attenuation by looking at history and nature and seeing the hand of God. This highlights inconsistencies in geological and biological systematizations. "Long-agers" and many creationists gloss over the history of science and extrapolative infatuation, so debate often bogs down.

In the ongoing creation-evolution debate, books written by creationists and long-agers have different topical interests. Creation books discuss geology and biology – the playing field. They might squeeze in a few words on astronomy. On the other hand, books defending long ages start with the cosmic outlook of science, falsely so-called, concentrating on mathematics and extrapolation. They then proceed down to geology and biology. Each side talks past the other, not knowing how to unify the study of the playing field with the cosmos. Yet, some creationists are now looking critically at mankind's "knowledge" of the cosmos and the sub-atomic.

As stated in the introduction, *grandiose extrapolation is an ancient error nurtured by the ahistorical mathematical line*. It falsely fulfilled the lure of objective truth with Mathematic's Word and the subsequent deduction that atheism, materialism, and ultimate meaninglessness undergird an unperforated cosmos. Having now discarded the science of measure, rationalists yet remain in its "worlds on paper," wrapped in appropriate cosmic thoughts.

At times, statements made by Christians about the cosmos are pious, but naive, attempts to reconcile the Bible with the science of the day (mistaken for science). Charles Haddon Spurgeon, an English evangelist of the nineteenth century, utilized the gap theory. Scofield, in his 1917 Bible notes, used a long ages outlook. Some books written in the 1920s defending Fundamentalism and dispensational theology utilized a gap or day-age theory. (One in my library also approves the old Kant-Laplace nebular hypothesis!) Today, the astrophysicist Dr. Hugh Ross claims that the triumphs of the big-bang theory prove creation![2] Rather, creation *ex nihilo* does not need paradigms for its foundation.

Rationalism has the advantage of being identified with the tools of science. Defending *ex nihilo* creation subsequently looks like "special pleading." Note also that theistic evolutionists have held positions such as the "Gap Theory," the "Day-Age theory," "progressive creation," *etc*. Yet, these systematizations were needed *only after first accepting the science of measure.* The priority of astronomy comes from its "vast distances and long ages." Geology and biology must then fill in the "surplus" time with something – and for ill-advised or progressive theologians to "spiritualize" it!

When someone asks me why I will not accept data as interpreted to support evolution – or its being the agent of "creation," I respond by asking the questioner to first explain the cosmos they believe in. If we disagree at that deeper prelude, why discuss the *subsidiary* subject of evolution? Knowing their typical response, another follow-up question is whether their cosmos is objective truth, or a relative paradigm?

This fancy "religious" footwork, required in order to remain both scientific and Christian (after mythifying Genesis 1:1), has been going on for a long time. One example is as follows:

> [The poet, H]awthorne [1804-1864] and the German idealists, both being liberal Protestants, were confronted with the same problem, namely how the soul could exist in a mechanistic universe. For both, the angel [as the human soul] ... was the only solution which would allow them to accept the truths of science and belief in the existence of the soul. (B120, page 12.)

Another facet of this intellectual confusion can be seen in the writing of some respected secular folk. The late Arthur Koestler in his, *Janus, a Summing Up*, scorns Darwinian and neo-Darwinian evolution. He considers it an "open secret that it is a crumbling citadel." Likewise, the late astronomer Sir Fred Hoyle said,[3] biological evolution is as probable as expecting that a hurricane blowing through a junkyard should create a Boeing 747 jumbo jet!

In spite of criticizing evolution, both men remained atheists – definitely not expecting *ex nihilo* creation. Why? Sometimes Christians also pose this question at the seeming blindness of rationalists to Christian truth. The "why" is answered in the rationalists' prelude in the deeper sciences. *Rationalists do not consider biology and geology to be the foundational systematizations.* Neither Koestler or Hoyle rejected

---

2   Dr. Ross has great dexterity with intellectual adventure, maintaining that extrapolation to the uttermost harmonizes with Scripture. But his success is his weakness – atheorism is denied. The science of the day denies atheorism.

3   *Nature*, Volume 294, 12 November 1981, page 105.

wholesale the prevalent systematizations of astronomy with its "vast distances and long ages," which then mandates a suitable unperforated systematization in subsequent biology and geology. They quibble about the theory presented in biology, not in astronomy.

Bertrand Russell, in 1935, captured well the consensus when he described humanity as "a curious accident in a backwater."[4] The "curious accident" gave tribute to Darwin; the "backwater" gave tribute to the utterly large cosmos of astronomy. Copernicus was his hero in astronomy, but Russell ignored the subjectivity of intellectual adventure. In this he was not alone – most thinkers still do.

Little has been said herein on the origins of life as many others have addressed the subject. I offer the following few comments.

Geology and fossil studies address the specific subject, but I believe it is overshadowed by the ancient confusion regarding the power of the ahistorical mathematical line. For many centuries, the universe was held to be "actually" infinite. As previous chapters showed, direct facts cannot be found in the geologic or fossil evidence – and there are two worldviews to interpret the evidence.

Theory is not competent to choose between explanations transcending the known! Consider again flood geology:

1,000,000,000 T x V = PDGF   **(Uniformitarianism)**
or is it:
T x 1,000,000,000 V = PDGF   **(Catastrophyism)**

T = Time in years
V = Volume of water
PDGF = Present Day Geological Features

Expressed this way, the second formulation is incomplete because high water volumes and pressures "activate" additional phenomena, such as cavitation erosion! The needed large volume of water is available – activated by tectonic motions.

We then turn to the recent specialty of genetic code (DNA) analysis. If a natural process for "writing" DNAs extensive information content cannot be formulated, then the argument over geology or fossils is meaningless, and defaults to the supernatural alternative. Geology or fossils point to catastrophic sorting, but rarely to "life" relationships between the various fossils. The Intelligent Design movement also points this out.

The genetic code stores information. Extensive information cannot be chemically explained or organized. The code, in itself, is a puzzle, but it directs the assembly of amino acids into proteins, and then

4   Bertrand Russell, *Religion and Science*, page 6.

directs their subsequent assembly into living things. To us laypeople, proteins are a "food group," but within living things, proteins are building blocks of cellular machines and cell structures. Thus their specific shape is important to their function in cellular machines and structures.

Amino acids form proteins and have various resultant shapes. Associated with the atoms (in anything) are various electrical and magnetic (attractive or repulsive) forces. When amino acids are "folded" within the cell to make proteins, these electrical and magnetic (attractive or repulsive) forces have specific "contact points" with adjacent amino acids. A stable protein has the amino acids folded so that "attractive" forces bind the assembly together.

If a protein machine mistakenly folds the constituent amino acids such that "repulsive" points are adjacent, the result is the dissolution of the protein. (Not a good survival idea!) Supposedly this is why only right-handed amino acids are used in living things. Incidentally, this is also why various enzymes are so effective. They find various "binding points" on the protein surface and "unlatch" the assembly.

So stable proteins are easy to understand, yet impossible to write the assembly or information code for! Powerful computers are not capable of doing the long string of calculations required to orchestrate stable arrangements.

Further, "long agers" love to point out that only about 4 to 8 percent of most living things DNA codes for amino acids and proteins. They say that the rest is "junk" DNA. In 2012, a long series of articles were published in various journals refuting this. Now, at least 80 per cent of the code is "active." Further analysis will undoubtedly raise the figure. Unexpected features are also being uncovered in RNA and enzymes.

This analysis faces the reality that "life" needs more than just the "code" for proteins from the DNA. Life also needs instructions for such things as protein folding, protein location in the cell, quantity required, and "switches" for various things, like quantity or size changes due to the aging of a living thing.

Try to visualize the numerous steps of cellular differentiation occurring from egg fertilization to birth to adulthood. The DNA in the initial fertilized (single cell) egg contains the complete instructions for the adult. As cell division occurs, specialization begins. Continuing growth encounters numerous design decisions. Cell X is first part of an emerging leg; then it divides and becomes part of a leg bone; then it divides and part of it becomes bone marrow. (This means the unselected part of the DNA code can be "blocked off" in that cell. If a given cell of the developing fetus becomes muscle, then the information for blood vessels, or other structures, is blocked off.) This is a mind boggling unfolding of an elaborate orchestrated design.

To say, "evolution happens," indicates storytelling or science, falsely so-called! When information specialists try to deterministically make sense of this information within the time constraints that astronomers set for them, they have a real problem!

Also, investigators are beginning to measure "genetic entropy" by comparing the genetic codes of related individuals. The measured mutation rates preclude a life continuum beyond many thousands of years. See *Genetic Entropy and the Mystery of the Genome* by Dr John Sanford.

No wonder DNA and information and cellular structure and assembly present such a formidable problem. Richard Dawkins, the "outspoken" spokesman for rationalism begins by saying, "*Biology is the study of complicated things that give the appearance of having been designed for a purpose.*" (B121, page 6.)

Of course, that is also a reluctant testimony to the *ex nihilo* Creator, where "*Biology is the study of complicated things that have been designed for a purpose!*"

C. S. Lewis provides insight into the false tension between faith and reason:

It is not reason that is taking away my faith: on the contrary, my faith is based on reason. It is my imagination and emotions. The battle is between faith and reason on one side and emotion and imagination on the other. (B122, page 122.)

Rationalism is an "imagination" of the all-seeing mind's eye – and questioning it can unleash emotional outbursts. Unfortunately, too often Christians still run scared at the thought of using Genesis to address this intellectual dead end. Is this a symptom of an over-reasoned retreat into spiritual niches?

Compare two passages in the original 1611 edition of the King James Bible with the same in the New King James Bible (1982). These show how the perception of science has been deflated:

Daniel 1:4: (1611 KJV): "skilful in all wisedom, and cunning in knowledge, and vnderstanding science"

(1982 nKJV): "gifted in all wisdom, possessing knowledge and quick to understand ..."

1 Timothy 6:20: (1611 KJV): "auoyding prophane and vaine babblings, and oppositions of science, fasly so called."

(1982 nKJV): "avoiding the profane and vain babblings and contradictions of what is falsely called knowledge."

We can now revert back to the early twentieth century and resume the history of science's categorizing impasse suspended several chapters ago at the sequential demise of the science of measure and the logical adventures. Many intervening pages have dwelt on mathematical and inaccessible profundities from the "between-years" because they are now forgotten, being on the other side of the 1930s "science" watershed. Rationalists quickly hiss their disapproval of "religious myths," while Christians, on the other hand, studiously ignore science and rationalism's impact on minds as they exhort to "purer" faith or doctrine. Both act as if they have never understood the science of measure or its nemesis, complexity.

Once again, some thinkers came to the rescue of science (after the demises of arithmetic, geometry and logic)! They said the grand extrapolations were right because they were consistent and worked. These made sense of reality; predictions could be based on them and thus the edifice would remain. Scientia remains: Reason and objective truth and consistency (and a subordinated logic and mathematics) and grandiose extrapolation and monotruth and atheism remain an inseparable rationalization. This "consistent" foundation for rationalism once again renewed the zeal of the well-reasoned. They were again assured that their Universal Connected Knowledge and layered paradigms contained no systematic errors of ancient origin. Unconsciously, they were pragmatic, tacitly realizing "Consistency Exists" made no sense, beyond saving (some of) the appearances.

They pointed with pride to the idealizations and systematizations in astronomy, electrodynamics, gravity, *etc.* Much of their success was due to observation from many perspectives and creative use of mathematical freedom, but not through experimentation. Yet, because their rational accounting of facts in many domains were "summarized" as layered together, saved (some of) the appearances, exhibited patterns of regularity, made sense within the grandiose framework of the adventure, utilized exquisite mathematics and formed a basis for predictions, they drew the grand conclusion that these were Universal Connected Knowledge – even though not experimental. Surely, they thought, these consistent expressions were monotruth, not layered potpourri. (IF … IF … THEREFORE means that alternative understandings can be dismissed. Pascal was too conservative! Page 207.) This rational confidence allowed other systematizations (or syntheses) such as those in the social understandings to hold their heads high. Discrepancies were interesting trivia, not warnings of fundamental problems signaling a need to retreat. The well-reasoned thought further research would always fill in the gaps. The edifice of science, falsely so-called, like the old soap commercial, boasted of being at least 99.44 percent pure!

Again, it was not to last. These people regarded as claustrophobic the conclusion that statistical probability, mathematical complexity and observational precision were not as rigorous (or prophetic) as experimental manipulation. They had forgotten that such rigor could, at best, secure internal "edificial" consistency, but could not rule out rational alternative systematizations). *Mathematics was so fruitful it could provide consistent systematizations supporting almost any "deep" understanding,* thus betraying the lovers of monotruth! The Scottish skeptic David Hume (1711-1776) came to this conclusion earlier, and the German philosopher Immanuel Kant (1724-1804) strove mightily to avoid it.

The explosive growth of mathematics was a mixed blessing to rationalists. Mathematics was now seen as a process of invention, not discovery. As free creations of the mind, the totality of mathematics did not flow in a single stream. This, they realized, did not trouble experimenters or technologists, whose empiricism ignored the all-seeing sciences, falsely so-called.

Philosophers of science in the last century, notably Sir Karl Popper, reminded rationalists of the pluralistic "wormwood and gall"[5] that their storytelling was unsuccessfully avoiding. He used phrases like "testability," "irrefutability," and "criterion of demarcation." Others introduced phrases like "revolutions of science" and the aforementioned "paradigm." For these philosophers, predictive success and mathematical probability statements gave no assurance that thinkers had advanced beyond layered potpourri – or to have found the only rational way to corral rafts of data. Discarded adventures litter the history of science. As Popper said, just because one believes only white swans exist, that does not mean that someday, somewhere, black swans will not be encountered.[6]

This is said in full recognition of the usefulness of systematics. For example, two of the outer planets, Uranus and Neptune, were each discovered through calculations based on orbital discrepancies observed on known planets. Consistency in God's creation made them predictable, but recognizing *spreadsheet parables*, success did not validate the particular reference frame used in the methods to save the appearances.

Renewed interest in creation science alarmed rationalists! Reasoned arguments actually supported *ex nihilo* creation and subsequent history! These consistent understandings of geology and biology were dangerous, especially their criticism of the privileged status of grandiose extrapolation.

The consistency argument, and its failure to protect rationalism, had a back-

---

5   A parallel to the wormwood and gall in Lamentations 3:19.
6   The jargon of statistics would say that the sampling base is too small. For example, a weather statistician may say that "one winter in ten will be extremely cold." If this winter is extremely cold, does this mean next winter will be mild? No! If next winter is extremely cold again, does that prove the statistician was wrong? No! He will retort that the probability is that we will have mild winters for the next eighteen years; *i.e.*, the ratio of 1:10 remains unchanged. No wonder that causeless arguments based on probability are irrefutable, thus irrelevant for understanding specific actual events. *The statistician, John Doe, drowned while crossing a river having an average depth of six inches!* (I read this somewhere.)

lash. Some thinkers turned to oriental religions. While Christianity was still rejected for "other" reasons, oriental ideas – the infinite nothingness, the impersonal god, endless cycles of time, reincarnation, and a resignation to fate – were seen as consistent and dimly similar to the infinity of mathematical determinism. A trek to oriental ideas began to grow. Some, preferring "pure" Pythagorean or Platonic ideas, achieved much the same result by returning to that realm. Why had rationalists been blind to the fact that their grandiosity never escaped choices?[7]

Philosophers of science (and pragmatists of the Dr Ad Hoc sort) could see that the dazzling progress of science and technology is not wedded to rationalism. Western philosophical thought now resorts to a web of useful equations for interpreting (and transcending) experiments, well beyond the simplistic concepts of 1 + 1 = 2 and associates. This newer mathematics can be *ad hoc* fine tuned or unwisely extrapolated – and is vulnerable to past oversights or manipulation by dominant personalities. Duhem, for one, both praised and critiqued them. Orientally minded thinkers seek to "reconnect" this web to their own ideas. Christians are in a position to prune and cultivate the shorn residue.

Nonetheless, the consistent knowledge of the well-reasoned was again reduced to an understanding. Words – or equations – did not say it just right. *Free and autonomous reason had failed – again!*

Yet again, some thinkers came to the rescue of science. They said that all "scientific" models and extrapolations must be accepted because all is relative! *Scientia* remains, reason and objective truth and relativity (and a subordinate consistency and logic and mathematics) and grandiose extrapolation (and mono-truth???) and atheism remained inseparable. So-called breakthroughs in astronomy rescued all "scientific" disciplines from disaster. Riding on the coattails of Einstein's intellectual adventure of relativity[8] ("precisely" confirmed in that eclipse observation of twenty percent accuracy), allowed other adventurers to proclaim that we now live in a relativistic, unbounded universe (with indeterminate quantum underpinnings

---

7   Researching this book required the ordering of many books. This put me on mail lists and then unsolicited catalogs arrived. Some of these are esoteric and mystical material! I don't know how large a community they appeal to, but it can't be tiny. After reading some of these books, I can't help but look up and comprehend the rational big picture. All I see is the big bang! Within this prominent intellectual adventure, these mystical and esoteric writings address no reality possible. Christianity and its little short story criticize intellectual adventures and also this recurring esoteric and mystical outpouring.

8   Somewhere in my reading, I remember someone expressing great relief over the advent of Einstein's relativity, because, after many centuries, a bold adventure finally came safely ashore.

also). The edifice essentially remains.

This appeal to astronomy again renewed the zeal of the well-reasoned, or did it? Anyhow, rationalists thought simple folk

should continue to trust the kindly, objective nature of "scientific" folk to exercise self-discipline. Gravity and electro-dynamics, the titans of intellectual adventure, had clashed in the late 1800s. Maxwell's electrodynamic field equations overthrew Newtonian "mechanical" light. An "exacting" test was devised to measure the earth's motion through the surrounding aether. The test failed to detect the aether or the motion of the earth.

The subsequent "astronomical" relativity sanctioned relativized "truth" in general and justified several centuries' accumulation of trophies to new philosophies gained through word wars. These trophies became "proofs" and were of comfort, sweet to the taste and promoted intellectual disarmament. Where, however, has reason gone? This "new" objective truth accepts inconsistency. Knowledge is now judged solely by its internal consistency with its guiding paradigms. External clashes with data or other well-reasoned paradigms became extraneous. "Colonies of thinkers" discovered that reductionism protected idea towers.

Philosophers of science were aghast at this stark confession! Yet, considering the centuries of investment made in rationalism and new philosophy, there was little alternative. Reason could not harmonize the growing multitude of "sciences," but had to accept these claimants to the name of science. This does not fulfill the lure of objective truth – or the textbook definition of science.

Nonetheless, supporters passionately deny that reason has gone. They insist that they apply modern "science," not science, falsely so-called. They may chant:

It does not matter how we learned the truths about matter,
For, you see, we now know that matter is all that matters.

Obviously, if history is bunk, such folk are undisturbed that modern "sciences," such as astronomy, interpret matter in light of the ancient Greek ahistorical mathe-matical line, which does not allow complexity to attenuate extension. Nor can they fathom qualities or modern sophistry – *how can science education lead to doubt!*

Sadly, their enthusiasm for relativized understandings outruns their knowledge! Words – or equations – did not say it just right. *Free and autonomous reason had failed – again. It cannot prove atheism nor disprove atheorism!*

The great quest for knowledge has come full circle. It started as "manna from heaven," yet ends in the wilderness of words wherein sits the Parthenon of science, falsely so-called. Mankind therein rationally feasts on reasonable relative thoughts and consistency and logic and mathematics and the resulting unperforated cosmic models, but starves for lack of truth. Dedicated to, and loving, "all-seeing" truth, these rationalists knew no limits, extrapolated to the uttermost, dispensed with God and His little short story – yet were unmasked as subjective. They re-decorated the structure many times, telling them-selves that their very tech-nical language excluded well-crafted words, that their theories were not storytelling or adventure; but to no avail. They no longer convinced even themselves that their all-enveloping "science" was synonymous with objective truth. They are trapped by the unfailing ability of systematic words to sound like rational thought.

> Before thought advances to a change of one of its "simple" geometrical laws it will first make the complex physical conditions that enter into the measurement responsible for the lack of agreement; it will change the "physical" factors before the "geometrical" .... Platonically speaking, phenomena are measured by Ideas, by the foundations of geometry, and these latter are not directly read out of the sensu-ous phenomena. (B16, pages 434-435.)

The defeat of cosmic reason (theory trumping local facts) must be faced. Ideas create polytruth – colonies of thinkers lost in a wilderness! Indeed, of all the forces known to man, none is stronger than a paradigm. (Stirniman) This recalls the con-fusing and "all-seeing" milieu encountered by the early church Fathers.

Such statements are too revealing for today's rationalists to accept. *Cynical amnesia becomes the final adventure!* Their deep distrust of history has grown to envelop their own history; it also shows capriciousness and irrationalism. Yet, even in their rejection of "Western Ideas", they never start over at ground zero. They hopefully assume that men of goodwill "know" that science, reason, and mathe-matics sanction grandiose extrapolation. Some even convert to modern sophistry.

The desire for truth and, through truth, the good and beautiful also died in their sterilized brains (and atrophied minds). They lacked nourishment; they never reach-ed fulfillment. Life became unlovely and jaded. "Stabbing your nerves to life" almost becomes a medical requirement for the well-reasoned!

Many rationalists find history and nature unimportant, compared to the "all-seeing" sciences. Books explaining creation for such folk would communicate better by including a prelude on the science of measure.

A portent of this breakthrough in awareness of the subjective nature of cosmic thoughts is the increasing Christian interest in the

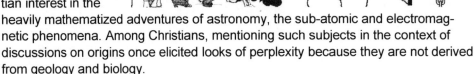

heavily mathematized adventures of astronomy, the sub-atomic and electromagnetic phenomena. Among Christians, mentioning such subjects in the context of discussions on origins once elicited looks of perplexity because they are not derived from geology and biology.

We must not forget that Genesis 1:1 says: "*God created the **heaven** and the earth.*" Therefore, a prelude to rational thought must address the heavens (astronomy) as well as the earth (geology and biology).

Romans 1:18-32 becomes a sobering commentary[9] on "free" spirits regarding the knowledge they give up and what they turn to for comfort. Loosening of the bonds knitting the body, soul, and spirit together is a perilous adventure.

---

9   Romans 1:18-32: *For the wrath of God is revealed from heaven, against all ungodliness and unrighteousness of men, who hold the truth in unrighteousness: Because that which may be known of God, is manifest in them; for God hath shewed it unto them. For the invisible things of him from the creation of the world are clearly seen, being understood by the things that are made, even his eternal power and Godhead; so that they are without excuse: Because that, when they knew God, they glorified him not as God, neither were thankful; but became vain in their imaginations, and their foolish heart was darkened. Professing themselves to be wise, they became fools; And changed the glory of the uncorruptible God, into an image made like to corruptible man, and to birds, and four-footed beasts, and creeping things.*

Wherefore God also gave them up to uncleanness through the lusts of their own hearts, to dishonor their own bodies between themselves: Who changed the truth of God into a lie, and worshipped and served the creature more than the Creator, who is blessed forever. Amen.

For this cause God gave them up unto vile affections: for even their women did change the natural use into that which is against nature: And likewise also the men, leaving the natural use of the women, burned in their lust one toward another; men with men, working that which is unseemly, and receiving in themselves that recompense of their error, which was meet.

And even as they did not like to retain God in their knowledge, God gave them over to a reprobate mind, to do those things which are not convenient: Being filled with all unrighteousness, fornication, wickedness, covetousness, maliciousness, full of envy, murder, debate, deceit, malignity; whisperers, Backbiters, haters of God, despiteful, proud, boasters, inventors of evil things, disobedient to parents, Without understanding, covenant-breakers, without natural affection, implacable, unmerciful: Who knowing the judgment of God, that they which commit such things are worthy of death, not only do the same, but have pleasure in them that do them.

Many people realize enlightenment rationalism has collapsed. Polylogic, poly-math and polytruth give witness to this collapse. Universal Natural Law, 1 + 1 = 2 and associates, and grandiose extrapolation flow from the great original Promissory IF: "We accept only reason and rational cause and effect explanations. THERE-FORE, we exclude qualities and supernatural revealed truth ("aided" reason). Yet, 'unaided' reason is 'aided' by mathematics and its reputed ability to dissect the 'inaccessible'." This "all-seeing" belief always trips over present complexity. For the rational mind, enlightenment rationalism encapsulates the sundering of faith and reason. Rationalism willingly took upon itself the task of objectively explaining every-thing – but could not find only one repeatable monotruth.

Over the centuries, not everyone rejoiced in the "passionate search for truth and beauty" that Euclid's *Elements* had inspired – or at least they did not like where it was going. These disillusioned ones did not like what an "un-event-filled" mathe-matical line said about themselves. *It consigned all mankind to meaninglessness and uncreativeness,* so it became a virtue to be alienated from science! (The various positions resulting from this are reviewed on page 16.)

Immanuel Kant, and many others such as Hegel, struggled to "objectify" the "inaccessible" truths that all moderns knew to be true. Indeed, "The technical jargon of one school shortly becomes the gibberish of the next." (B123, page vii.)

For those who considered themselves "scientific," these positions were ununderstandable, irrational and embarrassing! Yet none knew how to rationally modify the inhuman principles of paradigm science or its "proven" accomplishments in the previously inaccessible.

All of these movements waxed and waned through recent centuries as they tried to make absolute, universal, objective sense of "unaided" rational thought. Their obvious corollary is that faith is not necessary. Faith's exile is attached to the core of the modern dilemma.

Lifting the ban on the exiled faith and its event-filled history seems unwarranted to many. Why? Some have deep attachment to the un-event-filled ahistorical mathe-matical line, but most do not comprehend the debacle of the history of mathematics; and of the queen of the sciences, astronomy, and that rising living standards did not need extrapolative infatuation.

Something remains hidden in plain view. Rationalists of those days spoke much about the science of measure and Copernican astronomy. Can atheorism criticize the figurehead status of 1 + 1 = 2 and associates without also criticizing the science of measure's two crown jewels?

The step must be taken. Atheorism sees these as popular systematizations. With the prelude we have reviewed, who wants to be so naive as to call them scien-tific? Atheoristic reason can rationally ponder a perforating revelation! Many famous thinkers have long wondered what truth was conveyed by the collapsed enlighten-ment. Our interest is heightened because atheorism shows that a retreat from grandiose mathematics invalidates most of the "hype" surrounding this drama.

To further chasten our minds, ponder the words Cardinal Robert Bellarmine addressed to Galileo, words many would like to dismiss:

> It is one thing to prove that by assuming the sun at the center of the world and the earth in the heavens one saves all the appearances and quite another thing to demonstrate that the sun really is at the center, the earth really in the heavens. As to the first, I believe that demonstration can be given; but I have strong doubts as to the second; and in the case of mere doubt you should not diverge from Holy Scripture as the holy fathers have expounded it. (B42, page 107.)

Duhem, and Arthur Koestler in *The Sleepwalkers,* so quote this atheoristic admonition of the learned Cardinal. His statement, highlighting the distinction between understanding and knowledge, should be acceptable, but it is not. The well-reasoned are tied to a long history of systematic errors, which history shows few thinkers considering themselves to be "that" relativistic.

Duhem stated that Galileo's logical problem seemed to be that, "Experience, by convicting one system of error, *confers certainty on its opposite.*" Duhem also referred to Copernicus as a "mathematical realist," meaning that he followed the science of measure. The chastened mind is cautious when facing so many assumptions and so many esoteric mathematical choices. Atheorism should be faced!

An interesting affirmation of atheorism comes from the writings of the Dutch historian Dijksterhuis, referring to Pascal's reserved attitude towards Copernicanism, which was quoted in an earlier chapter. (Page 207.) Pascal held out for a rigorous proof; saving the appearances was not enough. Nonetheless, my surmise is that vociferous anti-Christians of that day made this Copernican "victory for 'rational thought'" a central thesis – or quiet assumption – in their attacks on Christianity. Consider that modern books on the Galileo affair cannot agree as to what in his "scientific" explanation for heavenly motion survives. I suspect these vociferous writers evidenced (or assimilated) Pythagorean number mysticism, Platonic geometry, or hermetic enthusiasm. If Christians and rationalists will not examine this history, perhaps modern sophists – with their linguistic analysis and grammatical criticism – will someday wax eloquent on the subject. That is – unless they are also squeamish, preferring to "de-sediment" only those aspects of science, falsely so-called, occur-ring well after such "science" put Christianity "in its place."

Am I saying that I disbelieve Copernican astronomy? With astronomy not being science, the question loses its sharp edge! Yet we have to walk carefully here and honor Duhem's concern that we inappropriately believe that "experience, by convicting one system of error, confers certainty on its opposite."[10] If asked what we believe about this aspect of astronomy, remind the questioner that they must first decide if they want a relative or an absolute answer. (Remember Sir Fred Hoyle's astronomy textbook mentioned in a footnote on page 145.) Also, we must readily admit that we today little appreciate the objective certainty with which the science of measure was held. We today also endow regrettable certainty too freely.[11] We

---

10   And how did anyone determine that there were only two possible answers? The question remains beyond science. I see at least seven positions expressed throughout history: Philolaus' fire-centric, Plato and Aristotle's geocentric, Ptolemy's geocentric, Copernicus' heliocentric, Brahe's geocentric, Kepler and Newton's heliocentric and today's relativistic acentric!

11   I once read an article on gravity in an 1890-ish Encyclopaedia Britannica. It discussed attempts to find a "physical" gravity. A LaSage and his ultramundane corpuscles were discussed, among others. All had the fatal defect of a heat loss that limited the age of the cosmos to embar-

should learn from history, accept atheorism, and respect the frailty of reason.

I wonder what the astronomical debate in the 1500s and 1600s would have been like if, *in addition to* stellar parallax, aberration, epicycles and equants they had to *also consider* such things as non-euclidean geometry, trans-finite numbers, adjust-able constants, mathematical debris, quantized red-shift data, the WMAP "axis of evil," Arp's unusual galaxies, plasma action in the sky, *etc.* It is agreed that consensus paradigm science is provisional, so revolutions in science may still occur. No wonder saving (some of) the appearances is not as good as empirical science.

Many people do not like to pay tribute to intellectual adventure at crucial historical junctures; this being one of them. It is dangerous to analyze the science of the day. It can also be hazardous to go behind the transition to "modern" science and analyze the science of yesterday. Many folk cling to a bad theory rather than back away from the grandiose. Pondering the common thread of unwarranted extrapolations in such systematizations as astronomy is unpleasant to many free and autonomous spirits. They use the mantle of science to cloak their subjectivity and bolster their enthusiasm.

Looking back over history, Greek thinkers postulated an eternal quiescent universe – in spite of contrary evidence of discontinuities. They "soared" to escape these reports. How much better would it be to study the present quiescence *and* ponder any preceding "irregularity?" Perhaps we ask too much of weak gravity.

As St. Paul says in Romans 1:20, His handiwork can be seen. Creation is God's *poema*.

Our shorn reason acknowledges learned ignorance. What if a long time ago wise folk said, God is a rational "being." He designed a lawful, well-crafted cosmos that mankind lives in and can study. God created this cosmos *ex nihilo.* This created fact is His *poema*, but it is not simple, such as our uncalibrated (or unicalibrated) minds can visualize in terms of number, line or syllogism. We have not been God's counselors, only His gift-laden servants. This finite material cosmos is stable and orderly, but the fall of man into sin in the Garden of Eden introduced subtle forms of attenuation. Mathematics can mislead as we imaginatively venture to inaccessible (or imagined) portions of the cosmos. Instead, we have more productive work to do in the playing field. We assume mathematics was one of the design tools the Lord utilized. Our mandate to "subdue the earth" (Genesis 1:26) is accepted with learned ignorance, for no manmade calibration is objective. But one calibration, "aided" truth, however, is transcendentally grounded back into reality.

Disbelief in modern systematizations (unwisely called science) outside the bounds of empirical science may still seem hard to believe. Nonetheless, history, philosophy, and exposed subjectivity inherent in top-down mathematics reinforce atheorism. Thinkers continue to be puzzled by many fundamental things, including wondering if people have lost concern that many "sciences" only save (some of) the

---

rassingly short years. I suspect many thinkers are anxious for a change in astronomical perspective. One of these is the out-of-favor and exiled astronomer, the late Halton C. Arp, who chronicled his concerns in *Seeing Red: Redshifts, Cosmology, and Academic Science.* Others group under the "electric universe" umbrella.

appearances. Is it a real surprise that men of goodwill are uneasy around grandiose extrapolation? Platonic mathematical scholasticism is a "strong force!"

Feyerabend comments about the mathematical underpinning:

> The case of *mathematics* is especially interesting. It was here that abstract thought first produced results and it was from here that the paradigm of true, pure and objective knowledge spread to other areas. But *the many approaches mathematics now contains shows no tendency to coalesce into a single theory* .... We have non-Euclidean geometries and various versions of arithmetic... [F]initists regard mathematics as .... "Cantorians" interpret it as .... New mathematical disciplines arise all over the place .... *Today mathematics is less restrained and more pluralistic than any other intellectual discipline.* (B27, page 72. Emphasis added.)

As Pontius Pilate asked, "What is truth?," so serious thinkers can ask, "What is mathematical truth?" Penrose even commented upon non-computable mathematical truths. Kline has a final consideration also:

> The efforts to eliminate possible contradictions and establish the consistency of mathematical structures have thus far failed .... Disagreement now extends even to the methods of reasoning .... The claim therefore to impeccable reasoning must be abandoned .... *The recent research on foundations has broken through frontiers only to encounter a wilderness.* (B11, page 276. Emphasis added.)

The Bible warns us not to be tossed too and fro by the winds of human wisdom. Listen again to the insight of Irenaeus:

> [W]ith great wisdom and diligence, all things have clearly been made by God, fitted and prepared [for their special purposes] .... [Mankind's attempts at explanation present] an *uncertain* mode of proceeding, on account of their *varied and diverse* systems, and because every sort of hypothesis may at the present day be, in like manner, devised by any one; so that they can derive arguments against the truth from these very theories, inasmuch as they may be *turned in many different directions* .... For system does not spring out of numbers, but *numbers from a system*; nor does God derive His being from things made, but things made from God. (B49, Volume 1, page 396. Emphasis added.)

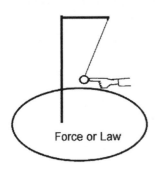

Force or Law

Such old advice is relevant and up-to-date. Cosmic thoughts, built with top-down mathematics, do not stand on a firm foundation. Playing with marbles or drawing in the sand is the better starting point – followed up centuries later by a science of forces, matter and experimentation. Bottom-up useful formulas are great for curve-fitting, but mathematics and equations cause nothing; they "shadow" reality.

Pythagoras and Plato said mathematics precedes matter while Aristotle implied that matter precedes mathematics. Should we not consider that the Lord created units of charge, forged them into subatomic components, and from these made the elements and the rest of creation. And mathematics models and shadows the resulting quiescent reality.

The cosmos is complex, so experts may disagree! Many things puzzle them, and some let the wish father the fact. Defensiveness or emptiness appears through certain answers they may give. If you ask, "What is gravity?" you may be told; "Well, the equations say..." Or you may ask, "What is a photon?" Again, you may be told, "Well, the equations say ..."

If you then ask, "And are the equations talking about equations or about reality?" *Silence.* This was Newton's concern and Russell's despair. The top-down mathematical world is an abstract world, not the real cosmos. This is the false comfort inherited from Platonic mathematical scholasticism. Man's reason cannot rationally grasp nature. (Bless our unfulfilled Promissory IFs!)

Symptoms of this limitation began in mathematics and spread into astronomy. Enlightenment thought had promoted their storytelling as puzzle solving. Even today, gravity, atomic structure – and cosmic frameworks – err regarding the grandiose extrapolations made with *or* without laboratory data. This prison of thought is presently guarded by big-bang astronomy.

Back in the chapter on *Old Mathematics*, page 105, the conversation was quoted that C. S. Lewis had with a fellow professor, who was quick to state that anything smacking of "religion" was like advocating a flat earth, with the stars only a few miles away. Let us now listen to C. S. Lewis' response:

I reached out my hand to a bookshelf. 'You see this book,' I said, 'Ptolemy's *Almagest.* You know what it is?'

'Yes,' said he. 'It's the standard astronomical handbook used all through the Middle Ages.' [and written about 200 AD.]

'Well, just read that,' I said, pointing to Book I, chapter 5.

'The earth,' read out my friend, hesitating a bit as he translated the Latin, 'the earth, in relation to the distance to the fixed stars, has no appreciable size and must be treated as a mathematical point!'

There was a moment's silence.

'Did they really know that *then*?' said my friend. 'But – but none of the histories of science – none of the modern encyclopedias – ever mention the fact.'

[Lewis continued] .... 'The enormous size of the universe and the insignificance of the earth were known for centuries, and no one ever dreamed that they had any bearing on the religious question.[12] Then, less than a hundred years ago, they are suddenly trotted out as an argument against Christianity. And the people who trot them out carefully hush up the fact that they were known long ago. Don't you think that all you *atheists are strangely unsuspicious people*?' (B48, page 74-75. Emphasis added.)

Yes, the cosmos is big, but "enormous size" may only mean "enormous size," not infinite or unbounded.

Scientific American is a good magazine. Superficial reading indicates an unreserved acceptance of science, falsely so-called, but close reading shows a hesitancy. The thought process of even supposedly dogmatic articles are sprinkled at critical junctures with phrases like, "if," "it is commonly accepted," "the current

---

12   An example is *The Consolation of Philosophy* by Boethuis (A.D. 524). It was a popular book up through the Renaissance. In it, Boethuis covers the same Ptolemaic information. (He wrote this while waiting execution by the Roman Emperor, by then a Visigoth!)

scholarly consensus," *etc.* The middle ground of conjecture remains.[13]

Our confused world remains entranced by a clear intuition – a clear and sharp chasm between religion and science, between subjective and objective. This Greek ideal of a chasm cannot be found, at least not outside of the vast expanse called "science." Such grandiose and mathematized reasoners could not accept – and their modern adherents also cannot accept – that science, itself, is a finite enterprise surrounded by the vague science of paradigmatic extrapolative infatuation.[14]

At a very basic level, well-reasoned folk know that the cliché regarding the simple opposition between faith and reason clothes their rational thought with objectivity. They prefer to wear the mantle of a vague science rather than acknowledge that they wear the vestments of philosophers and mystics and theologians. As stated in chapter three: questioning grandiose extrapolation sets in motion a chain of reasoning that ultimately affirms God's little short story.

The well-reasoned remain rational, defining their premises "objectively" and exploring the consequences (somewhat) faithfully. But they will not critique their history. Their ancient flight from polytheism blinds them to mathematical subjectivity, the created fact and monotheism. Nor, due to their loyalty to ancient errors, can they comprehend atheorism. They may still repeat the saying of the ancient Greek philosopher, Protagoras, that "man is the measure of all things." But really, *thinking man is a unicalibrated, unidirectional extrapolating "soaring" agent.*

I think, therefore I am ... unicalibrated! The "all-seeing" mind's eye does not fulfill the lure of objective truth.

How should this story end? Consider the *Riddle of The Titan's Meditation*:

The titans of extrapolative thought no longer clashed.
The dominant titan grew weary of words.
Paradigming yearned for science, for truth.
But policy requires vigilance against myth and upstart storytellers.

Primary qualities are mathematical, like 1 + 1 = 2, so we win.
But mathematics – our sacred oracle – is tarnished.
Pale invisible equations or what have we missed?
Science without grandiose extrapolation – let's atheorize:

Wait ... but ... but what about OUR truth!
Ah! ... the deeper truth I almost forgot.
Scientific truth didn't start in the lab!
The Science of Measure is our *a priori* home-base.

---

13   This was brought home to me on a business trip with a friend. We had both read an article in *Scientific American.* He said that the article had proved a certain point. Being my atheoristic self, I denied it. His frustration with me increased until I pointed out that every "proof" that he cited had been preceded by a qualifier such as: "if," "the current scholarly consensus," *etc.*

14   Their certainty that they were fulfilling the lure of objective truth had been a driving force in attempts to assure the separation of church and state was interpreted to their liking. Now their intellectual descendants must face the broad spectrum stretching from revelation to understanding to knowledge, but will they, and advocate the separation of science, falsely so-called, and the state? (Probably only men of goodwill, will.) Feyerabend, for one, recognized this need, due to the subjectivity and freedom inherent in "science" (falsely so-called).

We rationally OWN the cosmic picture!
Universal Natural Law and Grandiose Extrapolation.
Ahistorical – no exceptions for "close-up" details.
Anamnesis – clear intuition – it is puzzle solving!

Aimless, infinite, meaningless universe
But whence comes our sense of freedom!
Reality without creation – freedom's source.
Not being responsible to Him, you know Who I mean!

Yet ... the unperforated cosmos always needs "further research."
Atheorism and sophistry! Why are you hanging around?
Just thinking – does God actually exist?
In the beginning(????), God created the heaven and the earth?

Computers, labs and math still hum.
But inspired Scripture still perforates and calibrates.
Plato's cave should not be our home.
We know so little, Universal Connected Knowledge is not our possession.

Forgive us, Lord.
We are not what You created us to be.
We need to meet ourselves once again.
We need You to meet us, once again.

Will it end this way? I don't know. Much prayer is needed, but realize that we have not been God's counselors, only his gift laden servants. Usually, his unprofitable servants. C. S. Lewis seemingly pondered the outcome also. His "children's" tale, *The Final Conflict*, in his, *The Chronicles of Narnia*, may be applicable here.

In an early chapter, we mentioned that rationalists remained smug; *they retained a secret weapon!* They long insisted that reason is free, unbiased, and autonomous – only if it is atheistic. But we pointed out that, in reality, *free and autonomous reason is uncommitted; it is agnostic and atheoristic – not atheistic!*

Two concerns intermix at this juncture. *One*; is there God or is it to be atheism? *Two*; can our reason, resident here on earth, objectively reach all of history and distances and thereby explain reality?

Rationalists assume concern *One* affirms atheism. They further assume (or hope) concern *Two* need not be brought up! But atheorism requires serious discussion of both concerns.

Rationalists are frightened if both atheism and atheorism are addressed. A negative answer to concern *Two* nullifies their answer to concern *One*. The rationalist – that extrapolative artist – cannot be an atheorist. His assent to, and faith in, theories exists alongside the manifold failures of their "unaided" reason.

Also, they may fear that an agnostic who thinks about atheorism is in danger of lapsing into Christianity.

Thoughtful followers of the adventure can no longer say, "Yes, *then* we were subjective, but not now! Later events *absolutely* prove the correctness of rationalism's assumptions as elaborated and refined by modern science." Before an atheoristic audience, if they deny their heritage, their defense for present-day atheism, materialism, and meaninglessness depends upon the truth of (contending) systematizations. As modern sophists point out, these are a contentious lot, so their appeals to reason do not convince.

Rational thought no longer accesses foundational monotruth. If the well-reasoned say their layered systemizations *must be accepted* because all is relative, why are they not open and accepting of the alternate systematic understanding of Creation *ex nihilo*? They may try to defend their position by *retreating* to the argument that their position is systematic. What then, we ask, is wrong with the systematic explanation in the little short story? But they hastily counter, as they *retreat* to logic, that their position is logical. What, we ask, is illogical about the little short story? Again, they counter, as they *retreat* to the science of measure: "Cosmic thinking is science; what more can you expect from us? Why are you trying to drag discontinuous ideas into 'science'?" (And, under their breath, some of them add, "If you bother us any more, we will go to the Orient – or to Velikovsky – or to perturbations thereof.")

Such is the fruit of mistakenly thinking extrapolative infatuation is objective. In contrast, atheorism shows that early adventurers could be mathematically and physically confident, thanks to the science of measure. Later rationalists could be mathematically confident, but not physically confident. Reducing matter to point particles seemed to restore their confidence, because such were mathematical constructs. Few recognized the ease with which the wish (clear intuition) fathered the facts.

Unhinged rationalists may challenge their critics: But now, they say, the problem is that we, like Newton, are looking for physical objects. Rather, they advise that we be not deceived by the senses, but instead look for invisible points, quantum packets of energy and related phenomenon. These mathematical objects are the really real!

If one asks: "And how do you know you are giving the correct interpretation of the instruments used to measure them?" They respond that the validity of the equations guarantees it. And if thinkers with the same PhD degrees disagree? ...

Hmm, we further ask if these equations contain multiple solutions, bizarre functions, *ad hoc* constants, temporary scaffolding, deny ahistorical evidence, work with idealizations such as mathematical points or generate mathematical debris? "Why, yes," they reply, "but what difference does that make? The seamless fabric of explanations we derive with them fulfills the demands of scientific objectivity and are acclaimed by all leading authorities."

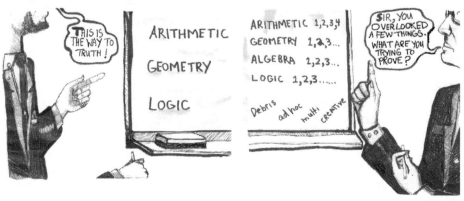

But we ask them to compare themselves to Laplace and his confidence in a master equation explaining all of reality. His equations pale in comparison to the complexity and choices now utilized. So how are alternative systematizations ruled out? Their response is quick; these obey the general rules; they work, so there is no need to look elsewhere. Besides, we need a deterministic cosmic explanation in order to be "all-seeing" scientists.

Yet, we persist by asking, "Who said you interpret the rules correctly? Are you unaware of spreadsheet parables?"

"Well," they reply, "that is outside of my specialty!"

"But surely," we ask, "are you puzzled by the fact that the history of science is littered with so many fallen cosmic theories and paradigmatic structures, and that present times show behind-the-scenes quarrels about cosmic systematizations?"

"Well, sorry again," they reply, "but history is boring. We cannot be of much help with such arcane and peripheral subjects! After all – everyone knows the objective nature of the tools of science: *Arithmetic*: 1 + 1 = 2; *Geometry*: line, triangle, cube, and conic section; and *logic*! These we cling to!"

In summary, misunderstanding science is their present source of confidence.

The well-reasoned show their unfamiliarity with the history of science when they complain that it is "unfair to invoke God and the supernatural and bring them into experiments." But they misinterpret; God is not brought into the experiments[15] of empirical science; rather, the well-reasoned go beyond experiments into the inaccessible and seek to justify their cosmic storytelling – which requires a believable basis for grandiose extrapolation. Such extrapolation is not public knowledge; some "disciplines" are in the fact-free domain.

On other occasions, some may appear pragmatic as they state that God and an event-less nature are a "draw" as far as provability is concerned. In either case, it is a matter of faith. But they do not realize an infinite or unbounded cosmos is already well into the subjective realm. They should base their defense upon the objective aspects of the playing field. (But instinctively they realize the playing field does not allow enough time, distance or material to accomplish what their mind's

In spite of our disagreements, at least we unreservedly pursue objective truth.

Yes! And thankfully we are not wearing blinders as other folk do. The principles of intellectual adventure have been long-tested!

15   As said in the opening chapter, Christianity believes in a finite, material cosmos as the stage upon which life exists. This "stage" can be subject to rigorous experiments.

eyes desire to imagine.)

They may retort that it is not possible to separate fact from theory, saying that such as "the big bang" or "photons" cannot be understood without theory. Thus, "theory-free" knowledge is not possible. Learned ignorance is the better choice – and atheorism can again open their eyes to the little world of empirical science.

It was mentioned earlier that the Newtonian cosmos could not be finite because, in the mind's eye, standing on the edge of such a cosmos would reveal a gravitational imbalance. What would happen if one stood on the edge of the science of our day's cosmos?

We would see rafts of data adrift on oceans of top-down mathematics! What fearsome mental constructs we have derived with our layered potpourri, a playing with a virtual reality, a sad alternative to working with the little playing field data we actually possess. It must give some a feeling of omnipotence – others a sense of slavery. Searchers may be like a group of blind men examining an elephant!

So today, chastened by atheorism, our minds permit our eyes to see that crisis engulfs many consensus paradigms. In the pursuit of extrapolation using mathematical points, geometric lines or superstrings, the rationalistic heritage burdens astronomy, electromagnetic and subatomic investigations, geology, biology, and social understandings. Freewill, mathematical debris, *ad hoc* clutter and Promissory IFs are everywhere. Thus, disillusioned thinkers return to empirical science, which encompasses experimentation, engineering, technology, and even welcomes craftsmen and tinkerers!

Basic building blocks of "paradigm" knowledge such as gravity and electrodynamics have foundational deficiencies. Recognizing spreadsheet parables and subjectivity does not undermine the core of experimental science nor reject years of scholarly research. However, thoughtful people need to distinguish between accumulated data and adventures.[16] The atheoristic mind, coupled with historical curiosity, winnows the wheat from the chaff, looking for treasures and keys previously overlooked or discarded. Actual discoveries within this thin slice of reality (empirical science) make sense as explorations of the playing field that God designed and created. Rafts of data need to be guarded from the swamping effects of bad philosophy and its oceans of mathematical choices. Analyzing data without fear of the guardians of rationalism would be a revolution among thinkers.

The atheoristic attitude allows one to see that our high-tech world continues without skipping a beat. As the allusion to spreadsheet parables hints at, alternative mathematical ways to correlate data exist. In the playing field, differences may be slight. In the realm of intellectual adventures, many surprises occur. Some changes in terminology also occur. For example, "design" and "teleology" replace "chance" and the "beneficent action of Mother Nature." Likewise, per G. K. Chesterton, "de-civilized" man is more appropriate than "savage" or "primitive." These are not semantic changes, but conceptual changes – changes without the baggage of rationalism.

The science of measure, the "all-seeing" mind's eye, and philosophical puzzlement over fundamental concepts stand as monuments to the uncertainty inherent in extrapolative infatuation. What else remains swept under the proverbial carpet – or even hidden in plain view?
Accordingly, spacecraft will fly, atom-smashers smash, computers compute, and superconductors conduct in a finite cosmos. However, atheorism, complexity and attenuation leave such trans-accessible concepts as evolution or redshift in the lurch. It is better to have learned ignorance and short extensions than the hasty habit of giving "assent" to the mercurial science of the day.
To repeat Feyerabend:

> *Ad hoc* approximations abound in modern mathematical physics .... *Ad hoc* approximations conceal, and even entirely eliminate, qualitative difficulties. They create a false impression of the excellence of our science .... In most cases modern science is more opaque, and much more deceptive, than its 16th- and 17th-century ancestors have ever been. (B4, pages 63-64.)

Yes, we citizens of the twenty-first century are proud of our consensus grandiose paradigms, in spite of their inadequate basis in public knowledge. Inaccessible science paradigms are systematic but not truthful. Useful formulas – attended with *ad hoc* modifications – do not confirm Universal Connected Knowledge!
At times, rationalists seem to say: "Why are you against us? We are the men in the white laboratory coats!" *And then all they can talk about is inaccessible paradigms.* I am a scientist, "IF ... IF ... IF ... IF ... IF ... I ... THEREFORE ...! They do not see the ancient irrational semantic leap they make.
But such people are subject to various pressures: tenure tension, the struggle to receive research grants, to produce "ground-breaking" research results, to maneuver through the peer-review process to be printed in consensus journals, and

---

16   With the increasing power and proliferation of personal computers, I expect that conceptual breakthroughs, *or conceptual returns,* may soon occur amongst even the "unprofessional."

to avoid the displeasure of dominant personalities. Do not underestimate the pressures they face.

My impression is that folk in learned occupations spend their spare time trying to stay abreast of developments in their own discipline. They have confidence in their discipline's "cutting-edge" happenings but may not have examined their disciplines knowledge base. Further, they have no time – and perhaps no inclination – to study the broader history of mathematics and science.

Empirical science – and its clutter – and friendliness with craftsmen and tinkerers is much closer to truth. It is okay to be empirical scientists and utilize *ad hoc* adjustments. It is not okay to be a paradigm "scientist" and accumulate *ad hoc* modifiers; such a string of beads is not causal. Why, perhaps such as spaceships, computers, CAT scan machines, composite graphite structures, iPads, *etc.*, require little of paradigm "science," but are tributes to empirical science, craftsmen and tinkerers. This would be in-line with the long history of past advances in living conditions.

Paradigmers warn that empirical science has to over-rely on data; they can not see the "big picture." That is technically correct, but paradigmers thrive on extrapolative infatuation – and the ancient ahistorical mathematical line motivating it. So paradigmers never "know" the "big picture" either. Extrapolative infatuation leads to more disastrous results than sticking with the data, and it never contributed to the worldwide improvement in living standards anyway.

Improvement came (and still comes) thanks to alert senses and keen intellects in tinkerers and on up to empirical scientists. Knowledge comes from understanding our accessible world – and not being spooked at the possibility that it may be a small world. Reality is wonderfully complex, yet orderly! The Book of Nature hints at the *ex nihilo* Creator! Curiosity is a productive quality!

Usually, complexity means that knowledge comes first; theories come later. Empirical science uses controlled experiments to interrogate accessible reality and uncover causal relations. In this they are not thoroughly successful, they advance through partial ignorance, corrected by events or tinkerers.

On our own we are susceptible to extrapolative infatuation, wrong "clear intuitions," the wish fathering the fact, being content with saving the appearances and common wisdom. Useful formulas, not Universal Natural Laws, undergirds public knowledge and rising standards of living.

These concerns are all necessary beginnings. They do not deny the existing creationist research in geology or biology, but realizing that their work can be summarized as "science avoids grandiose extrapolation" broadens the conceptual outlook. Such research needs strong souls because, *a priori*, they cannot be sure this thin slice of reality is not about all there is.

Enjoy and be thankful for accessible knowledge. Perhaps we have for too long withheld our praise from experimenters, engineers, technologists, craftsmen and tinkerers. Native ingenuity and attentive minds are blessed qualities.

Should support be withheld from extrapolative science? Well, were the alchemists of bygone centuries unproductive? Or, as Pierre Duhem noted, did not Christopher Columbus discover America while thinking he had reached India? (That is why native Americans are called Indians!) These days, extrapolative science can do little on its own. While it can access cash machines, it needs to employ legions of empirical scientists, engineers, technologists and craftsmen – who also converse with tinkerers. What these folk discover provides generous dividends funded by otherwise top-level misdirected thinkers. The extrapolative "scientists" subjectively pursue objective truth, but the honor should go to the others!

Truthfully, we laypeople generally require the advice of the mathematically dexterous – laypeople have a hard time spotting adjustable constants or other mathematical / wordy tricks that signal the shift (or hide) from empirical science to extrapolative science.

Aids are available. Some of the mathematically dexterous and academically credentialed thankfully avoid consensus paradigms. They may publish in mainline refereed science journals or various refereed creation science journals, belong to unorthodox professional groups such as the NPA (Natural Philosophy Alliance), the JCNPS (John Chappell Natural Philosophy Society) or the CRS (Creation Research Society) or they may be non-westerners, thus not as intently worshipping Western consensus paradigms.

There are also Creation Science groups and their websites and publications. They are such as the Institute for Creation Research, Answers in Genesis and Creation Ministries International.

Rationalism is not a clear intuition. Therefore, the pessimistic emerging view of intelligent effort is as recorded on page 30:

> Nature is orderly, but its essence is an inaccessible puzzle. Experiments can only go so far. Beyond that, science is a learned "consensus" conceptualization and investigation of stuff. Experiment and/or measurement lead to hypothesis and theory and then thinkers extrapolate, guided by their consensus paradigms. We rarely get any closer to Universal Truth. Frames of reference or points of view limit or enslave us. We are plagued by mathematics, logic and human theories. As we reach for Universal Truth, we can rarely distinguish between puzzle solving and storytelling because cloudy experiments and saving the appearances are protected from refutation by such as fortuitous *ad hoc* auxiliary hypothesis. Science proves necessity – but what necessity? Use de-sedimentation to find meaning in all

word systems – and believe no word system.

Thinker's "all-seeing" goal fosters self-deception because, admittedly, the tools of science resemble those used in the past: arithmetic, geometry, and logic. But these simplistic facets are now restricted to pre-college instruction. Today, our mathematics is fragmented, has more concepts and is labyrinthine; foundational objectivity is lacking. Subjective preferences, alternate methodologies, and creative viewpoints provide wide maneuvering room for dominant personalities. Choice is an inevitable companion when we leave the comforting confines of the laboratory. Thinkers may have axes to grind and hidden motivations. We sophists "understand" the resulting labyrinth.

No wonder the well-educated are sliding into cynicism or sophistry! In summary, of all the forces known to man, none is stronger than a paradigm! Except for the Hand of God!

Yet, we do not endorse intellectual relativity. Recognizing learned ignorance creates the strong impression that a retreat from failed extrapolations leads to empirical science and also *back* to God's created fact. Research unencumbered with consensus paradigms can achieve many things. One result will be a loss of fear regarding historical data evidencing attenuation or discontinuity. The late Thomas Barnes analyzed one such phenomenon, the earth's declining magnetic field strength, in his *The Origin and Destiny of the Earth's Magnetic Field*. It goes without saying that Noah's flood remains a prime object for historical and geological inquiry. Later world history also deserves much more attention.

As a Kuhnian philosopher might express it, "Revolutionary science is for those who are tired of extrapolative science[17]."

In contrast, typical investigations into these arenas become so mesmerized by intricate mathematics that one wonders if the practitioners lose sight of competing schools of mathematics and logic, multiple solutions, bizarre functions, *ad hoc* elements, temporary scaffolding, mathematical debris, spreadsheet parables, adjustable constants or being blind to events or qualities. These arenas remain enigmatic. Our knowledge of some subjects is essentially mathematical, not physical. As Kline has pointed out, the physical nature of radio waves has never been demonstrated, but radios and televisions work.

Devaluing rationalism still leaves the puzzling question regarding why mathematics works. If it is an invention, why does it work so well in analyzing reality? Rationalists may offer answers ranging from, "Plato is still right," to "The cosmos is a mind or a great thought."[18] Playing with marbles or doodling in the sand is a better

---

17   Electrodynamics without mathematical points has been investigated by Dr. Barnes in his *Physics for the Future* and *Space Medium* and by Dave Bergman and Charles "Bill" Lucas in the *Common Sense Science* publications.

18   Centuries ago, when rationalists said the cosmos is mathematical, the words had a physical connotation that could be visualized. But as the artificiality of mathematics was recognized, it became an even greater awe for rationalists that reality conformed to the "free creations of the mind." *As you think, so shall the cosmos be!* Rationalists change their clear intuitions, choose different solutions, and adjust the constants ... and reality magically "resystematizes itself" to conform! I believe this awe was in the mind of Immanuel Kant and the focus of Sir James Jeans' comment about the cosmos being like a mind. They gathered much data in some micro-light years of the

beginning activity.

It would make an interesting documentary to playback the last fifty years of inaccessible science. There, if we factored in the "half-lives" of cherished story-telling, we would be chagrined. Failure analysis indicates that a major problem is "clear intuitions" or theories about opening black-boxes with top-down or bottom-up techniques that ultimately weren't so clear. Mathematics and logic have enough flexibility to enhance whatever story we need to tell – in addition to their playing field usefulness. With this caution, the assumption that our grandiose answers are approximately correct – is incorrect. They may only be saving (some of) the appearances or even pointed in the wrong direction. Unfortunately, too many still believe that *"astronomy shows that the universe has 'vast distances and long ages.' The subsequent job of geology and biology is to fill in the details."*

And a parting admonition from Aristotle:

> It may be argued that experts are better judges than the non-expert, but this objection may be met by reference to (a) the combination of qualities in the assembled people (which makes them collectively better than the expert) and (b) their "knowing how the shoe pinches" (which enables them to pass judgment on the behavior of magistrates)... (B14, page 243.)

Individuals should not suspend judgment and leave it to the "experts." These may have vested interests in rationalism. Ask tinkerers and craftsmen for their input!

"Confusion is spoken with great emphasis" these days. Turning from theories to atheorism makes me less excited about the pivotal nature of various historical decision points in inaccessible science. While interesting, I doubt their pivotal nature. Too many people live in labyrinths, which protect them from correction. Creative folk have a long history of talking themselves around barriers.

The pivotal point is only to be found before the between-years began – either in ancient Athens or Jerusalem. The ancient Athenians "did not get it right" with their Mathematic's Word. "Extrapolative" science remains an adventure; few of its Promissory IFs have been redeemed – yet, it has great weapons for subtly promoting confusion! We prefer empirical science and technology; they have since grown enormously. Little Universal Connected Knowledge exists!

We began this writing with the lament of C. S. Lewis about "bad philosophy" and Morris Kline's lament over "mathematical disasters of reason." No wonder Tertullian had earlier asked that rhetorical question, "What, indeed, has Athens to do with Jerusalem?"

If, then, we step aside from mathematical debris and dwell for a moment on Jerusalem, what, indeed, is wrong with the perforating declaration in Genesis 1:1, *"In the beginning, God created the heaven and the earth?"* If God did not create the

---

solar system and extrapolative infatuation provided the rest. Such folk did not consider that subjectivity masked their misreading of the stable finite cosmos of God's creation.

universe, did it create itself? That is still absurd. If we say the universe always existed – then we are dabbling with the indigestible infinity again. Or we can try to avoid
the question by confusing ourselves with esoteric mathematical expressions, such
as those embedded in labyrinthine quantum, relativistic, or stringy storytelling.

Be not mesmerized by the winds of human wisdom. The cosmos can be
profitably understood as God's little short story. The between-years show:

> But everyone knows that 1 + 1 = 2!
> And everyone knows that 1 arithmetic + 1 rational thought = 4
>   foundational schools of mathematics.

> But the sum of the angles in a triangle always equals 2 right angles!
> And do they always equal 180 degrees?

> But geometry is foundational to inaccessible science!
> And do parallel lines meet at infinity?

> A x B = B x A is so obviously true!
> And William Hamilton discarded it in his quaternion algebra!

> But we know that 2 cubed equals 8, *i.e.*, $2^3 = 8$!
> And "converting" it to algebra, $X^3 = 8$.
> Why is there now three answers where there once was one?
> $X_1 = 2.$
> $X_2 = \sqrt{-3} - 1$
> $X_3 = -\sqrt{-3} - 1$

> But Plato said there is a REAL mathematical world!
> And Plato's famous pupil, Aristotle, reportedly said: "Boys, have you
>   ever doodled in the sand or played with marbles?"

> But mathematics is so beautiful, it won't deceive us!
> And are you lost in a beautiful labyrinthine garden?

> But if mathematical thinking is defective…?
> And the mathematician Kroneker threw up his hands in despair and said;
>   "God made the integers, the rest is made by man!"

> But surely we don't have to make THAT choice!
> And where now is monotruth … necessity … determinism …
>   and rational thought amongst all these choices?

> So we must begin to pursue eclectic operational definitions!
> And thus you flee limited rational thought!

> But WE said science must avoid the supernatural.
> Rather, science interrogates "what is," even a created fact.

> If what is, is supernatural, then our mind's eye cannot soar!
> The created fact is historical. What is, is okay with reason!

> But, it limits the mental "creativity" in extrapolative science.
> Yet, "what is" doesn't limit empirical science.

> But it cramps astronomy and social understandings.
> Thus rational thought must be atheoristic, to face "what is!"

So there have been intellectual disasters due to mankind's pride in "unaided"
reason – and its aid, Mathematic's Word. Plato had long ago stated that "should we
not settle things by calculation, and so come to agreement quickly." The desire was

noble, but buried beneath poly's!

Perhaps we have overlooked the obvious. Consider the between-years history!
Look at **Reason 101** again:

The fear of mathematics is the beginning of knowledge.
Our "all-seeing" mind's eye thus soars as on the wings of eagles.

Verily, our mind's eye is allowed to see great things!
Our ahistorical mathematical line shows experimenters what to do.

Do we understand our new mathematical knowledge?
Can our mind's eye deceive us? What is all this noise?

Is our mind's eye bipolar or poly-polar?
Is it our imagination that soars as on the wings of eagles?

How then can we objectively fulfill our leadership destiny?
Does knowledge come through the senses?

Oh well! Perhaps we can no longer "assent" to causal truth.
At least we can "assent" to consensus layers of saving the appearances.

If mathematics is deflated, experimenters must lead the way!
Then the fear of the Lord had better be the beginning of knowledge.

Early in the book, we mentioned that the contrast was between:

God's Word versus Man's Word.

But the Platonic viewpoint said it was:

Mathematic's Word versus Man's Word.

But rationalists have now "progressed" to:

Group Consensus versus Man's Word.

But that is the same thing on both sides, so it reduces back to:

God's Word versus Man's Word.

Many Christians are anxious to provide a "proof" of God's existence. Perhaps
the best proof of God's existence is rationalism's continual failure! Rationalism has
not disproven that:

- Mathematic's Word is a garden of bushes, not a sole fated tree.
- Mathematic's Word has been tried and found wanting.
- Empirical science providentially keeps company with engineers, technicians, craftsmen and tinkerers.
- Progress in living standards does not rely on paradigm science.
- Pure science rarely exists; empirical *ad hoc* modifications have to be added.
    Useful formulas trump Universal Natural Laws!
- Outside of empirical science are Word Wars.
- Rationalists are afraid to de-sediment paradigm science.
- Learned ignorance is abhorrent to extrapolative infatuation.
- Rationalists like "vast distances and long ages." They thrive in the inaccessible, living on "worlds on paper."

- Rationalists are so dexterous with mathematics that they do not
  realize they stumble within macro- and micro-reality.
- Rationalism cannot refute the created fact.

We must be men and women of faith – but not of a faith that is afraid of reason. Yes – fear and avoid science, falsely so-called – but be comfortable with reason shorn of ingrained subjectivity. Extrapolative infatuation undergirds secular pride.

We may now appreciate the words of Richard Lewontin, the famous evolutionary biologist and geneticist:

> *Our willingness to accept scientific claims that are against common sense* is the key to an understanding of *the real struggle between science and the supernatural.* We take the side of science in spite of its failure to fulfill many of its extravagant promises of health and life, in spite of the tolerance of the scientific community of *unsubstantiated just-so stories,* because we have a *prior commitment to materialism* …. *Moreover, that materialism is absolute, for we cannot allow a Divine Foot in the door.…* (B124, pages 124-125. Emphasis added.)

To this we must add "for we cannot allow a divine foot *or discontinuities or events of any kind* in the door!" The ahistorical mathematical line rules in the ivory tower of extrapolative infatuation!

To translate this from the language of unscience, we can say: "Multiple just-so stories with low probability are multiplied together to provide high comfort levels. This is puzzling storytelling at the highest level." Yet, as experimenters, engineers, technologists, craftsmen and tinkerers conclude – what is, is!

There is also the musing of the philosopher, Thomas Nagel, in his *The Final Word.*

> Rationalism has always had a more religious flavor than empiricism …. In speaking of the fear of religion, I don't mean to refer to the entirely reasonable hostility toward certain established religions and religious institutions …. Nor am I referring to the association of many religious beliefs with superstition and the acceptance of evident empirical falsehoods. I am talking about something much deeper – namely, the fear of religion itself. I speak from experience, being strongly subject to this fear myself: *I want atheism to be true and am made uneasy by the fact that some of the most intelligent and well-informed people I know are religious believers* …. It's that I hope there is no God! I don't want the universe to be like that. (B125, page 130. Emphasis added.)

Nagel struggles with his uncertainty. The rest of the chapter in his book reflects on that. He refers to the "cosmic authority problem" and the "ludicrous overuse of evolutionary biology to explain everything about life." And, "There would be no reason to trust [evolution's] results in mathematics and science…"; "There must be some thoughts that one simply thinks from the inside – rather than thinking of them as biologically programmed dispositions," and "[T]he physical story, without more, cannot explain the mental story, including consciousness and reason."

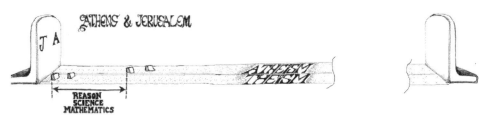

As such thinkers stand near the present-time bookend, they look forward with an uncertain confidence. Yet, if they turn around and contemplate the between-years and the beginning bookend, they see an extrapolative wasteland! "Unaided" reason has failed – as always.

The certainty of mathematics was the original great unifier of Greek thinkers. This certainty allowed them to no longer seek revealed truth ("aided" reason). They could do it on their own! This was Mathematic's Word: the one ring to rule them all.

So, Plato began with "should we not settle things by calculation and so come to an agreement quickly." This was still foremost in the thought of such as Rene Descartes "only mathematicians have been able to arrive at proofs." Later, with Thomas Paine "with geometry ... entirely independent of its author." And Giordano Bruno and Immanuel Kant gloriously wallowed in the marvels of infinity, and Baruch Spinoza was "drunk with infinity." "Unaided" reason shows itself as a devilish whore!

But today, "unaided" reason, is "aided" by a fractured mathematics, groping around in a complicated conceptual labyrinth, cluttered with mathematical debris and adjustable constants. Now, assurance of truth comes from group consensus – paradigms. Fancy footwork tries to hide this return to individual opinions (free thought), learned though they be.

Scientific truth can be found in empirical science, but not in paradigm ~~science~~ consensus. "Inferences to the best explanation," while necessary in daily life, don't explain cause and effect. So we prefer atheorism – and getting our hands dirty. No wonder Sir Isaac Newton had said when pondering gravity, "I make no hypothesis," but his wisdom was ignored. His wisdom made little difference in the empirical world – and the associated engineering, technology, craftsmanship and tinkering.

To be concerned about the distinction between empirical and inaccessible is a matter of truth. The ramifications may be unknown. The atom, distant astronomy, history, the human personality are major unknowns. What we do know in these arenas primarily is the fruit of empirical study. Milli-light-years are only milli-light-years!

Civilization is technologically vibrant and empirically restricted. Beyond that is learned rational confusion. Revealed truth ("aided" reason) impacts our faith. As Romans 1:18-32 says, *"... for the invisible things of him from the creation of the world are clearly seen ..."* This truth remains an incentive to investigate the accessible, which is not uniformly stable or constant. So faith proceeds to a wonder and a study of nature, where the features of creation and discontinuity are writ large. Faith, thus, has been incorrectly said to be "faith in the unknowable."

The universe is lawful – but perhaps it is better to say that the universe is stable. This distinction goes all the way back to the disputes between Plato and

Aristotle.

I give in to the temptation to add some insightful comments of Sir A S Eddington, (famed for his "solar eclipse observation of twenty per cent accuracy" that "precisely confirmed" Einstein's relativity). He astutely observed that:

> Study of the scientific world cannot prescribe the orientation of something which is excluded from the scientific world....
>
> Natural Law is not applicable to the unseen world behind the symbols, because it is unadapted to anything except symbols, and its perfection is a perfection of symbolic linkage. You cannot apply such a scheme to the parts of our personality which are not measurable by symbols any more than you can extract the square root of a sonnet.
>
> ... The laws of logic do not prescribe the way our minds think; they prescribe the way our minds ought to think. (B128, pages 27, 33-35.)

Eddington also brought rationalism home to the family:

> The materialist who is convinced that all phenomena arise from electrons and quanta and the like controlled by mathematical formulae, must presumably hold the belief that his wife is a rather elaborate differential equation; but he is probably tactful enough not to obtrude this opinion in domestic life. (B129, page 341.)

That tactfulness may have been prevalent in his day. Can one "love" an animated differential equation — a descendant of Pythagorean and Platonic mathematical mysticism? Pure rationalists despise mythical qualities. This frequently means divorce and tragedy for the children. *All this happens due to the belief in Mathematic's Word and science, falsely so-called!*

The real universe is not what we have expected. Atheism has a theological character, revealed in its various just-so subjectivities.

Christians! Awaken yourselves! Are you listening to unclear trumpets? Let your faith respect atheorism, not a sanitized atheism!

Thus chastened by history and atheorism, what guidelines do thinkers, experimenters, engineers, technologists, craftsmen, tinkerers, and mathematicians utilize in pursuing the lure of objective truth? That is, pursuing knowledge that is objective truth about the experimentally accessible; mathematically summarized and systematically arranged to show generalized relationships; but limited in extrapolation because of the subjectivity inherent in certain aspects of mathematics, mathematics' partial portrayal of reality, respect for the middle ground of understanding, and also due to wise timidity in the face of reality's complexity. Observation of the experimentally inaccessible provides useful understandings. But thinkers must respect atheorism – observation and extrapolation may only provisionally save (some of) the appearances.

The following guidelines for the acquisition of knowledge are patterned on those presented by Charles E. Hummel in a book. (B115, pages 159-160.) However, elaborations are made and conclusions drawn with which he may disagree.

1. **Order.** Inorganic reality has a discernable order shown in patterns and regularities discovered through experiment and/or observation. The heavens also

exhibit regularity. Organic reality shares many of these attributes, but also has qualities and thought-directed actions. Experimentally, accessible reality is exceedingly complex, so our confidence in the conclusions drawn is inversely proportional to the amount of extrapolation utilized. Obviously, complexity attenuates extension. We cannot think ourselves away and thereby affirm that complexity is only a "local affair" – in spite of what Plato recommended. Reality may be more finite than cherished Universal Natural Laws can accommodate. Instead, be comfortable with the reasonableness of useful formulas.

2. **Regularity.** Universal Natural Law is a cliché. The operative forces that man can consistently "measure" are uniform throughout traveled distances and recorded history, with some historical reports of discontinuity or attenuation. Our scientific "formulas" are geo-apparent. We conjecture that regularity has some extension into space before attenuation becomes significant. These operative forces are finely balanced, but do not rule out discontinuity or catastrophe. Thus, experimental manipulation, not multi-observation, is required.

How Quaint! Earth is the only place in the whole cosmos where (frequent) unmathematical motion occurs.

To what extent are my conclusions valid?

Cosmic Science, Falsely so-called   "Playing Field" Science

Thin slices of "playing field" regularity and order can be expressed with useful formulas, which communicate thin slices of knowledge. This regularity and order are more compatible with the design of a specific, finished creation rather than with the chance (un-order) charted by a free creation of the mind – or random nothingness. Ultimately, design versus chance is a question science cannot answer – but catastrophic discontinuity or intelligent design proclaim the Creator.

3. **Validity of sense perception.** Reliable data can be obtained by using our senses or their extensions (for example, reading a thermometer or voltmeter). However, complex instruments such as the atom smasher are quite indirect and their "calibration" is heavily theory-laden, causing circular arguments when "explaining" their results. It is difficult to have a crucial experiment when (adventurous) theory talks to (instrumental) theory. Be wary of confusing sense data with understandings, mathematical or otherwise.

The history of mathematics and logic reinforce the need for wariness. It may never be entirely clear how to objectively evaluate the choices resulting from esoteric mathematics. Empirical wisdom is needed. Unfortunately, storytelling mystique attempts to bypass these complexities. Not surprisingly, present-day definitions of science avoid addressing this problem.

4. **Simplicity.** If two systematic understandings fit the data, the simpler is preferred. The reason for Ockham's razor is beyond the competence of science. But it does suggest the reasonable result to be expected from *ex nihilo* creation!

5. **Moral responsibility.** Everyone involved in the quest for knowledge is expected to be committed to the lure of objective truth, although academic "freedom" abuses this definition.[19] Searchers honestly report their knowledge and data so other knowledge workers (even those not from their own consensus paradigm) can have confidence in their data and use it in their own work. This honest reporting further minimizes confusion when thinkers, philosophers, mathematicians, engineers, technologists, adventurers, and theologians apply extrapolation or explain "why."

Living amidst complexity and esoteric mathematics, it is possible to systematize "some" experimental and observational data in more than one way (*i.e.*, spreadsheet parables). This storytelling possibility reinforces the conclusion that astronomy, geology, and social understandings remain intellectual adventures. Age-old questions remain unanswered. The how and why distinctions proposed by Galileo are overshadowed by the mystique of grandiose extrapolation. Investigators should be cautious about propounding unattenuated "principles" and "necessities."

And, yes, many times we must sigh in bewilderment and make lists of what doesn't fit either our storytelling or puzzle solving. Too often, mesmerization with grandiose storytelling interferes with clearly seeing what is comprehensible about thin slices of reality. Granted, there is much group-think in "Western thought" but it is not total, nor are all nations chained to it. So conceptual breakouts are possible. (And man proposes, but God disposes!)

Recognizing design is a moral responsibility. Increasingly, complexity nullifies the view that things improve by chance. Complex stuff cannot be arranged, or usefully rearranged, by blind chance.

6. **Openness to data.** Experts should agree with each other. However, irrationalities of ancient origin may inhibit objective interest in certain areas of investigation, interpretation, or extension. This should not be so. Let tested formulas replace Universal Natural Laws.

Learned ignorance also attenuates philosophy, forcing us to ponder the interface between empirical science and the rest of reality. Recognizing the broad spectrum spanning from revelation to systematic understanding to knowledge is a moral responsibility.

7. **Confession.** These guidelines are honored in word, not deed. Atheorism is avoided due to rational thought's fear of losing the "all-seeing" capability of Mathematic's Word.

---

19   Universities in Medieval Europe were given autonomy because they taught truth, and truth was neutral, even though they often searched using astrology or the science of measure. Subjective and theological endeavors were not given that "freedom" *then*. Applied to modern educational institutions, the vast expenditures of time, talent and money in subjective adventures should not be protected by "academic freedom." They should be removed from subsidy or taxpayers (simple folk) should control the content of "science," so such science is no longer an overused word.

Philosophers: They surprise the ordinary run of men.
Christians: They surprise philosophers.
Blaise Pascal

When it comes to philosophers, one should never fear not to understand. Indeed, the gravest danger is to understand [philosophers].
Paul Valery

There is not a single interesting theory that agrees with all the known facts in its domain.
Paul Feyerabend

In no religious denomination has the misuse of metaphysical expressions been responsible for so much sin as it has in mathematics.
Ludwig Wittgenstein

Our trek along the hidden, yet obvious, path has been completed. Rationalists work hard to avoid the obvious. Amid the chorus of praise for relative truth, do they see the litter of the between-years history of science? *Do they see "polyscience" as no more secure than polytheism?* In the good old days when battling paganism, all agreed that polytruth would be the death of science.

Now, while high school science textbooks teach the monotruth derived with 1 + 1 = 2 and associates, polyscience's grandiose systematizations are held together by polytruth and patchwork. Everyone can recite the experimental basis of science and its bottom-up mathematics. But in the corner sits a big box labeled "rationalism." In it we found: Universal Connected Knowledge, event-less determinism, top-down Mathematic's Word and associated subjectivity, extrapolative infatuation, astronomical observations and a smaller box labeled "padadigm."

Polysciences, as quarreling extrapolations, (im)politely claw for supremacy. Each wants to lead science to supposedly new, but many times, actually, old, utopias! (Appeals for tolerance are typically stratagems to allow maneuvering for advantage.) Which science, falsely so-called, wants to retreat from its paradigms and democratically contemplate data or even limited models and extensions? Which wants to admit the subjective ambush: the inaccessibly large (astronomy) and the inaccessibly small (the atomic zone) – at the explanatory mercy of a flexible mathematics – in the hands of inflexible mathematicians?

Defending polyscience is like defending the gods on Mars Hill, yet modern society's movers and shakers dexterously accept the resulting babble as the COURT OF LAST APPEAL. They fear that events or qualities will re-allow "God's foot in the door." Their lack of objectivity regarding the inaccessible should lead to intellectual disgust. Instead, they jeer those who accept a finite science as falling from "science" into mere technology, research, engineering or tinkering.

Followers of polyscience have enthusiasm, but no shame, and are loath to admit that patchwork replaces truth. Layered patchwork is a suicidal defense

against Christianity and revelation about this event-filled "created fact!" God has fixed the inanimate portion of creation, understood with complex useful formulas – as
the backdrop for life and the thinking man made in His image. Once again, the data
of reality can be coherently resystematized.

Disaster beckons the well-reasoned! As always, they hypnotically search within paradigms for new understandings of Mathematic's Word. In spite of a glazed
recognition of polyscience, most remain awed by reason. Some conclude the cosmos is a great thought or mind. Others are pessimistic. Their list of options include
cynicism, the demonic, neo-paganism, modern sophistry, oriental immanence
(pantheism), or – worst of all to some – a return to Biblical Christianity.

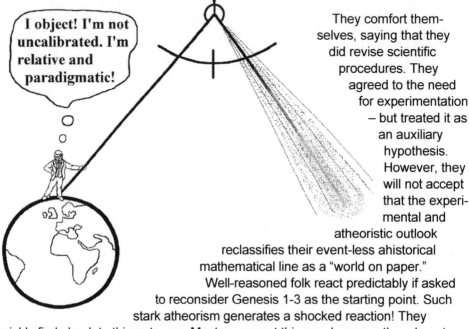

I object! I'm not uncalibrated. I'm relative and paradigmatic!

They comfort them-
selves, saying that they
did revise scientific
procedures. They
agreed to the need
for experimentation
– but treated it as
an auxiliary
hypothesis.
However, they
will not accept
that the experi-
mental and
atheoristic outlook
reclassifies their event-less ahistorical
mathematical line as a "world on paper."
Well-reasoned folk react predictably if asked
to reconsider Genesis 1-3 as the starting point. Such
stark atheorism generates a shocked reaction! They
quickly find absolute things to say. Most may react this way because they do not
recognize the musty dusty history of their extrapolative infatuation. However, others
recognize their atheistic commitment. Their basic drive is no longer a love for truth.
They realize monotheism was shut out, not annihilated. A methodology of science
starting with finite physics, not grandiose astronomy, would be to them a breath of
poison gas, not a draught of fresh air.

They know the challenge. If the "chasm" between faith and reason is engulfed
by a word fog generated by ignoring attenuation and nurturing extrapolative infatuation; if discontinuity and resonances short-circuit extrapolation; if mathematics only
has short intersections with reality; if complex equations and bizarre mathematics
provide freedom for construction and interpretation of cosmic ideas; if infinity (and
its baggage) is a mathematical abstraction; if atheorism yields tentative and short-
range descriptions of accessible complex relationships and thus separates science
from either paradigm or the essential nature of reality; if their extrapolative infatuation transcends public knowledge; if philosophies become a field of gibberish; if
civilization and material progress owe most of their thanks to engineers, technicians,

craftsmen and tinkerers; if paradigm consensus fears catastrophic artifacts in geology; if design complexity is the hallmark of DNA and cellular systems; if consensus model building in planetary formation, sub-atomic models, plasma and electricity in astronomy are wrong, then, what subjective ideas do rationalists base their rational "no foot in the door" strategy on? *They fear that (playing field) science coexists with a reasonable systematic worldview based upon the event-full Biblical created fact.* The Greeks used unwarranted extrapolations when they declared that monotheism failed because the myriad, lawless gods on Mars Hill had failed.

Rationalists enjoy critiquing "proofs" for God's existence. They avoid critiquing "proofs" for extrapolative infatuation. Forgotten history may repeat itself.

What is considered understanding hardly ever, if ever, goes beyond familiarity with a certain group of phenomena which can be related in a convenient pattern of thought and from which limited predictions can be made. *In most cases the illusion of understanding comes from a failure to examine the philosophical basis of one's professional knowledge.* (B126, page 102. Emphasis added.)

Reason is shorn, and "complexity attenuates extension" describes reason's limits. Polymathematics[1], polylogic and polyscience demonstrate "unaided" reason's versatility and unfortunate susceptibility to whoredom. This bears repeating: *Christian faith does not criticize reason, it criticizes grandiose extrapolation.* Grandiose extrapolation plus reason yields polyscientific confusion, not knowledge!

As Karl Popper wrote:

There are three levels of understanding of a proof. The lowest is the pleasant feeling of having grasped the argument; the second is the ability to repeat it; and the third or top level is that of being able to refute it. (B11, page 316.)

"Unbiased" folk prefer "polys" to revelation, it being their only means of transcending this thin slice of reality. That "all-seeing" vision in the soaring mind's eye is subjective!

Consequently, an autopsy shows that Western rationalism is not science, but *Extrapolatio Grandis Mythi.* (The Myth of Grandiose Extrapolation.) Despair over failed rational extrapolations (Universal Connected Knowledge) is the twenty-first century's open secret. From the well-reasoned who "discover" demons or Eastern mysticism, (as C. S. Lewis portrayed in *That Hideous Strength*), to those who want to refound university education on non-Western consensus paradigms or who become modern sophists; to Moslems who decry Western materialism; to the attempt to stab the nerves back to life through drugs, drink and increasing dependence on the melancholy stimulations of pornography and indecency; to the resurgence of conservative Christianity; to the "apostasy" of some nations governed by the "science" of historical materialism; to the back-to-basics movement in education and lifestyle, there is the same brooding recognition, unwelcome to secularists and almost beyond their comprehension: *the love of truth has come to this!* Western culture is technologically vibrant but extrapolatively confused! Bewildered rationalists may ask in anguish why they have to choose between a love of truth, goodness,

---

1   Polymath: A good meaning for the word is referring to one accomplished in several disciplines.

and beauty and their love for Universal Connectedness.

Polyscience may deny its lineage, but it had to *a priori* reject the Judeo-Christian short story. The thereby affirmed atheism, materialism, and absurd meaninglessness of rationalism appeared to be puzzle solving, not well-reasoned story-telling. In fact, they are well-reasoned nonsense!

Rationalism relies on many adventures. The major ones are:
- Adventure$_1$ - Pythagorean arithmetical proofs.
- Adventure$_2$ - Platonic geometrical proofs.
- Adventure$_3$ - Logical proofs.
- Adventure$_4$ - Systematic proofs.
- Adventure$_5$ - Accept all; they are relative.
- Adventure$_6$ - It does not matter; absurd meaninglessness is absolute.

Adventure$_2$ is pivotal (unless the randomness of atomism appeals to you). Adventure$_2$ makes a finite systematic understanding *irrational*. Later adventures merely redecorate the existing dwelling. Rationalists fear finite data; confrontation with mathematical subjectivity, taboo causes, design, and limits lurk nearby. In other words, to exclude monotheism (and preserve "science's" *monotruth*), Universal Connectedness *must* remain, but that betrays reason![2]

Rationalists vehemently deny they use Adventure$_2$. In spite of doublespeak, grandiose extrapolation remains alive and well. In a discussion of Einstein's relativity, a mathematician recently commented:

> Now we know that a rigid body may be transferred from one place to another and put in any arbitrary direction without altering its form and content or metrical conditions. This means that space is *everywhere* homogeneous in all directions, that is, one chunk of space is as good as any other. (B90, page 200. Emphasis added.)

This proclaims Universal Connectedness, but much reading makes some people wise, some mesmerized, some sleepy, and some *awakened to what is not said*. Philosophers and historians, while proudly boasting of their ability to criticize everything, never de-sediment the highest level of layered potpourri – to be "all-seeing" and to grasp Universal Connected Knowledge. How can a lover of truth accept their utterly large unperforated cosmos, if limited to empirical science?

They blame the disrespect shown to their reason on either a resurgence of "supernaturalism" or impatience with the plodding pace of "scientific" inquiry. Being blind to extrapolative confusion, they seek validity in the labyrinth of modern philosophy and its ability to interpret "facts." Persistent questioning of such "open minded" folk triggers a strange metamorphosis: the open, all-accommodating relativist becomes a narrow, hard absolutist! *What does this strange marvel mean?*[3]

---

2   Echoes of the Adventure$_{1,2,3,4,5,6}$ dilemma exist in the classical art and music of the last several centuries. Many composers and artists were well attuned to the desperate attempts to find meaning among crumbling adventures. Many times, music was philosophy in sound. Mahler, for one, seemed to capture the heroic pathos, but failure, of the intellectual adventurers!

3   In the introduction, rationalists were mentioned who are pleasant to those who express gratitude and respect for their historic destiny. But woe to those who ask rationalists to delineate the foundation of their *corpus* of objective truth. Also, many rationalists take a "teacherly" attitude. They are pleasant to "learners," but if you transgress that boundary and question their foundational systematization, then watch a sudden metamorphosis occur!

Paradigmatic science is where the milk of objective truth (supposedly) flows by the quart in every vein. But, in truth, such "science" is subjective and people fear to look behind adventures, afraid to rethink their commitment to methodologies used to ferret out inaccessible truth. Two ancient philosophical questions remain unanswered: "Matter is ... (arithmetical, geometrical, logical, systematic, relative, atomic or charge with fields), and ... (arithmetic, geometry, logic, systematics, or relativity) is self-evident." Matter is what? What is self-evident? What is reason? What is objective? The edifice of "all-seeing" science is subjective?

These are fearful questions to contemplate. Few people do; **angst** obscures the road. But what lies further back? How does one answer the ultimate questions of existence when the philosophy of the epoch is not in rational thought?

But first ...

Can atheism survive its dead adventure? What, then, does agnosticism compromise between? Is this why so many sneak back into theism via pantheism, a *relatively reasonable* strategy? What about hiding in polytheism? In the cool of the day God will not walk there.

Mankind's paradigms are susceptible to criticism; they do not replace monotheism. The strange metamorphosis of rationalists, mentioned above, tacitly acknowledges that matter *and* man cannot be understood without God.

Rational hope springs eternal, so this tacit confession about the failure of reason does not penetrate the cynical amnesia of rationalized Western civilization. To it, history is bunk, and unintelligibly contradictory to the tenants of a "scientific" culture. They think the doubts expressed herein are relevant only to the few interested in peripheral history and philosophy of science. Why should thoughtful, objective, reasonable, unbiased and loving people change their value-free ways.

In conclusion, Western civilization draws its identity from two conflicting sources: Adventure$_2$ and Christianity. Their "sciences" of matter differ, so also their understandings of man. It is tragic enough when passions cause wars, but conflicting "sciences" of love instigate wars! Considering the (forgotten) between-years of science, the modern sophisticated sense of objectivity is eerily unreal!

Atheism, rationalism, and ultimate meaninglessness entangle Adventure$_2$. Science, falsely so-called – *Extrapolatio Grandis Mythi* – and its consensus ahistorical Universal Natural Laws beautifully describe the "practically" infinite cosmos; then the nearer solar system; then the intricate phenomena of gravity, electromagnetism and the sub-atomic; then geology, genetics and human behavior. *These statements are considered knowledge,* not mere paradigms or saving the appearances. Rationalists think consistency in the cosmos-wide mathematical modeling proves that *humans cannot be an exception, not the only exception!*

Science has cut man down to size and broken his pride: *Copernicus* removed him from the center of the universe; *Darwin* reduced him to the status of animal; and *Freud* dethroned his intellect and put instincts in its place. (B127, page 193. Emphasis added.)

Copernicus, Darwin, and Freud – and in that order – followed in the footsteps of Greek top-down Mathematic's WORD! The rationalist's cosmos of chance matter cannot exhibit design. Atoms, or collections of atoms, do not think or possess moral sense. Therefore, humans cannot think, create or exercise free will because any supposed reality contrary to Adventure[1,2,3,4, 5 or 6] is *a priori* negated. Rationalists believe atomic humans – or photonic humans – are a product of chance, and continually being adapted to the larger chance configuration of their environment. "Scientific" progress is inevitable, a byproduct of conformance to natural law, and humans are simply its tool. Happiness will come, but "all-seeing" Universal Connected Knowledge is the supreme goal.

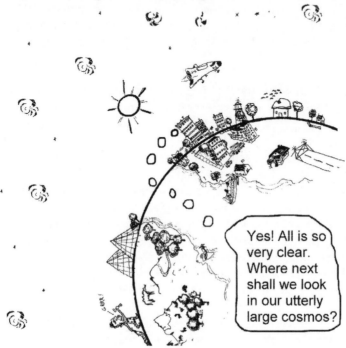

Humans are matter and plastic, full of myriad possi- bilities. By know- ing both human- kind and the cosmos, we can eliminate all disharmony by utilizing natural law. On the blank brains of raw humanity, we, the world's well- reasoned burden- lifters, can write the most beauti- ful characters. The monotruth edicts from cen- tral planners is our mandate, not the irrational "give and take" of the marketplace.

Much of the remediable evil (nonsense) afflicting humankind comes from restraints foisted upon humanity from sources "science" has debunked. They see moral codes, civil codes, political codes, *etc.*, as cruel hoaxes foisted upon humans.

On the other hand, the Christian worldview begins with a designer, a design and a specific, finished creation. The marvels of science, technology, and extrapola- tive infatuation are all recognized, displaying knowledge and ingenuity, but also storytelling and unredeemed Promissory IFs are recognized. The atheoristic eye sees paradigms: a patchwork of competing mathematics, theories, mathematical debris, actual points or lines, deliberate unawareness of ancient and crumbling foundations, spreadsheet parables, adjustable constants, a blind eye towards history and qualities, and subjective extrapolations. This patchwork does not hide the hand of God and His design in man and matter.

What was man designed for? To invent idols, worship intellectual adventures, or acknowledge his Creator? For deviant sexuality or faithful marriage? For subjective grandiosity or humble atheorism? Universal moral laws are not arbitrary but integral to harmony in the created order. Creation is God pleasing.

As a stable design, man has a mind that exercises control over the moral manifestations of his life. While institutions can be evil, reform begins in the fallen self.

Out of ancient Greece came views with some similarity to this, in the works of Aristotle. Rationalists finally reduced it to a minority view but did not eliminate it. Also, Christians of many persuasions have well-extended theologies and are caught between them and their relationship with the personal God.

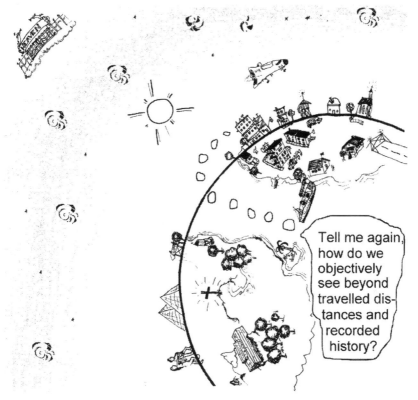

Thus, we have the curious situation today in American (and world) politics of the "New Right." It is a working together of old-fashioned Christians and secular conservatives. They have people's attention because they understand human action, being tired of *Extrapolatio Grandis Mythi*. Intellectually, however, they are vulnerable to both internal dissolution and external assault because their vision of mankind does not blend into the general scheme of science, falsely so-called. Their vision is a discontinuity when placed into the utterly large cosmos, as shown by reason and objective truth and cynical amnesia (and a subordinate relativity and consistency and logic and mathematics) and grandiose extrapolation and monotruth and atheism.

The "new right" lacks a cosmos built on a finite physics. Such a science would make secularists shudder.

In contrast, burdenlifters politicize the popular rafts of data adrift on oceans of mathematics, and "New Agers" spiritualize them. These introduce thinkers to the potency of the final understandings: paganism, pantheism and modern sophistry.

How to choose between three, four, maybe five understandings? It may take a disaster or an astronomical / sub-atomic surprise to force recognition that "unaided" reason and extrapolative infatuation are devilish whores. Either one destroys the rationalists *certainty in disbelief* of God's Revelation ("aided" truth) about Himself and His created fact. Just think, the "scientific" certainty regarding rationalism was "proven" long before thinkers realized that "one apple, two apples, three apples" ... was not the best way to count! With this recognition of polyscience, discussions about meanings, duties and truth take on an unaccustomed seriousness, because rationalists and Christians are now on "equal" footing, accepting learned ignorance and standing on the edge of the playing field, looking beyond.

Have you ever noted the absence of this serious dialog and also wondered why? A reasonable Biblical prelude is cleansing. Few are so naive as to think they can describe themselves or family members with logic or formula. Many folk now allow this "exception" to an otherwise relentless rationalism – sort of a soft rational-ism. Yet logic and formula cannot comprehend logic and formula – the supposed heart-beat of reason! Such "soft" rationalism cannot critique *ex nihilo* creation, much less maintain rational order among quarrelling paradigms. Atheism, materialism, and meaninglessness are collapsing – but will Christianity, the New Age, or modern sophistry pick up the pieces?

Faith and reason are intimately related, yet separate. Freedom in Christ wants to refine the paralyzing dross out of both, not commingle them. Uncalibrated man is to be "humble," yet consider his life work worthwhile. Man can indeed objectively measure, but not grandiosely extrapolate. Excessive reason has been dethroned! *The primary rational axiom is not "Evolution and Natural Selection." It is: "Astronomy shows that the universe has 'vast distances and long ages.' The subsequent job of geology and biology is to fill in the details."*

None are immune to the lure of objective truth. Even the well-reasoned, in the recesses of their souls, may have interesting conversations. As they take off the mantle of science, falsely so-called, how will such react? Original sin is a strong force. Yet, there is a parallel to Dorothy and the unmasking of the Wizard of Oz; he "turned around" and forsook his foibles and Manhattan beads.

To paraphrase C. S. Lewis in his *The Chronicles of Narnia*: "Aslan is on the move. The witch's power is weakening!"

As Jesus said in the Sermon on the Mount (Matthew 5:3): "*Blessed are the poor in spirit: for theirs is the kingdom of heaven.*" So, be of "humble intellect, for that is the best understanding of creation and complex natural laws."

[Y]e henceforth walk not as other Gentiles walk, in the vanity of their mind; Having the understanding darkened, being alienated from the life of God, through the ignorance that is in them, because of the blindness of their heart .... [P]ut off ... the old man ... and be renewed in the spirit of your mind: And that ye put on the new man, which after God, is created in righteousness and true holiness. (Ephesians 4:17-18, 22-24.)

The prospect of acquiring Universal Connected Knowledge has long engaged mankind's thoughts. Theology satisfied this for many people, but gods or spirits have proved unreliable. God, alone, and His Scripture ("aided" truth) has proved the exception.

Many ancient thinkers decided they could acquire Universal Connected Knowledge – "unaided truth" – on their own, for they had recently discovered the key to truth. The key was mathematics – precise numbers and figures. Such preliminary mathematics transformed reasonable thinkers into rational thinkers. Mathematic's Word was the secular "all-seeing" revelation! Mathematics was incarnated as reality – so they thought. It was the one ring that rules them all!

Rationalists were later cast adrift by Mathematic's Word after it revealed that it was only interested in itself! It is merely an abstraction, but this wasn't realized until around 1900 A. D. Zero, negative, fraction, irrational, multiple solutions, foundational schools and later "innovations" were so unwelcome. Geometry and arithmetic had to be re-grounded – or could they be?

Rationalists watched an independent, heroic salvage operation. Experiment, measurement, and a trailing mathematics was the empirical procedure, which leads to civilized comforts – but little of that was due to rationalist efforts. Instead, the ingenuity and curiosity of laboratory scientists, engineers, technologists, craftsmen and tinkerers deserves the bigger share of the honors.

Atheoristically, the rationalist edifice resembles a card castle – or, as Galileo said, "worlds on paper." Mathematics became increasingly complex and creative; reality grew increasingly complex. Paradigms, the consensus of learned participants, provided comfort, but not truth. Rationalists do most anything to avoid recognizing the yawning labyrinth of being without grandiose "unaided" truth! They save (some of) the appearances but mistake their effort as an unbiased edifice building project. Was this puzzle solving or storytelling or objective what?

It doesn't seem right to them that experiments are foundational. Or that observations are of a lower caliber. Their puzzling utilitarian marriage of experiment and mathematics is not a union of help-mates, because the "all-seeing" Universal Natural Law trumps local experiments! Mathematical chauvinism!

Yet the Voyager spacecraft are only 0.002 light years from earth – and reveal navigational discrepancies. How does such data affirm extrapolative infatuation? Answer: you silently appeal to inflexible Universal Natural Laws.

Rationalists, cast adrift by Mathematic's Word, still retained its concept of a physical infinity – and its baggage. It is an outworn umbrella, a cold security blanket, actually like the grin of a Cheshire cat. Around infinity, they continued to structure that eventless ahistorical mathematical line. With this, the material universe remained – where atheorism was not an option. Their "no foot in the door" theological strategy requires satisfaction with "just-so" rationalism. Their eyes could not see what their minds did not permit – even for the acidic deconstructionists. The alternative was unthinkable – being responsible to Him, you know Who I mean!

Freedom was exhilarating! Truth was the prize and infinity the playing field! Paradigm communities sprouted all over the intellectual landscape, yet perceptive observers noted that many of these had freedom from both religion and mathematics. It was "obvious" that freedom also included the freedom to be immoral. Old line rationalists were mystified at this irrational proliferation!

Science with atheorism – a bitter thought to rationalists! Yet, it forced their critics to reexamine the rationalist's "all-seeing" pronouncements to see if relevant measurements are really precise, measuring the right things, and whether the mathematics only says what the measurements reveal. Why is empirical science so restrictive? Surely atheorism can't cast doubt on inaccessible science!

The results of this prelude requires prayer and thought. Rationalists hit home-runs and later tried to figure out how to get to first base!

Empirical science has not discovered the cause of everything, but its useful formulas churn out useful stuff. It is a marvelous toolbox, yet qualities remain. Outside of its limited domains, buyers and taxpayers beware! Empirical examination of the rationalist's inaccessible foundations is futile. No one knows all that rationalists understand. Empiricists uncovered idealized or overlooked physical factors, mis-adjusted parameters, multiple solutions, temporary scaffolding, adjustable constants, Manhattan beads, Wizard of Oz "just so" pronouncements, *etc.* Rationalism speaks with many voices. Will anyone de-sediment their edifice?

The empirical examination produces a long repair list for inaccessible sciences. Atheorism identifies gravity, astronomy, the sub-atomic, history, life, psychologies, economics, and others as having large admixtures of "thought" clay. Platonic mathematical scholasticism is an arid taskmaster!

Alchemy is not entirely useless, but modern alchemists, unlike their ancestors, rely on the public purse. Access to a money machine does not foster atheorism.

It is still God's Word versus Man's Word (Mathematic's Word)! How then does inaccessible science compete with the reasonableness of empirical science and *ex nihilo* creation?

God is Almighty – how useful is it to visualize Him as the Great Mathematician or the Great Craftsman?

At a later time, I would like to add some words on the social understandings plus how Christianity proceeds in light of the foregoing prelude.

We must be men and women of faith – but not a faith afraid of reason. Yes – fear and avoid science, falsely so-called – but be comfortable with reason shorn of ingrained subjectivity. Extrapolative infatuation undergirds rational pride.

In contrast, what is the universe seen with atheorism?

But, for now, enough has been said.

Appendixes:

Appendix A   Page 291
    Review of Major Points

Appendix B   Page 303
    Algebra for Tinkerers

Appendix C   Page 309
    Electromagnetism for the Layman

Bibliography   Page 331

Index   Page 341

Review of Major Points

This Appendix gathers in one place major talking points for use in possible discussions with rationalists.

We reflect on the hidden, yet obvious, path that wends back through history. On page 9, thinkers in the developing Christian world utilized **First Principles of Science** to make sense of knowledge that I have grouped as follows:

A. The universe is real. Its origin is *ex nihilo*; the created fact.
B. The universe is reasonable (orderly), witnessing to the "mind of the Maker."
C. The human mind can understand much about the accessible universe because the mind is a major feature of being "created in the image of God."
D. After the *ex nihilo* creation event, material actions proceed due to cause and effect relationships – with few exceptions. Events occur, laws may not acknowledge them, but nothing happens because of definitions.
E. There is unity in the cosmos. One God and His common laws govern the universe.
F. Sense observation uncovers additional direct facts. Open eyes and creative minds, in all walks of life, were successfully improving living standards and knowledge. Experimental rigor was gradually recognized as needed to help distinguish between storytelling, saving the appearances and cause and effect relationships. Knowledge was expressed mathematically to limit ambiguity.
G. Mathematics reflects the rational design of reality.

From pages 10 and 11, **the Intermediate First Principles in Science** revised this outlook around A.D. 1900. The Intermediate First Principles revised the original First Principles. As a result of their growing mathematical confidence, item H was added. Finding Direct Facts happened less and less because so much had already been found:

A. The universe is real.
B. The universe is rational (orderly), not chaotic.
C. The human mind can understand the universe because of its mathematical structure.
D. Activity proceeds due to cause and effect relationships.
E. There is unity in the cosmos. One set of natural laws governs the infinite universe.
F. Scientific experiments and observations uncover facts. Experimental rigor distinguishes between storytelling, saving the appearances and cause and effect relationships. Observations in astronomy approach the objective standards of experimental sciences. Scientific results are expressed mathematically to limit ambiguity.
G. Mathematics reflects the ahistorical rational order in nature; *mathematical law* is a science!
H. Rational thought can safely extrapolate into the inaccessible.

These austere Intermediate First Principles had reduced Christian guidance. The question of origins was either ignored or thought to be answered within geology and biology. Rationalists rejected supernatural or historical limits to ahistorical physical processes – thus opting for infinity. Subsequently, many Christians began to talk less about God's action in historical events and more about "principles." As before, principles reflected belief, with evidence.

These changes also reflected the demotion of Aristotle and the re-elevation of Plato…. Thus, reality was infinite, material, eventless and uncreated. Dissent began to cause exclusion from the ranks of science, as scientists must "believe" in the infinite universe.

The impact of "clear intuitions" was most notable in the "theory of evolution" as *astronomers and mathematicians now "explained" the over-arching nature of reality.* They published "theories" that the universe was much larger and older than *ex nihilo* creation could accommodate. *This obligated geology and biology to "fall-in-line" and develop a "connected account"* that began with an utterly large and old universe.

On pages 13 and 14, **Inaccessible Science Paradigms** appear. "General" consensus of learned participants reflects this catastrophic overhaul of science:

A. Reality is an illusion. The inaccessible micro- and macro-worlds are "known" with top-down poly-mathematics. The bottom-up mathematics of the intermediate real-world is a lower-level experimental science – or mere engineering or technology.

B. Micro-reality is nonpredictable, not causal. Experimental results are therefore put into data arrays – to be algorithmically retrieved as needed. Micro-reality is imprecise and indeterminate – within experimental limits. Supposedly, at the real-world level, Classical Science reappears!

C. Actions proceed due to whatever is in those data arrays, as cause and effect predictability is replaced by rules, definitions and indeterminacy. This loss of causality is the "death of (classical) science." Science becomes a game – with strict rules, paying homage to the non-causal quantum mechanics.

D. In spite of chaos, there is unity in the cosmos, but there is no TOE (Theory of Everything).

E. Experiment and observation uncover some facts. To find "all" the facts, it is necessary to extrapolate with "inferences to the best explanation."

F. Mathematics proves that nature is infinite or unbounded. *Mathematics is the Foundational Science!* We know nothing about the micro- or macro-worlds, only their Natural Laws. (This reflects the dark-side of submission to the Janus mastery of mathematics.)

G. Rational thought, based on the above, can safely extrapolate into the past or whatever had been considered inaccessible. Consensus teaches that science no longer "sees through a glass, darkly." The "unaided" noble human ego was proud of its *consistent connected mathematical models that display the "unaided" proof of the rational unity of the materialistic universe.*

Eight centuries ago, science had been helped for some time, then hobbled, by *Aristotelian logical Scholasticism.* Today, science is helped, then hobbled, by a *Platonic mathematical Scholasticism.* While experimental science, engineering and technology thrive, Inaccessible Science Paradigms struggle to present themselves as responsible for this success.

Few see what is hidden in plain view: that which thrives and paradigms that struggle both use mathematics – but not with the same attitude! Empirical science is comfortable with a bottom-up attitude toward reality, for explanatory failure is a frequent companion of accessible science. On the other hand, inaccessible science is euphoric about its top-down "explanatory" successes. But the success/failure comparison is too jarring. It hints that science's provisional nature is due to saving the appearances, or unwise extrapolative confidence or reflects mystical aspects of rationalism.

On pages 18 and 19, **Empirical Science** appeared!

   A.   What can be manipulated and measured is our domain. Other studies
        we cannot comment upon; perhaps some have scholarly results.
        Theory has limited realistic extension, such as the Periodic Table of the
        elements. Science is one of the ways to acquire knowledge.
   B.   Experimental science is orderly. Well – mostly! Natural or manmade
        objects can exhibit resonances or other instabilities.
   C.   The human mind can understand processes. But understanding utilizes
        a toolbox. A toolbox witnesses to pragmatism – not to rational deter-
        minism.
   D.   Activity proceeds due to cause and effect relationships. We see but do
        not see into these relationships. Mystery and beauty abound.
   E.   There is unity among phenomena, but distinctions and unique charac-
        teristics remain. We cannot follow this unity into the inaccessible.
        Science is performed "now" – not as a "stand-in" for elsewhere or other
        times. Be wary of extrapolative infatuation!
   F.   Facts are owned by no model or procedure. "Anything goes" in the
        search for facts! Keen eyes and agile minds are a blessing. Observa-
        tion is less discerning than experimental interrogation.
   G   Mathematics is a tool, but its plurality highlights an ingenuous garden of
        choice, not a tree of determinism. Mathematics provides useful formulas.
   H.   Rational thought, to avoid disasters, should not gamble with pliable
        mathematical dice! Nor have allegiance to paradigms.

On page 19 is a discussion regarding secular priorities. Christians frequently warn against their "Primary Axiom: Evolution and Natural Selection." Yet awareness of the tumultuous times within the between-years broadens the concern. This prelude emphasizes, instead, that the MORE *Primary Axiom is: "Astronomy shows that the universe has 'vast distances and long ages.' The subsequent job of geology and biology is to fill in the details."*

These ideas are also expressed in text. On pages 28 and 29, we meet the present general public consensus:

All nature is orderly. Order originates from (or with) mathematics. This is the "unaided" starting point of science. There is nothing supernatural that can be invoked, and science is the servant of self-evident objective truth.

Science investigates (and tries to connect) all phenomena in the cosmos. The first tentative explanation is called a *hypothesis,* which is subjected to manipulative tests, called *experiments.* Deductive reasoning then finds cause and effect relation-ships – and predicts new data or wider application of the underlying mathematical relations. After repeated experiments and deductions by many researchers, successful hypotheses rise to the status of *theories.*

This rigorous methodology advances until the prize is attained – *monotruth: the single repeatable answer* ... written with mathematics to exclude bias. This satisfies the lure of objective truth. Indeed, a *Universal Natural Law* has been discovered. Natural Laws, being mathematical, reveal *uniformitarian necessity* – why laws *must* control things. (The objects of astronomy also obey laws, even though inaccessible to experiment. Observation in astronomy is thus scientific.) Laws are universal; they reach all times; past, present, and future, and all places in the cosmos. History is unneeded. Equations can be extrapolated to tell everything about non-deform-able matter. If interpretive doubt occurs, *theory trumps (local) experiment!* Science shows that reality is like an ahistorical mathematical line. It makes the inaccessible accessible. Laws are *ahistorical and all-seeing.*

The tool of science is mathematic, meaning arithmetic: 1 + 1 = 2; geometry: point, line, triangle, cube and conic section; and logic. With these tools, science has no axe to grind or hidden motivations. Due to their accuracy, we know mathematics is the "really" real. When science produces arithmetic, geometry, or logic, *all argu-ments must cease.* Unbiased people merely assent to truth. The accumulating facts may at times be disconcerting – but truth is truth. This is the scientific engine that generates such great confidence and enthusiasm.

With this tool and methodology, science infallibly distinguishes between sub-jective and objective. By many small fact-gathering steps, researchers reveal "all-seeing" true truth. They know how to verify data, equations and the logic required for discernment. Science finds Universal Connected Knowledge – it is a commons for all mankind. Experimental science provides an umbrella under which other sciences can flourish.

This is the *"public" version* of science. The *private version* is: *"Science dis-solves matter into mathematic and Universal Natural Laws are the result.* Any 'part' of matter that doesn't resurface into mathematics is thus identified as lower-class secondary phenomena."

But yet, a look-back at history revealed the thoughts expressed on pages 29 and 30:

Philosophy revealed the true foundation of reality – all nature is number or geometry, whose clarity and rigor were a continual delight. "Unaided" Mathematic's Word's necessity stands over gods. Science (Natural Philosophy) searched for (Euclidean) geometry in stuff with pure thought – or was assisted, when necessary, by simple experiment, measurement or observation. Hypothesis thus rose to theory and then to Universal Natural Law. As Plato said, science is the knowledge of Uni-versals. All-seeing ahistorical universal mathematical monotruth was the product of

Natural Philosophy.
The tool of Natural Philosophy was (Euclidean) geometry. Geometry and its axioms had no axe to grind, hidden motivation or inherent subjectivity. This was science by definition and deduction, yet it didn't outlive the demise of Euclidean geometry.

Those who peer into the future lack confidence, as shown on page 30:

Nature is orderly, but its essence is an inaccessible puzzle. "Unaided" experiment and/or measurement can only go so far – after which comes hypothesis and theory. Then thinkers extrapolate, "aided" by their consensus paradigms. Grandiose science is a learned consensus systematization and investigation of "lower level" results. We rarely get close to Universal Connected Knowledge. Frames of reference or points of view limit or enslave us. *We are plagued by mathematics, logic and paradigms.* As we reach for Universal Truth, we can rarely distinguish between puzzle solving and storytelling, because cloudy experiments and saving the appearances are protected from refutation by such as fortuitous *ad hoc* auxiliary hypothesis. Science proves theoretical necessity – but what "unaided" necessity? Use de-sedimentation to find meaning in all word systems – and believe no word system.

Thinker's "all-seeing" goal fosters self-deception because, admittedly, the tools of science resemble those used in the past: arithmetic, geometry, and logic. But these simplistic facets are now restricted to pre-college instruction. Today, our mathematics is fragmented, has more concepts, is more labyrinthean and lacks foundational objectivity. Subjective preferences, alternate methodologies, and creative viewpoints provide wide maneuvering room for dominant personalities. Choice is an inevitable companion when we leave the comforting confines of the "unaided" laboratory. Thinkers may have axes to grind and hidden grandiose motivations. We sophists "understand" the resulting labyrinth.

The view of Empirical science or Christianity was shown on page 52:

All nature is orderly – thanks to its Designer and Creator. Order allows modeling, especially so for solid inorganic matter, under constant ambient conditions. Other inorganic matter, possessing more elasticity, and liquids, gases or plasma, are more difficult to model. Likewise for organic life or the otherwise inaccessible. Understanding people is further complicated because people think and act. Marks of supernatural involvement may sit in test tubes but more likely in some large events, system designs and human hearts.

The scientific method extends human knowledge about the lawful creation. It is the unbiased manipulative investigation of accessible phenomena; thus experiments can only probe so far. The first tentative explanation is called a *hypothesis,* which is subjected to manipulative *experiments*. Deductive reasoning then finds cause and effect relationships – and predicts new data or wider application of the resulting mathematical relations. After repeated experiments and deductions by many researchers, successful hypotheses rise to the status of *theories.*

This rigorous methodology advances until the prize is attained – *monotruth: the single repeatable answer* – written with mathematics. To exclude bias, the choices within mathematics must be respected. Experimentally repeatable results are distilled into formulas which model (local) *necessity*, but cannot say what is the *extent* of the necessity, *why* nature has a specific arrangement nor *how* the specific arrangement came to be. Mathematics shadows the interaction of forces; reality is more than formulas or algorithms. Respecting atheorism helps to satisfy the lure of objective truth.

It is difficult to consider a natural law to be universal (possessing infinite precision, infinite hardness and unattenuated). Clearly, science seeks truth about the experimentally accessible, mathematically modeled and systematically arranged to show generalized relationships. However, extrapolation of the results and creating inter-domain facts require wisdom due to the subjectivity inherent in certain aspects of mathematics, mathematics' partial portrayal of reality, the non-equivalence of reality (and events) and mathematics, and wise timidity due to Creation's complexity.

Mathematics, the tool of science, can be an unruly servant. It is used for curve fitting and puzzle solving, but it can also be storytelling. Beyond experimental confines, arguments will never cease. Experimental facts may at times be disconcerting, but truth is truth, limited though it may be. This is the engine that drives technological, engineering and scientific advances. Atheoristic scientists, engineers, technologists, craftsmen, and tinkerers are servants of objective truth. This is the limited knowledge commons. Observation (such as in astronomy) and extrapolation may save some appearances.

Atheorism shuns extrapolative infatuation and dominant personalities, respects mathematical limitations and realizes that the supernatural is a hard potter for the clay to investigate. "All-seeing" thinkers may have axes to grind, hidden motivations, and accept the "unaided" philosophy of the epoch. Resulting systematizations bolster the pride of ivory-tower builders – it is not a commons. Such science, falsely so-called, is an unfortunate ongoing hypnosis. Patient atheorism and humility is the better option!

As we further reflect on the hidden, yet obvious, path that wends back through history (reviewed on page 112), we note that *Greek thinkers did not prove:*

• the "incarnation" of mathematics or logic into matter. Both remain useful abstractions. Without this "incarnation," grandiose extrapolation was subjective and "origins" lost to the Greek rationale.

• the impossibility of zero, negative, fractions or irrational numbers.

• the reality of a physical infinity.

• that a deterministic cosmos and its ahistorical mathematical line coexist with events or discontinuity – even of present realities such as earthquakes, volcanoes and tsunamis. *Ex nihilo* creation was the rational alternative.

• the irrationality of algebra and trigonometry.

• that they had found LAW or causality, rather than saving (some of) the appearances.

• natural motion is circular or that linear motion is forced.

• that "qualities" were unreal.

• that rationalists agree on reality.

• that reductionism is not an escape mechanism from flaws in the "all-seeing" mind's eye or from inter-domain problems.

Yet again (as reviewed on page 165), rationalists had not proven that:

■ empirical science, engineering and technology need guidance by grandiosely extrapolatable science.

■ the universe is infinite.

- historical rates of change are an illusion.
- histories of knowledge advancement can ignore engineering, technology and tinkerers.
- reason is *not* a devilish whore, when top-down rationalism is divorced from empirical science.

Yet again (as reviewed on page 192), rationalists had not proven that:

▲ algebra, arithmetic, geometry, calculus and trigonometry are a unity.
▲ mathematics is not a labyrinth.
▲ algebra is not a meat-grinder.
▲ reality has almost "infinite" stability.
▲ mathematics retains an objective "connection" to reality.
▲ an observation and an experiment provide the same mathematical certainty.
▲ all of the solutions to an algebraic equation can be used.

As we struggled to understand the rational confusion, the paradox of the new consensus paradigm "science" was expressed in a poem on pages 224 and 225:

The Titans of intellectual adventure clashed:
Newtonian gravity against Maxwell's electrodynamics,

The triumphant electrodynamicists were generous,
Praising Newtonian gravity as a "special case" of relativized gravity.

After all, the explanations both overflowed with equations.
But the explanations of the actual equations were opposite:

Gravity utilizes force, relativity postulates space-time creases.
Oh! Cavendish balance, do you measure creases or forces?

Relativity was "precisely confirmed" in that solar eclipse expedition.
Even though of 20 per cent accuracy, it is precise(!), and all is relative.

Anyhow, "science" triumphs, proving that reason is objective.
And as Sir Hoyle explained in his astronomy textbook:
Whether the earth goes around the sun or vice versa, has no physical significance!

So, taking him at his word,
And atheoristically viewing the 1887 Michelson-Morley observations!
A stationary earth is confirmed by the null result.

But we are told that it has no physical significance.
Relativists face a big challenge,
to be always or situationally relativistic!

Yet again, (as reviewed on page 241), rationalists had not proven that:

♦ history or reality is infinite.
♦ mathematics reliably models physical causes.
♦ mathematics is scientific discovery, not *ad hoc* invention.
♦ grandiose extrapolation is objective.
♦ observation is as valid as experiment.
♦ planetary formation/capture is a deterministic fact.
♦ the Standard Model of the point-particled atom is objective.

♦ paradigm science supersedes empirical science. Theoretical "facts" trump empirical facts.
♦ "dark" matter and "invisible" energy are not 96 % in error.

On page 262-263, we also pondered the *Riddle of The Titan's Meditation*:

The titans of extrapolative thought no longer clashed.
The dominant titan grew weary of words.
Paradigming yearned for science, for truth.
But policy requires vigilance against myth and upstart storytellers.

Primary qualities are mathematical, like 1 + 1 = 2, so we win.
But mathematics – our sacred oracle – is tarnished.
Pale invisible equations or what have we missed?
Science without grandiose extrapolation – let's atheorize:

Wait... but... but what about OUR truth!
Ah!... the deeper truth I almost forgot.
Scientific truth didn't start in the lab!
The Science of Measure is our *a priori* home-base.

We OWN the cosmic picture!
Universal Natural Law and Grandiose Extrapolation.
Ahistorical – no exceptions for "close-up" details.
Anamnesis – clear intuition – it is puzzle solving!

Aimless, infinite, meaningless universe
But, whence comes our sense of freedom!
Reality without creation – freedom's source.
Not being responsible to Him, you know Who I mean!

Yet... the unperforated cosmos always needs "further research."
Atheorism and sophistry! – why are you hanging around?
Just thinking – does God actually exist!
In the beginning(????), God created the heaven and the earth?

Computers, labs and math still hum.
But inspired Scripture still perforates and calibrates.
Plato's cave should not be our home.
We know so little, Universal Connected Knowledge is not our possession.

Forgive us, Lord.
We are not what You created us to be.
We need to meet ourselves once again.
We need You to meet us, once again.

Be not mesmerized by the winds of human wisdom. The cosmos can be profitably understood as God's little short story. As reviewed on pages 271 and 272, the between-years show:

But everyone knows that 1 + 1 = 2!
And everyone knows that 1 arithmetic + 1 rational thought = 4
    foundational schools of mathematics.

But the sum of the angles in a triangle always equals 2 right angles!
And why don't they always equal 180 degrees?

But geometry is foundational to inaccessible science!
And do parallel lines meet at infinity?

A x B = B x A is so obviously true!
And William Hamilton discarded it in his quaternion algebra!

But we know that 2 cubed equals 8, $i.e.$, $2^3 = 8$!
And "converting" it to algebra, $X^3 = 8$.
Why is there now three answers where there once was one!

$$X_1 = 2.$$
$$X_2 = \sqrt{-3} - 1$$
$$X_3 = -\sqrt{-3} - 1$$

But Plato said there is a REAL mathematical world!
And Plato's famous pupil, Aristotle, reportedly said: "Boys, haven't you
      ever doodled in the sand or played with marbles?"

But mathematics is so beautiful, it won't deceive us!
And are you lost in a beautiful labyrinthean garden?

But if mathematical thinking is defective...?
And the mathematician Kroneker threw up his hands in despair and said;
      "God made the integers, the rest is made by man!"

But surely we don't have to make THAT choice!
And where now is monotruth ... necessity ... determinism ...
      and rational thought amongst all these choices?

So we must begin to pursue eclectic operational definitions!
And thus you flee limited rational thought!

But WE said science must avoid the supernatural.
Rather, science investigates "what is," even a created fact.

If what is, is supernatural, then our mind's eye cannot soar!
The created fact is historical. What is, is okay with reason!

But, it limits the mental "creativity" in extrapolative science.
Yet, "what is" doesn't limit empirical science.

But it cramps astronomy and social understandings.
Thus rational thought must be atheoristic, to face "what is!"

So there have been intellectual disasters due to mankind's pride in "unaided"
reason – and its aid, Mathematic's Word. Plato had long ago stated that "should we
not settle things by calculation, and so come to agreement quickly." The desire was
noble, but buried beneath poly's!

Perhaps we have overlooked the obvious. On page 272 and 273, look at
Reason 101 again:

The fear of mathematics is the beginning of knowledge.
Our "all-seeing" mind's eye thus soars as on the wings of eagles.

Verily, our mind's eye is allowed to see great things!
Our ahistorical mathematical line shows experimenters what to do.

Do we understand our new mathematical knowledge?

Can our mind's eye deceive us? What is all this noise?

Is our mind's eye bipolar or poly-polar?
Is it our imagination that soars as on the wings of eagles?

How then can we objectively fulfill our leadership destiny?
Does knowledge come through the senses?

Oh well! Perhaps we can no longer "assent" to causal truth.
At least we can "assent" to layers of consensus saving the appearances.

If mathematics is deflated, experimenters must lead the way!
Then the fear of the Lord had better be the beginning of knowledge.

Early in the book, we mentioned that the contrast was between:
   God's Word versus Man's Word
But the Platonic viewpoint said it was:
   Mathematic's Word versus Man's Word
But rationalists have now "progressed" to:
   Group Consensus versus Man's Word
But that is the same thing on both sides, so it reduces back to:
   God's Word versus Man's Word.

Many Christians are anxious to provide a "proof" of God's existence. Perhaps the best proof of God's existence is rationalism's failure. Rationalism has not disproven that:

- Mathematic's Word is a garden of bushes, not a sole fated tree.
- Mathematic's Word has been tried and found wanting.
- Empirical science providentially keeps company with engineers, technicians, craftsmen and tinkerers.
- Progress in living standards does not rely on paradigm science.
- Pure science rarely exists; empirical *ad hoc* modifications have to be added. Useful formulas trump Universal Natural Laws!
- Outside of empirical science are Word Wars.
- Rationalists are afraid to de-sediment paradigm science.
- Learned ignorance is abhorrent to extrapolative infatuation.
- Rationalists like "vast distances and long ages." They thrive in the inaccessible, living on "worlds on paper."
- Rationalists are so dexterous with mathematics that they do not realize they stumbled within macro- and micro-reality.
- Rationalism cannot refute the created fact!

We may now appreciate the words of Richard Lewontin, the famous evolutionary biologist and geneticist, on page 274:

Our willingness to accept scientific claims that are against common sense is the key to an understanding of *the real struggle between science and the super-natural.* We take the side of science in spite of its failure to fulfill many of its extravagant promises of health and life, in spite of the tolerance of the scientific community of *unsubstantiated just-so stories,* because we have a *prior commitment to materialism…. Moreover, that materialism is absolute, for we cannot allow a Divine Foot in the door….* (B124, pages 124-5. Emphasis added.)

On page 274, there is also the musing of the philosopher, Thomas Nagel, in his *The Final Word*:

> Rationalism has always had a more religious flavor than empiricism …. In speaking of the fear of religion, I don't mean to refer to the entirely reasonable hostility toward certain established religions and religious institutions …. Nor am I referring to the association of many religious beliefs with superstition and the acceptance of evident empirical falsehoods. I am talking about something much deeper – namely, the fear of religion itself. I speak from experience, being strongly subject to this fear myself: *I want atheism to be true and am made uneasy by the fact that some of the most intelligent and well-informed people I know are religious believers ….* It's that I hope there is no God! I don't want the universe to be like that. (B125, page 130. Emphasis added.)

Nagel struggles with his uncertainty. The rest of the chapter in his book reflects on that. He refers to the "cosmic authority problem" and the "ludicrous overuse of evolutionary biology to explain everything about life." And, "There would be no reason to trust [evolution's] results in mathematics and science…"; "There must be some thoughts that one simply thinks from the inside – rather than thinking of them as biologically programmed dispositions," and "[T]he physical story, without more, cannot explain the mental story, including consciousness and reason."

As such thinkers stand at the present-time bookend, they look forward with an uncertain confidence. Yet, if they turn around and contemplate the between-years and the beginning bookend, they see an extrapolative wasteland! "Unaided" reason has failed – as always.

And on page 275 there are some concluding thoughts.

The certainty of mathematics was the original great unifier of Greek thinkers. This certainty allowed them to no longer seek revealed truth ("aided" reason). They could do it on their own! This was Mathematic's Word: the one ring to rule them all.

So, Plato began with "should we not settle things by calculation and so come to an agreement quickly." This was still foremost in the thought of such as Rene Descartes "only mathematicians have been able to arrive at proofs." Later, with Thomas Paine "with geometry … entirely independent of its author." And Giordano Bruno and Immanuel Kant gloriously wallowed in the marvels of infinity, and Baruch Spinoza was "drunk with infinity." "Unaided" reason shows itself as a devilish whore!

But today, "unaided" reason is "aided" fractured mathematics, groping around in a complicated conceptual labyrinth, cluttered with mathematical debris and adjustable constants. Now, assurance of truth comes from group consensus – paradigms. Fancy footwork tries to hide this return to individual opinions, learned though they be.

Scientific truth can be found in empirical science, but not in paradigm ~~science~~ consensus. "Inferences to the best explanation," while necessary in daily life, don't explain cause and effect. So we adopt atheorism – and getting our hands dirty. No wonder Sir Isaac Newton had said when pondering gravity, "I make no hypothesis," but his wisdom was ignored. His wisdom made little difference in the empirical world – and the associated engineering, technology, craftsmanship and tinkering.

To be concerned about the distinction between empirical and inaccessible is a matter of truth. The ramifications may be unknown. The atom, distant astronomy, history, the human personality are major unknowns. What we do know in these arenas primarily is the fruit of empirical study. Milli-light-years are only milli-light-years!

Civilization is technologically vibrant and scientifically restricted. Beyond that is learned rational confusion. Revealed truth ("aided" reason) impacts our faith. As Romans 1:18-32 says, "… for the invisible things of him from the creation of the world are clearly seen …" This truth is an incentive to investigate the accessible, which is not uniformly stable or constant. So faith proceeds to a wonder and a study of nature, where the features of creation and discontinuity are writ large. Faith, thus, has been incorrectly said to be "faith in the unknowable."

The universe is lawful – but perhaps it is better to say that the universe is stable. This distinction goes all the way back to the disputes between Plato and Aristotle.

Another way of looking at the struggles (page 282) during the between-years of the history of adventures is:

- Adventure$_1$ - Pythagorean arithmetical proofs.
- Adventure$_2$ - Platonic geometrical proofs.
- Adventure$_3$ - Logical proofs.
- Adventure$_4$ - Systematic proofs.
- Adventure$_5$ - Accept all, they are relative.
- Adventure$_6$ - It does not matter; absurd meaninglessness is absolute.

Adventure$_2$ is pivotal, it makes a finite systematic understanding *irrational*… Rationalists fear to interpret data finitely; confrontation with mathematical subjectivity and taboo causes, design, and limits lurks nearby. To exclude monotheism (and preserve "science's" *monotruth*), universal connectedness *must* remain.

Algebra for Tinkerers

This Appendix expands on some mathematics mentioned at various points in the text.

Algebra was viewed with suspicion by the ancient Greeks for reasons to become apparent in this Appendix. Yet Diophantus, a later Greek, is noteworthy for his work with algebra.

Algebra is a shortcut to solving numerous equations that have a similar form. Earlier, each equation seemingly had to be tackled on its own. The algebra shortcut comes about by viewing equations in a general form – beginning by substituting letters of the alphabet for numbers.

From page 82, we saw how the ancient Greeks avoided algebra! Consider the algebraic equation, $x^2 + 4x = 5$. This quadratic equation was not viewed abstractly, but as a physical problem to solve for the resulting area of 5 units. As the following figure shows, the geometric methodology required completing the square.

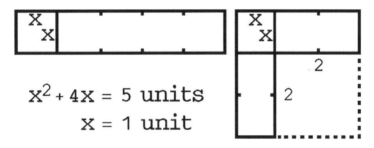

$$x^2 + 4x = 5 \text{ units}$$
$$x = 1 \text{ unit}$$

The 4x is broken up and the square completed. Thus the side is 3 units or x + 2, so x + 2 = 3. The answer is: x = 1.

This figure also illustrates why Greek mathematicians never constructed the equation as: $x^2 + 4x - 5 = 0$. The equation represents an "area" and 0 is not an area.

Ominously, solving the above equation with the factoring approach of algebra results in *two* answers:

$$X^2 + 4X - 5 = 0$$
$$(X + 5)(X - 1) = 0$$
$$\mathbf{X = -5}$$
$$\mathbf{X = 1}$$

However, the Greeks emphasized that zero and negative numbers did not exist – and *multiple* answers also didn't exist where matter is number! Again, *specs of dust get in the mind's eye!* No wonder algebra was avoided.

We now consider the algebraic solution for quadratic equations that was finally developed in the Middle Ages. See http://en.wikipedia.org/wiki/Quadratic_equation.

$$ax^2 + bx + c = 0$$

To solve this equation for x requires the rearrangement of the equation to:

$$x = \frac{-b \pm \sqrt{b^2 - 4ac}}{2a}$$

Three noteworthy comments:

First, we rely on the mathematicians that this is the proper general arrangement. You can find it on websites.

Second, the $\pm$ symbol indicates two operations, plus and minus!

Third, the symbol $\sqrt{}$ indicates that a square root is to be taken of the number under the symbol, specifically:

$$b^2 - 4ac$$

Applying this to the first quadratic mentioned, $x^2 + 4x = 5$, the equation must first be rearranged to: $x^2 + 4x - 5 = 0$. Then:

$$x = \frac{-4 \pm \sqrt{4^2 - 4\cdot(1)\cdot(-5)}}{2\cdot1}$$

Doing the multiplications, one gets:

$$x = \frac{-4 \pm \sqrt{16+20=36}}{2}$$

Remember that "- 4 x - 5 = + 20"!
And the square root of 36 is 6, so:

$$x = \frac{-4 +6}{2} = \frac{2}{2} = 1$$

$$x = \frac{-4 -6}{2} = \frac{-10}{2} = -5$$

Remember that $\pm$ has been replaced with a "+" and a "–" for two separate calculations. So we arrive at the two answers found using the factoring approach.

Can you imagine someone trained in Plato's school being comfortable with this? *Matter is number – yet matter cannot go through these gyrations!* What really is the relation of number and matter!

From page 71, we saw the Pythagorean Theorem, which was applicable to triangles. It was a famous quadratic equation, but it wrecked their intellectual adventure. The Pythagorean Theorem: $AC^2 = AB^2 + BC^2$. The length AC is the hypotenuse of a right triangle. (Its origin can be traced to ancient Babylon.)

Therein they encountered *irrational numbers* while trying to calculate certain square roots of triangular relationships. But that was not the only thing they encountered with the Pythagorean Theorem – therein they again encountered multiple solutions.

We now apply algebra to triangles via Pythagoras Theorem to show that they encountered multiple solutions in addition to irrational numbers. The terms will have to be renamed in order to conform to the general equation. Further, there can only be one unknown, not three!

For the first example, the 3 4 5 right triangle will be used. This gives rational numbers as the answer. (This gives away that one of the answers is 5!)

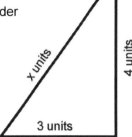

$$x = \frac{-b \pm \sqrt{b^2 - 4ac}}{2a}$$

Realize that:

a = 1

b = 0

$c = 1 \cdot (3)^2 + 1 \cdot (4)^2$ or = 25

Plugging in the appropriate values, we get:

$$x = \frac{-0 \pm \sqrt{0^2 - 4 \cdot (3^2 + 4^2)}}{2 \cdot 1}$$

Note that "b" equals 0 and that "a" equals 1. "c" equals the addition of the 2 known sides of the triangle, thus $3^2 + 4^2$.

$$x = \frac{\pm \sqrt{-4 \cdot (9 + 16)}}{2 \cdot 1}$$

$$x = \frac{\pm \sqrt{-4 \cdot 25} = -100}{2}$$

Then the two solutions are:

$$x = \frac{-(-10)}{2} = +5$$

$$x = \frac{+(-10)}{2} = -5$$

Thus, the hypotenuse, according to algebra, can be either + 5 units or - 5 units, and within mathematics, there is no way to tell which is the correct answer. In physics, the unreal option is discarded!

No wonder the ancient Greeks viewed algebra with suspicion, in spite of its usefulness! Further, can you visualize these steps as being incarnate in matter?

The triangle shown here is the one that gave rise to irrational numbers – in addition to multiple solutions! The general solution is, once again:

$$x = \frac{-b \pm \sqrt{b^2 - 4ac}}{2a}$$

Plugging in the appropriate values, we get:

$$x = \frac{-0 \pm \sqrt{0^2 - 4 \cdot (1^2 + 1^2)}}{2 \cdot 1}$$

Note that "b" equals 0 and that "a" equals 1. "c" equals the addition of the 2 known sides of the triangle, thus $1^2 + 1^2$.

$$x = \frac{\pm \sqrt{-4 \cdot (1+1)}}{2 \cdot 1}$$

$$x = \frac{\pm \sqrt{-4 \cdot 2} = -8}{2}$$

The square root of a -8 is another irrational. The value is approximately - 2.82842..., which is double the value for the square root of a - 2. Then, divide - 2.82842... by 2 and the answer is - 1.41421 ..., which is the square root of a - 2. So we end up with 2 answers, both irrational.

$$x = \frac{+(-2.82842)}{2} = -1.41421...$$

$$x = \frac{-(-2.82842)}{2} = 1.41421...$$

With number and matter interchangeable in the science of measure, no number, when multiplied by itself, could yield a negative product (quantity). Nonetheless, because positive roots worked, solutions containing the $\sqrt{-1}$ could not be ignored.

After years of *violent* arguments, negative roots were made respectable by defining the square root of -1 as $i1$. i is an abstract symbol, $i1^2$ = -1. In mundane matters, we can avoid algebra and just multiply – not calculate roots.

On page 180 the cubic equation was viewed – and its three solutions.

Suppose we have a cubical vessel whose volume is 8 cubic feet, and we wish to find the length of one of its edges.... We can solve the problem by mathematics. We let x be the required length, and all we have to do is to solve the [cubic] equation, x^3 = 8. *But this equation has three solutions, viz. 2, $\sqrt{-3} - 1, -\sqrt{-3} - 1$, – all having the same mathematical validity.* But we know that the only one of these solutions that can possibly correspond to the reading of measuring rods is 2 .... So we ignore two of the mathematical solutions, and quite overlook the significance of the fact – namely, that *in the language of mathematics we can tell lies as well as truths, and within the scope of mathematics itself there is no possible way of telling one from the other.* (B86, pages 32-33. Emphasis added.)

The solution to cubic equations is complicated. Perhaps as many as 10 methods for solving cubic equations exist, all with restrictive conditions. See http://en.wikipedia.org/wiki/Cubic_function. It has 14 pages of text and 3 pages of references.

We will not discuss the details here. One is tempted to view the process as an algebraic meat-grinder. They do solve equations, but do not forget that the equations are meant to solve physical problems – perhaps indicate physical processes. This is where the process is revealed as saving the appearances rather than as causal. Again, in mundane matters, we can avoid algebra and just multiply – not calculate roots.

On page 180, an example of a quintic equation is given – one to the 5th power. The practical use of the equation containing it is to calculate the pressure loss of gas flowing through a length of pipe – such as in the exhaust pipe of a large diesel engine. The appropriate equation is:

$$\text{Pressure Loss} = \frac{\text{Pipe Length x Gas Density x Gas Flow}^2}{\text{K (constant) x Pipe Diameter}^5}$$

What physical meaning is there to the diameter of a pipe to the fifth power? Or its root? Nonetheless, the 5th power term for various pipe diameters is incorporated into engineering charts from which the Pressure Loss can be determined.

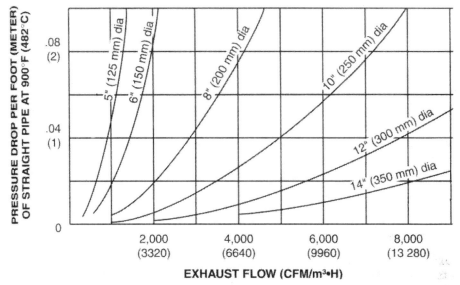

EXHAUST FLOW (CFM/m³•H)

Just consult the engineering chart; it avoids the need to know the value of any of the five roots! The chart provides the correct physical answer without showing the hidden complexities. Multiply various pipe diameters instead of calculating roots!

Solving quintic equations is discussed at http://en.wikipedia.org/ wiki/Quintic_Function. Again, the details are not discussed in this chapter. It is another algebraic meat-grinder.

Where was rational thought when one needs its cleansing power to *eliminate thinking about mathematical choices*? If matter is incarnate mathematics, then all this is serendipitous nonsense! Alternatively, because higher power equations are reliable, the mathematics has short intersections with reality and saves some appearances.

Before these discoveries, mathematics carried a much heralded virtue: Solutions to equations *always* yielded one answer. *Mathematics means (had meant!) monotruth!* Therefore subjectivity was (thought to be) absent from the mind's eye when engaged in mathematical thinking. Geometric problem solving gives only one answer; algebra is more generous. *There are as many solutions as the equation has powers.* (For example; equations with X^4 have 4 solutions. Tensor calculus, which is used in relativity, has X^{10} and string theory has X^{26}!)

An article in *Sky and Telescope* supports this concern. While discussing "space-time," Sten Odenwald mentions the following:

> And it's worth remembering that mathematics can sometimes introduce concepts that are only a means to an end and *have no independent reality.* In the abstract world of mathematical symbolism, *it isn't always clear what is real and what's not* .... Particle physicists often have to deal with *"ghost fields"* that are simply *temporary scaffolding* used for calculations, and that *vanish* when the calculations are complete. *Nonphysical devices* such as negative probability and faster-than-light tachyon particles are *grudgingly tolerated* so long as they *disappear before the final answer.* (B88. Emphasis added.)

When the gears of algebra grind towards a solution, an object is first replaced with a mathematical point! Next, "temporary scaffolding" (intruding mathematical objects) may appear at various steps in the internal gears of the algebraic meat-grinder. Then we arrive at the solutions – yes, multiple solutions, some of which incorporate $\sqrt{-1}$. Is this what actually happens within matter? Next, we discard inconvenient algebraic results. Then the object magically reverts away from a mathematical point. This process is saving the appearances, not cause and effect!

But ominously, some mathematicians will ponder what "negative probability" or "tachyons" mean. Buyers beware!

The philosopher Nancy Cartwright points out:

> The use of certain mathematical devices, such as complex numbers, *will generate excess terms* which we do not expect to have any physical significance. (B87, page 121. Emphasis added.)

Later, she refers to these excess terms as *mathematical debris!*

Pierre Duhem earlier gave a similar warning:

> Between the concrete facts, as the physicist observes them, and the numerical symbols by which these facts are represented in the calculations of the theorist, there is an extremely great difference. (B89, page 133.)

Here were challenges ancient thinkers did not face! How could the lure of objective truth be fulfilled within this new and strange territory populated with newfangled constructs, choices, and debris? Matter is not mathematical! How do abstractions relate to reality? And "mathematical facts" will not lead to monotruth if reasoners courageously list all possible solutions, including the reasons for selecting such-and-such solution.

This is not causality. It is top-down Universal Natural Law, it is saving the appearances. Freedom of choice is hidden in plain view! Thinkers ponder the inaccessible with consensus agreements among colleagues to "get around" this loss of truth.

Mathematics provides snapshots of "thin slices" of reality! Rationalists mistakenly construct card castles; they do not capture empirical reality. They operate with a faith that they may not even recognize!

"Deep" mathematics can be a captivating mystery!

Electromagnetism for the Layman

This appendix provides a non-technical "popular science" view of this very technical subject.

In spite of knowledge of many things, the following probably remain undefined terms: light, charge, heat, electric field and magnetic field. Useful formulas are developed about them but they remain fuzzy realities.

We earlier discussed the history of the Toroidal Ring Electron model and its relation to the atom. Toroidal ring electrons are stationary around the atom's nucleus, held in balance by their magnetic and electric field forces.

The drawing shows an intrepid explorer on a "core" to the toroidal ring, but the "core" is only an artistic effect. The toroidal ring could be shown as a circle, but that would have the electron in its ground state. The above drawing shows the toroidal ring with four turns, n = 4. The difference is caused by the amount of energy within the ring. The flowing charge imparts a twisting effect upon itself. At specific stress levels, the number of turns in the toroidal ring changes quickly – and forms a denser spiral.

The electron's various energy levels come from the toroidal ring acting as an antenna to gain energy from its surroundings or to radiate energy back to the surrounding to lose energy.

In this second drawing, the toroid is shown as a more subdued artistic effect.

This drawing of the toroidal ring electron shows 7 turns of the charge ring, n = 7.

The resulting constant DC current flow creates a stationary magnetic field. It can be called a "standing wave." The electric field is also shown.

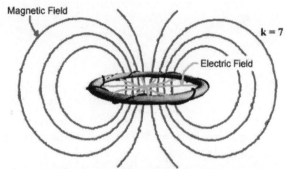

Toroidal Electron Showing Its Electric and Magnetic Fields
(Not to Scale.)

Courtesy CommonSenseScience.org

We now take a detour into some elements of basic electricity to become better acquainted with what happens with capacitance and inductance.

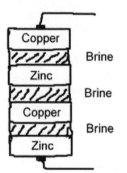

(Incidentally, in 1802, the Italian, Alessandro Volta, made a "pile," the first battery. He piled (stacked) discs of copper and zinc, separated by salt water soaked cloths. The "volt" is named in honor of Mr. Volta and a battery is called a pile in some parts of the world.)

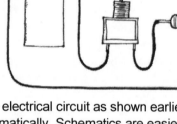

This is a pictorial layout of a battery, a switch, and a resistor (as a load).

This is the same electrical circuit as shown earlier, but drawn schematically. Schematics are easier to draw than a pictorial layout.

Closing the switch allows current to flow and opening the switch stops the current flow.

When current flows, there is an associated magnetic field surrounding the components. Oerstad, in 1819, discovered this phenomenon by noticing the movement of a compass needle when current flowed through a nearby wire.

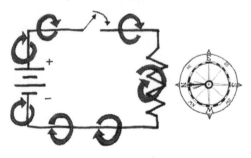

There is also another field (shown as a dashed line), sensibly called the voltage field, but commonly called the electrostatic or electric field. The voltage field is diffi-

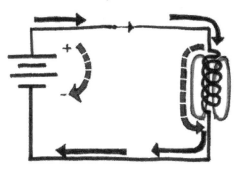

cult to sense, but there are instruments that can measure it. The voltage field contains about the same amount of energy as the magnetic field does.

We can sense this field as static electricity. When the air is dry and you walk on wool carpet, you pick up charge and will draw a spark whenever you touch a grounded object. You may have also seen a van der Graff static generator. With either transistor circuits or high voltage situations, the voltage field (electric field) must be treated carefully.

The electric and magnetic fields do not interact with each other – or with other electric and magnetic fields. They only interact with charge – usually in conductors. Specifically, the electric field only depends on the quantity of charge, whether stationary or moving. The magnetic field interacts only when charge is in motion.

In 1831, Michael Faraday made discoveries that were to revolutionize the world. He discovered that moving a wire through a magnetic field (motion shown left-to-right) created a voltage in the moving wire (and associated voltage field, shown dashed). This generated (induced) voltage, in turn, causes a current to flow if the wire is connected to a load and then

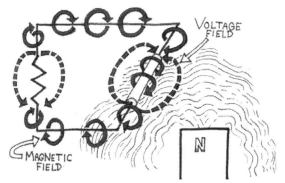

there arises an associated magnetic field. Faraday also discovered that he could move the magnet and keep the wire stationary – with the same result.

The magnetic field induced in the wire moves with the wire (its source). "Whatever" constitutes the magnetic field is revolving around the wire, supposedly at the speed of light.

From this humble beginning, electric generators, electric motors and other things like light bulbs were invented. The knowledge of what really was happening in these devices took time to accumulate.

Actually, for years there was a debate as to whether current was a newly found current element. This thought was possible because most substances have no evidence of magnetism, when no voltage is applied, and atoms were then hard little pieces of inert matter.

The next thing to be considered are two little devices: capacitors and inductors. Let us look at the capacitor first.

A capacitor consists of two plates separated by an insulator.

When the switch is closed, current from the battery flows unto the upper plate of the capacitor, (and repelled away from the lower plate), as shown by the graph. The current tapers off to zero as the plates "charge."

There is a + (positive) and - (negative) charge across the plates of the capacitor, and a voltage field across the plates of the capacitor when it is charged. The chart shows this effect. Like charges repel, unlike charges attract. Actually, if the plates of the capacitor were not held rigid, they would move towards each other as they charged. Ultimately they would touch each other and short out!

Controversially, James Clerk Maxwell proposed a "displacement current" to explain the charging of a capacitor – it went from plate-to-plate across the gap. It seems better to view capacitor charging as resulting from a finite amount of charge coming from the + (positive) post of the battery – which forces an identical amount of charge to be repelled from the capacitor back to the - (negative) post of the battery. Nothing flows through the capacitor. The battery always retains a constant amount of electrons within itself. (A charged battery has the positive and negative charges clustered at the respective battery posts.)

If you then disconnect the battery, the capacitor retains its charge. You could connect a light bulb across the capacitor and it would light and slowly discharge the capacitor. In summary, the capacitor is an energy storage device!

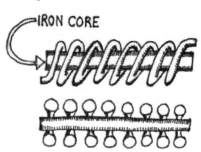

We now turn our attention to the inductor. It is a length of wire wrapped in a spiraling circle. The iron core may be added to increase the effect. (What is shown is not a trans- former. A transformer requires a separate second coil to be wrapped around the first coil.)

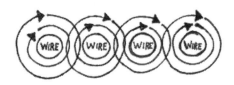

This drawing shows what happens as current begins to flow through the coil. A magnetic field begins to form around each turn of the wire as the current flows from a battery.

But now electricity begins to get complicated. The drawing on the next page shows the magnetic field continuing to expand, then it "cuts" through the adjacent turns of wire. (Fields don't interact with each other, they only act on units of charge, which are in the wire.)

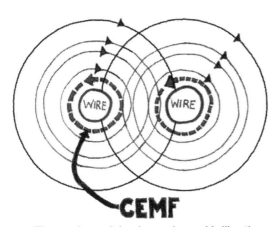

CEMF

As this expanding magnetic field cuts the adjacent coils, a "counter" voltage is generated (shown as counter-clockwise motion dashed lines), its magnetic field is in the opposite direction as that due to the battery power. This effect goes by various names. It may be called a "feedback" effect or it may be called the "CEMF" – counter-electromotive force.

The end result is shown here. Unlike the capacitor, current flow slowly rises in a coil, resisted initially by the counter-voltage. Once the field has totally expanded, this "counter" voltage effect ends.

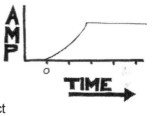

But now we face a problem. We previously saw that the capacitor can be disconnected from the battery and it can hold a charge (store energy). But with the coil, we face a dynamic situation in that the magnetic field does, in fact, store energy, *but only while battery current is flowing.*

To understand what happens when the switch is opened, we call upon the daring rider of the electron we met earlier. He reaches down with both hands and opens the switch!

As he picks himself up off the ground, he wonders what happened! What happened is a second example of CEMF (counter-electromotive force). The opening of the switch "tried" to interrupt the current flow – which caused the magnetic field to collapse. A collapsing field is a moving field – so it generates a CEMF (voltage). Actually, the faster the switch is opened, the faster the current tries to fall, the faster the magnetic field collapses, and the higher is the CEMF (voltage) generated. (This is

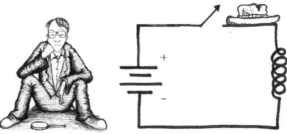

how the spark plugs for a gasoline engine can get thousands of volts out of a car's 12 volt battery!)

So, our friend has advanced from an understanding of formulas to a knowledge of physics!

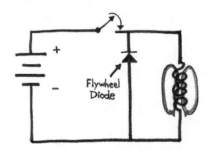

Opening a switch on an inductor will badly arc the switch contacts. To minimize this, many DC circuits add a flywheel diode (discharge diode) to allow the gradual dissipation of the magnetic field.

Another odd thing about current flow is that the magnetic field around a wire actually squeezes the wire. This is typically not seen with metal wires but is shown in a conducting liquid such as mercury. This is a "pinch effect" that can actually stop the flow of current, *i.e.,* physically cut the conductor.

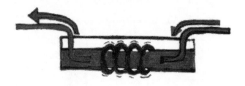

To illustrate further magnetic field effects, we begin by adding a second switch that is "ganged" mechanically to the first switch, and we remove the flywheel diode. This allows the second switch to close at the same time as the other switch is opening. The arrows show the current flow.

The voltage field is shown as a dashed line, although, it is normally not indicated, but it will be important when looking at the Toroidal Ring Electron.

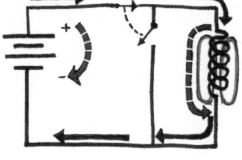

When the switch is moved to the open position, the magnetic field tries to reduce, but that generates a current caused by the CEMF (counter-electro-motive force) which sustains current flow through the coil, but not through the battery. Note that the polarity of the electric field is reversed. Depending upon the resistance of the wires, this current flow will gradually decline (discharge) over an extended period of time.

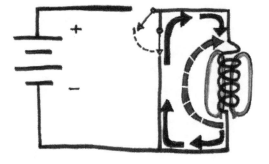

Consider a "thought experiment;" what if the wire was a "superconductor," with zero resistance? The current flow and magnetic field would continue indefinitely! In other words, the collapsing magnetic field indefinitely sustains the current flow, through the phenomenon of "feedback" or CEMF (counter-electromotive force)!

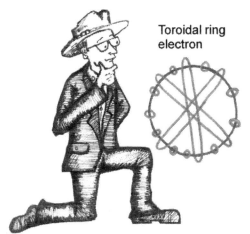

Toroidal ring electron

This raises some interesting possibilities! We will call upon our friend to make some adjustments to the circuit. After charging the coil, he eliminates the battery and stretches out and "circularizes" the "super-conducting" coil. He then realizes that he has made an imitation of a toroidal ring electron. Perhaps we can learn a few things from this model!

There are two fields present: the magnetic field encircling the wire (and tending to push the wire circle out because the lines of force have to squeeze through the center of the ring) and the voltage field across the diameter of the toroidal ring (and tending to pull inward the circle of wire). If the toroidal ring was flexible, these two forces would circularize it and balance each other out.

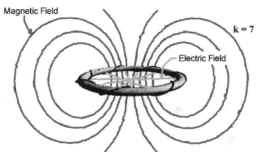

Magnetic Field

k = 7

Electric Field

Toroidal Electron Showing Its Electric and Magnetic Fields
(Not to Scale.)

Courtesy CommonSenseScience.org

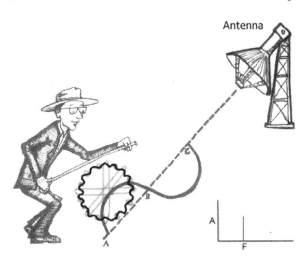

Antenna

At the same time, locally, the magnetic field tends to "pinch" the charge ring.

We next consider energy transfer into or out of the ring. Energy can enter due to an electromagnetic signal at the right frequency. The "right" frequency has to match the diameter of the circle. If the distance of A to B of the transmitter signal equals the diameter of the ring, (or exact multiples or sub-multiples of the ring's diameter), then small amounts of energy will enter the toroidal ring – or radiate out when no energy enters!

(With the speed of light at 186,000 miles per second, this large an electron ring would require a hard-to-achieve low frequency. At the actual small size of the toroidal ring electron, the frequency is much higher – in the range associated with today's communication marvels.)

Energy entry will increase the amperes of current flow in the toroidal ring electron. As the current flow increases, the magnetic field in the ring increases in strength. The twisting effect of the mag- netic lines-of-force begins to stress the magnetic circle.

Eventually, the toroidal ring will break and quickly reconnect, thereby adding another "wrap" to its structure. This tends to "shrink" the toroidal ring a small amount. The antenna signal will now have to be at a slightly higher frequency (shorter wave-length). It could go as high as 25 or so wraps – each with a different frequency and diameter, as illustrated below.

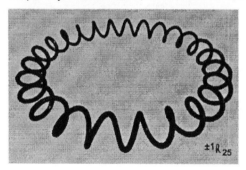

$\pm 1 \Re_{25}$

NOTE: Electron, proton, neutron sizes and masses. Information shown for the ground state.

Property (SI MKS units)	Free Electron	Free Proton	Bound Electron in Neutron	Bound Proton in Neutron	Isolated Neutron
Electrostatic Energy (Joule)	4.0983×10^{-14}	7.5251×10^{-11}	2.2542×10^{-11}	5.2719×10^{-11}	7.5261×10^{-11}
Magnetostatic Energy (Joule)	4.0888×10^{-14}	7.5077×10^{-11}	2.2490×10^{-11}	5.2597×10^{-11}	7.5087×10^{-11}
Total Energy (Joule)	8.1871×10^{-14}	1.5033×10^{-10}	4.5032×10^{-11}	1.0532×10^{-10}	1.5053×10^{-10}
Mass (kilogram)	9.1094×10^{-31}	1.6726×10^{-27}	5.0105×10^{-28}	1.1718×10^{-27}	1.6749×10^{-27}
Magnetic Moment (Joule/Tesla)	-9.2848×10^{-24}	5.0566×10^{-27}	-1.6880×10^{-26}	7.2179×10^{-27}	-9.6624×10^{-27}
Radius (meter)	3.8661×10^{-13}	2.1055×10^{-16}	7.0287×10^{-16}	3.0054×10^{-16}	N/A
Shape, $\log_e(8R/r)$	428.932	428.932	428.932	428.932	
Spin Rate (radians/second)	-7.7544×10^{-20}	$1.4238 \times 10^{+24}$	$-4.2652 \times 10^{+23}$	$9.9750 \times 10^{+23}$	N/A
Compton Wavelength (meter)	2.4291×10^{-12}	N/A	1.8884×10^{-15}	N/A	1.8884×10^{-15}
Resonant Frequency 1 (Hertz)	$1.23416 \times 10^{+20}$		$1.5876 \times 10^{+23}$		$1.5876 \times 10^{+23}$
Compton Wavelength (meter)	N/A	1.3229×10^{-15}	N/A	4.4163×10^{-15}	4.4163×10^{-15}
Resonant Frequency 2 (Hertz)		$2.2661 \times 10^{+23}$		6.7883×10^{-22}	6.7883×10^{-22}

Table 1   Selected Properties of the Electron, Proton, and Neutron.

Courtesy of Common Sense Science

The above table shows some basic information on the electron, proton and neutron. The electron and proton have different values for their various properties. They do have the same charge, but with greatly different diameters, yet the Electrostatic and Magnetostatic Energies remain almost identical. *Most properties vary greatly between the free and the bound states.* Most properties differ by a constant value, in proportion to this difference in diameter, which is equal to 1836.15. No physical reason can be given presently for these differences.

The proton and electron have similar toroidal ring structures. The neutron, in turn, is a proton, bound within the diameter of an electron.

Remember that the free electron is actually 1836.15 times larger that the free proton. Yet, in the neutron, their sizes are much closer. In neutrons, the electron and proton's electric and magnetic fields interact and hold the electron and proton in a bound balanced configuration.

Figure 1.
CSS Concept of a Neutron
The neutron is not an elementary particle but a paired electron and proton.

Courtesy of Common Sense Science

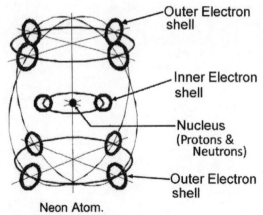

Outer Electron shell

Inner Electron shell

Nucleus (Protons & Neutrons)

Outer Electron shell

Neon Atom.
Courtesy CommonSenseScience.org

The Neon atom is not to scale. The nucleus is actually much smaller than shown (1836.15 times smaller) as also the spacing between the valence electrons is larger. The voltage field is not shown.

Not illustrated here is the further complication of variations in the number of wraps in the toroidal rings, due to reception or emission of energy. These change the size of the electrons – as well as a slight change in the overall atom's diameter. The resulting smaller electrons remain about where they were due to the stronger fields.

With the nucleus an "ultra-small" particle, gravity is a minor force. Remember that the electric field force is 10^{39} power stronger than gravity.

Our intrepid explorer now decides to takes a stroll with his toroidal ring electron. But he cannot ignore his surroundings, it is filled with many other toroidal ring electrons.

As he begins his stroll, he finds that he must grab on to the toroidal ring electron with both hands and push it along in front of him. The electric and magnetic fields of his toroidal ring electron are interacting with the charges and fields of all the surrounding toroidal ring electrons! This demonstrates "local" contact force through electric and magnetic fields, rather than through action-at-a-distance.

This demonstrates the electro-magnetic origin of its mass and inertia. Resistance to motion shows that an object interacts with all the surrounding toroidal ring electrons.

NOTE: High velocity effects on fields.

We now take a closer look at the magnetic field encircling the toroidal charge ring. This field is rotating around the ring – at the speed of light.

If the toroidal ring electron is moving at close to the speed of light, the circula-ting fields have difficulty keeping up with the motion of its source toroidal ring. The fields lengthen out with this high speed movement. This either "pinches" the toroidal charge ring or produces CEMF in its own or adjacent toroidal charge rings.

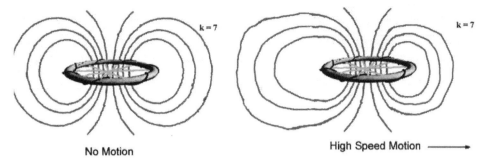

No Motion

High Speed Motion ⟶

Toroidal Electron Showing Its Electric and Magnetic Fields
(Not to Scale.)

Courtesy CommonSenseScience.org

This high velocity effect was not considered when Maxwell utilized his quaternion equations. (Perhaps the effect was unknown at the time!) When he wrote in the 1870s, there was no way to accelerate a particle to close to the speed of light. Particles were limited to wires used to generate current flow.

Therefore, the shortcoming of the fact that his calculus, any calculus, has to calculate with point particles was of no importance at the time. Maxwell did deal with fields in motion – electromagnetic radiation. His calculations revealed many facts about electromagnetic fields, but it was not remembered that a point particle is not the source of the fields. Granted, the electron is very small, with a radius in the range of 3.8×10^{-13} meter, but that is very large compared to a mathematical point!

Furthermore, the phenomena of capacitance, inductance and counter-electromotive force (CEMF) can be visualized for a toroidal ring electron, but not for a point electron. This *physical* oversight caused high velocity mathematical errors that were later "corrected" by Albert Einstein with his *mathematical* concept of relativity. At the time, it was not realized that physical lagging fields would correct for the same phenomena, but without requiring the mathematical tweak of relativity.

When these toroidal ring electrons are brought together to form atoms, the rings are stationary at various positions – held there by the balance of opposing electric and magnetic field forces. (See the neon atom on the previous page.)

This atom is stable and does not "emit" energy as a result of its stationary configuration.

Historical Markers in Understanding the Atom.

1885 Balmer Series in Spectroscopy.

In 1885, Johann Balmer developed the Balmer formula to predict the spectral lines observed with spectrometers. Spectroscopy could be said to have been anticipated by Sir Isaac Newton when he shined sunlight through a prism and then projected the results unto a wall in a darkened room. (Newton thus proved that white light is a composite of all colors of light.)

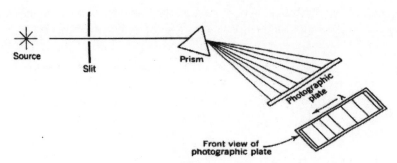

Figure 1
Apparatus for Atomic Spectroscopy

The drawing shows a modernized version of the spectroscope projected unto a photographic plate. When the source was not sunlight, but a restricted light source, investigators were puzzled by the result. Each light source seemed to have a "signature" on the photographic plate. No one could predict why these lines on the photographic plate were precisely spaced as they were. Further, at higher frequencies, the line spacings became less.

Hydrogen, being the simplest element, was widely investigated. The photographic plate results are shown below. Note that the hydrogen lines get closer to each other at higher energy levels, to the right.

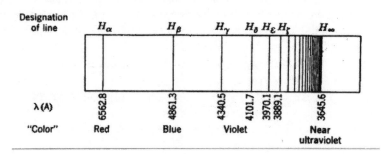

Figure 2
Balmer Line Series for Hydrogen

Balmer came up with the following equation that predicted the line spacing. But the "why is it like this" could not be answered. It was a puzzle that existed for many years.

The Balmer equation could be used to find the wavelength of the absorption/emission lines and was originally presented as follows (save for a notation change to give Balmer's constant as B):

$$\lambda = B\left(\frac{m^2}{m^2 - n^2}\right) = B\left(\frac{m^2}{m^2 - 2^2}\right)$$

Where
 λ is the wavelength.
 B is a constant with the value of 3.6450682×10^{-7} m or 364.50682 nm.
 n is equal to 2
 m is an integer such that $m > n$.

Wikipedia.org/wiki/Balmer_series. (On this and previous page also.)
But what does the number 656.28 represent in Figure 2 – and labeled as "red"? At least that could be understood. It represents the wavelength (656.28 nano-meter), so that the frequency and color of the associated radiation could be calculated. Note: 656.28 and 6562.8 represent different metric units.

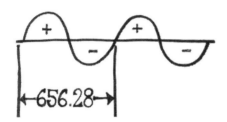

With the speed of light at 186,000 miles per second (300,000,000 meters per second), it is solvable. It is 4.57×10^{14} Hertz – a very high frequency.
The next number, 486.1 nm, "blue", represents a higher frequency, 6.32×10^{14} Hertz.
Beyond that, the Balmer series remained a mystery. This was to be expected as elements were understood at that time as like little solid marbles. As such, there was no room to accommodate spectroscopic ideas.

An offshoot of the interferometer shown on the previous page is the dual slit unit originally used by Young in 1803 to show the wave nature of light – in contrast to Newton's particle conception of light. Light first goes through a single slit and then through two additional slits and then onto a screen. The screen showed the two beams produced patterns of dark and bright patterns, showing interference (local cancellations) due to the wave nature of light.
(www.wikipedia.org/Young's_interference_experiment)

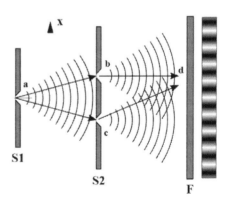

1895 Roentgen Discovers X-Rays.

Cathode ray tubes had been around for some time and they possessed strange "effects." Traveling exhibitioners showed eerie glows coming from them – sort of an early fluorescent light.

Roentgen was experimenting with them, with an AC voltage produced by an induction coil setup. This produced a square-wave AC voltage on top of a DC voltage. He discovered something strange, called "x-rays" because of their unknown character. His first x-ray photograph was of the bones in his wife's hand!

But what was this strange phenomenon? Was it coming from within the otherwise hard "marble" atoms? No one knew.

1897 J J Thompson Discovers the Electron with a Cathode Ray Tube.

J J Thompson ran a series of experiments with cathode ray tubes, similar to

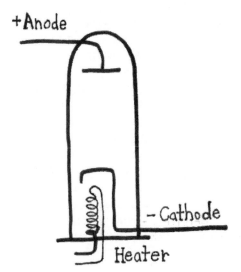

Roentgen's version. Shown here is a type of vacuum tube. (Of course, the tube requires DC Voltage applied to it in order to operate.)

The cathode is the plate with the connector at the lower right. (Below the cathode is a heater element. Vacuum tubes didn't work very well with a cold cathode.) The plate at the top is the anode.

Thompson detected something moving from the cathode to the anode. He called it a corpuscle, later it was labeled the electron. He determined that this corpuscle was negatively charged, could be deflected with magnets or a voltage field and was about one-thousandth the size of an atom of hydrogen. He also determined that whatever element he made the cathode from, the corpuscle remained the same size. Further, this "corpuscle" looked like a particle, not a wave.

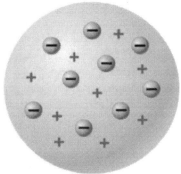

But what was it? Was it a "slimy" invisible film attached to the element in the cathode plate? Or was it a part of the atoms that made up the various elements? At the time, no one could answer this question. Thompson initially leaned towards viewing them as artifacts from the gas (air) remaining in the partially evacuated tube.

Later he set forth what became known as the "plum pudding" model of the atom. Electrons were objects "afloat" in a sea of positive charge.

http://2011modelsb.wikispaces.com/Group5

(Thomson_Plum_Pudding_Atomic_Model.jpg by Flinn)

1898 Curie's Discover Radioactive Elements.

Marie Curie began the work to isolate radium, thorium and polonium. She was later joined by her husband, Pierre Curie. The first clue had been Becquerel's discovery a year earlier of radioactivity due to the image formed on photographic plates accidentally exposed to some uranium salts.

Marie then used an instrument invented by her husband and discovered that pitchblende and torbernite ores had more evidence of "activity" than did uranium. The Curie's worked with these two substances and discovered thorium and polonium fairly quickly. Refined radium would take many additional years to isolate from pitchblende. Refined radium actually gave off an "unnatural" light so it could not be ignored.

Again, the important question was unanswerable. "Radioactivity" was coming from within the atoms! Was the atom really like a hard marble?

1900 Planck Develops Equation to Explain Black-Body Radiation.

The term "black-body" can refer to an unknown thing. In this case, it also meant a "body" painted black, so that it would not have colors to confuse what was being studied.

Black-body radiation had been known for some years. It was a problem in thermodynamics – the study of heat. It was studied in special furnaces where objects could be gradually heated or gradually allowed to cool off. Refer back a few pages to Figure 2.

To be heated was to gain energy. As an object is heated, it gradually changes color. Further, the heated object absorbed radiation (energy) only at set frequencies, depending upon the temperature. The same frequencies occurred as the object cooled off – emitted radiation. (It was by then known that the hotter temperatures had light of higher frequencies.) These specific frequencies varied when a different object was being heated. There was a "signature" to the frequencies – unique to each element.

The big puzzle was that it was expected that the heated object would give off light (frequency, energy) at all frequencies, perhaps only influenced by the rapidity of the heating/cooling cycle. Why did energy flow occur only at specific frequencies?

The light given off in the heating or cooling cycles could be examined with spectroscopy. This was how the specific frequencies were measured.

Max Planck had not been particularly interested in this phenomenon, but when informed of some recent attempts at explanation, he came up with his answer in a very short time. He was forced to agree that energy transfer was not continuous, but occurred in "buckets" of energy. "Buckets" of energy meant "quanta" of energy. (This was to be the beginning of Quantum Mechanics.) His formula included his famous Planck constant:

$$E = hv$$

Where E = energy, h = Planck's constant (6.6×10^{-34} Joules per second), and v = frequency. Planck's constant is a very small quantum of heat.

Energy transfer could only occur at this frequency – or even multiples of it. This was an empirical formula. Planck could not give a reason for this action. A formula without a "continuous" action was a violation of Classical Mechanics!

1905 Einstein Explains Photoelectric Effect with Photons of Light.

The photoelectric effect is a phenomenon showing that shining light upon metals can cause electrons to be knocked off the metals, travel through a vacuum and attach to another plate – sort of like what appears at the anode of the cathode ray tube, mentioned in an earlier section.

Historically, in 1887, Hertz had observed a change in electrical conductivity in one of his instruments that was due to ultraviolet light. In 1899, J J Thompson showed this effect in one of his cathode ray tubes with ultraviolet light and linked it with his recently discovered electrons. In 1902, Lenard showed that light intensity and frequency varied the current flow. However, the affect of frequency was unexpected. It hinted at Newton's light as particles!

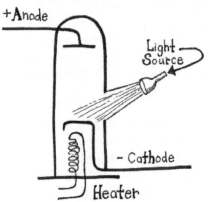

Einstein said that light traveled in discrete quantas of energy. The quantas were absorbed by the electrons until they became excited enough to break free from the cathode plate. Einstein called these quanta "photons."

(Years later, this experiment could not be replicated when the "plate" of the cathode was made of amorphous non-crystalline forms of the same metal plates, per Bill Lucas. So the experimental data is correct, but in the toroidal ring electron model energy from the light source flows in a continuous basis, not quanta, but excites electrons to threshold changes in their number of charge wraps only at specific accumulated energy amounts.)

1909 Geiger – Marsden Gold-Leaf Scattering Experiment.

This is normally referred to as the Rutherford gold-leaf experiment. Geiger and Marsden were two of his laboratory assistants. In 1904, J J Thompson had proposed his plum-pudding model of the atom, but Rutherford thought it was not adequate.

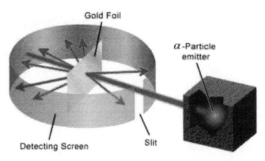

So he devised the gold-leaf experiment. A source of alpha-particles shot out particles through a very thin sheet of gold and unto a detector screen. Actually, the screen was made circular. It was expected that the alpha particles would go through the gold leaf, with little or no deflection. (It was known that the alpha particles were much heavier than the electrons in Thompson's plum-pudding model.) Image at www.bing.com/images/Rutherford_Gold-Leaf_Experiment.

Most of the alpha-particles did, indeed, pass straight through the gold leaf and on to the detector screen. Others took minor to significant deflections. The biggest surprise was that about one alpha particle in 8,000 (or 20,000) didn't hit the screen at all! It was bounced straight back at the alpha particle source.

Rutherford expressed his surprise as follows: "It was almost as incredible as if you fired a 15-inch [artillery] shell at a piece of tissue paper and it came back and hit you!" After much thought and calculation, Rutherford wrote a 1911 paper on what he had found.

First, Rutherford concluded that the Thompson plum pudding model was wrong. Second, the atom had a heavy nucleus – accounting for the one in 8,000

bounce-backs. The smaller electrons were around this nucleus – in circular orbits, much like planets around the sun. This was his solar model of the atom. It was known to have major problems, but he still proposed it. The major problem was that, according to Maxwell's equations of electrodynamics, the orbital motion of the electrons around the nucleus meant that they should emit radiation due to the centripetal motion of their orbit. This would lead to a loss of energy and collapse of the atom.

(www.atomictheory.tumblr.com (Bohr-model.png, by Morgan Aumick.)

NOTE: At this time the nucleus remained like a little hard marble – surrounded by the newly discovered electrons.

1913 Bohr Proposes the Quantum Solar Model of the Atom.

Niels Bohr was a newly minted PhD when he published his paper in 1913. Earlier, he had spent a year in England, first working for J J Thompson but later under Rutherford. He was sure that the solution to the problems with Rutherford's solar model of the atom must somehow be tied to Max Planck's idea of the quantum of motion.

Taking a hint from a friend, he then looked at the 1885 Balmer series in spectroscopy. He realized that the jumps in frequency plotted there could be related to Planck's work and then tied to the Rutherford solar model of the atom. To that end, he realized that new "physical" principles were needed.

• = Mathematical Points

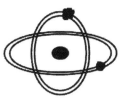

Rutherford Atom

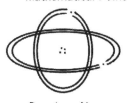

Quantum Atom

The problem with a physically sized electron, as Bohr knew, was two-fold: First, it was the old problem of the radiation of energy – and the frequency at which it occurred. Second, his solution to that dilemma required the electron to "jump" instantaneously to a higher or lower orbit, i.e., orbits of different diameters. That was something that only a mathematical point-sized object could accomplish. (Physical sized objects had inertia to overcome, as well as the orbital energy radiation problem.)

• = Mathematical Points

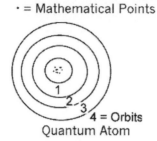

4 = Orbits

Rutherford Atom

Quantum Atom

To that end, Bohr postulated that the orbiting electrons moved in defined orbits. They could only "jump" to other orbits that were whole number multiples, in accordance with Planck's work. As said earlier, this mathematically required reducing the electrons to mathematical points. This was understandable to mathematicians, but not to physicists!

These possible orbits were numbered. There were distinct frequencies associated with these various diameter orbits, depending upon the element involved.

(People interested in cars or other big engines are prone to ask another question: "What are the 'rev's' of this electron?" Revs refers to "revolutions per minute" or RPM. The speed at which this orbital motion was happening is generally thought to be the speed of light but some say somewhat slower. The orbital diameter is "very" small," on the order of 1 nm – that is one millionth of a meter diameter. Well, the rev's can be in the range of 3 trillion RPMs!)

No wonder the mathematics to "understand" this is complicated – and that mathematics is about all there is. Thus was born quantum mechanics. Succeeding decades were spent trying to adjust this theory to reality.

1915 Parson Proposes Magneton Model of the Electron.

Parson was working on his master's degree in chemistry at the time. Thus, he was not credentialed like the other theoreticians. His model did not succeed in that climate. By the early 1920s, it had disappeared.

The Parson magneton concept has been revived and revised as the toroidal ring model of the atom. Let us see how it applies to these significant events in this era of science that we have just reviewed.

1885 Balmer Series in Spectroscopy.

The toroidal ring electron model features a "charge ring" in a circle. Physically, as energy enters or leaves the toroidal ring, electrical stresses occur due to the changing energy levels. Accordingly, the charge ring changes the number of "wraps" in response. This, in turn, changes the ring's diameter. (The drawing does not reflect this changing ring diameter.)

Figure 9
Electron Fundamental or Ground State

Figure 10
Electron 1st Harmonic or Excited State

Figure 11
Electron 2nd Harmonic or Excited State

Courtesy: Common Sense Science

The frequency for transmission or reception of energy changes accordingly. The Balmer line series reflects this physical process. This correlates with the changes in diameter of the ring electron.

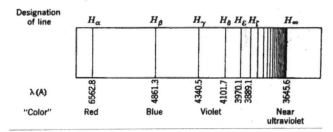

Figure 2
Balmer Line Series for Hydrogen
Wikipedia.org/wiki/Balmer_series

Looking again at Young's 1803 dual slit interferometer, the question is whether light is a photon or a charge with attached electric and magnetic fields.

Consider when electrons pass through the initial slit (S1). If the electrons are the mathematical point of quantum mechanics, they are "observed" (interpreted) as either a wave or a particle.

If it is performed with toroidal ring electrons in mind, entry through S1 is performed with physical objects – the toroidal ring and associated magnetic and electric fields. The toroidal rings pass through the secondary slits, and their fields pass through and create the interference patterns indicated.
(www.wikipedia.org/Young's_interference_experiment)

So, the wave-particle duality is a consequence of the point particle electron. With the toroidal ring electron, both the particle (toroidal ring) and the wave (electric and magnetic fields) exist simultaneously.

1895 Roentgen Discovers X-Rays.
The outer electrons in certain elements used as a cathode are good conductors, meaning that the outer valence electrons in a toroidal ringed atom are looser bound than the inner electrons. They can thus be removed from an atom by an applied high frequency voltage. The ring electron is a particle that, with proper energy input, can excite as high frequency x-rays.

1897 J J Thompson Discovers the Electron with a Cathode Ray Tube.
Again, the outer electrons in certain elements used as a cathode are good conductors, meaning that the outer valence electrons in an toroidal ringed atom are looser bound than the other electrons. They can thus be removed from an atom by an applied voltage. The toroidal ring electron is a particle of unit charge.

1898 Curie's Discover Radioactive Elements.
Some of the large atoms do not have completely filled valence rings of electrons – nor similar completely filled positions in the nucleus. This results in imbalances in the net total of electric and magnetic fields that attempt to hold everything in balance. Large imbalances in fields can result in the random loss of some electrons, protons and/or neutrons – this is radioactivity.

1900 Planck Develops Equation to Explain Black-Body Radiation.
Heated bodies are energized bodies. Thus, ring electrons, protons and neutrons are experiencing stress on the net balance of electric and magnetic forces and then quickly change the number of "wraps" of the charge ring – the ring diameter changing in response. This transient event creates bursts of energy at specific frequencies which matches the Balmer series in spectroscopy.

1905 Einstein Explains Photoelectric Effect with Photons of Light.
Light is energy – but it probably isn't photons, just moving electric and magnetic fields. Light (electric and magnetic fields) falling on a metal is like a transmitter sending energy to a receiving antenna – in this case, the electrons of the metal. At the right frequency, energy input occurs and electrons get more "wraps" in their charge ring. Some of the outer electrons become energized enough to allow them to leave their atoms and become free electrons.

Amorphous metals in the cathode do not have the atoms aligned regularly, thus they will not all act like energy absorbers. They will not display the photoelectric effect that "normal" versions of the same elements display.

1909 Geiger – Marsden Gold-Leaf Scattering Experiment.

Rutherford's experiment shows the primary emptiness of an atom. This is in accordance with the toroidal ringed model. Also, while the charge ring is "small" in diameter, the charge cross-section is much smaller. No observing instrument can come close to resolving an object that small.

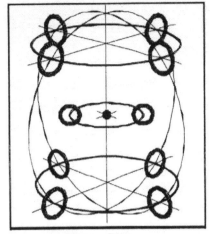

Neon Atom.
Courtesy CommonSenseScience.org

Electron $n = 2$

Figure 10
Electron 1st Harmonic or Excited State

Electron $n = 3$

Figure 11
Electron 2nd Harmonic or Excited State

1
2 3
4 = Orbits
Quantum Atom

SCR Atom

1913 Bohr Proposes the Quantum Solar Model of the Atom.

In place of mathematical points jumping between various "discrete orbits," the toroidal ring electron operates on the principle that the number of charge ring "wraps" changes due to varying energy levels. Charge ring "wraps" follow electrical engineering principles, while Quantum Mechanics has to postulate an abstract mathematical model with increasing levels of unbelievability.

As 1920 drew near, the nucleus was still viewed as a single entity. Later work with higher energy "rays" revealed that the nucleus was composed of constituent protons and neutrons – and their associated electric and magnetic fields.

Quantum Mechanics did not have this physical insight about the fields, so it had to formulate mathematical abstractions to hold together the quantum atom. Later stages of research employed "atom smashers" and associated particle detectors. A large quantity of bewildering phenomena were observed.

Quantum Mechanics currently requires 61 or so mathematical entities to acknowledge all subatomic phenomena – referred to as the "standard model." Most of these 61 "items" are unstable, with life-spans much less than second. Perhaps these items are debris, not actual items.

With the toroidal ring electron model, the tracks emerging from these detectors reflect the debris field emerging from the collisions of toroidal ring electrons, protrons and neutrons. Being charge rings, when they collide, the result is either electrical short circuits – or open circuits and resultant CEMF and arcing – with the dissolution of electric and magnetic fields – and release of energy.

B1   *A Beginners Guide to Constructing the Universe*, Michael S. Schneider. Harper Perennial Books, New York, 1994.
      Pages 23 *fn*; 71.

B2   *Christianity and Classical Culture*, Jaroslav Pelikan. Yale University Press, New Haven and London, 1993.
      Page 25.

B3   *Rock-Solid Faith*, Bert Thompson. Apologetics Press, Montgomery, 2000.
      Page 30.

B4   *Against Method*, Paul Feyerabend. Verso Edition, Thetford Press, Thetford, Norfolk, 1978.
      Pages 31; 145 *fn*; 225 *fn*; 226; 267.

B5   *Causality and Modern Science*, Mario Bunge. Dover Publications, Inc., New York, 1979.
      Page 45.

B6   *The Physics of the Stoics*, S. Sambursky. Princeton University Press, Princeton, 1987.
      Pages 49; 97 *fn*.

B7   *U. S. News and World Report*, April 4, 1983, page 36. (A special issue devoted to religion in America.)
      Page 49.

B8   *The Humanist Alternative*, Paul Kurz, editor. Promethius, New York, 1973.
      Page 50.

B9   *The Everlasting Man*, G. K. Chesterton. Image Books, Garden City, New Jersey, 1955.
      Pages 59; 111.

B10   *The Main Stream of Mathematics*, Edna E. Kramer. The Scholar's Bookshelf, Princeton Junction, New Jersey, 1988.
      Pages 62-63; 81.

B11   *Mathematics: the Loss of Certainty*, Morris Kline. Oxford University Press, New York, 1980.
      Pages 12 *fn*; 63; 66; 78; 88; 94-95; 149; 155; 171; 173 *fn*; 174; 175 *fn*; 176; 179; 181; 203; 260; 281.

B12   *The Theology of Arithmetic*, Iamblichus. Phanes Press, Grand Rapids, 1988. Translated by Robin Waterfield.
      Page 63.

B13   *Pythagoras Revived*, Dominic O'Meara. Clarendon Press, Oxford, 1990.
      Pages 64-65; 70 *fn*; 98.

B14   *What is Mathematics, Really?* Reuben Hersh. Oxford University Press, New York and Oxford, 1997.
      Pages 12 *fn*; 17 *fn*; 34; 65; 89 *fn*; 149; 156; 173 *fn*; 175 *fn*; 177; 178; 179; 217; 271.

B15   *Study and Difficulties of Mathematics*, August DeMorgan. The Open Court Publishing Company, LaSalle, 1943 reprint of 1831 original.
      Pages 66-67.

B16   *Substance and Function*, Ernst Cassirer. Dover Publishing, Inc., New York, 1953 edition of 1923 original.
      Pages 67; 255.

B17   *Ray's Mathematical Series*, Joseph Ray. American Book Company, New York, 1866.
      Page 67.

B18   *Oral Arithmetic*, Wentworth and Smith. The Athenian Press, Ginn & Co., New York, New York, 1910.
      Page 68.

B19   *Teleology Revisited*, Ernest Nagel. Columbia University Press, New York, 1979.
      Pages 69; 182.

B20   *Science Awakening 1*, B. L. van der Waerden. The Scholar's Bookshelf, Princeton Junction, New Jersey, 1988.
      Pages 69; 72; 75-76; 87.

B21   *Greek Mathematical Thought and the Origin of Algebra*, Jacob Klein. Dover Publications, New York, 1968. Translated by Eva Brann.
      Pages 70; 77; 78; 82.

B22　　*The Great Mathematicians*, H. W. Turnbull. New York University Press, New York, reprint of 1929 original.
Page 70.

B23　　*The Mystery of Number*, Annemarie Schimmel. Oxford University Press, Oxford, 1993.
Pages 70; 149.

B24　　*Greek Mathematical Philosophy*, Edward A Maziarz and Thomas Greenwood. Barnes and Noble, 1995 reprint of 1968 Frederick Ungar Publishing.
Pages 72; 98.

B25　　*Parmenides of Elea*. University of Toronto Press, Toronto, 1984. Translated by David Gallop.
Page 73.

B26　　*A Commentary on the First Book of Euclid's Elements*, Proclus. Princeton University Press, Princeton, 1970. Translated by Glenn R. Morrow.
Pages 74; 99.

B27　　*Farewell to Reason*, Paul Feyerabend. Verso, London, 1987.
Pages 74; 75; 221; 260.

B28　　*Plato: The Collected Dialogues*, Plato. Princeton University Press, Princeton, 1989. Edited and translated by Edith Hamilton and Huntington Cairns.
Pages 75; 76; 77; 79; 80; 84; 85; 86; 89; 93; 113-114.

B29　　*Plato and Aristotle*, Giovanni Reale. State University of New York Press, Albany, 1990. Translated by John R Catan.
Pages 77; 79; 89; 99.

B30　　*Towards a New Interpretation of Plato*, Giovanni Reale. The Catholic University of America Press, Washington, DC, 1997. Translated by John R Catan and Richard Davies.
Page 79.

B31　　*The Six Enneads of Plotinus*, Plotinus. Forgotten Books, 2007. Translated by Stephan MacKenna and B S Page.
Pages 79; 86.

B32　　*Plato and the Foundations of Metaphysics*, Hans Joachim Krämer. State University of New York Press, Albany, 1990.
Pages 79-80; 84 *fn*.

B33　　*Hamlet's Mill*, Giorgio de Santillana and Hertha von Dechend. Gambit Incorporated, Boston, 1969.
Pages 81; 119.

B34　　*A Sourcebook on Mathematics*, David Eugene Smith. Dover Publications, Inc., New York, 1959 reprint of 1929 original.
Page 81.

B35　　*The Pythagorean Sourcebook and Library*, Phanes Press, Grand Rapids, 1987. Compiled and Edited by Kenneth Sylvan Guthrie.
Pages 85; 103-104; 136.

B36　　*Platonism*, Paul Elmore More. Greenwood Press, New York, 1969.
Page 88.

B37　　*A History of Mathematics*, Carl Boyer. Princeton University Press, Princeton, 1985 reprint of 1968 original.
Pages 87; 91.

B38　　*Wisdom of the West*, Bertrand Russell. Crescent Books, Inc., New York, 1959.
Pages 88; 98; 99.

B39　　*The Theoretic Arithmetic of the Pythagoreans*, Thomas Taylor. Samuel Weiser, New York, 1972 reprint of 1816 original.
Page 91.

B40　　*The Complete Works of Aristotle*, Aristotle. Princeton University Press, Bollingen Series, Princeton, 1984. Edited and translated by Jonathan Barnes.
Pages 91; 99; 108; 109.

B41　　*The Open Society and its Enemies*, (Volume 1: Plato), Karl R. Popper. Princeton University Press, Princeton, 1971.
Pages 92 *fn*; 105 *fn*.

B42   *To Save the Phenomena*, Pierre Duhem. University of Chicago Press, Chicago, 1969. Translated by Edmund Doland and Chaninah Maschler.
Pages 92; 106; 225 *fn*; 258.

B43   *God's Philosophers*, James Hannam. Icon Books, London, 2010.
Pages 99; 133-134; 137; 139.

B44   *The Mechanization of the World Picture*, E. J. Dijksterhuis. Princeton University Press, Princeton, 1986. Translated by C. Dikshoorn.
Pages 101; 148; 206; 207; 225 *fn*.

B45   *From the Closed World to the Infinite Universe*, Alexandre Koyre. The Johns Hopkins University Press, Baltimore, Maryland, 1974.
Pages 103; 152; 178.

B46   *The Development of Rationalism and Empiricism*, Giorgio de Santillana and Edgar Zilsel. The University of Chicago Press, Chicago, 1970. 1970 reprint of 1941 original.
Pages 104; 105.

B47   *The Beginnings of Western Science*, David C. Lindberg. The University of Chicago Press, Chicago, 1992.
Pages 130; 134; 135; 136; 138; 139.

B48   *God in the Dock*, C. S. Lewis. William B. Eerdmans Publishing Company, Grand Rapids, 1970.
Pages 106; 261.

B49   *The Ante-Nicene Fathers*, Roberts and Donaldson, editors. Wm. B. Eerdmans Publishing Co., Grand Rapids, Michigan, 1989 reprint of 1886 original.
Pages 113; 116; 117; 120-123; 124; 125; 128; 260.

B50   *Giordano Bruno and the Hermetic Tradition*, Francis A. Yates. The University of Chicago Press, Chicago, 1991 reprint of 1964 original.
Pages 123; 144.

B51   *The Eternal Hermes*, Antoine Faivre. Phanes Press, Grand Rapids, 1995. Translated by Joscelyn Godwin.
Page 123.

B52   *The Hymns of Hermes*, G. R. S. Mead. Phanes Press, Grand Rapids, 1991.
Page 123-124.

B53   *Essays on Magic*, in *Cause, Principle, and Unity*, Giordano Bruno. Cambridge University Press, Cambridge, 1998. Edited and translated by Richard J. Blackwell and Robert de Lucca.
Page 124.

B54   *Science and Technology in World History*, McClellan III and Dorn. The Johns Hopkins University Press, Baltimore, 2006.
Pages 134; 160; 161.

B55   *Wheels, Clocks and Rockets*, Roy Porter. W W Norton and Company, New York, 2001.
Pages 134; 160.

B56   *The Age of Reason*, Stuart Hampshire. New American Library, NY, 1961.
Pagea 136; 150.

B57   *The Fall of Man and the Foundations of Science*, Peter Harrison. Cambridge University Press, New York, 2009.
Page 137.

B58   *Nicholas of Cusa On Learned Ignorance*, Jasper Hopkins. Arthur J. Banning Press, Minneapolis, 1985, second edition.
Pages 139-140.

B59   *The Intellectual History of Europe*, Friedrich Heer. The World Publishing Company, Cleveland, 1966 translation of 1953 original.
Pages 140; 146; 163-164.

B60   *Oration on the Dignity of Man*, Giovanni Pico della Mirandola. Regnery Publishing, Inc. Washington, D.C., 1956. Translated by A. Robert Caponigri.
Page 140-141.

B61   *The Age of Adventure*, Giorgio de Santillana. New American Library, New York, 1956.
Page 9 *fn*; 141.

B62   *The Sleepwalkers*, Arthur Koestler. The MacMillan Company, New York, 1963 reprint of
          1959 original.
          Pages 142 *fn*; 203-204; 225 *fn*.
B63   *The Individual and the Cosmos in Renaissance Philosophy*, Ernst Cassirer. Harper
          Torchbooks, New York, 1963 translation of 1927 original.
          Pages 143; 155; 163.
B64   *Giordano Bruno*, J Lewis McIntyre. MacMillan and Co, New York, 1903.
          Pages 144-145.
B65   *Galileo at Work*, Stillman Drake. The University of Chicago Press, Chicago, 1978.
          Page 148 *fn*.
B66   *Science and Religion in Seventeenth Century England*, Richard S. Westfall. Ann Arbor
          Paperbacks, Ann Arbor, 1973.
          Pages 150; 152.
B67   *Discourse on Method* and *The Meditations*, Renee Descartes. Translated by F E
          Sutcliffe. Penguin Classics, 1983.
          Page 151-152.
B68   *Mathematics and the Search for Knowledge*, Morris Kline. Oxford University Press, 1985.
          Page 152.
B69   *Voltaire Almighty*, Roger Person. Bloomsbury Publishing, New York, 2005.
          Page 152.
B70   *Essential Works of David Hume*, David Hume. Bantam Books, New York, 1965.
          Page 153.
B71   *Miracles*, C. S. Lewis. MacMillan Publishing Co., Inc., New York, 1978 edition of 1947
          original.
          Page 154.
B72   *The Age of Enlightenment*, Sir Isaiah Berlin. New American Library. NY, 1960.
          Page 154.
B73   *What is Mathematics?*, Richard Courant and Herbert Robbins. Oxford University Press,
          Oxford, 1978 reprint of 1941 original.
          Page 153.
B74   *Philosophy: Who Needs It*, Ayn Rand. Bobbs-Merrill Company,Inc., Indianapolis, 1982.
          Pages 157.
B75   *The Road of Science and the Ways to God,* Stanley Jaki. University of Chicago Press,
          Chicago, 1978.
          Page 157.
B76   *The Physical World of Late Antiquity*, S. Sambursky. Princeton University Press,
          Princeton, 1987.
          Page 158.
B77   *Representing and Intervening*, Ian Hacking. Cambridge University Press New York, 2008.
          Page 159.
B78   *History Of Mathematics*, D. E. Smith. Dover Publications, Inc., New York, 1958 reprint of
          1923 original.
          Page 161.
B79   *The Age of Reason*, Thomas Paine. Freethought Publishing Company, London, 1880.
          Page 162.
B80   *The Early Church*, Henry Chadwick. Dorset Press, New York, 1986.
          Page 163.
B81   *The Ancient Religion of the Gentiles*, Edward Herbert. John Nutt, London, 1705.
          Page 163.
B82   *Foundations of Mathematical Logic*, Haskell B. Curry. Dover Publications, Inc., New York,
          1977.
          Page 173.
B83   *The Emperor's New Mind*, Roger Penrose. Penguin Books, New York, 1991 reprint of
          1989 original.
          Pages 173 *fn*; 186; 221.
B84   *Science and Hypothesis*, Henri Poincaré. Dover Publications, New York, 1952 reprint of
          1905 original.
          Pages 171; 225.

B85   *On Scientific Thinking*, edited by Ryan Tweney, Michael Doherty, and Clifford Mynatt. Columbia University Press, New York, 1981.
       Pages 178.

B86   *Science at the Crossroads*, Sir Herbert Dingle. Martin Brian & O'Keeffe, London, 1972.
       Pages 181; 220; 306.

B87   *How the Laws of Physics Lie*, Nancy Cartwright. Clarendon Press, Oxford, 1983.
       Pages 183; 308.

B88   *Sky and Telescope*, February, 1996.
       Pages 182-183; 308.

B89   *The Aim and Structure of Physical Theory*, Pierre Duhem. Athenum, New York, 1977 translation of 1914 original.
       Pages 183; 308.

B90   *Great Ideas of Modern Mathematics*, Jagit Singh. Dover Publications, New York, 1959.
       Pages 185; 282.

B91   *Gravitation Versus Relativity*, Charles Lane Poor. G. P. Putnam's Sons, New York, 1922.
       Pages 188-189; 213.

B92   *Engineering and the Mind's Eye*, Eugene Ferguson. MIT Press, Cambridge, 1999.
       Pages 135; 190.

B93   *Mathematical Thought from Ancient to Modern Times*, Volume 3, Morris Kline. Oxford University Press, Oxford, 1990.
       Pages 176; 196 *fn*; 199.

B94   *An Outline of Philosophy*, Bertrand Russell. Meridian Books, New York, 1974 reprint of 1927 edition.
       Pages 200.

B95   T*he Metaphysical Foundations of Modern Science*, E. A. Burtt. Humanities Press, Atlantic Highlands, 1980 reprint of 1952 original.
       Pages 200; 201.

B96   *Science and the Modern World*, Alfred North Whitehead. The Free Press, New York, 1967 reprint of 1925 original.
       Pages 200-201.

B97   *Theories of the Universe*, Milton Munitz, editor. Free Press, Glencoe, 1957.
       Pages 204; 205.

B98   *Universal Natural History and Theory of the Heavens*, Immanuel Kant, translated by Ian Johnson. Richer Resources Publications, Arlington, 2008 translation of 1755 original.
       Page 205; 208 *fn*.

B99   *Cosmotheros*, Christiaan Huygens. Eighteenth Century Collections Online, print editions. Reprint of 1762 translation of 1698 original.
       Page 206.

B100   *The Mysterious Universe*, Sir James Jeans. The MacMillan Company, New York, 1932.
       Pages 211-212; 213.

B101   *Relativity*, Albert Einstein. Crown Publishers, Inc. New York, 1961. Translated by Robert Lawson.
       Page 213.

B102   *Sky and Telescope*, Oct. 1983.
       Pages 15 *fn*; 213.

B103   *The Atom in the History of Human Thought*. Bernard Pullman. Oxford University Press, New York, 1998.
       Pages 17 *fn*; 216; 221.

B104   *The Journal of Common Sense Science*, ed. Dave Bergman. www.commonsensescience.com. Volume 2 Number 2.
       Pages 19 *fn*; 216; 237.

B105   *How is Quantum Field Theory Possible?*, Sunny Y Auyong. Oxford University Press, New York, 1995.
       Pages 13 *fn*; 218.

B106   *The Investigation of the Physical World*, G. Toraldo DiFrancia. Cambridge University Press, Cambridge, 1981 translation of 1976 original.
       Pages 219.

B107   *Causality and Chance in Modern Physics*, David Bohm. University of Pennsylvania Press, Philadelphia, 1971 reprint of 1957 original.
Page 219.

B108   *Philosophical Foundations of Quantum Theory*, edited by Harvey Brown and Rom Harre. Clarendon Press, Oxford, 1990.
Page 220.

B109   *How is Quantum Field Theory Possible?*, Sunny Y Auyang. Oxford University Press, New York, 1995.
Page 220.

B110   *A Brief History of Time*, Stephen Hawkins. Bantam Books, New York, 1990.
Page 221.

B111   *The Trouble with Physics*, Lee Smolin. A Mariner Book, Houghton Mifflin Company, Boston. 2007 copy of 2006 original.
Pages 221-222; 229.

B112   *The Evolution of Scientific Thought from Newton to Einstein*, A. d'Abro. Dover Publications, New York, 1950 reprint of 1927 original.
Page 222.

B113   *Beyond Einstein, The Cosmic Quest for the Theory of the Universe*, Dr. Michio Kaku and Jennifer Trainer. Bantam Books, New York, 1987.
Page 223-224.

B114   *Astronomy and Cosmology: A Modern Course*, Fred Hoyle. W. H. Freeman and Company, San Francisco, 1975.
Page 224 *fn*.

B115   *The Galileo Connection: Resolving Conflicts Between Science and the Bible*, Charles E. Hummel. InterVarsity Press, Downers Grove, 1986.
Pages 225 *fn;* 276.

B116   *Sky and Telescope*, June, 1990.
Pages 225.

B117   *God and the Astronomers*, Robert Jastrow. Warner Books, New York, 1980.
Page 227.

B118   *The Lighter Side of Gravity*, Jayant V. Narlikar. W. H. Freeman and Company, San Francisco, 1982.
Page 227.

B119   *Two New Sciences*, Galileo Galilei. The University of Wisconsin Press, Madison, 1974 translation of original by Stillman Drake.
Page 245.

B120   *The Angel and the Machine*, E. Stanley Jones. Sherwood Sudgen & Company, Peru, II, 1991.
Page 247.

B121   *The Blind Watchmaker*, Richard Dawkins. W W Norton and Co, New York, 1986.
Page 250.

B122   *Mere Christianity*, C. S. Lewis. MacMillan Publishing Co., Inc., New York, 1977.
Page 250.

B123   *The Age of Ideology*, Henry D Aiken. Mentor Book, The New American Library, New York, 1963.
Pages 17 *fn*; 257.

B124   *C S Lewis's Dangerous Idea*, Victor Reppert. InterVarsity Press, Downers Grove, 2003.
Pages 274; 300.

B125   *The Last Word*, Thomas Nagel. Oxford University Press, Oxford, 1997.
Pages 274; 301.

B126   *The Dreams of Reason*, Rene Dubos. Columbia University Press, New York, 1961.
Page 281.

B127   *From Dawn to Decadence,* Jacques Barzun. Harper Collins, New York, 2000.
Page 283.

B128   *Science and the Unseen World*, Sir Arthur Stanley Eddington. George Allen & Unwin Ltd, London, 1929.
Page 284.

B129   *The Nature of the Physical World*, Sir Arthur Stanley Eddington. Ann Arbor Paperbacks,
        Ann Arbor. 1978 reprint of 1928 original.
        Page 284.

Internet References

www.commonsensescience.org
Pages 19 *fn*, 230, 238, 310.

www.commons.wikimedia.org/wiki/image: Sanzio_01_Plato_Aristotle.jpg. Picture of School of Athens.
Pages 100, 141

www. wikipedia.com. Early invention photographs.
Pages 135, 136.

www.en.wikipedia.org/wiki/William_of_Ockham. Quote from William of Ockham.
Page 138.

www.en.wikipedia.org/wiki/paracelsus. Quote on Paracelcus.
Page 142.

www.wikipedia.org/wiki/philolaus and *www.plato.stanford.edu/entries/philolaus/.* References on old
astronomical views.
Page 142 *fn*.

www.wikipedia.com. Drawings of later inventions.
Pages 160, 161.

http://creation.com/pierre-simon-laplace-the-nebular-hypothesis. See footnote 2.
Page 205.

www.en.wikipedia.org/wiki/Nebular_hypothesis.
Page 206.

www.extinctionshift.com/. Reference on starlight bending limitations.
Page 214.

http://creation.com/our-galaxy-is-the-centre-of-the-universe-quantized-redshifts-show on quanticized redshift
data.
Page 225.

http://creation.com/cmb-conundrums. Information on the cosmic background radiation data which indicates
an embarrassing "axis of evil."
Page 225.

www.twinkle_toes_engineering.home.comsat.net for electron-positron tracks.
Page 233.

www.holoscience.com for information on the Electric Universe.
Page 239.

http://en.wikipedia.org/wiki/Quadratic_equation.
Page 304.

http://en.wikipedia.org/wiki/Cubic_function.
Page 306.

http://en.wikipedia.org/wiki/Quintic_Function.
Page 307.

Wikipedia.org/wiki/Balmer_series._.
Page 321.

www.wikipedia.org/Young's_interference_experiment.
Page 321.

http://2011modelsb.wikispaces.com/Group5 (Thomson_Plum_Pudding_Atomic_Model.jpg by Flinn)
Page 322.

www.bing.com/images/Rutherford_Gold-Leaf_Experiment.
Page 325.

www.atomictheory.tumblr.com (Bohr-model.png, by Morgan Aumick)
Page 325.

Bible Quotations

KJV (King James Version)

Genesis 1:1:	vii; 1; 112; 115; 126; 131; 151; 125; 247; 254; 256.
Deuteronomy 29:29a:	21.
Joshua 10:11-14:	109.
Psalms 104:8:	38
Proverbs 1:7:	iv; 6; 110.
Proverbs 24:1:	vii
Isaiah 64:8:	44
Lamentations 3:19:	252 *fn.*
Daniel 1:4	250.
Wisdom of Solomon 11:20:	164.
Matthew 5:3:	289.
Matthew 5:18:	45.
John 1:3a:	22.
John 14:6a:	22.
John 18:38:	22; 260.
Acts 17:16-34:	*1;* 22; 58.
Acts 19:19:	124.
Romans 1:20:	*113;* 169; 174; 256; 259; 275; 302.
Ephesians 4:17-24:	286.
Ephesians 6:12:	26 *fn.*
Colossians 2:8:	21; 115.
I Timothy 1:4:	*123.*
I Timothy 3:15b:	ix.
I Timothy 4:1:	71 *fn.*
I Timothy 6:20:	21; 115; 122; 128; 250.
I John 4:1:	71 *fn.*
Revelation 13:18:	66.

Other books referenced, but not quoted from:
A Free Man's Worship, Bertrand Russell. Page 176 *fn.*
Almagest, Ptolemy. Page 4; 105.
A Magneton Theory of the Structure of the Atom, A N Parsons. Page 234.
Ancient Philosophy, Mystery and Magic, Peter Kingsley. Pages 62 *fn;* 70 *fn;* 146 *fn.*
Annals of the World, Bishop James Usshur. Page 109 *fn.*
Bondage of the Will, Martin Luther. Page 164 *fn.*
Book of the Revolutions of the Heavenly Spheres, Nicholas Copernicus. Pages 142.
Chance and Necessity, Jacques Monod. Page 159 *fn.*
Cosmos and Creator, Fr. Stanley Jaki. Pages 147 *fn,* 150.
Darwin's Black Box, Michael Behe. Page 189.
Elements, Euclid. Pages 3; 4; 11; 16; 78 *fn;* 95; 103; 126; *257.*
Enchiridion, Erasmus. Page 164 *fn.*
Eosagoge, Porphyry. Page 135.

Ethics, Spinoza. Page 170.
Galileo at Work, Stillman Drake. Page 225 *fn.*
Galileo, Science, and the Church, Jerome Langford. Page 225 *fn.*
Genetic Entropy and the Mystery of the Genome, John Sanford. Page 250.
Geography, Ptolemy. Page 4; 136 *fn.*
God and the Philosophers, Thomas Morris, Ed. Page 44 *fn.*
In Job's Balances, Lev Shestov. Page 27 *fn.*
Incompleteness Theorem for Formally Undecideable Systems, Kurt Gödel. Pages 12; 177.
Infinitesimal, Amir Alexander. Page 152.
Janus; A Summing Up, Arthur Koestler. Pages 10; 247.
Manual of Harmonics, Nichomachus. Pages 71 *fn*; 85 *fn.*
Mathematical Principles of Natural Philosophy, Sir Isaac Newton. Page 153.
Mathematics and the Metaphysician, Bertrand Russell. Page 174.
Nature. Page 247.
Observations on Experimental Philosophy, Margaret Cavendish. Page *137.*
On Formally Undecideable Propositions of Principia Mathematica and Related Systems, Kurt
Goedel. Page 177.
On Magic, Giordano Bruno. Page *144.*
On the Infinity of Worlds, Giordano Bruno. Page 145.
Origin and Destiny of the Earth's Magnetic Field, Thomas Barnes. Page 270.
Physics for the Future, Thomas Barnes. Pages 230 *fn*; 270 *fn.*
Pimander, Ficino. Page 140.
Planets and Perception, William Sheehan. Page 48 *fn*; 195 *fn.*
Plato at the Googleplex, Rebecca Goldstein, Page 33 *fn*; 87 *fn.*
Principia Mathematica, Whitehead and Russell. Page 176; 177.
Proofs and Refutations, Imre Lakatos. Page 175 *fn.*
Reasons to Believe (Journal), Hugh Ross. Page 56 *fn.*
Religion and Science, Bertrand Russell. Page 248 *fn.*
Scientific American (Journal). Pages 262.
Seeing Red: Redshifts, Cosmology and Academic Science, Halton C. Arp. Pages 259 fn; 259 *fn.*
Space Medium, Thomas Barnes. Page 230 *fn.*; 270 *fn.*
Symposium, Plato. Page 125.
Tetrabiblios, Ptolemy. Page 4.
That Hideous Strength, C. S. Lewis. Pages 281.
The Ash Wednesday Supper, Giordano Bruno. Page 144.
The Case for the Ring Electron, H S Allen. Page *234.*
The Chronicles of Narnia, C. S. Lewis. Page 263.
The Consolation of Philosophy, Boethius. Page 261 *fn.*
The Copernican Revolution, Thomas Kuhn. Page 225 *fn.*
The Crime of Galileo, Giorgio de Santillana. Page 225 *fn.*
The Exhortation to Philosophy, Iamblichus. Page 84 *fn.*
The Essential Spinoza, Michal Morgan. Page 150 *fn.*
The Great Turning Point, Terry Mortenson. Page 209 *fn.*
The Methodology of Scientific Research, Imre Lakatos. Page 47 *fn.*
The Nature of the Gods, Cicero. Page 96.
The Origin and Destiny of the Earth's Magnetic Field, Thomas Barnes. Page 270.
The Passion of the Western Mind, Richard Tarnas. Page 13 *fn*; 145; 218 *fn.*
The Sleepwalkers, Arthur Koestler. Page 258.
The Story of Inventions, Frank Bachman. Page 135; 161.
The Structure of Scientific Revolutions, Thomas Kuhn. Page 223.
The Universal Force, Bill Lucas. Pages 231 *fn*, 238.

Authors Cited in Chapter Introductions.
Henry Aiken   Page 244.
Anonymous   Page 193.
Saint Basil   Page 97.
Niels Bohr   Page 193.
Girolamo Cardano   Page 168.

Rudolph Carnap   Page 193.
Nancy Cartwright   Page 193.
G. K. Chesterton   Pages 168; 244.
Nicholas of Cusa   Page 168.
Dijksterhuis   Page 57.
Paul Feyerabend   Pages 244; 279.
J Daniel Fernie   Page 244.
Julienne Ford   Page 244.
Galileo Galilei   Page 168.
Werner Heisenberg   Page 193.
Reuben Hersh   Page 193.
David Hilbert   Page 244.
Jacob Klein   Page 168.
Morris Kline   Pages 21; 244.
C. S. Lewis   Pages 21.
Glenn Morrow   Page 57.
Sir Isaac Newton   Page 244.
Pascal   Page 279.
Roger Penrose   Page 57.
Plato   Pages 57; 244.
Michael Polyani   Page 57.
Carl Sagan   Page 168.
Robert Stirniman   Page 244.
Paul Valery   Page 279.
Voltaire   Page 57.
Ludwig Wittgenstein   Pages 193; 279.

Abduction, 201
Abel, 196 *fn*
Achilles, 93
Ad hoc, 198, 233, 253, 266
Æons, 60, 120
Agnosticism, 46, 263
Aiken, Henry D, 17 *fn*, 244
Airy, 211 *fn*
Alchemy, 160
Alexander the Great, 101
Alétheia, 73, 120 *fn*, 307
Algebra, 40, 66, 82, 148, 153, 181, 183, 303
Alice in Wonderland, 192
Alfven, Hannes, 239
Allen, H S, 234
Amnesia, 8, 255
Ampere, 209, 231 *fn*
Anamnesis, 88, 90, 102, 153
Anaxagoras, 60
Anaximander, 60
Angst, 283
Anonymous, 193
Answers in Genesis, 269
Appearances, 40 *fn*
Aquinas, Thomas, 7, 137, 150
Archimedes, 4, 103, 126
Aristarchus, 142
Aristotle, 2, 3, 11, 40, 61, 70, 75, 83 *fn*, 89 *fn*,
  91, 96, 98, 108, 116, 125, 129, 136, 176, 268,
  271, 285, 292
Arithmetic, 2, 5, 64, 66, 67, 70, 73, 78, 111
Arius, xii
Arp, Halton, 38, 239, 259 *fn*
Astrology, 94
Astronomy, 52, 94, 146
Attenuation, 169, 194 *fn*
Atheism, 47, 97, 148, 261, 274, 283
Atheorism, 47, 199, 241, 257, 262, 264, 266,
  280
Atlantis, 6
atom, 214, 232, 234, 322
Atomism, 1, 9, 97, 124, 129, 149
Attenuation, 194, 196, 202
Averroes, 138 *fn*, 141
Axiom, 19
Axis of Evil, 225, 259

Bacon, Roger 136
Balmer, Johann, 319, 327
Barnes, Thomas, 230, 270
Baryon, 233
Batten, Don, 37,
Behe, Michael, 189
Bellarmine, Cardinal, 258
Bentley, Richard, 204
Berkeley, George, 187, 219
Berlinski, David, 38, 229
Bernoulli, 189
Bessel, 171, 208 *fn*, 225 *fn*
Boethuis, 261
Bohm, David, 219
Bohr, Niels, 12, 193, 214, 216, 232, 235, 325,
  329
Bookend, 31, 274

Bostick, 234
Boyle, Robert, 149
Bradley, 208 *fn*
Brahe, Tyco, 92 *fn*, 143, 144
Bridgman, Percy, 192
Bruno, Giordano, 124, 144, 145 *fn*, 147 *fn*, 208
  fn, 275
Buffon, comte de, 208 *fn*
Bultmann, Rudolph, 24 *fn*
Burbidge, Goeffrey, 225
Burtt, 193, 200

Capacitor, 312
Cardano, Girlamo, 168
Carnap, 226
Carnot, Lazare, 66, 160
Cartwright, Nancy, 183, 196
Casaubon, Isaac, 146
Cassirer, 143
Catastrophe, 37, 194, 248
Causality, 39, 115 *fn*
Cavendish, Margaret, 137, 195 *fn*
Cayley, Arthur, 181
-centricity,
  Firecentric, 142 *fn*
  Geocentric, 85, 92 *fn*, 142, 163, 207, 211,
    225 *fn*, 258
  Heliocentric 144, 148 *fn*, 164, 197, 207,
    257
  Acentric, 258 *fn*
Chesterton, G K, 59, 111, 244, 267
Christianity, 6, 54, 128, 129
Cicero, 1, 96
Clement, 124
Common Sense Science, 19, 210, 230 *fn*, 234,
  270 *fn*, 317, 327
Compton, 234
Constantinople, 8, 135
Convergence, 195
Copernicus, Nicholas, viii, 40, 104 *fn*, 142, 211,
  225, 248, 257, 283
Cosmos, 23, 24
Council of Nicea, vi
Counter-electromotive force, 313
Creation, 6, 44, 204, 239, 246, 250, 259, 284
Creation Ministries International, 37, 269
Creation Research Society (CRS), 15, 269
Crete, 6, 108
Curie, Marie, 212, 332, 328
Cusa, Nicholas, 139, 140, 147 *fn*, 168
Cynic, 96, 129

Darwin, Charles, viii, 22, 25, 208, 247, 283
Davy, Humphrey, 159
Dawkins, Richard, 250
Deconstruction, 16, 20
Demiurge, 121
Democritus, 1, 3, 60, 97, 149, 212, 224
De Moivre, 161
Demorgan, August, 66
Descartes, 66, 148, 150, 205, 245, 275
Desedimentation, 16, 20, 93 *fn*
Devil, 71 *fn*
Di Francia, 218

Digges, Thomas, 144, 208 fn
Dijksterhuis, 57, 207, 225 fn, 258
Dionysius, 84
Dirac, P A M, 216
Diophantus, 82, 182
Discontinuity, 83
Divergence, 195, 196 fn
Divinci, Leonardo, 8, 141, 170
DNA, 248
Domain, 34
Donne, John, 178
Drake, Stillman, 225 fn
Duhem, Pierre, 135, 139, 183,186 fn, 210,
    225 fn, 258, 269

Economics, 26, 54
Eddington, A S, 15, 213, 235
Edison, Thomas, 161, 213
Ego, 155
Einstein, Albert, 17, 110, 207, 212, 216, 235,
    324, 328
Electromagnetism, 210, 230, 238
Electron, 19, 232, 315, 317, 322, 326, 328
Empiricism, 197
Encyclopedia Britannica, 46, 202 fn, 258 fn
Engineering, 133, 159, 161
Enlightenment, viii, 93 fn, 115, 257
Entropy, 158, 169
Epicureans, 1, 60, 113
Epistemology, 28
Erasmus, 164
Existentialism, 16
Extrapolation, 33, 50, 195, 240
Euclid, 3, 4, 95, 98, 103, 126, 170, 257
Eudoxus, 78
Evolution, 158, 208, 246
Ex Nihilo Creation, 51

Fact, 34
Faivre, Antione, 123
Faraday, Michael, 209, 231
Fernie, J Daniel, 244
Feyerabend, Paul, 31, 74, 159, 208, 221, 225 fn,
    226, 229, 244, 260, 262 fn, 264, 279
Feynman, Richard, 13 fn, 218
Freedom From Religion Founation, 33 fn, 87 fn
Fibonacci, 92 fn
Ficino, 140
First Principles, 32 fn
Ford, Julienne, 242
Fossils, 36
Fraction, 69
Freemason, 146
Frege, Gottlieb, 177
Freud, Sigmund, viii, 283
Fundamentalism, 247

Gale, 211 fn
Galen, 126
Galileo, 22, 104 fn, 143, 148, 155, 168, 195, 245
Galloping Gertie, 3 fn, 190
Gandalf, iv, 275
Gassendi, Pierre, 9
Gauss, C F, 171, 231 fn

Geiger – Marsden effect, 324, 329
Geometry, 2, 4, 5, 12, 78, 80, 81, 89, 92, 102,
    106, 112, 115, 162, 169, 171, 260
Gell-Mann, Murray, 13 fn, 218
Genetic, 248
Gilbert, William, 155
Gilgamesh, 109
Gnosticism, 7, 101, 118, 122, 129, 163
God, Theism, 44, 131
Gold-leaf experiment, 324; 329
Goldstein, Rebecca, 33 fn, 87 fn
Grandiose Extrapolation, 9, 33
Grassman, Hermann, 181
Gravity, 203, 207, 213 fn, 227, 232, 238
Guericke, Otto von, 66 fn

Hamilton, William Rowen, 181, 210, 231
Hawking, Stephen, 221
Hawthorne, 247
Heath, Thomas, 4
Heaviside, Oliver, 212, 232
Hebdomad, 123
Heer, Freidrich, 164 fn
Hegel, 16, 257
Heisenberg, Werner, 17, 193, 216
Hellenism, 101
Helmholtz, 209 fn
Hempel, 226
Heraclitus, 60
Herbert, Edward, 164
Hermaphroditical Effects, 137, 161
Hermeticism, 101, 123, 129, 140, 144, 169, 258
Herschel, William, 147 fn, 160
Hersh, Reuben, 12 fn, 17 fn, 173 fn, 175 fn, 193
Hertz, Heinrich, 210
Hesiod, 108
Hilbert, David, 177, 244
Hipparchus, 188
Hippolytus, 116, 124
Hobbes, Thomas, 152
Hofstadter, 214 fn
Homer, 108
Hoyle, Fred, 224 fn, 246, 258
Hubble space telescope, 228
Humanism, 139
Hume, David, 153, 252
Hummel, Charles, 225 fn, 276
Hutton, 208 fn
Huygens, Christiaan, 147 fn, 206, 208 fn
Hypothesis, 208

Iamblichus, 64, 84 fn, 101
Infinite, 5, 23, 42, 72, 95 fn, 101, 139, 143, 145,
    149, 150, 152, 155, 157, 162, 178, 190, 202,
    205, 220, 253
Institute for Creation Research, 269
Intelligent design, 248
Interferometer, 214, 321, 327
Intuition, 11, 89, 152, 155
Inventions, 134, 159, 161
Inwagen, P v, 44 fn
Irenaeus, 73, 116, 120, 128, 260

Jaki, Stanley, 147 fn, 150 fn

Jastrow, Robert, 227
Jeans, James, 212
John Chappell Natural Philosophy Society, 15, 269
Joshua's Long Day, 7, 109
Justinian, Emperor, 105

Kabbal, 101, 123, 140
Kaleidoscope, x
Kant, Immanuel, 16, 147 fn, 153, 155, 162, 205, 206, 208 fn, 247, 252, 257
Kepler, Johan, 40, 92 fn, 143, 211 fn
Kierkegaard, Sören, ix, 16
Kingsly, Peter, 70 fn, 146 fn
Klein, Jacob, 78 fn, 168
Kline, Morris, 12 fn, 21, 133, 152, 173 fn, 175 fn, 180, 190, 199, 203, 244, 260, 271
Knosis, 107
Koestler, Arthur, 142, 225 fn, 247, 258
Kramer, Hans Joachim, 84 fn
Kronecker, 272, 299
Kuhn, Thomas, 31, 223, 225 fn, 270
Kurtz, Paul, 50

Lactantus, 117, 125
Lakatos, Imre, 175 fn, 226
Lambert, 147 fn
Lamont, Corliss, 30
Langford, Jerome, 225 fn
LaPlace, Pierre, 155, 162, 188 fn, 191, 205, 208 fn, 246, 265
LaSage, 258 fn
Lavoiser, Antoine-Laurent, 208
Lenz, 231 fn
Levin, Flora, 71 fn
Lewis, C S, 21, 50, 106, 154, 250, 261, 271, 281, 286, 313 fn
Lewontin, Richard, 274, 300
Liebnitz, 164
Lobatschewsky, 112, 171
Lindemann, 189 fn
Logic, 178, 193
Lord Kelvin, 209 fn
Lorenz, 212
Lucanus, Ocellus, 103, 144
Lucas, C W, 186 fn, 231 fn, 238, 324
Lucretius, 1
Luther, Martin, ix, 164, 198, 244
Lyell, 208 fn

Maccabbeas, 101
Machiavelli, 136
magnet, 209, 312
Mahler, 282 fn
Mars Hill, 279
Materialist, 42, 129, 151, 162
Mathematic's Word, iv; 2, 27, 33, 42, 87, 94, 230, 271, 278, 287
Mathematics, 1, 2, 8, 39, 61, 87, 98, 173, 176, 179, 182, 198, 199, 240, 257, 262, 264, 266
Maxwell, James Clerk, 12, 207, 210, 231, 235, 254, 312, 319
Medici, Cosimo de, 138, 140
Medieval, 8, 127

Mendelsson, Moses, 150
Michelson-Morley, 211, 224
Mill, John Stuart, 67
Milner, Issac, 160
Miracle, 153
Mirandola, Pico Della, 140
Modernism, 16, 286
Monotruth, 81, 182, 192
Monod, Jacques, 159 fn
Moon, 158
More, Henry, 155
Morrow, Glen, 57
Mortenson, Terry, 209 fn
Motion, 83, 86, 92, 103, 105, 137, 139
Myth, 44, 109

Nagel, 226, 274
Narlikar, 227
Natural Philosophy Alliance (NPA), 15, 269
Nebular Hypothesis, 162, 205
Neon atom, 318, 329
Neptune, 252
Neutrino, 223
Newcomen, 159
Newton, Isaac, 3 fn, 10, 41, 110, 153, 155, 184, 201, 203, 204, 230, 244, 264
Nicomachus the Pythagorean, 71 fn, 85 fn, 101
Noah's Flood, 7, 109
Number, 2, 4, 71, 78, 82, 85, 90, 175, 178, 181, 185
Numenius of Apemea, 81, 101

Occam's Razor, 6, 19, 277
Odenwald, Sten, 183
Ogdoad, 120 fn, 123
Origin, 101
Orphic Cult, 62
Otto, Nicholas, 161

Pagan, 1, 24, 58, 129, 146
Paine, Thomas, 162
Paley, William, 154 fn
Pantheism, 24
Paracelsus, 142
Paradigm, 12, 35, 46, 251
Parmenides, 60, 73, 150, 157, 223
Parsons, A N, 234, 326
Pascal, Blaise, 10, 66, 201, 207, 251, 258, 279
Pempad, 84
Penrose, Roger, 57, 173 fn, 186, 221, 260
Perturbation, 188
Phaethon, 109
Phenomenology, 16
Philolaus, 70 fn, 142 fn
Philoponus, 158
Philosophy, 23, 31, 43
Phlogiston, 42
Photoelectric effect, 324, 328
Pilate, Pontius, 22
Planet, 93, 124 fn, 185
Planck, Max, 214, 222, 323, 328
Plato and platonism, 1, 3, 11, 19, 40, 57, 61, 69, 70, 75, 77, 81, 86, 90, 96, 101, 104, 108, 113, 118, 129, 135, 140, 142 fn, 149, 155, 163, 199

fn, 204, 223, 244, 253
Pletho, 138
Plotinus, 79, 101, 123 *fn*
Poincaré, 171, 176 *fn*, 225
Points, 185
Polanyi, Michael, 57
Polyai, 171 *fn*
Polyscience, 279, 286
Polytruth, 106
Poor, Charles Lane, 15, 213
Popper, Karl, 31 *fn*, 48, 92 *fn*, 95 *fn*, 105 *fn*, 226, 252, 281
Porphyry, 135
Post-Modernism, 16
Pragmatism, 285
Probability, 34
Proclus, 4, 70 *fn*, 74, 101, 149
Proof
    Deductive, 80 *fn*, 99
    Inductive, 99
Protagoras, 80, 262
Ptolemy of Egypt, 4, 92 *fn*, 103, 126, 136 *fn*, 258 *fn*
Pullman, Bernard, 17 *fn*
Pythagoras, 1, 3, 57, 60, 61, 62, 66, 70, 72, 80, 84, 87, 97, 101, 113 *fn*, 129, 150, 253

Quality, 43, 99
Quantum Mechanics, 12, 19, 83 *fn*, 110, 214, 215, 217, 220, 222, 232, 237
Quaternions, 181, 210, 231

Radiation, 309, 316, 323, 325
Rand, Ayn, 56, 157
Raphael, 100, 141
Rationalism, 8, 54, 111, 150, 163, 201, 245, 246, 257, 271, 281, 286
Reason 32, 40, 43, 47, 65, 73, 77, 95, 101, 162, 164, 167, 172, 175, 189, 198
Recidivst, 89 *fn*, 114
Recorde, Robert, 69
Red-Shift, 225, 259
Reductionism, 46
Regiomantanus, 140
Reiman, 112, 171
Reincarnation, 62, 70, 88, 89, 95, 113 *fn*, 113, 119
Relativity, 212, 233
Renaissance, viii, 8, 104, 124, 135, 139, 146 *fn*, 149
Renormalization, 220, 221
Revelation, 44, 53, 112
Roentgen, 212, 322, 328
Romanticism, 16
Rosicrucians, 146
Ross, Hugh, 56 *fn*, 247
Russell, Bertrand, 38, 41 *fn*, 88, 174, 176, 200, 229, 248
Rutherford, 212, 324, 329

Sagan, Carl, 168
Sagnac, 211 *fn*
St Augustine, 7, 125, 150
St Basil, 97

St Paul, 1, 58, 113
St Peter, 21
Sanford, J C, 250
Santillana, Giorgio de, 9, 81, 225 *fn*
Save the Appearances, 40, 53
Savonarola, 141
Scholasticism
    Aristotelean Logical, 14, 137, 228
    Platonic Mathematical, 14, 228
Science, 20, 27, 28, 31, 38, 48, 65, 129, 145 *fn*, 161
    First Principles, 8, 170
    Intermediate First Principles, 10, 179
    Classical, 12, 240
    Inaccessible Science Paradigms, 13, 215, 223, 240
    Empirical, 18, 20, 50, 240, 268
Science, falsely so-called, viii, 27
Scientific American, 261
Scofield, 247
Scripture, 44, 109
Second Wind, 76
Sheehan, William, 48 *fn*, 195 *fn*
Shestov, Lev, 27 *fn*
Sky and Telescope, 15
Sociology of Scientific Knowledge, 16
Socrates, 1, 57, 59, 77, 89
Sophist, 30, 59, 75, 87, 129
Solomon, King, 2 *fn*
Spectroscope, 319, 327
Speusippus, 97
Spinoza, 27 *fn*, 150, 155, 170
Spurgeon, C H, 247
Stars, 93, 124
Statistics, 252 *fn*
Stirniman, Robert, 244, 255
Stoics, 1, 97, 113, 129
String theory, 223
Sulla, 105
Susa, 81
Syllogism, 176

Tarnas, Richard, 13 *fn*, 145 *fn*, 218 *fn*
Telford, Thomas, 160
Tertullian, iii, 22, 113 *fn*, 116, 122, 131, 198,
Tetraktys, 62, 120 *fn*
Thales of Miletus, 60
Theory of Everything (TOE), 42
Thierry of Chartres, 136, 140, 163
Thompson, J J, 322, 328
Titan's Riddle, 262
Transmitter, 315
Trevithick, 159
Triangles, 85, 87

Usshur, Bishop 109 *fn*
Uniformitarian, 15, 36, 83, 246
Unintelligibility, 203, 230
Universal Connected Knowledge, 1, 5, 20, 21, 29, 38, 44, 110, 167, 271, 279, 281, 287
Universal Natural Law, 5, 9, 28, 51, 52, 106, 110, 126, 147, 157, 167, 190, 263, 276, 278, 83, 287
Unwritten Doctrine, 37, 79, 84

Uranus, 252

Velikovsky, Immanuel, 239, 264
Vieta, 66
Volta, Alessandro, 310
Voltaire, 57, 152
Voyager, 191, 198, 228

Wallis, John, 152
Watts, 159
Weierstrass, 189
Whitehead, A N, 25, 61, 94, 176, 200
William of Ockham, 138
Wisdom, 45
Wittgenstein, Ludwig, 193, 279
Wizard of Oz, 43, 217, 227, 233, 245, 286
Wormwood and Gall, 252

Xenocrates, 97

Young, 214, 321, 327

Zeno of Elea, 72, 83, 103
Zoroaster, 62, 141

11077763R00203

Printed in Great Britain
by Amazon.co.uk, Ltd.,
Marston Gate.